Communications
in Computer and Information Science   1867

Rationale

The CCIS series is devoted to the publication of proceedings of computer science conferences. Its aim is to efficiently disseminate original research results in informatics in printed and electronic form. While the focus is on publication of peer-reviewed full papers presenting mature work, inclusion of reviewed short papers reporting on work in progress is welcome, too. Besides globally relevant meetings with internationally representative program committees guaranteeing a strict peer-reviewing and paper selection process, conferences run by societies or of high regional or national relevance are also considered for publication.

Topics

The topical scope of CCIS spans the entire spectrum of informatics ranging from foundational topics in the theory of computing to information and communications science and technology and a broad variety of interdisciplinary application fields.

Information for Volume Editors and Authors

Publication in CCIS is free of charge. No royalties are paid, however, we offer registered conference participants temporary free access to the online version of the conference proceedings on SpringerLink (http://link.springer.com) by means of an http referrer from the conference website and/or a number of complimentary printed copies, as specified in the official acceptance email of the event.

CCIS proceedings can be published in time for distribution at conferences or as post-proceedings, and delivered in the form of printed books and/or electronically as USBs and/or e-content licenses for accessing proceedings at SpringerLink. Furthermore, CCIS proceedings are included in the CCIS electronic book series hosted in the SpringerLink digital library at http://link.springer.com/bookseries/7899. Conferences publishing in CCIS are allowed to use Online Conference Service (OCS) for managing the whole proceedings lifecycle (from submission and reviewing to preparing for publication) free of charge.

Publication process

The language of publication is exclusively English. Authors publishing in CCIS have to sign the Springer CCIS copyright transfer form, however, they are free to use their material published in CCIS for substantially changed, more elaborate subsequent publications elsewhere. For the preparation of the camera-ready papers/files, authors have to strictly adhere to the Springer CCIS Authors' Instructions and are strongly encouraged to use the CCIS LaTeX style files or templates.

Abstracting/Indexing

CCIS is abstracted/indexed in DBLP, Google Scholar, EI-Compendex, Mathematical Reviews, SCImago, Scopus. CCIS volumes are also submitted for the inclusion in ISI Proceedings.

How to start

To start the evaluation of your proposal for inclusion in the CCIS series, please send an e-mail to ccis@springer.com.

Matthes Elstermann · Anke Dittmar ·
Matthias Lederer
Editors

Subject-Oriented Business Process Management

Models for Designing Digital Transformations

14th International Conference, S-BPM ONE 2023
Rostock, Germany, May 31 – June 1, 2023
Proceedings

 Springer

Editors
Matthes Elstermann
Karlsruhe Institute of Technology
Karlsruhe, Germany

Anke Dittmar
University of Rostock
Rostock, Germany

Matthias Lederer
Technical University of Applied Sciences
Weiden, Germany

ISSN 1865-0929 ISSN 1865-0937 (electronic)
Communications in Computer and Information Science
ISBN 978-3-031-40212-8 ISBN 978-3-031-40213-5 (eBook)
https://doi.org/10.1007/978-3-031-40213-5

This Springer imprint is published by the registered company Springer Nature Switzerland AG
The registered company address is: Gewerbestrasse 11, 6330 Cham, Switzerland

Preface

Our current societies are subject to a continuous digital transformation. Models of existing realities have to inspire the design of envisioned ecosystems. As designers, we emphasize the importance of ideas and speculations being realized in diverse forms such as models or prototypes and explored together with all stakeholders. At the same time, we know that the design and use of future-oriented technologies will be essential for economic and social progress. The typical workday of modern businesses and knowledge workers is increasingly influenced by interactive technologies that are changing the way work gets done.

Business processes are central here: they encapsulate the behavior of people and things. They are key to the design of workflows and situations we experience in everyday life. Their representation(s) form the basis for the exchange, exploration, and ultimately the implementation of new developments or dynamic adaptations in societies.

After many trends such as integration, modularization, standardization, contextualization, and open interfaces, the design of all the described process aspects in a dynamic changing world is coming to the center of attention with the increasing technological progress. Under the motto " Models for Designing Digital Transformations", the 14th International S-BPM ONE Conference 2023 provided a discussion forum for the basic questions of holistic modelling of processes. Researchers and practitioners addressed innovative approaches on how organizations and societies can support their stakeholders to holistically design processes and all their relevant aspects and thus become more involved in the value creation framed by process technologies and their (digital) design tools.

The original call for contributions included the following topics (but not limited to):

- Process change & transformation
- Autonomous digital workplace design
- Explainable and transparent process design
- Accountable process engineering
- Multi-/interdisciplinary perspectives on process engineering
- Examples and cases of (subject-oriented-) BPM research & practice
- Collaboration & communication
- Value streams
- Modeling, transformation, and execution
- Internet of Things
- Transformation intelligence
- Design systems
- Continuous design
- Intelligent process design
- Digital twins
- Organizational design
- Sensemaking through perfect design

- Sustainable design
- Design principles for Industry 4.0 | Smart Cities | Healthcare | Smart Logistics | Hyper Automation CPS
- Tasks & scenarios
- Stories & business processes
- Modelling dynamic behavior

All submitted 24 papers were reviewed by at least two members of the international program committee. As a result, after the double-blind peer review, 10 papers could be accepted as research contributions in this conference volume (acceptance rate of 45%). Additionally, 7 contributions were originally submitted or accepted as short paper contributions.

On another note, a successful conference is always based on the interaction of many contributors, who we would like to thank at this point:

- All presenters and contributors of research reports, all of whom have advanced the knowledge of innovation in and with business processes.
- All reviewers, who have checked the academic quality of the contributions and with their many hints increased it further.
- All participants on site in Rostock for the constructive discussions at a high scientific level.
- The two keynote speakers, who offered highly topical and exciting insights into the world of real subject orientation.
- Finally: All readers of this conference series, who strengthen the value of the discipline with their interest in questions of (subject-oriented) business process management.

Lastly, we would also like to thank the University of Rostock and the many helping hands who created a pleasant environment for the conference. Likewise, our thanks go to the Institute for Innovative Process Management, which provided the framework for the conference.

June 2023

Matthes Elstermann
Peter Forbrig
Anke Ditmar
Matthias Lederer
Stefanie Betz

Organization

General Chairs

Anke Dittmar   University of Rostock, Germany
Matthes Elstermann   Karlsruhe Institute of Technology, Germany
Stefanie Betz   University of Applied Science Furtwangen, Germany
Matthias Lederer   Technical University of Applied Sciences Amberg-Weiden, Germany
Peter Forbrig   University of Rostock, Germany

Steering Committee

Albert Fleischmann   InterAktiv Unternehmensberatung, Germany
Werner Schmidt   Technische Hochschule Ingolstadt, Germany
Christian Stary   Johannes Kepler University Linz, Austria

Program Committee

Antunes, Pedro   Victoria University of Wellington, New Zealand
Becker, Jörg   Universität Münster, Germany
Betz, Stefanie   Hochschule Furtwangen, Germany
Dittmar, Anke   University of Rostock, Germany
Elstermann, Matthes   Karlsruhe Institute of Technology, Germany
Fischer, Herbert   TH Deggendorf, Germany
Fleischmann, Albert   InterAktiv Unternehmungsberatung, Germany
Forbrig, Peter   University of Rostock, Germany
Gadatsch, Andreas   Hochschule Bonn-Rhein-Sieg, Germany
Helferich, Andreas   ISM International School of Management, Germany
Höppenbrouwers, Stijn   HAN University of Applied Sciences, Germany
Hvannberg, Ebba   University of Iceland, Iceland
Koch, Stefan   Johannes Kepler University Linz, Austria
Komarov, Mikhail   HSE University, Russia
Kurz, Matthias   Germany
Lamersdorf, Winfried   Hamburg University, Germany

Lederer, Matthias   Technische Hochschule Amberg-Weiden,
                                    Germany
Lawall, Alexander   IU Internationale Hochschule, Germany
Märtin, Christian   Hochschule Augsburg, Germany
Matzner, Martin   Universität Erlangen-Nürnberg, Germany
Neubauer, Matthias   University of Applied Sciences Upper Austria,
                                    Austria
Oppl, Stefan   Donau University Krems, Austria
Proper, Henderik   TU Wien, Austria
Schaller, Thomas   Hof University, Germany
Schieder, Christian   Technische Hochschule Amberg-Weiden,
                                    Germany
Schmidt, Werner   Technische Hochschule Ingolstadt, Germany
Stary, Chris   Johannes Kepler University Linz, Austria
Strecker, Florian   actnconnect, Germany
Turetken, Oktay   Eindhoven University of Technology,
                                    The Netherlands
Winckler, Marco   Université Côte d'Azur, France
Zemaitaitiene, Gintare   Mykolas Romeris University, Lithuania

Contents

(S-)BPM Management Issues and People

Impact of Subject Orientation for Current Developments of Business
Process Management - A Qualitative Assessment 3
  Matthias Lederer, Reinhard Gniza, and Albert Fleischmann

Boosting the Maturity of Agile Process Teams: A Complete Model
for Assessing and Increasing Self-Organization in BPM 17
  Julia Thummerer and Matthias Lederer

Exploring Potential Barriers for the Adoption of Cognitive Technologies
in Industrial Manufacturing SMEs – Preliminary Results of a Qualitative
Study 45
  Thomas Auer, Stefan Rösl, and Christian Schieder

Business Process Automation for Data Teams - A Practical Approach
at Handelsblatt Media Group 55
  Ana Moya, Michael Hein, and Janina Reimann

(S-)BPM Development and Requirements

An Approach to Create a Common Frame of Reference for Digital
Platform Design in SME Value Networks 63
  Jakob Bönsch, Svenja Hauck, Matthes Elstermann, and Jivka Ovtcharova

The Role of Stories in Software Development and Business-Process
Modeling 83
  Peter Forbrig, Alexandru Umlauft, Mathias Kühn, and Anke Dittmar

Can a 'Metaverse by Design' Benefit from Digital Process Twins? 91
  Christian Stary

Approach of Partial Front-Loading in Engineer to Order 111
  Konrad Jagusch, Jan Sender, David Jericho, and Wilko Flügge

Addressing the Data Challenge in Manufacturing SMEs: A Comparative
Study of Data Analytics Applications with a Simplified Reference Model 121
  Stefan Rösl, Thomas Auer, and Christian Schieder

Improving Interoperability in the Exchange of Digital Twin Data Within
Engineering Processes 131
    Constantin Liepert, Christian Stary, Axel Lamprecht, and Dennis Zügn

Credit to Machine Learning – Performance of Credit Card Fraud Detection
Models 151
    Andreas Widenhorn and Paramvir Singh Gaawar

(S-)BPM Modeling, Technology and Infrastructure

Comparing BPMN 2.0 and PASS: A Review and Analysis of Previous
Research 163
    Christoph Piller

Modelability of Agile Development Projects - An Assessment
of the Opportunities and Limitations of BPMN and S-BPM 180
    Matthias Lederer, Stefanie Betz, Werner Schmidt,
    and Matthes Elstermann

Proposal for a Recursive Interpreter Specification for PASS in PASS 187
    Matthes Elstermann

Handling Cross-Cutting Concerns in Subject-Oriented Modeling:
Exploration of Capabilities and an Aspect-Oriented Enrichment 202
    Thomas Ernst Jost, Christian Stary, and Richard Heininger

Autonomy as Shared Asset of CPS Architectures 223
    Richard Heininger, Thomas Ernst Jost, and Christian Stary

Using OPC UA for Integrating and Tracing Data Flows in the Insurance
Industry 240
    Udo Kannengiesser, Florian Krenn, and Harald Müller

Code Generation for Cloud-Based Implementation of Public Sector
Processes Using a Pattern-Based Approach 250
    Jan Gottschick, Anna Opaska, Petra Steffens, and Jaouhara Zouagui

Revisiting the ALPS - An Investigation of Abstract Layered PASS 263
    Matthes Elstermann and Jivka Ovtcharova

Author Index 285

(S-)BPM Management Issues and People

Impact of Subject Orientation for Current Developments of Business Process Management - A Qualitative Assessment

Matthias Lederer[1]([⊠]), Reinhard Gniza[2], and Albert Fleischmann[3]

[1] Technical University of Applied Sciences Amberg-Weiden, Hetzenrichter Weg 15, 92637 Weiden, Germany
ma.lederer@oth-aw.de
[2] Actnconnect, Frankenstr. 152, 90461 Nürnberg, Germany
[3] InterAktiv Unternehmensberatung, Burgfriedenstr. 16, 85276 Pfaffenhofen, Germany

Abstract. The subject-oriented business process management (S-BPM) paradigm, with its basic idea that actors form a business processor choreography or orchestration, has impact on many modern trends in BPM. The modelling, encapsulation, communication orientation, and executable environment can not only support trends, but may also provide a new approach to technological and organizational developments to the point of potentially solving open issues in progress. This paper discusses the contribution of S-BPM to particularly important current BPM trends (such as IoT, BPM platforms, NLP, Process Mining) and the solutions that the subject-oriented paradigm can provide.

Keywords: Subject-oriented paradigm · Business process management · BPM trends · Impact analysis · Value network

1 Introduction

The S-BPM paradigm has stimulated new process models through its innovative core idea, namely the communication-oriented and implementation independent view of subjects (subjects with implementation are called smart actors) whose internal behavior can be defined and synchronized [1, 2]. Many of the explicitly designed components ensure good application in business practice, such as the reduction to five essential symbols and the possible translation into the execution of actions on objects. But also, inherent properties of S-BPM promote practicality, e.g. the encapsulation of behavior and the orientation towards natural language [3].

It is recognized in academia that general paradigms as well as concrete techniques for modeling (like S-BPM) must address classical requirements [4]. These can range from abstract recommendations (heuristics) to specific rules [5, 6]. In addition to these scientific demands, it is necessary to continuously demonstrate the added value and importance - as well as to evolve the artifacts if necessary [7]. This can happen (i) exemplarily through concrete applications in the context of simulations, case studies or

M. Elstermann et al. (Eds.): S-BPM ONE 2023, CCIS 1867, pp. 3–16, 2023.
https://doi.org/10.1007/978-3-031-40213-5_1

frameworks. (ii) Furthermore, it is possible to demonstrate practicality in general with thought experiments and reflections along new trends [8, 9].

Complementing the many publications for the first approach (see, among others, [10–13], and [14]), the purpose of this paper is to demonstrate in general terms the relevance S-BPM can have for emerging new trends in process management (BPM). The discussions of this contribution are intended to demonstrate to practitioners and researchers the value of S-BPM to current issues in process management and to encourage the development of further case studies and exemplary implementations.

2   Method

Two methodological decisions have to be made for the described objective of this paper.

First, the BPM trends to be considered must be selected for which the use of S-BPM must be discussed. The findings of [14, 15] and [16] are used for this purpose. The authors of these publications come from the S-BPM community and have identified explicit trends in their three-stage study based on a systematic analysis of current BPM conferences. According to their findings, eleven BPM trends are currently of particular importance to researchers. Likewise, by surveying BPM practitioners in addition to rigour, the authors were also able to systematically assess the relevance of these eleven trends.

Second, the methodology of analysis and documentation in a narrower sense needs to be defined. For this purpose, this paper used a researcher triangulation (more precisely, an investigator triangulation) in the technical implementation of a three-stage Delphi analysis [17–19]. Three experts evaluated the current and future importance of S-BPM for each BPM trend along two guiding questions:

- What contribution can subject orientation/S-BPM make to the successful realization of the trend?
- How can the paradigm of subject orientation/S-BPM contribute to new issues in the trend?

The selection of experts to collect, process and evaluate the application of S-BPM to the trend was made according to profile-analytical aspects. The following experts were included in the elaboration:

- Expert 1: Founder of S-BPM.
- Expert 2: Experienced BPM and S-BPM practitioner.
- Expert 3: Experienced BPM and S-BPM researcher.

The operational implementation of investigator triangulation followed the recommendations of [20] and [21] as a three-stage Delphi study. One expert undertook the profile-analytic interpretation according to the leading questions, which was then presented again to the next expert according to the latter's preliminary considerations. This step was repeated at least two times (so that all three experts argued on the application for each trend) or if there were no more significant deviations in the textual assessment. The text presented in this report on the importance and influence of S-BPM on current BPM trends thus represents an interpretation agreed between the three experts as the result of a gradual approach.

3   Results

The results for interpreting the influence and added value of S-BPM are discussed trend by in this section. The texts represent the status of the final discussion of the researcher triangulation.

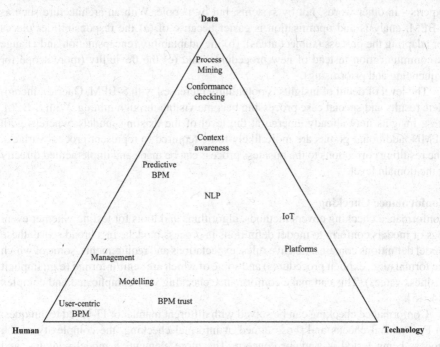

Fig. 1. Relevant BPM trends to be discussed against S-BPM [16]

Process Mining

Process mining refers to approaches that aim to extract information from real process flows (usually recorded in event logs of information systems such as ERP). Therefore, existing systems such as ERP, workflow and cloud determine what information can be extracted and thus analysed. Due to a strong focus by research groups and a large presence of tool vendors, process mining is seen as a solution to many BPM challenges (e.g. cost optimisation, identifying bottlenecks, uncovering anomalies or creating transparency, ensuring compliance) [14, 15].

This trend shows first of all that there is a great need to know one's own business processes and then to analyse them down to the smallest activity in order to generate improvements. Subject-oriented business process management is fundamentally based on the same objective: To design and implement processes in such a way that they can be easily understood and analysed. For process mining, which is mainly based on events and activities, the challenge is that for business-oriented processes (a) communication between actors and (b) internal behaviour of actors have to be considered.

Overcoming this technical (possibly different systems, no central event registry) and organisational (possibly hidden or encapsulated behaviours) hurdle opens up several possibilities. Today, process mining tools are often only used to represent processes that are already known (because they exist in systems). If S-BPM is used consistently, this step can be overcome and analysis can be performed directly. In most cases, despite the use of mining tools, process optimisation is done by consultants, analysts and business experts - in other words, not by systems, but by people. With an architecture such as S-BPM, analysis and optimisation is easier because of (a) the responsibilities/places for adapting the process (subject areas), (b) the adaptability (encapsulation and change of communication instead of new procedures) and (c) the flexibility (more scope for sequencing and prioritising).

The level of detail of insights is potentially increased with S-BPM. Queries, incomplete results and special case processing become visible through mining. With S-BPM, these insights may already emerge at the level of the existing models, whereas with BPMN, additional graphs are more likely to be required to represent process variants. The resulting corrections to the business process can be made and implemented directly at the domain level.

Conformance Checking

Conformance checking covers methods, algorithms and tools for testing whether event logs or models conform to model definitions in process models. In a broad sense, these model definitions contain extensive rules, expectations and requirements, some of which are formal (e.g., explicit procedures) and some of which are semi/informal (e.g., implicit business values). This can make conformance checking very complicated and complex [14, 15].

Conformance checking can be solved with different manual or IT-based techniques. (i) For manual checks and those aimed at informal checking, the complexity of the process being tested is a major concern. The more elements a model contains, and the more variants of a sequential process exist, the more complex the audit. In the conception of S-BPM, this aspect was the main driver for the requirement that a business process model be described in such a way that this description automatically results in an executable program. This applies to the subjects as well as to the set of subjects that make up a business process. The compliance checking is facilitated by the fact that the description language needs only five symbols in the core. This circumstance leads to the fact that this language can be learned fast and thus this check does not have to be made by programmers but by persons from the specialized divisions concerned with sufficient logic knowledge. (ii). If a company has a rules engine, it is integrated directly into the process via subjects. An automatic check of whether the rules of the engine are correct is not yet known in the previous research on S-BPM. For S-BPM research it will be relevant to describe more precisely in which form rules are to be specified in order to use them for checking. It will also be relevant to make existing mining tools and especially their visualization and analysis functions usable for S-BPM.

If these aspects are thought through to their logical conclusion, the well-known goal of information systems "Code is Law" can be achieved with the basic concept.

Context Awareness

Context Awareness stands for approaches that aim to consider more - or preferably all - aspects in the surrounding execution system in a more comprehensive and holistic way when performing BPM activities. It includes developments, analyses, and meta-models that allow specific contexts to be used for situational and environmental information about people, places, and things, and to be integrated directly into business processes. Spoken for BPM, there must be a basic structure in which events outside the processes can be seamlessly integrated and in which the actual business processes can be continuously expanded without system interruptions in process execution [14, 15].

The context of a business process has two dimensions. One dimension describes the relations to other processes e.g. which process starts the execution of the considered process. This type of context is called horizontal context.

The other dimension covers the infrastructure and resources required to execute the activity sequences defined in the process procedures. This is the vertical context.

In S-BPM, subjects are loosely coupled by message exchange. Therefore, it is easy to couple a process with other business processes. A subject in a process just sends a message to a subject in another process.

Looking at the horizontal context, the basic structure of S-BPM systems is fundamentally designed and prepared for such use cases. A business process consists of a set of autonomous subjects, which synchronize themselves independently via their communication. The rules for communication are implemented in each subject and thus form an essential part of the choreography of the subjects – and thus of the business process. A context-related event from another process therefore requires only one addressee (subject) in the business process, which receives the context information, processes it and, from its side, influences the business process accordingly from this moment on. So, a business process must be extended to include a subject that receives context information and changes the business process in a context-related manner. Since in an S-BPM system a business process arises from the communication of the involved subjects, a subject can be added or exchanged individually for the case of new context information.

This first interpretation refers to all contingencies that happen in the system boundary of the business processes. In the wider environment - usually called the context boundary - changes in the operational, business, social and general environment are taken into account. The integration of such events is also possible in the basic structure of S-BPM via the described mechanism. The recording of these events and also their interpretation (including the derivation of adjustments in processes) is of course more challenging.

In S-BPM the process procedures are separated from the infrastructure and resources required for executing of the activities which are entities of the procedures. The vertical context of a process describes which resources are required to execute a subject and how the object classes used by a subject are implemented. In this context it is defined whether a subject is executed by people, software, physical devices or combinations of these resource types. Analog it is described in which way object classes are implemented. This allows that business people must not have an understanding how a business process may be implemented. Implementation can be delegated to corresponding specialist or automated by a business process and thus simplified to such an extent that this function can also be performed by the business department.

This separation of concerns makes it easier to define and to implement business processes. Case studies or reference works could help the S-BPM community to (a) better draw the context boundary, (b) organize the capture, and (c) systematically derive the implications. Agility and flexibility may reach a new dimension with this basic architecture in both cases.

Predictive BPM

Predictive BPM stands for data analysis approaches that aim to predict future behavior of any kind. Studies and case studies have often shown in the past that predictive systems using simple process data provided too inaccurate predictions. Today, two current trends are heavily discussed [14, 15].

On the one hand, there are attempts to use patterns and extend taxonomies to translate predictions into known knowledge/new areas of knowledge. On the other hand, other researchers are interested in individual and specific analysis methods using single predictions without patterns. Although there are still approaches that focus on classic KPI-based predictions with standard sets, many researchers are trying to explore individualized measures. These mostly originate from performance management and are currently only partially linked to concrete application scenarios.

These developments in Predictive BPM show how complex, extensive, and therefore difficult to grasp in research and practice this topic area is. In practice, it is still difficult to make predictions about business processes - and this presupposes the existence of usable internal and external data traces (see discussion in sub-section on Process Mining).

The S-BPM approach is to lay the basis for well-founded statements. This means not only to record the results and intermediate results of a business process, but also to make the entire content communication of the subjects of a business process with the respective version of the subjects (programs) available for evaluations. It now becomes possible, for example, to identify weak points in the process path that are dependent on the input content and to implement any capacity or process changes as a result. This analysis becomes more complex, but also more powerful, the more sub-processes are analyzed simultaneously. In this way, an extensive business process might automatically adapt flexibly to the start events in terms of performance.

For the future, it will rather be decisive to provide convincing answers based on the S-BPM paradigm whether and how an automatic construction of business processes can take place with the help of AI. In a narrower sense related to S-BPM, artifacts are needed that can describe how AI can also be used to create and design subjects automatically.

IoT

IoT (Internet of things) systems make it possible to connect the physical world with the digital world. They combine hardware and software technologies to network devices and sensors, collect and process information, and use knowledge based on this to develop intelligent services or products [14, 15, 22].

While in classical approaches such as UML or BPMN many elements of an IoT-ecosystem are considered passive, S-BPM includes many more active subjects. This becomes necessary because IoT systems must coordinate and realize there goals actively (e.g. production of physical products) with many process partners. Referring to the essential paradigm, S-BPM can provide support especially where many subjects have to contribute their individual behavior to realize a process.

In S-BPM subjects are abstract entities which define the sequence of messages which are sent to other subjects, received from other subjects and the execution of operations of subject internal object. IoT is one way to implement subjects. The IoT behaves like it is defined in the related subject. This means that during the specification of a IoT system it is not required to take care which subjects or objects are implemented in technology. In a later implementation step, suitable technology is assigned to a subject (see also the discussion in the sub-section Context Awareness).

While it is obvious for company departments or even higher-level units (e.g., an entire smart factory or a smart city) to have their own behaviors (e.g., because they also set and control their own goals), it is often not yet common for smaller entities (e.g., individual sensors, orders,). In a classic IoT environment, a centrally optimized process with its instances uses the services of the integrated agents (see Fig. 2).

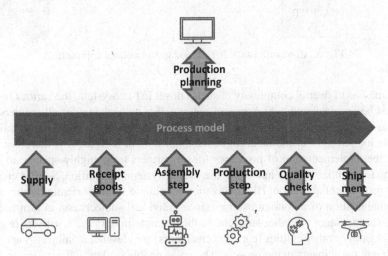

Fig. 2. Configuration of IoT in an in a classic approach

S-BPM gives the chance to have many parallel processes and especially many active elements instead of a sequential sequence and especially instead of many passive elements in an active network. The maturity level of IoT orientation will increase as more autonomous systems are mapped with intelligent subjects. With the proliferation of intelligent behaviors (e.g., not only the robots have artificial intelligence, but also the processed parts, the job to be processed, and the underlying control tool), it will be necessary to accept (or even encourage) that many parallel behaviors and actions will be choreographed. Processing, transport, exchange, and even consumption steps are characterized in an IoT ecosystem by being self-optimizing in a Data optimized way (e.g., through pattern recognition, expert systems, neural networks, etc.). Via the asynchronous exchange of messages, a process is realized that is built up from intelligent behavior in each step. Figure 3 shows such a process described with various subjects exchanging messages, where each subject is implemented in a different way. The supplier subject is implemented by a truck which sends message like "ready to unload in five minutes" to the warehouse agent.

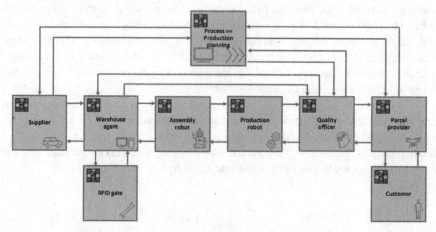

Fig. 3. Configuration of IoT in a subject-orientated approach

For reasons of overall complexity of such a novel IoT ecosystem, the various behaviors must be encapsulated, which in turn requires that an exchange of all partners can take place as simple as possible (e.g., only via simple messages) so as not to have to intervene too strongly in the local implementations. With S-BPM, it is therefore possible in the implementation of processes for all partners to be highly specific to each other and to optimize their behavior for the overall system. In addition, S-BPM enables another form of collaboration. Hierarchization (or simple service orientation) becomes the communication of autonomous units since individual subjects can in turn use the services (or messages) of other subjects. In the example in the Fig. 3, sensors (e.g., of the RFID gate) or other entities (e.g., end customers) are elevated to subjects - and thus to intelligent participants in the process. These can enable further optimization on both a small and large scale. If new intelligence (e.g., smarter software for the RFID gates) or new information (e.g., customer request for different delivery) is available, it is possible to take this into account without changing the central process configuration (from Fig. 1).

Platforms

Platforms are a cornerstone of digitization. They bring together supply and demand for products, services, information, etc. and support transactions between buyers and sellers. Thus, platforms facilitate digital business models and enable ICT-supported execution of business processes [14, 15].

BPM platforms are basically nothing more than marketplaces or exchanges. They bring together the supply of process resources and the demand for them. The parts of a process (e.g., materials, processing capabilities, people or skills) are coordinated on an as-needed basis through a transaction rather than a hierarchy, rather than a complete understanding of the full complexity of a process. In S-BPM terms, this means: All resources to be acted/exchanged can be elevated to active elements (subjects) instead of being managed as passive "unintelligent" entities (e.g., an order, a material, a role, a public BPMN pool). Rather, subject orientation means that these actors bring their own behaviors to process instances. Their own behavior ensures that they act not only in sequence according to the events or inputs received, but also according to their own priorities, rather than sequentially, as would be the case in classical process and SOA architectures. For example, the price on the platform, agreements or even other properties of the shared process can determine the priority.

From an S-BPM point of view, a platform can be seen as a marketplace. It offers different ways to implement a business process. Subject-orientation is not limited to types or domains. Therefore, there is no restriction on the use of S-BPM for platforms. Rather, a focus on working in a network seems to be encouraged. This promotes competition on the one hand and the adaptability of BPM platforms on the other. Competition for the best process actor can ensure further process innovation, because it is not a lengthily negotiated service level agreement that decides how subjects are addressed. Instead, it is the subject behavior that is best suited to the respective process instance (based on its value/price ratio). The absence of central process control - as in classical processes with a flat sequence - also ensures adaptivity. A coordination center will hardly be able to anticipate all events in dynamic and uncertain environments.

A new level of process adaptivity could be achieved by combining BPM platforms (dynamic selection of appropriate resources) and S-BPM (more events and contingencies can be mapped to improve the world). The encapsulation of behavior would not only make the complexity of modern processes manageable, but also solve the problems of interfaces between the many IT systems of process partners around the world and across industries.

S-BPM can also be used to build an alternative to central platforms (like predominant marketplaces). Since S-BPM has fully defined subjects and the communication between subjects is a communication within complex applications, there are efforts to standardize this communication. If this is successful, this standardization would mean a new level in the ISO 7 layer model of communication and with it every subject (in this case an smart actor) would become addressable and thus reachable from any point in the world [23]. The goal is the creation of an interoperability network of autonomous subjects/smart actors.

NLP

Techniques for the automatic handling of natural (spoken or written) language are described as natural language processing (NLP). NLP techniques are used to support the capture, interpretation, and verification of natural language, or even the automatic realization of this direct communication between humans and computers [14, 15].

There are two levels to the current and future contribution of S-BPM to this BPM trend.

At the *operational level*, NLP can be used in subject-oriented models where messages are currently in the form of non-machine-readable text (e.g., voice instructions) and made available to a (non-human) subject. As the number of subjects will increase in more complex structures (e.g. IoT, SOA, global value chains), the four general options described in Fig. 4 will become more important in the future. (1) Since subjects run

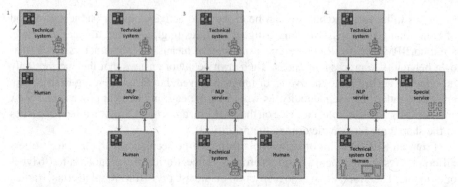

Fig. 4. Major operational deployment options of NLP in subject-oriented models.

their own routines, it is possible to implement NLP techniques in the subjects. Thus, natural language messages can be converted into machine-readable form and made usable for communication, either when sending or receiving. This is always of interest when humans are to act as subjects, in order to reduce the effort at the interface to a dialog system. (2) It is also possible to encapsulate NLP in a subject that, for example, receives human messages as full text as a shared service and then passes them on to the technical system in machine-readable form. When the subjects agree on their communication rules, it must be clarified which additional services the NLP subject provides (e.g., removing information irrelevant to the technical system). As with all services, this has the advantage of reusability. At the same time, it has the disadvantage of increasing complexity. (3) A significant strength of S-BPM also arises when people can make natural language entries in a dialog system (e.g. ratings in a web shop). These can be stored there and presented to human subjects. However, if other systems require a machine-readable form (e.g. CRM system to measure positive and negative comments), a subject can be inserted for translation as in option 2. This encapsulation allows for different views of a program - a key advantage of S-BPM. (4) In the previous options, the focus was on the mere translation performance of the NLP subject. However, S-BPM can also help to professionalize the behavior. Due to the increasing diversity in the technical and business environment and thus in the natural language to be translated, NLP techniques are faced with increasing challenges (e.g. more and mixed languages and dialects, more complex instructions in speech, scaling challenges such as processing peaks). This may require the NLP service itself to call on the help of specialized services. This can also be mapped in S-BPM and flexibly adapted in a process flow. In summary, S-BPM provides operational support by: (a) models that already place special emphasis on communication (to be supported by NLP), and (b) by precisely locating the NLP behavior in a separate or existing actor.

On a *conceptual level*, S-BPM as a paradigm already stands for an NLP method. It is based on spoken language for the mapping of models. This makes it easier to transfer natural language requirements for systems or the description of processes into models, because all important components of a natural language sentence have corresponding equivalents. What S-BPM lacks, however, is an automatic solution that translates textual executions directly into models. This has been desired for many years in information systems disciplines such as software engineering. For BPM, solutions such as low-code platforms are the main approach to this challenge. However, these do not offer automatic translation, as S-BPM could potentially do. Instead, they lower the barrier to implementation. S-BPM can lead the way here if it succeeds in automatically linking the advantages of easy-to-understand language with human explanations.

Management

Management is the identification of a company's mission, goals, procedures, rules, and manipulation of resources, including the company's employees, in order to contribute to the company's success. This common definition shows: Managing an enterprise or parts of it is a complex task. Separation of concerns is a common method to overcome this complexity. Employees are at the center of management. In order to produce the added value of an enterprise, they must understand the goals, carry out the procedures and follow the rules. In general, employees are also seen as resources. They are supported by other resources such as tools, machines, and software systems [14, 15].

Procedures and rules that are independent of specific resources are the focus of the separation of concerns in subject orientation. In a first step, the procedures and rules are defined. They are independent of specific resources and people executing the procedures. Abstract resources are introduced in this specification. Abstract resources, called subjects, execute procedures. The resources on which the operations are to be executed are called objects. A subject communicates with other subjects to contribute to the goals of an enterprise in addition to performing operations on objects.

Subject Orientation focuses on the tasks performed by a procedure and on communicating with other subjects. Specific resources are assigned to subjects after defining the procedures executed by the abstract resource subject.

Subject orientation separates work logic from resources. Each of these aspects can be managed in a nearly independent way from each other. The work logic of a subject can be changed without changing the resources assigned to it. Conversely, subject behavior can be changed without replacing resources. Sure, there may be times when both aspects need to be adjusted for major process changes. However, each change can be assigned to either process logic or resource aspects. In this way, the management of the continuous improvement process is easier.

Modeling

According to [24], at the beginning of creating a model of something, you have to make a pragmatic decision. This is about what aspects of the world you will have in mind. What part of the world you want to understand and what part you want to change [14, 15].

A first decision has been made by the definition of management (see above). The definition contains the aspects of the world we want to consider. We have divided them into process and resource aspects. The definition of procedure aspects is the first step in the modeling of business processes. The subject-oriented modeling of procedure aspects considers two main types of entities in the world: Active entities called subjects and passive entities called objects. A verb connects subjects and objects.

Tests show that people who have to describe events non-verbally follow the order: "Agens Patiens Act", which means subject, predicate object.

A subject is the initiator of an event, and the event defines what the operation to be performed on the object will be [25]. Object Oriented Modeling follows this basic pattern. It looks like this natural sequence developed by evolution. Object-oriented modeling begins with the identification of the object. A subject contains the sequence of events that it can initiate (verbs). The subject-predicate descriptive pattern is also consistent with the recommendation of [26], that is beginning a main sentence with a subject and a predicate.

In a nutshell, subject-oriented modeling follows the natural human pattern of beginning descriptions of events with the subject. As long as humans are predominantly involved in developing and revising processes (see also explanations in the section on Mining and Platforms), subject-oriented modeling will remain a good paradigm for modeling.

BPM Trust

As mentioned above, the separation of procedures from resources is an important feature of subject orientation. The only connection between them is the mapping of resources to subjects and objects, respectively. The corresponding rights can be specified based on the actions contained in the different procedures executed by subjects. Access rights to the objects manipulated by the assigned subject are granted to active resources executing subjects. This means that a subject-oriented specification implicitly covers the specification of access rights. These access rights must be implemented by assigning specific resources.

If questions of trust in the broader sense (e.g., also in function, integrity, protection of data, identification of subjects) are also taken into consideration, further areas of research for the S-BPM community can be identified that go beyond pure communication. The detailed questions about trust in subjects will not diminish with increasing digitalization and IT security challenges. Possible starting points for could be analogous to the explanations of NLP.

User-Centric BPM

In the user-centic BPM, there can be found many approaches that use the potential of stakeholders (e.g., participants, customers, and partners) to innovate or mature workflows. They include recommendations how to collect ideas for process adoption, the organization of such initiatives (e.g., case management), and the understanding of models by humans [27].

The most important modeling aspect in S-BPM are subjects. Subjects execute activity sequences. Activity sequences define the order in which messages will be sent to other subjects or received from other subjects, and the order in which local actions will be performed on objects that are the property of a subject. A subject definition does not include its implementation. That is, what means are used to execute a subject. A means is a person who executes the defined sequence of activities. Subjects are the definition of the role of the people who are involved in the execution of the corresponding process.

Summing up, S-BPM is user-centric by its basic philosophy. Processes are defined from the point of view of the people involved. Each process participant knows who they are receiving messages from, who they are sending messages to, and what actions they must perform on local objects. In terms of the overall research area ("user-centic

BPM"), this has meant that S-BPM provides a notation as well as a paradigm that can be integrated into all the major approaches of the field. Upcoming research can address the concrete incorporation into emerging approaches from this field.

4 Summary

In this paper, we have used the most important BPM research trends to discuss how S-BPM contributes to each of these. The discourses on the value, importance and context of S-BPM for major process developments (e.g., IoT, mining, user-centric BPM, NLP, etc.) are the result of research triangulation.

In summary, we can say: The shift from a centralized organization to a communication-oriented view of processes is driving many trends. Instead of assuming that many elements of the process are rigid and passive, as in classical process orientation, S-BPM makes its contribution through encapsulated and active subjects – each can be active nodes of a value network.

At the same time, however, the impact analysis also reveals general open questions. These should be pursued by the BPM community. For S-BPM researchers in particular, many open questions are mentioned. These can be groundbreaking for subsequent studies to keep the pulse on the development of the subject orientation.

References

1. Fleischmann, A., Stary, C.: Whom to talk to? A stakeholder perspective on business process development. Univ. Access Inf. Soc. **11**(2), 1–28 (2011)
2. Fleischmann, A.: Subjektorientiertes Prozessmanagement. Hanser, München (2011)
3. Fleischmann, A.: What is S-BPM?. In: Proceedings of the 1st S-BPM ONE 2010 - Setting the Stage for Subject-Oriented Business Process Management (2010)
4. Hogrebe, F., Nüttgens, M.: Rahmenkonzept zur Messung und Bewertung der Gebrauchstauglichkeit von Modellierungssprachen. Universität Hamburg, Hamburg (2009)
5. Thomas, O., Becker, J., Jannaber, S., Riehle, D., Leising, I.: Collaborative Specification Engineering: Kollaborative Entwicklung einer Sprachspezifikation der Ereignisgesteuerten Prozesskette (EPK) unter Verwendung einer wikibasierten Onlineplattform. Münster: WWU (2018)
6. Frank, U.: Outline of a method for designing domain-specific modelling languages. Duisburg-Essen: ICB-Research (2010)
7. Elstermann, M., Fleischmann, A., Moser, C., Oppl, S., Schmidt, W., Stary, C.: Ganzheitliche Digitalisierung von Prozessen. Springer Vieweg, Berlin (2023)
8. Fleischmann, A., Oppl, S., Schmidt, W., Stary, C.: Contextual Process Digitalization: Changing Perspectives – Design Thinking – Value-Led Design. Springer International Publishing, Cham (2020). https://doi.org/10.1007/978-3-030-38300-8
9. Fleischmann A., Friedl A., Großmann D., Schmidt W.: Modeling and implementing of industrie 4.0 scenarios. In: Proceedings of the Conference Modelling to Program: Second International Workshop, M2P 2020 (2020)
10. Fleischmann, A., Schmidt, W., Stary, C. (eds.): S-BPM in the Wild. Springer International Publishing, Cham (2015). https://doi.org/10.1007/978-3-319-17542-3
11. Bönsch, J., Reh, K., Ovtcharova, J.: Subject-oriented business process models of SMEs: case study, best practices and evaluation. InL Proceedings of the International Conference on Subject-Oriented Business Process Management S-BPM ONE (2022)

12. Elstermann, M., Betz, S., Lederer, M., Schmidt, W., Bührer, L.: Subject-Oriented Reference Model for Virtual Factory Operations Commissioning. In Proceedings of the BPMDS International Conference on Business Process Modeling, Development and Support (2021)

13. Neubauer, M., Stary, C. (eds.): S-BPM in the Production Industry. Springer International Publishing, Cham (2017). https://doi.org/10.1007/978-3-319-48466-2

14. Lederer, M., Betz, S., Schmidt, W.: Proceedings of the International Conference on Subject-Oriented Business Process Management S-BPM ONE (2018)

15. Lederer, M., Elstermann, M., Betz, S., Schmidt, W.: Technology-, human-, and data-driven developments in business process management: a literature analysis. In: Proceedings of the International Conference on Subject-Oriented Business Process Management S-BPM ONE (2020)

16. Lederer, M., Betz, S., Schmidt, W., Elstermann, M.: Are BPM practitioners and researchers friends? current questions of process professionals and the impact of science. In: Proceedings of the International Conference on Subject-Oriented Business Process Management S-BPM ONE (2022)

17. Denzin, N.K.: The Research Act. Aldine, A Theoretical Introduction to Sociological Methods, Chicago (1970)

18. Archibald, M.M.: Investigator triangulation: a collaborative strategy with potential for mixed methods research. J. Mixed Methods Res. 10(3), 3 (2015)

19. Settinieri , J.: Forschst Du noch, oder triangulierst Du schon? In Elsner, D., Viebrock, B. (eds.), Triangulation in der Fremdsprachenforschung (pp. S. 17–35). Frankfurt, Kolloquium Fremdsprachenunterricht (2015)

20. Whitehead, D., Ferguson, C.: Mixed-methods research. In Whitehead, D., Ferguson, C., LoBiondo-Wood, G., Haber, J. (eds.), Nursing and Midwifery Research: Methods and Appraisal for Evidence-Based Practice, pp.237–251. Elsevier, Amsterdam (2020)

21. Loo, R.: The Delphi method: a powerful tool for strategic management. Policing Internat. J. 25(4), 762–769 (2002)

22. Kett, H., Lehmann, K., Renner, T.: IT-Plattformen für das Internet der Dinge (IoT). Fraunhofer Verlag, Stuttgart (2017)

23. Gniza, F., Strecker, F.: Interoperability network - the internet of actors. In: Proceedings of the International Conference on Subject-Oriented Business Process Management S-BPM ONE (2019)

24. Stachowiak, H.: Allgemeine Modelltheorie. Springer Vienna, Vienna (1973). https://doi.org/10.1007/978-3-7091-8327-4

25. Wilson, E.O.: The Social Conquest of Earth. Liveright Publishing, New York (2013)

26. Roy, P.C.: Writing Tools. Little, Brown and Company, New York (2006)

27. Lederer, M.: Digitalisierungs-Cluster für Geschäftsprozesse – Prozessinnovationen, Forschungsdiskurse und praktische Relevanz. In: Bulitta, C. (ed.): Forschungsbericht 2023. Amberg: Ostbayerische Technische Hochschule Amberg-Weiden (2023)

Boosting the Maturity of Agile Process Teams: A Complete Model for Assessing and Increasing Self-Organization in BPM

Julia Thummerer and Matthias Lederer[✉]

Technical University of Applied Sciences Amberg-Weiden, Hetzenrichter Weg 15, 92637 Weiden, Germany
ma.lederer@oth-aw.de

Abstract. Agile methods are often used to make initiatives for adaptation or working in business processes more flexible. A particular challenge in the many practices of agile business process management is to establish the necessary self-organization in teams. This is a particular challenge for many companies because the actual state of self-organization is unknown and very many areas (e.g., communication, collaboration, work distribution) are affected. Both challenges can be addressed with the maturity model developed in this paper. The literature-based artifact allows measuring the degree of self-organization in processes in eight design fields for 31 concrete indicators. Using a questionnaire, teams can identify a development path to more agile process management.

Keywords: Agile Business process management · self-organization · maturity model · agile process teams

1 Introduction

Companies face the challenge that the environment of processes is changing faster. Technological, social and economic change [1] are reasons why agile approaches to analyzing and improving processes are being used more frequently. The trend towards agile process management stands for incremental and iterative adjustments of company processes, so that their design (e.g. process models) and implementation (e.g. roll-out of processes in teams or IT systems) can happen at shorter intervals and along changes in the company context. In agile process management, not all phases of the classical process life cycle are planned in advance, but agile methods are used to adapt processes in a feedback-oriented and, above all, iterative way [2, 3]. This often promotes customer orientation, continuous improvement and dealing with increasing complexity as well as growing internationalization [4]. In this point, the self-organization of teams basically starts at the same point where the accepted process management approaches BPM 2.0 or case management have been known for years.

M. Elstermann et al. (Eds.): S-BPM ONE 2023, CCIS 1867, pp. 17–44, 2023.
https://doi.org/10.1007/978-3-031-40213-5_2

Studies show that the implementation of agile techniques must be supported by a suitable team organization in the sense of suitable work coordination [5]. The appropriate team work coordination - for agile BPM this applies (A) to the process team within the workflows as well as (B) to the team that organizes the BPM initiatives in the life cycle of the process - promotes performance to a high degree [6]. A particularly important requirement in the agile manifesto and practices is that both teamwork levels should be self-organized [7]. As described comprehensively in the previous study [8], it is primarily the demand for self-organization that often is challenging for companies. As described in [8], two aspects are critical in the transition to self-organized BPM teams: (1) First, it is well known that moving too quickly to agile values and practices often leads to failure and frustration. This means that even if, in the agile approach to BPM, teamwork is to be predominantly self-organized [7], the current state of self-organization must first be determined and then gradually and successively extended. (2) Furthermore, companies are often overwhelmed with the introduction of self-organizing teams for BPM because it requires a profound change [3, 9]. Many organizational, technical, and social aspects of a team and an organization (be it the process [see A] or the project [see B]) need to be considered and holistically designed.

To answer both challenges, a previous study developed the first steps of a maturity model [8]. Together with the findings from this paper, this will answer the following research question:

How can a team's level for self-organization in BPM be assessed?

This maturity model helps managers, teams, and the organization to take a realistic look at the level of self-organization of BPM teams and incrementally increase agility. According to the design science approach in the discipline of information systems [10], the decision to answer the question by a maturity model helps for both challenges: (1) The model can be used to assess the current state and at the same time provides a suitable development path to more self-organization. (2) According to common standards for maturity models, several design areas of an organization are evaluated in a balanced way and developed further. In accordance with the underlying methodology (see Sect. 3), the design areas ("categories" and "factors") of the maturity model were already developed in the previous study. Likewise, specific indicators were derived for all identified areas. Both were the result of a systematic literature review, which is comprehensively presented in the next section (section "Related Work"). The remaining content to complete the maturity model (in particular a calculation model, the levels of maturity, a questionnaire for evaluating the current state and the levels of the model) is the content of the fourth section (section "Results").

2 Related Work

The significance of agile BPM and in particular the importance of self-organization in theory and corporate practice has already been described comprehensively in the preliminary study. For these fundamentals, reference should therefore be made to [8].

According to the parts necessary in this second study to complete the maturity model artifact, the state of the art on agility and self-organization shall be described in this section. In addition, the design areas, factors and indicators (sub-section "Previous results") will be described as an important basis for the section on "results".

State of the Art

As transitioning to Agile is both demanding and time-consuming, implementing the appropriate tools and methods can save a lot of energy and time [11]. By assessing the readiness level of self-organization, possible barriers can be identified and addressed to accelerate the change. Thus, several structured adoption frameworks and indices have been proposed to measure an organization's and a team's agility level respectively.

[12] developed the Agile Adoption and Improvement Model (AAIM) for the adoption, assessment and improvement of an agile software development process, which can be used as a gradual roadmap for an agile adoption approach. The AAIM is organized in three agile blocks, six agile stages and an agility measurement model [12, 13] presented a model for the transition of a team to an agile method in a distributed environment within the four stages of evaluation, inception, transition and steady state [14].

Furthermore, [15] propose a 4-step roadmap to lead teams to agility in five essential values, which consider both the project and organizational level. The researchers evaluate the degree of agility of an organization using the Agile Measurement Index. The first stage of this index is to identify Discontinuing Factors that indicate an organization is not ready to adopt Agile. By providing an extensive questionnaire, a project-level assessment and the evaluation of the organizational readiness can be conducted. Afterward, agile practices, which the organization should adopt, are suggested [15]. Similar steps can be found in [11] and [13].

[14] argue that, while researchers have developed various assessment tools and frameworks, current agile adoption frameworks have several characteristics in common. They are incremental, combine both bottom-up and top-down strategies and are composed of stages, e.g., the assessment of the ability of the organization to adopt agile methods and the selection of the suitable agile practices to be implemented. Furthermore, they provide mechanisms for implementation [14]. However, there does not exist a consensus on the proposed adoption stages [16].

In contrast to the previous frameworks, [5] designed an instrument that addresses key concerns and characteristics of teamwork in agile software development. The status of the self-organizing team is reviewed by the researchers and presented in a radar plot along five dimensions. The score of each dimension is generated by conducting interviews and each dimension is assigned a score from zero to ten [5]. Likewise, [17] developed an assessment of team agility for Internet of Things projects to evaluate a team's agility level using Multi-grade Fuzzy Analysis and Importance Performance Analysis. The authors uncovered several attributes that influence the team agility level, which also can be rated on a ten-point scale [17].

While agile adoption frameworks and teamwork agility models have several similarities in the structure and evaluation of the dimensions and attributes, the theoretical frameworks can only be applied in business practice, if a well-founded maturity model with a scientific basis and a questionnaire are provided. So, a holistic index for assessing a team's self-organization level that considers these aspects must be designed.

Previous Results

This contribution makes use of the findings of the preliminary study, which will be summarized and substantiated here.

Categories and Factors

In developing an index for self-organizing teams, multiple dimensions need to be considered to obtain a complete and valid assessment of the as-is statis. After a systematic review of the relevant literature, six critical categories that enable self-organization were identified in the previous study [8]. It is assumed that when all categories are sufficiently mature, a team has achieved readiness for self-organization in BPM initiatives or daily BPM work. Table 1 summarizes the identified categories.

Table 1. Factors indicating a Team's Level Self-organization [8]

Category	Factor	Category	Factor	Category	Factor
Autonomy	F1: Minimum Critical Specification	Learning and development	F11: Knowledge Sharing	Team orientation	F20: Participatory Goal Setting
	F2: Decision-Making Authority		F12: Continuous Feedback		F21: Shared Vision
	F3: Self-Assignment		F13: Team Reflection		F22: Mutual Trust
	F4: Management Support		F14: Agile Training		F23: Crystallized Team Norms
	F5: Team Capability		F15: Commitment to Change		F24: Agile Planning
	F6: Informal Org. Structures		F16: Collective Responsibility	Collaboration and communication	F25: Effective Communication
Cross-functionality	F7: Team Size	Team leadership	F17: Shared Leadership		F26: Task-related Communication
	F8: Skill Variety		F18: Clear Roles and Responsibilities		F27: Porous Communication
	F9: Redundancy		F19: Adoption of Informal Roles		F28: Conflict Management
	F10: Team Flexibility				F29: Member Personality
					F30: Customer Collaboration
					F31: Team Distribution

Indicators

As presented in the Related Work section, in order to evaluate the Self-Organization Index, there must be a list of assessable factors that can be used in operational BPM practice. To this end, the factors were transformed into 80 specific indicators for which a concrete statement can be made when evaluating BPM teams (see [8]). Looking at the resulting indicators from the "Autonomy" category again, it can be seen, for example, that the factors mentioned ("Minimum critical specification") now become more precise ("Management does not interfere in day-to-day activities ") and are finally made assessable by BPM experts or BPM teams. In a nutshell, this partial artifact of the maturity model bases on the literature review and provides a set of indicators that can now be used to shape the subsequent artifacts of the overall model [8]. Most important aspects for each indicator will be summarized in the following sub-sections.

Autonomy

Minimum Critical Specification (F1): For a team to be able to self-organize, top management should only define the critical factors that are needed to lead the team. This is referred to as minimum critical specification [40]. A team possesses high external autonomy when executives provide it with the freedom to manage and assume responsibility for the tasks and not interfere with the teams' day-to-day activities [19, 41] also

Table 2. Indicators for measuring a Team's Self-organization Readiness

Factor	Indicator	Indicator	Max score	Factor Weight
F1	F1I1	Management only specifies minimum project criteria [67]	8	0,166
	F1I2	Management does not interfere in day-to-day activities [19]		
F2	F2I1	The team must refer back to several stakeholders (management, client, other teams) before making a decision [20]	8	0,166
	F2I2	The team was involved in the project planning from the beginning [53]		
F3	F3I1	Team members control the scheduling and implementation of their tasks [71]	8	0,166
	F3I2	Tasks are clearly outlined [71]		
F4	F4I1	Management provides sufficient infrastructure and resource support for effective functioning [45]	8	0,166
	F4I2	Management supports the team when the schedule needs to be bent [22]		
F5	F5I1	Team members have the skills and expertise to accomplish the tasks [23]	16	0,166
	F5I2	Team members can handle the workload [22]		
	F5I3	The team doesn't lose resources to other projects [45]		
	F5I4	The team feels it has the ability to self-organize		
F6	F6I1	The organization has informal structures [45]	12	0,166
	F6I2	Management is directly accessible by all employees and maintains an open-door policy [45]		
	F6I3	Team members are free to voice their opinions and raise concerns [46]		
F7	F7I1	Teams have no more than 5–9 members [48]	8	0,25
	F7I2	Teams have enough members to accomplish a task [47]		
F8	F8I1	Team members come from different training and backgrounds [51]	8	0,25

(continued)

Table 2. (*continued*)

Factor	Indicator	Indicator	Max score	Factor Weight
	F8I2	Team members accumulate knowledge in other areas than their own [67]		
F9	F9I1	It is easy for a team member to complete someone else's task [24]	8	0,25
	F9I2	It is easy to shift workload among team members [25]		
F10	F10I1	Team members are easily added removed [26]	8	0,25
	F10I2	The team can organize itself according to the current challenges [27]		
F11	F11I1	Information is shared with the whole organization [28]	16	0,2
	F11I2	Teams set aside exclusive time for learning [18]		
	F11I3	Team members accumulate knowledge in other areas than their own [18]		
	F11I4	The team has daily meetings [29]		
F12	F12I1	Team members regularly give feedback on a co-worker's work [24]	8	0,2
	F12I2	Team members ask for input and suggestions on their work [24]		
F13	F13I1	The team regularly contemplates what they are doing and how they are working together [30]	8	0,2
	F13I2	Team members can question given concepts and organizational processes [31]		
F14	F14I1	The team can apply agile methods [22]	8	0,2
	F14I2	The team is encouraged to use agile methods and self-organizing practices [46]		
F15	F15I1	The team introduces changes in their work to help the organization achieve its change goals [34]	12	0,2
	F15I2	Change is intensively and transparently communicated throughout the whole organization [22]		

(*continued*)

Table 2. (*continued*)

Factor	Indicator	Indicator	Max score	Factor Weight
	F15I3	Team members provide recognition when they see people implementing new ways of doing things [34]		
F16	F16I1	The accountability for the whole project is shared among team members [33]	4	0,25
F17	F17I1	Every team member is involved in the decision-making process [32]	16	0,25
	F17I2	Leadership is rotated to the person with the knowledge, skills and abilities for the issues at the time [5]		
	F17I3	Team members listen to the concerns of other team members [51]		
	F17I4	Team members explain to other team members what is needed from them [51]		
F18	F18I1	Every team member has clear roles and responsibilities [35]	8	0,25
	F18I2	Team members seek out new responsibilities [35]		
F19	F19I1	The team identifies members who jeopardize the productiveness and initiates their removal [46]	16	0,25
	F19I2	The team has a member that understands both business language and technical terms [46]		
	F19I3	The team has a representative of the agile cause that advertises agile methods with the clients and management [46]		
	F19I4	The team has a representative that manages clients' expectations and guides the collaboration of the client and the team [46]		
F20	F20I1	The team has clear and common team goals [20]	12	0,2
	F20I2	Team members actively participated in the identifying and setting of the team's goals [68]		
	F20I3	The team values and considers alternative suggestions in team discussions [20]		
F21	F21I1	The team has a shared vision [20]	8	0,2

(*continued*)

Table 2. (*continued*)

Factor	Indicator	Indicator	Max score	Factor Weight
	F21I2	Team members are committed to the vision [20]		
F22	F22I1	Team members believe that every member will perform their role [25]	16	0,2
	F22I2	Team members can admit to mistakes [25]		
	F22I3	Team members feel respected by others [25]		
	F22I4	Communication mostly happens face-to-face [7]		
F23	F23I1	The team approves or disapproves of behaviors [47]	8	0,2
	F23I2	Team members adapt their behavior to the team's behavior [47]		
F24	F24I1	The team is involved in the planning process [20]	16	0,2
	F24I2	The team has a product delivery strategy and continuously delivers the product within small releases [23]		
	F24I3	The team has daily meetings [60]		
	F24I4	The team is proud of its agile prioritization and planning procedure [37]		
F25	F25I1	Communication and negotiation in the project mostly happen face-to-face [7]	16	0,143
	F25I2	The team works in an open workspace [60]		
	F25I3	The current project status and project requirements are visualized [60]		
	F25I4	Information is shared daily [60]		
F26	F26I1	Team members know what other team members are currently working on [35]	4	0,143
F27	F27I1	Team members know what other teams in the project are currently working on [38]	4	0,143
F28	F28I1	The team knows what to do when conflicts between team members arise [39]	8	0,143
	F28I2	The team can avoid the negative aspects of conflict before they occur [62]		
F29	F29I1	Most of the team members are very conscientious [64]	12	0,143

(*continued*)

Table 2. (*continued*)

Factor	Indicator	Indicator	Max score	Factor Weight
	F29I2	Most of the team members are very agreeable [58]		
	F29I3	Most of the team members are motivated [105]		
F30	F30I1	The customer considers themselves responsible for elements of the project [46]	8	0,143
	F30I2	The customer provides feedback regularly [46]		
	F30I3	The team has a product delivery strategy and continuously delivers the product within small releases [23]		
F31	F31I1	The team is geographically closely located [23]	16	0,143
	F31I2	The team is dedicated to a single project [74]		
	F31I3	The team works in an open workspace [22]		
	F31I4	The team loses resources to other projects [45]		

highlight the importance of freedom given by senior management for a team to have the ability to self-organize.

Decision-Making Authority (F2): External influence is not only the influence of management but also that of others outside the team. In this context, external influence means the influence that disrupts teamwork [32]. Too much dependency on others was identified as a barrier to self-organization because a team would need to find consensus with too many stakeholders, experts and other teams, which limits its decision-making power [20]. For example, a cutback of decision-making authority could occur if the software architecture prompts many technical dependencies, leading to an increased coordination effort with other teams [42].

Self-Assignment (F3): Individual autonomy of a team member is critical for the development of self-organization [5]. It is the amount of freedom a team member is given to accomplish assigned tasks. Team members with high individual autonomy have few rules and procedure constraints and high control over their work nature and pace [43]. In a self-organizing team, individual autonomy is established when team members can assign a task or user story to themselves.

Management Support (F4): Executive support was found to be a critical environmental factor influencing self-organizing agile teams [44]. [5] also identified the lack of a support system as a barrier to self-organization as it may lead to reduced autonomy. [22] also mention that management support is an absolute necessity when release schedules need to be bent or additional resources are needed for training and coaching. Likewise, the team must be financially sponsored in the form of infrastructure support such as setting up an open-plan workplace and providing tools for electronic communication and collaboration [21, 45].

Team Capability (F5): Team capability was found to be a success factor of autonomous agile teams. Team members need to have high competence and expertise in their field and at the same time be highly motivated to accomplish the task [23,45] also highlight that the team needs to be dedicated to self-organize. Dedication can emerge from the knowledge to be able to manage the workload. Hence, the workload must be adjusted to facilitate the change process. If people are overloaded, they will feel less committed and will not be able to change their behavior [22].

Informal Organizational Structures (F6): The ability of a team to self-organize is also influenced by the organizational structure. Self-organizing teams require structures without hierarchical boundaries that could prevent the free flow of information. This informality promotes openness because management is directly accessible to all employees [45]. Team members can voice their opinions and concerns, ask management for assistance in solving problems, make decisions together and adapt to change, which is essential to achieving and maintaining team autonomy [46].

Cross-functionality

A team is said to possess cross-functionality when it is composed of individual members with varying specializations, thought processes and behavior patterns [19].

Team Size (F7): Team size refers to the appropriate number of members to perform the task [47]. In the agile approach, team size is a common issue as it is difficult to find the optimum [48]. According to [49], the number of people in a self-organizing team must be kept as small as possible, while teams typically vary from five to 15 members. Other researchers also found out that an individual team size of five to 17 people contributes to high dynamism [50].

Skill Variety (F8): [40] states the team "must embody critical dimensions of the environment with which they have to deal so that they can self-organize to cope with the demands they are likely to face". This means that members of a self-organizing team must have the ability to work across different functional areas. Individuals with high skill variety have different backgrounds and expertise in several areas, including financial and technical knowledge and interpersonal skills [51]. Therefore, a team ready for self-organization consists of members with high skill variety [52].

Redundancy (F9): [40] outlines that redundancy is required for the creation of innovation and development in a self-organizing team. Redundancy is necessary because team members need to be able to do each other's work so they can organize in response to emerging requirements [52]. This is often referred to as backup behavior, which means team members need to be aware of another's tasks and have equivalent skills to perform or substitute them if necessary [5].

Team Flexibility (F10): Team flexibility is directly associated with cross-functionality as well as redundancy of tasks [53]. A team is flexible if it can organize itself repeatedly to meet new arising challenges [27]. According to [26], a key design feature of externally oriented and highly adaptive teams is flexible membership. Unlike traditional teams that protect their group identity by maintaining a stable membership, agile teams can easily change members. As changes occur, new members are added or removed [26].

Learning and Development

For a self-organizing team to respond quickly to changing market conditions, it must go through a continuous process of trial and error to limit the alternatives. Team members also need to obtain knowledge and diverse skills to create a cross-functional team [19].

Knowledge Sharing (F11): Self-organizing teams gather and share knowledge through multi-learning across individual, group and organizational levels, through multifunctional learning across roles and through the transfer of learning across different departments [21]. For example, if teams want to achieve shared leadership, both vertical leaders and the team members themselves need training and development [5].

Continuous Feedback (F12): Agile teams strive for fast and continuous feedback, which was found to be a key factor for success in agile projects [54]. Feedback from team members can lead to individuals becoming more aware of their performance, which in turn can increase team performance. As feedback is essential in agile teams, members need to monitor their performance mutually. This is the ability to keep track of a team members' work while carrying out their own assignments.

Reflective Practices (F13): According to [30], self-organizing teams need to regularly reflect on what they are doing and how they are working together as a team. This can improve teamwork, productivity, team learning and development and is found to be a necessary element of the feedback and learning cycle in agile practices. It also helps team members to get to know each other better and develop a higher degree of trust [30].

Agile Training (F14): Several studies have revealed that training in agile methods improved the chances of succeeding with the transition. It also helped team members be more positive about the new way of working and enthusiastic to change. Without agile training, some studies stated the change would have failed [22]. Also, it has been discovered that inadequate and dysfunctional training was one of the critical issues that affected the agile transformation process [55].

Commitment to Change (F15): For teams to be able to self-organize, there must be a strong commitment to change by clarifying that there can be no return to the old ways of working [22]. Team members demonstrate commitment to change by communicating in both words and actions their support for the change. Commitment to change is displayed if employees try to learn more about change initiatives, encourage others to embrace change, explain the rationale behind the change, provide recognition to those who have changed their behavior or introduce changes in their work [34].

Factors for Team Leadership

A traditional team following a plan-driven model usually has a specialized leadership role. With this form of leadership, one person has more influence than the other members. In contrast to that, leadership can be seen as a collective social influence process among all members of a team [56]. Following this, leadership should be distributed rather than centralized in a self-organizing team [5].

Collective Responsibility (F16): Collective responsibility is defined as the state in which members have a collective sense that they have the responsibility and the authority to control their work [57]. This emergent state was found to be a critical mediator of high-performing autonomous teams [58]. Collective responsibility is an important element of psychological safety as the team shares responsibility for the product. However, it does not undermine individual accountability [59].

Shared Leadership (F17): Shared leadership can also be described as internal autonomy, which refers to the degree to which all team members jointly share decision authority [32]. However, [5] add that not every decision must be made collectively with equal involvement by every team member. [60] point out that shared leadership is supported by a lead-and-collaborate principle.

Clear Roles and Responsibilities (F18): In a self-organizing team, members will shift from being employees with job descriptions to individuals with different roles and responsibilities. Positions will no longer exist as the goal-oriented roles are responsible for tasks [35]. To accomplish this, every team member must understand and accept their roles as well as the roles of the other team members. While role clarity will allow the team to work effectively, a lack thereof can create friction that disturbs the self-organizing work team [66].

Adoption of Informal Roles (F19): While members have clear roles and responsibilities in a self-organizing team, a study by [67] revealed that there exist six informal, implicit, transient and spontaneous roles in agile teams that enable self-organization. The absence of a manager leads to team members with good communication skills taking on the roles of Coordinator and Translator. Likewise, the Champion and Promoter role must be filled with individuals promoting the team with senior management and customers. While the role of the Mentor is encouraging the use of agile and self-organizing practices, the Terminator has the task to remove disruptive team members.

Factors for Team Orientation
Team Orientation is reflected by the acceptance of team norms, the level of group cohesiveness, assigning a high priority to team goals as well as the attitude towards another.

Participatory Goal Setting (F20): [20] observed not having clear and common goals as a barrier to self-organization. If objectives are ambiguous, team members will try to figure out what is supposed to be achieved [20]. This happens when top management frequently sets goals without including the team, which in turn leads to team members equating goals with deliverables and deadlines or not committing to them at all. Hence, participation in identifying goals is an essential feature of a self-organizing team [68].

Shared Vision (F21): One of the characteristics of self-organizing teams is the understanding of each other's strengths and weaknesses [45]. This shared understanding is frequently referred to as shared mental models that allow anticipating each other's needs and realizing the team's goals [25]. In this context, a shared vision can be described as a mental model of a future state of a team, which builds the basis of team motivation, planning and goal setting [69].

Mutual Trust (F22): Mutual trust refers to the shared belief that each member of a team will perform their roles and protect the interests of the other team members. If team trust exists, members of a team are more willing to share information as well as to admit to mistakes and accept feedback. Trust becomes especially relevant in environments with high interdependence, close cooperation, teamwork, and requirements for flexibility [25].

Crystallized Team Norms (F23): Team norms are standards shared by the team members that manage their behavior. A norm is well crystallized when the whole team approves or disapproves of a particular behavior. In consequence, self-organizing work teams are likely to have better crystallized norms than other teams to regulate member behavior [47]. Additionally, it was established that diversity in norms is a barrier to self-organization. This is especially important as the norms serve as informal rules that guide the team. In a self-organizing team, they are not left to emerge by themselves, but established together with all team members [20].

Agile Planning (F24): Agile planning means projects use an iterative process to realize incremental delivery. The product delivery can be divided into multiple releases that have two-to-four weeks iterations. The deliverables of these iterations are described as user stories. With a continuous delivery strategy, customers can see functions more quickly and give feedback [70].

Communication and Collaboration

The category Communication and Collaboration refers to how members interact and represents the mechanisms that inhibit or enable the ability of team members to combine their capabilities and behavior.

Effective Communication (F25): Effective communication is one of the key factors that establishes self-organizing practices within teams [36;71]. As the Agile Manifesto states, the most efficient and effective method of conveying information to and within a team is the face-to-face conversation [7]. While face-to-face interaction requires co-location, a suitable alternative for distributed teams is video conferences that capture the visual aspect of communication such as facial expression and gestures [72]. Effective communication is also supported by the concepts of an open workspace, sharing information daily as well as having information radiators and visualizing the process.

Task-related Communication (F26): In a self-organizing team, work is organized through formalized meetings that are task-related [35]. At the beginning of the agile transition, these meetings require a lot of time and tend to be highly formalized with set agendas, which limits the interaction possibilities. As self-organization raises the question regarding the usefulness of these meetings and their frequency, each role should be able to decide for themselves if it is necessary to participate in each meeting (35).

Porous Communication (F27): [61] observed the theme of porous communications in self-organizing teams. The term means increasing communication paths and interaction across teams by allocating the resources accordingly. The challenge of planning porous communication lies in trying to address all the requirements from the standpoint of individuals as well as business units. The strongest form of porous communication is achieved by tactically organizing team members in the different teams to increase communication paths and thus, a high interaction frequency amongst teams (61).

Conflict Management (F28): To enable self-organization, a team is required to know how to deal with conflict because increased collaboration also generates interpersonal conflict [39]. Since most conflicts arise at the team level, they should be dealt with there so that the team can learn and mature. Research has shown that autonomous teams must implement conflict resolution techniques to manage internal conflicts and disagreements efficiently [62]. [63] found out that interpersonal conflict affected project outcomes less when teams had well-functioning conflict management in place. Moreover, interpersonal conflict is negatively connected to the agile team practices Iterative Development and Customer Access [39]. Thus, a structure for intra-team conflict is needed so team members discuss the conflicts as early as possible before they become personal [62].

Member Personality (F29): Having the right people, in terms of member personality, is believed to be key to success factors in agile teams. On the one hand, conscientiousness was found to be a critical driver of autonomous work team behaviors [64]. The personality trait provides organization and direction for achieving the team's goals [65]. In highly interdependent teams, individual contributions are essential to overall team success. Therefore, conscientious individuals will more likely perform multiple roles, perform their roles with a minimum of oversight, avoid social loafing and engage in greater cooperative behavior [64]. On the other hand, studies show that agreeability also relates to better teamwork [58].

Customer Collaboration (F30): For an agile project to be successful, customer involvement is necessary as maintaining a good customer relationship is essential in a self-organizing team [23]. Some studies suggest that a customer representative needs to be on-site who can be consulted if needed [44].

Team Distribution (F31): Not only the proximity to the customer was seen as a driver of self-organization practices but also co-location of the whole team is deemed as a success factor for agile teams [23] and proved to influence communication [73]. [74] state that team members need to be co-located and dedicated to a single project to effectively self-organize. [45] support this claim by observing that team members need to be allocated to one project as a split across multi-projects has a negative influence on the team's ability to perform and self-organize. Not only the co-location but also the physical arrangement of the workspace was discovered to enable self-organization.

3 Method

For the overall answer to the research question, a multi-criteria maturity model is to be developed. In addition to an assessment of the already existing degree of self-organization, it should also guide a development path towards more of this agile practice and thus promote agile process management. The general suitability of a maturity model for such an objectives following the principle of design science research [10, 75] and is generally affirmed in scientific discussions of the information systems discipline [76, 77, 78, 79]. The exact research design towards the maturity model follows the recommendation of [80] and is described in Fig. 1. Many details of the holistic study design have already been published in [8] - the reader interested in the in-depth methods is in this respect referred to this previous publication.

Overall, the first step is to collect design areas of self-organization on the basis of scientific findings. Indicators make the gradual achievement of the path toward an ideal self-organization for agile process management measurable. A provided questionnaire serves the operational collection of the indicators on the part of the users of the model, that is the BPM team. The internal complexity of the model remains hidden to them (e.g. scientific indicators of self-organization), because they only agree or disagree with

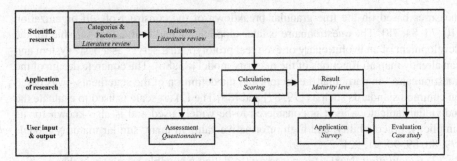

Fig. 1. Research design to create the maturity model [8]

practical statements in the evaluation. The developed scoring provides a quantitative measurement of the current degree in comprehensible maturity levels. A final evaluation could assess the added value of the maturity model.

The steps highlighted in white in Fig. 1 were already part of the first study. There, based on a systematic literature analysis in scientific databases, a total of 31 factors for a high degree of self-organization in process teams were derived. In the Realted Work of this paper, the related indicators were presented. Their development and compilation followed the rules according to [80–82]:

(0) *Indicators*: In order to obtain usable (calculable) factor values for the model, specific requirements must be placed on the indicators of the factors. In addition to the requirement that the indicators must be applicable across processes, teams and organizations, they must also be able to be handled by the target group without much effort. This increases the acceptance of the model through usability and traceability [81]. On the one hand, the objectification of the indicators used is intended to ensure that they can be easily and clearly determined and used as applied performance indicators. The metrics therefore follow the assessment of [82] according to which they have to quantify certain characteristics of the investigated object (e.g., the team organization) and also translate phenomena (e.g., lack of self-organization) into quantifiable parameters. For an accurate assessment of the target dimension (in this case agile process management), indicators of self-organization are to be derived from several data points that are aggregated into an index by measurement rules [82]. For this purpose, the compilation follows [83], who distinguishes between two types of indicators: On the one hand, factors that can be quantitatively measured by scalable parameters are considered and, on the other hand, indicators that capture the good or bad quality of a factor, such as the presence of an agile event or a certain ceremony [80].

In this paper, we now document three further steps to complete the overall research project:

(1) *Assessment*: In order to appropriately assess the identified factors for desirable self-organization, a standardized assessment is recommended. Statements are developed for the indicators, which the BPM teams or team leaders can gradually agree to. A self-assessment system in the form of a questionnaire was developed for this purpose. This makes it possible to (a) use the maturity model as a reference framework, (b) simultaneously measure the actual state of self-organization, and (c) prioritize improvement

measures based on the fine-granular breakdown of the construct of self-organization [10, 75, 84, 78]. The questionnaire is later (application and evaluation) suitable for the development of an evolutionary or even real prototype that serves as a basic system and can already map all functions of the maturity model [85, 86]. The concrete design of the questionnaire - in particular the sectors and the definition of the statements - was based on common standards such as [79, 87] and [88].The Likert scale is used to evaluate the individual indicators, as it is considered to be widely used and is also known for its simplicity, practicability, and high informative value in many similar maturity models [79, 88, 89, 90, 91, 92].

(2) *Calculation*: Next, it is necessary to define a suitable rating scale that enables the user evaluation from the questionnaire to be transferred into values and, finally, also to determine a maturity level as a rather simple (possibly even striking) means of describing the current status. This seems to be warranted despite no quantitative research in the strict sense, as [83] argues, for example, that the quality of processes can rarely be measured directly, but that the use of rating scales is possible as a suitable method for self-assessment [80]. (a) For calculation purposes, it is first assumed that the assessment of the state of self-organization is multicriteria, so various factors must be considered in weights. The evaluation scheme (i.e., statements and rating on the scale) from (1) provides the basis for this. As a result of an evaluation of suitable multicriteria decision methods, the simple additive weighting (SAW) method described by [93] is used for the model construction of this paper [80, 94]. Other alternatives proposed in the literature to determine the weights (e.g., direct ranking, the pairwise comparison, the trade-off method, or the swing method) seem much less appropriate for the question of self-organization [95]. Rather, the results of the categorization should be used to distribute equal weights between the indicators [79, 80, 96, 97].

(3) *Result (maturity levels)*: A classification according to five successive maturity levels has become established in BPM maturity models. For example, [98], [99, 100] and [101] do this, as [79] has compiled. This gradual classification seems very appropriate for very IT-centric perspectives on digital transformation [92, 102, 100, 103], however, this differentiation seems too fine-granular for people-centric questions. Mock inaccuracies arise, as social conditions are less objective to capture, and even the classical interpretations of the five levels (e.g., following CMMI's explanations) would be of little help in the case of self-organization (for example, at level 4: What would quantitative measurement of self-organized team mean?).This is why, the exact levels of the maturity model of this contribution bases on the more social-driven recommendations by [104]. The author specifies that three different self-organization levels can be distinguished [104] and should be sufficient for agile levels.

4   Results

Calculation
The scoring of the index is divided into several steps, which will be explained in the following. At first, the factors needed to be made assessable for use in business practice. For this reason, a set of indicators which is presented in Table 2, was defined for each factor based on the literature review.

In the next step, the input from the model needed to be made applicable. As readiness was discovered to be best measured by using a 5-point Likert scale, each indicator was transferred into a Likert-type response item. The translation to a nominal score was done by mapping the ratings to a nominal value. These nominal values are then used to evaluate a particular indicator. Table 3 shows the mapping rule that was applied to make the items assessable.

Table 3. Nominal Values

Linguistic measure (5-point Likert scale)	Strongly Disagree	Tend to Disagree	Neither Disagree nor Agree	Tend to Agree	Strongly Agree
Applied mapping rule	0	1	2	3	4

After the mapping rule application, the highest achievable score for each of the factors could be calculated. Depending on the number of indicators, the maximum scores per factor were computed as follows:

Maximum score per factor = highest possible rating (=4) x number of indicators per factor.

The maximum score then acts as a basis to determine the Factor Maturity Level:

Factor Maturity Level = Sum of the rating of each indicator / maximum score per factor.

In the next step, each factor was assigned a weight with a value between 0 and 1 with the weights of all factors of a category equaling 1. While the example in Table 2 assumes that all factors have equal weight, index users can assign higher weights if they subjectively deem a factor as more or less important than others. The weights were computed as follows:

Factor weight = 1/number of factors per category.

By multiplying the Factor Maturity Level with the factor weight, the weighted factor is determined:

Weighted factor = Factor Maturity Level x factor weight.

Finally, the last step is to calculate the Category Maturity Level:

Category Maturity Level = Sum of the weighted score of each factor.

The assignment rule served as a guide for classifying the maturity levels achieved. It is assumed that strong agreement with the indicators implies self-organization readiness. Thus, if the indicators are rated on average from 0 (strongly disagree) to 2.4 (strongly neither agree nor disagree), teams have achieved 0–60% of self-organization readiness. If teams tend to agree with the statements with an average of 2.5 to 3.4, they have achieved 60–85%. If most questions are answered with "strongly agree" (3.5–4), the result is 85–100%, which means the team is ready to self-organize.

Therefore, a team is ready for self-organization when all categories have a minimum of 85%. In theory, if only one or two categories have reached 100% and the others only 30%, self-organization readiness will not have been achieved. Table 4 presents the self-organization levels that can be attained and their associated values and descriptions.

On the first level, hierarchies and a strong formal culture define the work of a team [104]. It is not ready to self-organize and has only reached up to 60% in all the categories. These teams are new to agile methods and must first learn basic agile development practices. Typically, they retain many of their previous ways of working, while some individuals are perceived as resistant to change. In new agile teams, individuals are risk-averse and prefer a manager-driven approach. Team members feel more secure when management assigns tasks to them, so they do not have to make decisions voluntarily or independently. Project management practices such as requirements specification

Table 4. Levels of Self-organization

Self-organization Readiness	Category Maturity Level	Self-organization Level
Not Achieved	0%–60%	The team itself decides the things that directly affect it such as personnel deployment, content and distribution of work. Hierarchies, clear disciplinary responsibilities, a strong formal culture and rules are part of this level [104]. Team members show a lack of knowledge of Agile values and practices [21, 45]. The following practices are displayed at this level [16]: Traditional Software Development Practices, Manager-Driven Team Practices, Driving Management Approach, Limited Reflective Practices, Hierarchical Culture
Partially Achieved	60%–85%	The team is familiar with the Agile methods and practices and confident to work in the Agile environment [21, 45]. It sets itself flexible goals, actively works on its improvement and discloses all work processes. While hierarchies exist, managers see themselves more as consultants and coaches. Strategic decisions continue to be made by top management [104]. The following practices are displayed at this level [16]: Hybrid Software Development Practicesc, Manager-Assisted Team Practices, Adopting Management Approach, Focused Reflective Practices, Evolving Culture

(continued)

Table 4. (*continued*)

Self-organization Readiness	Category Maturity Level	Self-organization Level
Largely / Fully Achieved	85%–100%	The team is organized in a completely decentralized manner so that it acts as a company within a company. It continues to actively exchange information with the other teams. There are no hierarchies, instead, everyone follows a clear self-governing code [104]. Team members are likely to think positively about their team, project, management and customers and strong team culture has been developed [21, 45]. The following practices are displayed at this level [16]: Agile Software Development Practices, Team-Driven Team Practices, Empowering Management Approach, Embedded Reflective Practices, Open Culture

and prioritization as well as effort estimation are mostly performed by managers and customers without involving the team, which only focuses on the implementation of the tasks. Management is often seen as the driving force when working with customers and as a problem solver for the team. Teams on this level are limited in their reflective practices and highly focused on implementation. Although learning opportunities are available, learning-oriented tasks are often seen as time-consuming [17].

Self-organization readiness is partially achieved when the Category Maturity Levels have attained 60–85%. The team sets itself flexible goals and works on its improvement [104]. Teams on this level move away from their previous practices toward agile practices, while learning and reflection are more common. Project management activities are alternatively determined by the manager or the team. Task assignments can take the form of assisted assignments where team members are directed by their technical leads or project managers to improve individual autonomy. Teams can communicate and collaborate directly with their customers [16].

If the team has a score of 85–100% across all the categories, it is ready to self-organize. On this level, the team is organized in a decentralized manner and every member follows a self-governing code [104]. These teams use agile practices such as pair programming, testing, frequent releases, daily stand-up meetings and retrospectives. The team self-assigns its tasks and handles the requirements specification, clarification, prioritization and estimation on its own. The empowering management approach includes aspects such as encouraging teams, removing external barriers, keeping the team informed and helping the team focus by protecting them from disruption. Managers in self-organizing teams expect direct team-customer collaboration and relinquish control to the team. Reflective practices are firmly embedded in the daily work routine.

At the organizational level, agile methods are adapted to the respective context and specific constraints and learning opportunities are created in the form of organization-wide initiatives [16].

Application

The guide now to be developed serves as a handbook for the application of the index in management practice. It proposes an index questionnaire for better identification of weak and strong points and provides a usage guide that explains when and how to use the index.

Lastly, references to tools and methods are made that can improve a team's self-organization readiness. The index questionnaire, whose items were generated by evaluating the indicators, is shown in Table 5. It consists of 71 questions that were grouped

Table 5. Questionnaire to evaluate the maturity of self-organization

Factor	Statement to be rated	Factor	Statement to be rated
Team Goals, Vision and Cohesion			
F20I1	Our team has clear and common team goals	F22I2	I feel I can admit mistakes
F20I2	I actively participated in identifying and setting team goals	F22I3	I feel respected by my team members
F21I1	I feel our team has a shared vision	F23I1	Good/bad behavior is addressed within the team
F21I2	I feel committed to the vision	F23I2	I adapt my behavior to the team's behavior
F6I3	Team members are free to voice their opinions and raise concerns	F22I1	Every team member performs their role to the best of their ability
Team Organization			
F7I1	We work in small teams (no more than 5–9 members) in our projects	F17I1	Every team member is involved in the decision-making process
F7I2	We have enough capacity to accomplish the tasks	F16I1	The accountability for the whole project is shared among team members
F18I1	Every team member has clearly defined roles and responsibilities	F19I1	Our team identifies members who jeopardize the productiveness and initiates their removal
F9I3	It is easy to shift workload among team members	F10I1	Team members are easily added or removed
F10I2 F17I2	Leadership in our team is given to the person with the knowledge, skills and abilities required for the issues at the time		

(continued)

Table 5. (*continued*)

Factor	Statement to be rated	Factor	Statement to be rated
Communication and Collaboration			
F22I5 F25I1	Communication and negotiation in our project happen mostly face-to-face	F27I1	I know what other teams in the project are currently working on
F11I4 F24I3 F25I4	Our team has daily meetings	F12I1	I regularly give feedback on a co-worker's work
F20I3	Our team values and considers alternative suggestions in team discussions	F12I2	I regularly ask for input and suggestions on my work
F28I1	Our team knows what to do when conflicts between team members arise	F17I4	I explain to other team members what is needed from them
F28I2	Our team can avoid the negative aspects of conflict before they occur	F19I4	Our team has a representative who manages clients' expectations and guides the collaboration between the client and the team
F13I1	Our team regularly contemplates what we are doing and how we are working together	F30I1	I feel the customer considers themselves responsible for elements of the project
F25I3	The current project status and requirements of my team are clearly visualized	F30I2	I feel the customer provides feedback regularly
F26I1	I know what other team members are currently working on		
Planning and Strategy			
F1I1	Management only specifies minimum project criteria	F24I2 F30I3	Our team has a product delivery strategy
F1I2	Management doesn't interfere in our day-to-day activities	F31I2	I am dedicated to a single project
F4I2	Management supports our team when the schedule needs to be bent	F5I3 F31I4	Our team doesn't lose resources to other projects
F2I1	Our team has to refer back to many stakeholders before making a decision	F6I1	Our organization doesn't have hierarchical structures
F2I2	Our team was involved in the project planning from the beginning	F4I1	Management provides sufficient infrastructure and resources for effective operations

(*continued*)

Table 5. (*continued*)

Factor	Statement to be rated	Factor	Statement to be rated
F24I1	Our team collectively estimates and plans iterations	F6I2	Management is directly accessible by all employees and maintains an open-door policy
F24I4	Our planning process can work as a model for others	F11I1	Information is shared with the whole organization
F3I1	I control the scheduling and implementation of my tasks	F25I2 F31I3	Our team works in an open workspace
F3I2	Tasks are clearly outlined so that I can easily perform them	F31I1	Our team is geographically closely located
Knowledge and Skills			
F5I1	I have the skills and expertise to accomplish the tasks	F8I1	Team members come from different training and backgrounds
F5I2	I can handle the workload	F19I2	Our team has a member that understands both business language and technical terms
F11I2	I set aside exclusive time for learning	F29I1	The majority of my team members are very conscientious
F8I2 F11I3	I accumulate knowledge in other areas than my own	F29I2	The majority of my team members are very agreeable
F9I2	It is easy to complete someone else's task	F29I3	The majority of my team members are motivated
Agility and Change			
F13I2	It is easy to question given concepts and organizational processes	F15I3	I provide recognition when I see people implementing new ways of doing things
F18I2	I seek out new responsibilities	F15I1	I introduce changes in my daily work to help the organization achieve its change goals
F14I2	Our team is encouraged to use agile methods and self-organizing practices	F15I2	Change is intensively and transparently communicated throughout the whole organization
F14I1	I feel it is easy to apply agile methods	F5I4	I feel our team can self-organize
F19I3	Our team has a representative of the agile cause who advertises agile methods with the clients and management		

into six topics. If a team leader, change or project manager wants to assess a team's self-organization readiness, the proposed survey needs to be answered by the members of this team. In the questionnaire, the interviewees indicate their agreement with a given statement on a 5-point Likert scale. For each statement, it is recommended to record an assessment (response) following the linguistic measure described in Table 5. The introductory phrase "To what extent do you agree with the statements" can be used.

5 Discussion and Summary

In this paper, a maturity model for self-organized BPM teams was developed based on a preliminary study. The artifact created uses the self-reporting of process teams or BPM project managers to be able to precisely determine what level of self-organization already exists. For this purpose, the assessments from a questionnaire are successively compared with factors for a well-organized team known from the literature and finally quantified on the basis of a maturity level.

Although the model is an attempt to measure self-organization, the research presented is in tension between quantifiable objectivity and qualitatively vague characteristics of teams and its performance. In this respect, the scales used as well as the few maturity levels are to be understood as a compromise for the quantification of facts that are difficult to quantify. The same applies to the factors, which may be well-founded and literature-based, but can certainly never completely cover all relevant factors for effective teamwork in self-organization. Moreover, this leads to the missing part of the maturity model - namely the evaluation to fully cover the research design and also the claim of the design science paradigm. Initial case studies in IT consulting processes have already been undertaken by the authors. These were able to demonstrate for very different processes and process teams that (i) filling out the questionnaires was very easy and that (ii) the assessments matched the previously queried states of experts on the self-organization of the processes under investigation. In addition, (iii) guidance towards more agile process management was very easy possible through the criteria list. Even though the case studies cannot be published here due to confidentiality and because they were not designed for a study report, they have at least practically and exemplary demonstrated the added value of the overall model very well.

Self-organization is not the only agile practice that needs to be considered in BPM. Nevertheless, the model set up can be understood as a further building block towards agile process management, with which the current state of self-organization (as part of agile BPM) and also a path to an ideal target state can be described.

References

1. Saynisch, M.: Beyond frontiers of traditional project management. Proj. Manag. J. **41**(2), 21–37 (2010)
2. Kosieradzka, A., Rostek, K.: The Multifaceted Character of Process Management in Organizations. In: Process Management and Organizational Process Maturity, pp. 1–33. Springer, Cham (2021). https://doi.org/10.1007/978-3-030-66800-6_1
3. Gebhart, M., Mevius, M., Wiedmann, P.: Business process evaluation in agile business process management using quality models. Int. J. Adv. Life Sci. **6**(3/4), 279–290 (2014)

4. Perminova, O., Gustafsson, M., Wikström, K.: Defining uncertainty in projects – a new perspective. Int. J. Project Manage. **26**(1), 73–79 (2008)
5. Moe, N., Dingsøyr, T., Røyrvik, E.A.: Putting agile teamwork to the test - a preliminary instrument for empirically assessing and improving agile software development. Lecture Notes Bus. Inform. Process. **31**, 114–123 (2009)
6. Högl, M., Gemuenden, H.G.: Teamwork quality and the success of innovative projects: a theoretical concept and empirical evidence. Organ. Sci. **12**, 435–449 (2001)
7. Fowler, M., Highsmith, J.: The agile manifesto. Software Development **9**(8), 28–34 (2001)
8. Lederer, M., Thummerer, J.: Organizing a Self-Organized Team: Towards a Maturity Model for Agile Business Process Management. In: Proceedings of the S-BPM ONE (2022)
9. Bernstein, E., Bunch, J., Canner, N., Lee, M.: Beyond the holacracy hype. Harv. Bus. Rev. **94**(7), 38–49 (2009)
10. Hevner, A.R., March, S.T., Park, J., Ram, S.: Design science in information systems research. MIS Q. **28**(1), 75–105 (2004)
11. Qumer, A., Henderson-Sellers, B.: A framework to support the evaluation, adoption and improvement of agile methods in practice. J. Syst. Softw. **81**(11), 1899–1919 (2008)
12. Qumer, A., Henderson-Sellers, B., McBride, T.: Agile adoption and improvement model. In: Proceedings of the European and Mediterranean Conference on Information Systems (2007)
13. Sureshchandra, K., Shrinivasavadhani, J.: Adopting Agile in Distributed Development. In: IEEE Proceedings of the Int. Conference on Global Software Engineering (2008)
14. Rohunen, A., Rodriguez, P., Kuvaja, P., Krzanik, L., Markkula, J.: Approaches to Agile Adoption in Large Settings: A Comparison of the Results from a Literature Analysis and an Industrial Inventory. In: Ali Babar, M., Vierimaa, M., Oivo, M. (eds.) Product-Focused Software Process Improvement. PROFES 2010. Lecture Notes in Computer Science, vol. 6156. Springer, Heidelberg (2010)https://doi.org/10.1007/978-3-642-13792-1_8
15. Sidky, A., Arthur, J., Bohner, S.: A disciplined approach to adopting agile practices: the agile adoption framework. Innov. Syst. Softw. Eng. **3**(3), 203–216 (2007)
16. Hoda, R., Noble, J.: Becoming Agile - A Grounded Theory of Agile Transitions in Practice. In: Proceedings of the 39th International Conference on Software Engineering (2017)
17. Patil, M.R., Suresh, M.: Assessment of team agility in internet of things projects. Webology **18**, 137–148 (2021)
18. Hoda, R., Noble, J., Marshall, S.: Self-organizing roles on agile software development teams. IEEE Trans. Software Eng. **39**(3), 422–444 (2013)
19. Takeuchi, H., Nonaka, I.: The new new product development game. Harv. Bus. Rev. **64**(1), 137–146 (1986)
20. Stray, V., Moe, N.B., Hoda, R.: Autonomous agile teams: Challenges and future directions for research.In: Proceedings of the 19th International Conference on Agile Software Development, pp. 1–5 (2018)
21. Hoda, R.: Self-organizing agile teams. Victoria University, Wellington (2011)
22. Dikert, K., Paasivaara, M., Lassenius, C.: Challenges and success factors for large-scale agile transformations. J. Syst. Softw. **119**, 87–108 (2016)
23. Chow, T., Cao, D.: A survey study of critical success factors in agile software projects. J. Syst. Softw. **81**, 961–971 (2008)
24. Marks, M.A., Mathieu, J.E., Zaccaro, S.J.: A temporally based framework and taxonomy of team processes. Acad. Manag. Rev. **26**(3), 356–376 (2001)
25. Salas, E., Sims, D.E., Burke, C.S.: Is there a "big five" in teamwork? Small Group Res. **36**, 555–599 (2005)
26. Ancona, D., Bresman, H., Caldwell, D.: The X-factor: Six steps to leading high-performing X-teams. Organ. Dyn. **38**, 217–224 (2009)

27. Cockburn, A., Highsmith, J.: Agile software development - The people factor. Computer **11**, 131–133 (2001)
28. Babb, J.S., Hoda, R., Nørbjerg, J.: Embedding reflection and learning into agile software development. IEEE Softw. **31**(4), 51–57 (2014)
29. Qureshi, M.R., J., Abass, Z.: Long term learning of agile teams. Int. J. Softw. Eng. Appl. **8**(6), 1–18 (2017)
30. Lamoreux, M.: Improving agile team learning by improving team reflections. In: Proceedings of the Agile Development Conference (2005)
31. Kröll, M.: Innovations, agile management methods and personnel development. In: Nazir, S., Ahram, T., Karwowski, W. (eds.) Advances in Human Factors in Training, Education, and Learning Sciences. AHFE 2020. Advances in Intelligent Systems and Computing, vol. 1211. Springer, Cham (2020)https://doi.org/10.1007/978-3-030-50896-8_43
32. Högl, M., Parboteeah, K.P.: Autonomy and teamwork in innovative projects. Hum. Resour. Manage. **45**(1), 67–79 (2006)
33. Thorgren, S., Caiman, E.: The role of psychological safety in implementing agile methods across cultures. Res. Technol. Manag. **62**(2), 31–39 (2019)
34. Cinite, I., Duxbury, L.E.: Measuring the behavioral properties of commitment and resistance to organizational change. J. Appl. Behav. Sci. **54**(2), 113–139 (2018)
35. Schell, S., Bischof, N.: Change the way of working. Ways into self-organization with the use of Holacracy: an empirical investigation. Europ. Manage. Rev. **21**(5), 1–15 (2021)
36. Karhatsu, H., Ikonen, M., Kettunen, P., Fagerholm, F., Abrahamsso, P.: Building blocks for self-organizing software development teams: a framework model and empirical pilot study. In: Proceedings of the 2nd Software Technology and Engineering (2010)
37. Whitworth, E., Biddle, R.: Motivation and cohesion in agile teams. In: Concas, G., Damiani, E., Scotto, M., Succi, G. (eds.) Agile Processes in Software Engineering and Extreme Programming. XP 2007. Lecture Notes in Computer Science, vol. 4536. Springer, Heidelberg (2017).https://doi.org/10.1007/978-3-540-73101-6_9
38. Keller, R.T.: Cross-functional project groups in research and new product development: diversity, communications, job stress, and outcomes. Acad. Manag. J. **44**(3), 547–555 (2001)
39. Gren, L.: The Links Between Agile Practices, Interpersonal Conflict, and Perceived Productivity. In: Proceedings of the 21st International Conference on Evaluation and Assessment in Software Engineering (2017)
40. Morgan, G.: Images of organization. Sage, Beverly Hills (1986)
41. Hoda, R., Noble, J., Marshall, S.: Developing a grounded theory to explain the practices of selforganizing Agile teams. Emp. Softw. Eng. **17**(6), 609–639 (2012)
42. Gundelsby, J.H.: Enabling autonomous teams in large-scale agile through architectural principles. Proceedings of the 19th International Conference on Agile Software Development Companion (2018)
43. Langfred, C.W.: The paradox of self-management, individual and group autonomy in work groups. J. Organ. Behav. **21**(5), 563–585 (2000)
44. Grossman, F., Bergin, J., Leip, D., Merritt, S., Gotel, O.: One XP experience: introducing agile (XP) software development into a culture that is willing but not ready. In: Proceedings of the Conference of the Centre for Advanced Studies on Collaborative research (2004)
45. Hoda, R., Noble, J., Marshall, S.: Supporting self-organizing agile teams. In: Sillitti, A., Hazzan, O., Bache, E., Albaladejo, X. (eds.) Agile Processes in Software Engineering and Extreme Programming, pp. 73-87. Springer, Heidelberg (2011).https://doi.org/10.1007/978-3-642-20677-1_6
46. Hoda, R., Noble, J., Marshall, S.: Balancing acts: walking the Agile tightrope. In: Proceedings of the 2010 ICSE Workshop on Cooperative and Human Aspects of Software Engineering (2010)

47. Cohen, S.G., Ledford, G.E., Spreitzer, G.: A predictive model of self-managing work team effectiveness. Human Relations **49**(5), 643–676 (1994)
48. Almadhoun, W., Hamdan, M.: Optimizing the self-organizing team size using a genetic algorithm in agile practices. J. Intell. Syst. **29**(1), 1151–1165 (2018)
49. Brown, D.R., Harvey, D.F.: An experiential approach to organization development. Pearson, New York (2011)
50. Lemon, B., et al.: Applications of simulation and ai search: assessing the relative merits of agile vs traditional software development. In: Proceedings of the ASE 24th IEEE/ACM International Conference (2009)
51. Moe, N.B., Dingsøyr, T., Dybå, T.: Overcoming barriers to self-management in software teams. IEEE Softw. **26**(6), 20–26 (2010)
52. Nerur, S., Balijepally, V.: Theoretical reflections on agile development methodologies. Commun. ACM **50**(3), 79–83 (2007)
53. Moe, N.B., Dingsøyr, T., Dybå, T.: Understanding self-organizing teams in agile software development. In: 19th Australian Conference on Software Engineering, pp. 76–85 (2008)
54. Dybå, T., Dingsøyr, T.: Empirical studies of agile software development: a systematic review. Inf. Softw. Technol. **50**, 833–859 (2008)
55. Gandomani, T.J., Zulzalil, H., Abdul Ghani, A.A., Sultan, A.B.M., Meimandi Parizi, R.: The impact of inadequate and dysfunctional training on Agile transformation process: a Grounded Theory study. Information and Software Technology **57**, pp. 295–309 (2015)
56. Yukl, G.: Managerial Leadership - a Review of Theory and Research. J. Manag. **15**(2), 251–289 (1989)
57. Mathieu, J.E., Gilson, L.: Empowerment and team effectiveness: an empirical test of an integrated model. J. Appl. Psychol. **91**(1), 97–108 (2006)
58. Powell, A., Pazos, P.: Building high-performing autonomous teams in complex manufacturing settings. Eng. Manag. J. **29**(7), 1–14 (2017)
59. Valentine, M.A., Edmondson, A.C.: Team scaffolds: How mesolevel structures enable role-based coordination in temporary groups. Organ. Sci. **26**(2), 405–422 (2015)
60. Karhatsu, H., Ikonen, M., Kettunen, P., Fagerholm, F., Abrahamsso, P.: Building blocks for self-organizing software development teams: a framework model and empirical pilot study. 2nd Software Technology and Engineering (2010)
61. Thummadi, B.V., Khapre, V.D., Ocker, R.: Unpacking Agile Enterprise Architecture Innovation work practices: a Qualitative Case Study of a Railroad Company. In: Twenty-third Americas Conference on Information Systems (2017)
62. Gren, L., Lenberg, P.: The importance of conflict resolution techniques in autonomous agile teams. In: 19th International Conference on Agile Software Development (2018)
63. Barki, H., Hartwick, J.: Interpersonal conflict and its management in information system development. MIS Q. **25**(2), 195–228 (2001)
64. Morgeson, F., Reider, M., Campion, M.: Selecting individuals in team settings: the importance of social skills, personality characteristics, and teamwork knowledge. Pers. Psychol. **58**, 583–611 (2005)
65. King, E.B., George, J.M., Hebl, M.: Linking personality to helping behaviors at work: an interactional perspective. J. Pers. **73**(3), 585–607 (2005)
66. Barke, H., Prechelt, L.: Role clarity deficiencies can wreck agile teams. Peer Journal Computer Science 5 (2019)
67. Hoda, R., Noble, J., Marshall, S.: Self-organizing roles on agile software development teams. IEEE Trans. Softw. Eng. **39**(3), 422–444 (2013)
68. Moe, N.B., Dahl, B.H., Stray, V., Karlsen, L.S., Schjødt-Osmo, S.: Team Autonomy in Large-Scale Agile. In: Proceeding of the 52nd Hawaii International Conference on System Sciences (2019)

69. Nanus, B.: Visionary Leadership: Creating A Compelling Sense of Direction for Your Organization. Jossey-Bass, San Francisco (1992)
70. Zhong, S., Liping, C., Tian-en, C.: Agile planning and development methods. In: 3rd International Conference on Computer Research and Development (2011)
71. Hoda, R., Murugesan, L.K.: Multi-level agile project management challenges: a self-organizing team perspective. J. Syst. Softw. 117(06), 245–257 (2016)
72. Dorairaj, S., Noble, J., Malik, P.: Understanding the importance of trust in distributed agile projects: a practical perspective. In: Sillitti, A., Martin, A., Wang, X., Whitworth, E. (eds.) Agile Processes in Software Engineering and Extreme Programming. Springer, Heidelberg (2010)https://doi.org/10.1007/978-3-642-13054-0_14
73. Hummel, M., Rosenkranz, C., Holten, R.: The role of communication in agile systems development. Bus. Inf. Syst. Eng. 5(5), 343–355 (2013). https://doi.org/10.1007/s12599-013-0282-4
74. Hänninen, K., Haapasalo, H., Kaikkonen, H.: Characteristics of self-managing teams in rapid product development projects. Int. J. Value Chain Manage. 9(1), 1–25 (2018)
75. Peffers, K., Tuunanen, T., Rothenberger, M.A., Chatterjee, S.: A design science research methodology for information systems research. J. Manag. Inf. Syst. 24(3), 45–77 (2007)
76. Mettler, T, Rohner, P.: Situational maturity models as instrumental artifacts for organizational design. In: Proceedings of the 4th International Conference on Design Science Research in Information Systems and Technology (2009)
77. Pöppelbuß, J., Röglinger, M.: What makes a useful maturity model? a framework of general design principles for maturity models and its demonstration in business process management. In: Proceedings of the 19th European Conference on Information Systems (2011)
78. Van Looy, A., Poels, G., Snoeck, M.: Evaluating business process maturity models. J. Assoc. Inf. Syst. 18(6), 461–486 (2017)
79. Flechsig, C., Lohmer, J., Voß, R., Lasch, R.: Business process maturity model for digital transformation: an action design research study on the integration of information technology. Int. J. Innov. Manag. 26(3), 1–39 (2022)
80. Lederer, M., Meier, J., Heider, L.: A Multidimensional indicator system for quantifying business process interface problems. Int. J. Manag. Pract. 13(3), 295–320 (2020)
81. Schuh, H.: Entscheidungsverfahren zur Umsetzung einer nachhaltigen Entwicklung. Beiträge zur Betriebswirtschaftslehre, 45 (2001)
82. Kütz, M.: How to introduce KPIs and scorecards in IT management. In: Sheta, A.F., Ayesh, A., Rausch, P. (eds.). Business intelligence and performance management - Theory, systems and industrial applications. Springer, London (2013). https://doi.org/10.1007/978-1-4471-4866-1_5
83. Scheermesser, S.: Messen und Bewerten von Geschäftsprozessen als operative Aufgabe des Qualitätsmanagements. Beuth, Berlin (2003)
84. Tarhan, A., Turetken, O., Reijers, H.A.: Business process maturity models: A systematic literature review. Inf. Softw. Technol. 75, 122–134 (2016)
85. Laudon, K.C., Laudon, J.P., Schoder, D.: Wirtschaftsinformatik. Pearson, München (2010)
86. Pomberger, G., Blaschek, G.: Grundlagen des Software Engineering. Hanser, München (1993)
87. Schumacher, A, Nemeth, T., Sihn, W.: Roadmapping towards industrial digitalization based on an Industry 4.0 maturity model for manufacturing enterprises. Procedia CIRP 79, pp. 409–414 (2019)
88. Wagire, A.A., Joshi, R., Rathore, A.P.S., Jain, R.: Development of maturity model for assessing the implementation of Industry 4.0: learning from theory and practice. Production Plann. Contr. 32(8), 603–622 (2021)
89. Hammer, M.: The process audit. Harv. Bus. Rev. 85(4), 111–123 (2007)

90. Harmon, P.: Evaluating an organization's business process maturity. Business Process Trends **2**(3), 1–11 (2004)
91. Mettler, T., Rohner, P., Winter, R.: Towards a Classification of Maturity Models in Information Systems. In Atri, A.D., de Marco, M., Braccini, A.M., Cabiddu, F. (eds.). Management of the Interconnected World. Physica, Heidelberg (2010)
92. Nygaard, J., Colli, M., Wæhrens, B.V.: A self-assessment framework for supporting continuous improvement through IoT integration. Procedia Manufact. **42**, 344–350 (2020)
93. Yoon, K.P., Hwang, C.L.: Multiple attribute decision making: An introduction. Sage University, Thousand Oaks (1995)
94. Zangemeister, C.: Nutzwertanalyse in der Systemtechnik: Eine Methodik zur multidimensionalen Bewertung und Auswahl von Projektalternativen. Wittemann, München (1976)
95. Eisenführ, F., Weber, M., Langer, T.: Rational decision making. Springer, Berlin (2010)
96. Schreier, M.: Qualitative content analysis in practice. Sage, Los Angeles (2012)
97. Muckel, P.: Die Entwicklung von Kategorien mit der Methode der Grounded Theory. In Mey, G., Mruck, K. (eds.). Grounded theory reader. Verlag für Sozialwissenschaften, Wiesbaden (2011)
98. Tomanek, D.P., Schröder, J.: Analysing the value of information flow by using the value added heat map. Bus. Logist. Modern Manage. **17**, 81–91 (2017)
99. Leyh, C., Schäffer, T., Bley, K., Forstenhäusler, S.: Assessing the IT and software landscapes of Industry 4.0-enterprises: the maturity model SIMMI 4.0. In Ziemba, E. (ed.) Information Technology for Management: New Ideas and Real Solutions. Springer, Cham (2017)https://doi.org/10.1007/978-3-319-53076-5_6
100. Mamoghli, S., Cassivi, L., Trudel, S.: Supporting business processes through human and IT factors: a maturity model. Bus. Process. Mahag. J. **24**(4), 985–1006 (2018)
101. Siedler, C., et al.: Maturity model for determining digitalization levels within different product lifecycle phases. Prod. Eng. Res. Devel. **15**(3–4), 431–450 (2021). https://doi.org/10.1007/s11740-021-01044-4
102. Gollhardt, T., Halsbenning, S., Hermann, A., Karsakova, A., Becker, J.: Development of a Digital Transformation Maturity Model for IT Companies. In: 22nd Conference on Business Informatics (2020)
103. Schallmo, D., Williams, C.A., Boardman, L.: Digital Transformation of Business Models - Best Practice, Enablers, and Roadmap. Int. J. Innov. Manag. **21**(8), 1–17 (2017)
104. Hofert, S.: Agiler führen. Springer Fachmedien Wiesbaden, Wiesbaden (2016). https://doi.org/10.1007/978-3-658-12757-2

Exploring Potential Barriers for the Adoption of Cognitive Technologies in Industrial Manufacturing SMEs – Preliminary Results of a Qualitative Study

Thomas Auer[✉], Stefan Rösl, and Christian Schieder

Technical University of Applied Sciences Amberg-Weiden, Hetzenrichter Weg 15, 92637
Weiden, Germany
{t.auer,s.roesl,c.schieder}@oth-aw.de

Abstract. While small and medium-sized enterprises (SMEs) make up 99% of registered companies in Germany, only a fraction of them is engaged in Internet of Things (IoT) and Artificial Intelligence (AI) as part of their Industry 4.0 initiatives. Despite the potential of IoT and AI, the prerequisites to use these technologies may not be met by SMEs, or the benefits expected may not be aligned with their needs. This research paper identifies typical characteristics of SMEs in the manufacturing sector through a literature review. In addition, we conducted a brainwriting workshop and discussed the findings among interdisciplinary researchers. Our qualitative research approach revealed 19 distinct barriers classified into three key dimensions. Our findings can assist technology managers and production departments in evaluating their organizations and addressing the identified adoption barriers. Additionally, the results can be used in further research to set up practice-oriented guidelines that support the holistic adoption of IoT and AI in manufacturing SMEs.

Keywords: Internet of Things · Artificial Intelligence · Industry 4.0 · SME · Characteristics · Manufacturing

1 Introduction

Within industrial manufacturing, digitalization appears as a technology-driven transformation, proliferating technologies like the Internet of Things (IoT) and Artificial Intelligence (AI). These innovations play a crucial role in the advancement of Industry 4.0. Furthermore, they enable the manufacturing industry to tackle challenges, such as decreasing labor costs or promoting sustainable production by enhancing quality, minimizing waste, or reworking more effectively [1].

Industry 4.0 includes a wide range of current concepts, the assignment to a precise discipline and delineation of which is not possible. One of the fundamental concepts involves cyber-physical systems (CPS), which describe the merging of the digital and physical levels. Another concept is self-organization, in which existing manufacturing

M. Elstermann et al. (Eds.): S-BPM ONE 2023, CCIS 1867, pp. 45–54, 2023.
https://doi.org/10.1007/978-3-031-40213-5_3

systems are increasingly decentralized. Both concepts reflect the retrofit in small and medium-sized enterprises and are therefore addressed in this paper [2].

As a third concept cognitive technologies cover a broad spectrum, including subgroups such as AI, IoT, high-performance computing, and advanced analytics [3]. In general, cognitive technologies are extensively discussed in the context of the fourth industrial revolution and the development of Industry 4.0 [4]. We define the term cognitive technology as AI in conjunction with the IoT and its relationship to the fourth industrial revolution, specifically the development of Industry 4.0.

By combining AI and IoT, the possibilities and potential of both can be further expanded. As IoT generates data, AI has the potential to find valuable insights within that data. Without AI, the data generated by IoT would be useless, as it is impossible for a human to find information within it. Furthermore, when a new pattern is discovered within the data, the machine can learn on its own, which is impossible for an IoT system without AI. Therefore, IoT must rely on AI in order to be effective [5].

According to the EU fact sheet 2022, 99.6% of registered companies in Germany are classified as SMEs [6]. Despite the enormous potential, AI and IoT are hardly applied there. Only 9% use at least one AI application and a mere 5% are fully committed to AI and IoT, triggering questions about why SMEs do not use these technologies [7]. One reason is that introducing cognitive technologies is a significant challenge with extensive, unidentified barriers [8].

Türkeş [9] presents opinions and perceptions of SME managers in Romania on the barriers and drivers of Industry 4.0 technology adoption in business development. They conclude that regardless of industry, the most significant barriers were the lack of knowledge on Industry 4.0 and the focus on operations at the cost of developing the company. Concerning the relevance and adoption of AI technologies in SMEs, another study among 283 companies shows that contextual factors such as industry and degree of digitization play a significant role in SMEs' decision-making processes [10]. From a management and marketing perspective, the barriers and benefits of AI in SMEs have been perceived six foremost factors in AI applications [11]. These were technical AI competencies, poor financial position, organization size, the orientation of business promoters, awareness of AI benefits, and data quality [11]. A review of 37 studies examining the adoption of Industry 4.0 technologies in SMEs in the manufacturing sector revealed 27 determinants, divided into technological, organizational, and environmental factors, and act as barriers or drivers depending on their characteristics [12].

So far, the studies do not deal with the implementation of AI/IoT in industrial manufacturing in general. Some deal only with country-specific characteristics or explore the issues from a solely technological or entrepreneurial perspective. The extensive acceptance of SMEs regarding existing cognitive technologies is not given, and the potential gap of barriers in the context of manufacturing processes in SMEs needs to be identified. In this study, we thus seek answers to the following research question (RQ):

RQ: *What are the potential barriers for SMEs to adopt AI and IoT in industrial manufacturing and how can SMEs counteract these barriers?*

The remainder of the paper is structured as follows: first, the methodology applied is described. Then, in chapter 3, the results are presented and categorized into three key dimensions. Next, each key dimension and barrier is discussed individually. Finally, the conclusion discusses the summarizing results, limitations, and future research opportunities and emphasizes their significance.

2 Methodology

We conducted a brainwriting workshop to explore the first part of the RQ. Therefore, the methodology consists of two subsequent qualitative research steps and is presented in Fig. 1. For preparation, we used an organizational framework to cluster the characteristics of SMEs. Our paper utilizes a literature review to identify characteristics of SMEs in the manufacturing sector following the approach of Mayring 2019 [13]. Together with the organizational framework, these literature-based findings were utilized as input for a workshop with senior IT experts from academia, which followed the approach of Wilson 2013 [14].

Based on the research discussion and the summarized, merged results, three key dimensions were identified, along with strategies to counteract barriers, to fully address the RQ. The goal is to provide recommendations for SMEs in industrial manufacturing, and further research is incentivized.

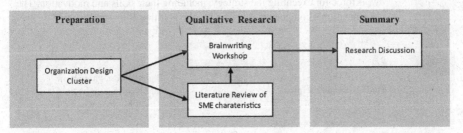

Fig. 1. Methodology

2.1 Organization Design Cluster

To reduce ambiguity, we refer to the widely used and well-established 7S organization design model. This framework considers the interplay of seven key elements. They are divided into hard elements (strategy, structure, and systems) and soft elements (shared value, style, staff, and skill) to describe the organizational design of an enterprise [15].

To avoid confusion in the following workshop, we combined the elements "Skill" and "Staff" as they have overlapping meanings, particularly within the context of SMEs. Table 1 summarizes the definition of the core elements according to the applied research approach followed by the original 7S framework.

2.2 Literature Review

To ensure an assessment of the current understanding of SME characteristics, a literature review has been conducted. The search string is shown in Fig. 2 and was used on the databases Data Science, EBSCOhost and IEEEXplore, ACM, and Springer Link.

Table 1. Definition of organizational core elements based on McKinsey 7S [15].

Dimension	Definition
Strategy	Outlines the company's actions and strategies for adapting to environmental shifts and securing a lasting competitive edge through sustainability
Structure	Concerns the organizational structure of departments and work processes, as well as the allocation of responsibility, reporting, and authority to make decisions
Systems	Refers to all supporting procedures that assess the organization's efficiency, including systems for control, information management, and production
Shared Value	The standards and norms that are actively practiced within the organization. These values guide behavior at all levels and influence the mindset of employees
Style / Culture	Represents the leadership style of top management in the company, how they manage the organization, present themselves to stakeholders, and the company's identity
Staff & Skill	Concerns about the company's human resource system and the necessary workforce for executing the strategy, including their skills and motivation. The organization's competencies are tied to the abilities of its employees

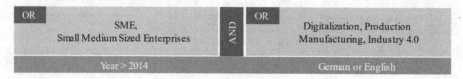

Fig. 2. Search string

After filtering on abstract, keywords, and region, 34 papers remained. Finally, after reviewing the remaining research articles, we determined eight relevant research papers. Additionally, the database was extended by three papers due to the inclusion of valuable studies based on the background knowledge and further reviews of the researchers. The results of the analysis of the typical characteristics of SMEs are shown in Table 2. For clarification, the characteristics have been mapped with the previously described 7S dimensions.

2.3 Brainwriting Workshop

The results of the literature review on SME characteristics were then used as input for a brainwriting workshop, where they were presented and validated in a group discussion. This ensured that all participants had a common understanding of the organization's design dimensions. To address the RQ, participants were briefed on the brainstorming topic to create ideas about potential barriers to each dimension of organizational design and how to counteract these.

Table 2. Characteristics of SMEs mapped by organization design dimension.

Dimension	Typical characteristics of SMEs	References
Strategy	C1: Lack of strategic orientation and digitalization strategy C2: Inconsistent competitive position and mostly in a specific market C3: Lack of government support C4: Digitalization strategy is often a task of management	[16–18]
Structure	C5: Owner-managed company, with all responsibilities at management C6: Centralized decision-making C7: Patriarchal management C8: Flat hierarchies with short ways of communication	[8, 17, 19, 20]
Systems	C9: Low degree of formalization and administrative effort C10: Relatively low quantities in production but high specialization C11: Heterogeneous manufacturing technologies and IT systems C12: Brownfield environment	[8, 18, 19, 21]
Shared Value	C13: Strong personal relationships C14: Low redress options in case of wrong decisions C15: Accumulation of functions (one person has many roles) C16: Limited financial possibilities	[16, 22, 23]
Style	C17: High flexibility due to person-related instruction and control C18: High improvisation and intuition C19: High workload due to a wide range of tasks C20: Direct involvement with small decision-making authority	[22, 24]
Staff & Skill	C21: Relatively high job satisfaction C22: Limited human resources (less academics, highly skilled workers) C23: Mainly technical background (less knowledge of methodologies) C24: Lack of resources for process optimization and digitalization	[8, 17, 18, 23–25]

Every group received handouts to assist them. Following a well-established best practice, the initial round was conducted with extended time and the opportunity to address any lingering questions. Upon completion of the final round, participants were given the chance to discuss particularly significant findings or emphasize exceptional aspects of individual elements. Furthermore, this collaborative discussion allowed for the exchange of diverse perspectives, enhancing the overall understanding and outcomes of the workshop.

3   Results and Discussion

The following section summarizes and categorizes the results of the brainwriting workshop. Subsequently, the key dimensions are presented and discussed, focusing on potential barriers for SMEs in adopting AI and IoT. Finally, we provide a brief comparison of our identified barriers to those found in a systematic review and outline strategies to counteract them.

3.1   Potential Barriers

The 19 barriers were accumulated using components of the research approach, a) brainwriting and b) researcher discussion. Table 3 shows the final compilation of all identified barriers mapped to the previously defined organization design dimension.

The organizational dimensions based on the 7S model were used to classify the characteristics of SMEs. However, thematic overlaps became visible when analyzing individual barriers, and further grouping was needed. The new aggregation became incompatible with the 7S model because topics are spread across multiple organizational dimensions. Thus, a new classification has been made in different key dimensions, representing SMEs' primary keys of action.

3.2   Key Dimensions

In Table 4, we present the correlation between the adoption barriers encountered by SMEs in the manufacturing industry (as documented in Table 3) and the key dimensions. These are divided into technology, strategy/management, and organizational change. According to this study, the key dimensions are relevant to address the development of a guideline that supports the adoption of AI and IoT in manufacturing SMEs.

A significant proportion of the items correspond to the organizational and managerial categories. This can be explained by the focus on identifying new barriers based on the typical characteristics of SMEs in combination with the defined organization design dimensions (see Table 2). In the following, we will discuss the key dimensions and provide suggestions to overcome the barriers.

Organizational Change Several barriers to AI and IoT adoption in SMEs include issues related to organizational change, like communication challenges, resistance to change, data-driven application acceptance, lack of skills and knowledge of IoT and AI, and fear regarding both technologies. Employees are afraid of being replaced by AI or AI experts. Management should promote positive attitudes towards change and improve communication to address these barriers. A technologically progressive organizational culture encompassing all employees and the need for alignment between the established corporate culture and required technical expertise is essential for successfully adopting

Table 3. Summarized and categorized results of the brainwriting workshop.

Dimension	Potential barriers to SMEs in adopting AI and IoT technologies in the context of industrial manufacturing
Strategy	B1: Lack of understanding of the technologies (IoT and AI) B2: Missing strategy for knowledge acquisition and skill building B3: Fear of decreasing competitiveness (time and cost-consuming)
Structure	B4: Concerns about data-driven decision-making and resistance to acceptance B5: Fear of organizational transformation triggered by new technologies B6: Resistance to change due to insufficient employee involvement/communication
Systems	B7: Missing status quo: need for analysis of processes and systems B8: Lack of standard integration procedures for existing systems B9: Concerns about sustainability, ROI, and reliability of systems
Shared Value	B10: High financial costs related to the rapidly aging technologies B11: Concerns about first-mover risks when integrating emerging technologies B12: Missing or unclear value proposition B13: Limited success stories
Style / Culture	B14: Organizational style fit and fear of change among owners B15: Lack of standardized methodology for innovative work styles B15: Issues with communication style and low-key communication
Staff & Skill	B16: Fear of job loss or change due to AI and AI experts B17: Gap in specialized skills, including AI and soft skills B18: Shortage of skilled professionals in SMEs B19: Discrepancy between traditional and modern roles

Table 4. Mapping of SME barriers to key dimensions.

Key Dimension	SME adoption barriers
Technology	B7, B8, B9, B10
Strategy and Management	B2, B3, B4, B11, B12, B13, B14, B18
Organizational Change	B1, B5, B6, B15, B16, B17, B19

AI and IoT in SMEs. A basic understanding of the technologies should be disseminated among all employees to reduce fears and reservations.

Strategy and Management A shortage of skilled professionals puts SMEs in a disadvantageous position compared to larger companies. To address this, companies should develop a strategy for employee skill-building and retention, along with innovative and standardized work procedures. In addition, employees need to grasp AI's benefits to fulfill their job duties. This ensures them to be more willing to adopt the new technology.

Additionally, the decision-making and strategy dilemma poses a challenge for managers. They are concerned about the risks of pioneering new technologies but also fear missing out on the trend and losing competitiveness. The management often waits due to a lack of clear monetary value propositions and limited success stories. To overcome this, the technical side must demonstrate promising progress and applications, reducing the perceived risks for early adoption. There must be transparent and standardized methods for using and adopting AI that deliver traceable and measurable results. These methods must be validated and documented beforehand so decision-makers can compare their investments with the possible results.

Technology Based on the technology dimension, the brainwriting workshop results reveal barriers to a comprehensive understanding of the systems' current state and future readiness, including physical assets and software systems. In preparation for IoT and AI adoption, processes and systems must be analyzed to determine their current state and whether and how compatibility with the new technologies is possible. That is not easy to accomplish in SMEs due to the brownfield environment with disparate systems and a need for standards. To counteract these barriers, standardized and evaluated guidelines must be developed and tailored specifically to the needs of a SME. Other barriers include uncertainty about future availability, reliability concerns, sustainability issues, and the financial viability of rapidly aging technologies.

In comparison to the systematic review of barriers of Industry 4.0 technology adaption from Ghobakhloo et al. [12], we identified new potential barriers. Furthermore, we focused solely on AI and IoT, thus achieving a more detailed and clearer picture. Among the previously neglected barriers were (1) fear of job loss or replacement by AI and AI experts, (2) concerns about data-driven decisions and limited success stories to which executives can refer and finally, (3) the lack of status quo processes and systems. This is especially a problem for SMEs, where existing equipment is already in use. Therefore, SMEs must first analyze and identify their status quo processes before adopting AI and IoT.

4 Conclusion

Our paper identifies potential new barriers to AI and IoT adoption in industrial manufacturing SMEs and suggests how these barriers can be countered. To answer the presented RQ, first typical SME characteristics were derived from a literature review and a group discussion. Afterward, they were clustered into an organizational design model. Based on these characteristics, a brainwriting workshop was conducted. As a result, 19 barriers were identified and mapped into three key dimensions: organizational change, management/strategy, and technology. Finally, the barriers were discussed and compared to those identified in a systematic review, and strategies to counteract them were explored to comprehensively address the research question.

The most significant new barriers are fear of job loss or replacement by AI and AI experts, concerns about data-driven decisions, limited success stories to which executives can refer, and the lack of status quo processes and systems due to the characteristic brownfield environment in SMEs. Our research paper highlights the significance of considering the presented key dimensions and barriers and guides companies and decision-makers to encounter the barriers.

It should be mentioned that our research approach is limited due to the need for more participants in the brainwriting workshop. Therefore, future research should aim to validate these results using larger samples and investigate other possible limitations. Based on the results of this paper and the analyzed studies, a guideline for the adoption of AI and IoT in manufacturing SMEs should be developed to explore the full potential of cognitive technologies in SMEs.

References

1. Zeba, G., et al.: Technology mining: Artificial intelligence in manufacturing. Technological Forecasting and Social Change, vol. 171 (2021). https://doi.org/10.1016/j.techfore.2021. 120971
2. Lasi, H., Fettke, P., Kemper, H.-G., Feld, T., Hoffmann, M.: Industry 4.0. Bus. Inf. Syst. Eng. 6(4), 239–242 (2014). https://doi.org/10.1007/s12599-014-0334-4
3. Elia, G., Margherita, A.: A conceptual framework for the cognitive enterprise: pillars, maturity, value drivers. Technology Analysis & Strategic Management, vol. 34 (2022). https://doi.org/ 10.1080/09537325.2021.1901874
4. Hollowell, C., Kollar, B., Vrbka, J., Kovalova, E.: Cognitive Decision-Making Algorithms for Sustainable Manufacturing Processes in Industry 4.0: Networked, Smart, and Responsive Devices. Econ. Manage., Financial Markets, 14(4), 9–15 (2019). https://doi.org/10.22381/ EMFM14420191
5. Ghosh, A., Chakraborty, D., Law, A.: Artificial Intelligence in Internet of Things. CAAI Trans. Intell. Technol., 3(4), (2018). https://doi.org/10.1049/trit.2018.1008
6. European Commission: 2022 SME Country Fact Sheet Germany (2022). https://ec.europa. eu/docsroom/documents/50688
7. Bauer, W., et al.: Künstliche Intelligenz in der Unternehmenspraxis. Studie zu Auswirkungen auf Dienstleistung und Produktion. Fraunhofer Verlag, Stuttgart (2019)
8. Bischoff, J., et al.: Erschließen der Potenziale der Anwendung von Industrie 4.0 im Mittelstand. agiplan, Mülheim an der Ruhr (2015)
9. Türkeş, M., et al.: Drivers and Barriers in Using Industry 4.0: A Perspective of SMEs in Romania. Processes, 7(3), 153 (2019). https://doi.org/10.3390/pr7030153
10. 1Ulrich, P., Frank, V.: Relevance and Adoption of AI technologies in German SMEs – Results from Survey-Based Research. Procedia Computer Science, vol. 192, 2152–2159 (2021). https://doi.org/10.1016/j.procs.2021.08.228
11. Kuldeep, B., Anuj, K., Arya, K., Purvi, P.: A Study of Barriers and benefits of Artificial Intelligence Adoption. In: Small and Medium Enterprise. Academy of Marketing Studies Journal, vol. 26 (2022)
12. Ghobakhloo, M., et al.: Drivers and barriers of Industry 4.0 technology adoption among manufacturing SMEs: a systematic review and transformation roadmap. JMTM, vol. 33(4) (2022). https://doi.org/10.1108/JMTM-12-2021-0505
13. Mayring, P.: Qualitative Content Analysis: Demarcation, Varieties, Developments. Qualitative Content Analysis, vol. 20 (2019). https://doi.org/10.17169/FQS-20.3.3343
14. Wilson, C.: Brainstorming and Beyond. A User-Centered Design Method. Elsevier Science, Amsterdam (2013)
15. Guenzi, P., Storbacka, K.: The organizational implications of implementing key account management: A case-based examination. Indust. Market. Manage. 45, 84–97 (2015). https:// doi.org/10.1016/j.indmarman.2015.02.020

16. Ihlau, S., Duscha, H.: Besonderheiten bei der Bewertung von KMU. Planungsplausibil-isierung, Steuern, Kapitalisierung. Springer, Wiesbaden (2019). https://doi.org/10.1007/978-3-658-18675-3

17. Wiesner, S., Gaiardelli, P., Gritti, N., Oberti, G.: Maturity Models for Digitalization in Man-ufacturing - Applicability for SMEs. In: Moon, I., Lee, G.M., Park, J., Kiritsis, D., von Cieminski, G. (eds.) APMS 2018. IAICT, vol. 536, pp. 81–88. Springer, Cham (2018). https://doi.org/10.1007/978-3-319-99707-0_11

18. Peschke, F., Eckardt, C.: Flexible Produktion durch Digitalisierung. Entwicklung von UseCases. Carl Hanser Verlag, München (2019)

19. Ludwig, T., et al.: HMD Praxis der Wirtschaftsinformatik 53(1), 71–86 (2015). https://doi.org/10.1365/s40702-015-0200-y

20. Steinmüller, K.: Methoden der Zukunftsforschung – Langfristorientierung als Ausgangspunkt für das Technologie-Roadmapping. In: Möhrle, M.G., Isenmann, R. (eds.) Technologie-Roadmapping. V, pp. 29–46. Springer, Heidelberg (2017). https://doi.org/10.1007/978-3-662-52709-2_3

21. Sames, G., Diener, A.: Stand der Digitalisierung von Geschäftsprozessen zu Industrie 4.0 im Mittelstand. Technische Hochschule Mittelhessen, Gießen (2018)

22. Mittal, S., Khan, M.A., Romero, D., Wuest, T.: A critical review of smart manufacturing & Industry 4.0 maturity models: Implications for small and medium-sized enterprises (SMEs). J. Manufact. Syst. 49, 194–214 (2018). https://doi.org/10.1016/j.jmsy.2018.10.005

23. Dickmann, P.: Schlanker Materialfluss mit Lean. Kanban und Innovationen. Springer, Berlin (2015)

24. Schebek L.: Ressourceneffizienz durch Industrie 4.0. VDI Zentrum Ressourceneffizienz, Berlin (2017)

25. Teichmann, M., Ullrich, A., Wenz, J., Gronau, N.: HMD Praxis der Wirtschaftsinformatik 57(3), 512–527 (2020). https://doi.org/10.1365/s40702-020-00614-x

Business Process Automation for Data Teams - A Practical Approach at Handelsblatt Media Group

Ana Moya[1](✉), Michael Hein[2], and Janina Reimann[1]

[1] Handelsblatt Media Group, Toulouser Allee 27, 40211 Düsseldorf, Germany
a.moya@handelsblattgroup.com
[2] Datatoolbox, Scheurenstr. 43, 40215 Düsseldorf, Germany

Abstract. This paper discusses the increasing importance of automating business processes, with a particular focus on data integration challenges required for data analytics at a larger organization. In this context, the paper introduces the concept of integration-Platform-as-a-service (iPaaS) solutions and highlights their key principles and advantages. It further presents a practical case study by the data team of Handelsblatt Media Group (HMG) to showcase how iPaaS can significantly increase efficiency of organizations. This paper not only serves as a valuable case study for iPaaS implementation for data teams, but also contributes to the broader discourse on the role of iPaaS technology in enhancing business performance.

Keywords: Business Process Automation · Integration Platform as a Service · Digital Transformation · Data Analytics · Workflow Automation

1 Introduction

In today's fast-paced business environment, modern organizations rely on numerous applications and undertake diverse business processes to drive the growth of their organizations. Nevertheless, many of these processes are still performed manually, leading to a slow and error-prone system. To address this issue, it is imperative to standardize and automate business processes. The increasing demand for business process automation has led to a growing need for businesses to integrate data across disparate systems, and the advent of cloud-based services and software-as-a-service (SaaS) applications has further fueled this trend.

However, implementing automation projects can be challenging, as modern business processes are agile and dynamic, and technical issues can exacerbate the situation by inducing system downtime, loss of data, and other such issues that negatively impact the business. In response to these challenges, Business Process Automation (BPA) refers to the use of technology to simplify and automate repetitive and manual processes in a business. It involves the use of software applications to automate routine tasks, such as data entry, document processing, and workflow management, and to reduce

M. Elstermann et al. (Eds.): S-BPM ONE 2023, CCIS 1867, pp. 55–60, 2023.
https://doi.org/10.1007/978-3-031-40213-5_4

the need for human intervention [1]. One type of software that is often used in BPA is integration-Platform-as-a-service (iPaaS). IPaaS facilitates a collaborative and integrated technical ecosystem, allowing efficient data transfer and workflow automation across diverse applications [2].

In this paper, we aim to highlight the growing importance of iPaaS solutions for business process automation and to outline the core concepts and benefits of using iPaaS systems from the perspective of a data expert at Handelsblatt Media Group (HMG). In this context, we will also provide a practical case study from the data team of HMG to demonstrate how the implementation of a standardized request management process using iPaaS solutions resulted in significant efficiency improvements. By showcasing the benefits of iPaaS solutions, we hope to encourage other organizations to consider similar implementations to optimize their business processes and enhance their overall performance.

2   Benefits and Constraints of iPaaS

In the present data-centric era, there has been a noticeable rise in the demand for professionals in the field of data analytics. Data teams are essential for any organization, as they provide valuable insights through the analysis of data, in other words turning data into actionable insights and decisions. By analyzing data, data teams can also identify improvements in business processes and increase the efficiency and productivity of organizations. However, business processes often have challenges in managing and integrating data from various sources and involving different departments. That's where iPaaS comes in.

IPaaS is a cloud-based solution it enables businesses to integrate and automate their workflows and business processes without the need for extensive coding or IT expertise. In essence, iPaaS allows different applications, systems, and data sources to communicate with each other, thereby streamlining business processes and increasing operational efficiency [3].

As data experts, we can attest to the fact that traditional methods of data integration and automation typically require a high degree of technical skill and experience. This often results in a situation where non-IT professionals are unable to fully leverage the benefits of automation and data-driven decision making. iPaaS, on the other hand, offers a user-friendly interface that makes it possible for non-technical users to easily connect and automate various data sources and applications.

Therefore, a key benefit of iPaaS is that it can help businesses to reduce the time and cost associated with traditional data integration projects. Instead of developing custom integration solutions from scratch, iPaaS platforms typically offer a range of pre-built connectors and integrations to popular business applications such as Jira, Slack, Salesforce and Microsoft 365 tools that can be easily configured and deployed. This can significantly reduce the time and cost associated with integration projects, while also reducing the risk of errors and downtime as well as facilitating communication across departments and teams.

Another key benefit of iPaaS is that it is designed to be scalable and flexible, which means that it can handle large volumes of data and adapt to changing business requirements. It can also help organizations to become more agile and responsive to changing market conditions. This, in turn, can lead to increased employee motivation and productivity.

However, there are also several limitations of iPaaS that organizations should consider before adopting this integration solution. Since iPaaS relies on pre-built connectors and templates, it may not support all the customizations necessary for complex integration scenarios. This poses a potential challenge for organizations that require a high degree of customization in their integration processes.

Another limitation of iPaaS is related to data security. As iPaaS is cloud-based, there may be concerns about the security of sensitive data during integration. It is therefore critical for organizations to evaluate the security measures implemented by the iPaaS provider and ensure that appropriate security measures are in place to protect their data.

Disruptions in internet connectivity can also impact the performance and availability of integrations. Hence, organizations must consider the reliability and availability of internet connectivity when utilizing iPaaS.

Vendor lock-in risks are yet another consideration when adopting iPaaS. The process of switching to a different iPaaS provider or reverting to on-premises integration can be resource-intensive and expensive. Therefore, it is vital for organizations to carefully evaluate the vendor's pricing model, contract terms, and exit strategy to avoid potential vendor lock-in situations.

In conclusion, iPaaS offers many benefits and can be a useful integration solution for data teams and organizations. However, it is important for organizations to carefully assess the limitations of iPaaS and evaluate their specific integration requirements before choosing this solution.

3   Case Study

At Handelsblatt Media Group, the demand for data analysis and insights has been increasing constantly in recent years due to factors like digital transformation and the growing recognition of the importance of data for business development and strategy. Therefore, it is particularly important for our data team to have an efficient and comprehensible request management. Clear processes for accepting, prioritizing and managing requests from stakeholders, along with establishing clear communication channels, are important to avoid delays and inefficiencies and at the same time to ensure that all stakeholders are informed of progress and priorities. However, this can be challenging due to limited resources and a lack of standardization and automation.

We at HMG have defined clear processes for the acceptance and management of requests from stakeholders. The key objective was to create a user-friendly workflow that was easily comprehensible and transparent for all parties involved. To achieve a high degree of standardization and automation in the data collection, organization, and communication process, various applications and tools were employed. These included a Sharepoint website as a central hub for users to access the system, which we have shown in Fig. 1. To correctly cluster our requests in advance, we have classified them into three types: Incidence-Requests, Ad-hoc-Requests and Project-Requests.

In order to ensure the most efficient implementation of our projects and requests, we follow a standardized process. This is intended to simplify communication, make processes and responsibilities transparent, better understand requirements and focus on adding value.

Please choose the type of your request:

Data Incident   **Ad hoc**   **Project**

Requests related to dashboards   Requests related to ongoing   Requests related to new projects
and tools   projects

Fig. 1. SharePoint Website for all types of data requests

Besides the SharePoint Website, we have used several other applications, such as Microsoft Forms for data entry, Microsoft Lists as database, Slack and Jira for communication and processing. Although there are a variety of iPaaS solutions available on the market, we have used Microsoft Power Automate for data integration. As a result, all requests are reported and handled consistently through all applications. This workflow could usually involve various manual steps, such as data validation, data transformation, and authentication. Figure 2 provides an illustration of the applications we have used in the entire request process.

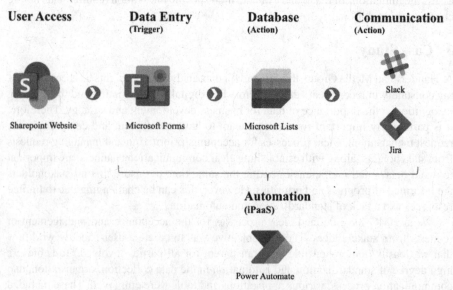

Fig. 2. Applications used in the request process

Triggers and actions are the two primary building blocks used to create iPaaS automations. A trigger is an event that initiates the integration workflow. An action, on the other hand, is a task that is performed in response to the trigger. Figure 3 shows our workflow within Microsoft Power Automate.

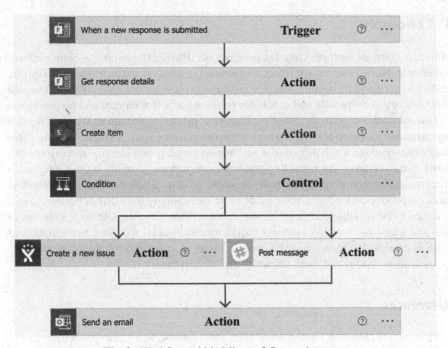

Fig. 3. Workflow within Microsoft Power Automate

The trigger of this workflow is the submission of a Microsoft form. The form is designed to standardize the communication and requirements when reporting a data request based on its request type. This standardization helps to reduce confusion and miscommunication between stakeholders involved in the incident reporting process.

The first two actions taken by the workflow are to get the response details and store the form entries in a SharePoint list. The SharePoint list serves as a centralized database what makes it easier to categorize requests, understand the issues and assign responsibilities.

The third action taken by the workflow is either to send a message to a Slack channel (Incidence-Requests) or to create a new issue in Jira (Ad-hoc-Requests and Project-Requests) that is controlled by a condition element within Power Automate. All stakeholders involved in the process can see updates on the status of the request in real-time. This transparency helps to reduce the need for stakeholders to ask questions repeatedly. Finally, an automated email notifies the data team that a new request has been received, which serves as a starting point for the remaining process.

Overall, this approach has allowed us to achieve a high degree of standardization and automation in our data collection and processing efforts. By utilizing a variety of technologies and applications, we have created a streamlined workflow that is easy to understand and use for everyone involved. This has resulted in increased efficiency, reduced errors, and improved data quality, ultimately enabling our team to make better informed decisions based on reliable data.

4   Conclusion

Although, there are far more complex use cases for iPaaS automation, our main goal was to demonstrate the basic idea of iPaaS solutions using a real-world example and to inspire readers to create their own customized business process automations. We believe that iPaaS offers a user-friendly and accessible solution for both technical and non-technical users to take advantage of the benefits of business process automation. We also like that organizations can monitor and manage their integrations from a single location. This makes it easy to track the progress of automation projects and identify and resolve any issues that may arise. By providing pre-built integrations, simplifying the integration process, and accelerating digital transformation efforts, iPaaS can help businesses to stay competitive and achieve their goals in an increasingly data-driven economy. It is designed to be scalable and flexible, which means that it can handle large volumes of data and adapt to changing business requirements. Finally, we think the adoption of iPaaS is expected to increase in the coming years, as organizations always continue to seek solutions to improve their efficiency and effectiveness.

References

1. Mohapatra, S.: Business Process Automation. PHI Learning, Neu-Delhi (2009)
2. Blokdyk, G.: Ipaas A QuickStart Guide. CreateSpace Independent Publishing Platform (2017)
3. Hyrynsalmi, S.: The State-of-the-Art of the Integration Platforms as a Service research. In 5th International Workshop on Software intensive Business: Towards Sustainable Software Business (IWSiB 2022), Pittsburgh, PA, USA. ACM, New York (2022)

(S-)BPM Development
and Requirements

An Approach to Create a Common Frame of Reference for Digital Platform Design in SME Value Networks

Jakob Bönsch, Svenja Hauck, Matthes Elstermann(✉), and Jivka Ovtcharova

Karlsruhe Institute of Technology, Karlsruhe, Germany
{boensch,matthes.elstermann}@kit.edu
http://www.imi.kit.edu

Abstract. Platform economy is well established in the business to customer domain. However, digital platforms are lacking in the business to business realm, especially for SMEs. This work presents a way to create a common frame of reference, that is inevitably needed to efficiently design a digital platform. Following the principles of a Design Thinking approach, models are created, that can be used as communication tool for a large group of diverse stakeholders. The approach includes the two means of initial collection of knowledge: exploratory user stories and capturing of use-case processes. A subject-oriented, unified Synthesis Model is created on his basis. By enriching this model with another layer of information from the user stories and their context, another form of a graphical representation is realized. The presented approach proofs valuable in a big research consortium with about 25 organisations (companies, research institutes, and authorities; mainly SMEs). The models are used to design platform architecture as well as platform processes and link them to one another. In addition intangible assets for digital platform development for SMEs are identified.

Keywords: S-BPM · Subject-Orientation · Digital Platform · SME · Design Thinking

1 A Digital Platform for SMEs

Tomorrows mobility is created today. Electrification of the drive-train, lightweight design, new concepts of energy storage and *Mobility as a Service* are just some of the arising challenges. Disruptive change to the entire automotive sector is thereby inevitable. Additionally *Manufacturing-X* is emerging as a new paradigm for highly efficient and more effective production. Satisfying the resulting requirements of both of these trends is one of the major tasks for the big automotive companies. However, especially in Germany, many small and medium sized enterprises (SME) are present in this sector as well. How can they cope with the new general conditions of the field? How do they adapt to new technologies? How can they stay competitive?

M. Elstermann et al. (Eds.): S-BPM ONE 2023, CCIS 1867, pp. 63–82, 2023.
https://doi.org/10.1007/978-3-031-40213-5_5

One answer to these questions supposedly is collaboration of SMEs in intelligent value networks [14].[1] One way to support such value networks are digital platforms and ecosystems. This paper builds on findings from the German research project IntWertL[2] and is a report on how a design thinking approach can be (and is) utilized to design a digital collaboration platform for SMEs. More concretely the IntWertL solution: an engineering- and production platform for use-case-specific mobility solutions.

Platform economy makes economies of scale accessible to SMEs [3]. Intelligent networking of a diverse number of players makes the result more than the sum of its parts [2]. In particular SMEs can jointly provide services that could not be offered individually. However, it is not clear how a platform is to be designed in order to properly support inevitably changing business processes in the new environment [8, 12, 13]. This work is result of a research project that aims to build a digital platform for SMEs in the automotive sector. Technically, this development and production platform serves as a data hub and central interaction and collaboration tool. A shared data space enables digital interoperability across the entire end-to-end product creation process. Building on this, new, (partially) automated IT services are available in conjunction with artificial intelligence (AI) that streamline processes, expand existing business models and enable entirely new types of value creation. The research consortium consists of about 25 organisations, including engineering, production and IT companies, research institutes as well as territorial authorities. Unsurprisingly, these various organisations have different needs and initially didn't have a common understanding of the functionality. Therefore, an important task was to identify roles and processes on the platform and to shape a comprehensive and consistent interaction model, that all stakeholders could agree upon. A unified view was generated through a design thinking approach which synthesized different understandings and needs into one common model.

This work was conducted in the context of the automotive industry, nevertheless the focus here is not on vehicle production. Many industries can and will benefit of new digital platforms and according business models. We present a feasible way to create a common frame of reference for a diverse group of individuals and organisations from various backgrounds.

2   Related Work

This chapter will introduce the three main concepts that have been employed in the here presented research. First, the reasoning behind relying on a subject-oriented approach is indicated. Second, the principal idea of design thinking is

---

[1] Value networks are to be understood as progression from rigid value chains. Theoretically they allow for greater flexibility in the collaboration between their participants. Heterogeneous and diverse relationships as well as constantly changing roles allow for a better fit of all participants to achieve a common goal.

[2] Intelligent value networks for lightweight vehicles in small quantities (German: Intelligente Wertschöpfungsnetzwerke für Leichtbaufahrzeuge geringer Stückzahl).

discussed. And at last, the application of user-stories in the scrum methodology is explained.

2.1   Subject-Orientation

In a nutshell the paradigm of subject-orientation is "*a modeling or description paradigm for processes that is derived from the structure of natural languages. It requires the explicit and continuous consideration of active entities within the bounds of a process as the conceptual center of description. Active entities (subjects) and passive elements (objects) must always be distinguished and activities or task can only be described in the context of a subject. The interaction between subjects is of particular importance and must explicitly be described as exchange of information that cannot be omitted* [4]. The paradigm is closely related to the wider approach of Subject-Oriented Business Process Management (S-BPM) and can practically be applied with help of the Parallel Activity Specification Schema (PASS), a specifically subject-oriented, graphical process modeling language.

The theory of [5] and [4] analyzed why and how this approach is very suitable as a method in the design for Information Systems or rather the socio-technical processes that are supposed to be executed by them.

2.2   Design Thinking

The general approach of this research follows the Design Thinking Methodology as defined in [11]. Design thinking is a general concept or approach centered around iterative development, executed by an interdisciplinary team of people working in a "creativity-inducing environment" in order to derive creative solutions for arbitrarily given problems.

While the methodology itself usually encompasses more aspects, for this work as part of the overall research project we consider our research and development process to be in or located around the Design Thinking Task Areas[3] of *Observation* and *Synthesis*, with the side goals of achieving/generating understanding and ideas among the involved people. Since the research project itself has not yet progressed far enough, neither prototyping nor testing of prototypes of any solutions have yet been conducted.

2.3   User Stories in SCRUM

In agile software development, the concept of *user stories* is usually used to develop a so-called *backlog*. The backlog in SCRUM is a collection of the currently known specifications of all requirements and features, that are still to be implemented in a software development project. It is changing with time and

---

[3] Sometimes these Task areas are also referred to as Design Thinking "Phases". However, as can be seen from Fig. 1, due to every activity aspect being interwoven with basically every other aspect, the linear concept of 'phases' that follow upon each other does not really befit the conceptual nature of Design Thinking.

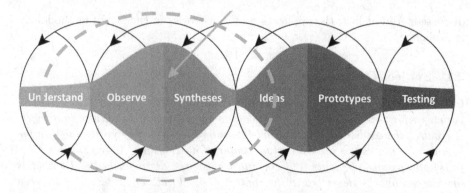

Fig. 1. Task-Areas of Design Thinking according to [7]

constantly updated. This software specification is typically indirect and is commonly divided into different themes, which are referred to as *epics*. Each epic can include several user stories. A user story shall always just be related to one singular feature and describe it from a user perspective (hence only indirectly detailing the software design). Therefore, user stories are often times created for different roles. By including a test case for every user story the validation of successful implementation is considered [10].

Requirements elicitation by means of user stories represents a bottom-up approach. Well-defined goals are sought at the individual level of each project partner. A user story represents the most concrete and singular wish of a user, including the reasoning behind it. Often it has the form: "As [role] I would like [functionality], so that I [reason]", whereby details can be noted. A clear formulation and a sufficient level of detail are necessary for a common understanding in the team. It is also important to prioritize the entries on an ongoing basis, which can be used to guide the development of a functionality or the entire project [10].

3   Methodical Approach

This research follows the principles of Design Thinking as understood by [6]. In our case the problem at hand being the design of an information system. This includes many processes that are supposed to be supported. In consequence to the iterative nature of the Design Thinking approach it took several months, a multitude of interviews and countless step-wise improvements to develop the later presented results. As seen in Fig. 1, generally, Design Thinking has four main objectives: Understand and Observe, Synthesise, Ideate, and Prototype and Test. This report mainly focuses on the first two objectives: Understand and Observe and Synthesise, however it is also shown how the created support (the synthesis model in Fig. 3) is then used to start ideation. The following section further details out the actual employed method. This method aligns with the basic principals described in Sect. 2. However, adaptions have been made to better fit the problem at hand. Especially these deviations from common applications are described.

3.1 Understand and Observe

Following the Design Thinking approach, the first step to create a digital platform is all about observing and understanding of the given problem. This area of observing and understanding is divided into two thematic fields, the use cases and the user stories. To generate a common understanding of the functionality provided by the digital platform three use-cases, that are used to validate the digital platform, are captured. They provide a top-down view on what kind of interaction has to be supported by the platform. Additionally, explorative user stories enable all stakeholders to include their very own interests into the big picture and provide a bottom up approach to designing a common model.

Capturing of Use-Cases. The research project connected to this work has three use-cases for validating the digital platform. Each of which is concerned with one small-series lightweight electronic vehicle. However, all three use-cases have their originate from different companies. Accordingly all three use-cases come with a different set of requirements for the digital platform. To better identify these requirements, interviews with the respective use-case responsible are conducted. The gathered information includes presentations, documents, pictures, CAD-files and minutes of meetings. On top of that, a trained process expert was on hand for every interview to model the described procedures and interactions. The parallel activity specification schema (PASS) is used as modeling language for this use-case capturing. The choice of modeling language is determined because of the benefits of a subject-oriented approach proposed in [4]. However, since the use-case responsible does not know all connections beforehand, only incomplete models are derived. The level of detail of the three models varies greatly and the focus is different in each of them. Nevertheless, the use-case specific models help to show the big picture and give a rough understanding of how the digital platform is to be designed.

Elicitation of User Stories. In contrast to the conventional application of user stories in the context of SCRUM (see Sect. 2.3, here they are used as a tool to explore the different areas of interest for various stakeholders. Traditional user stories are a great way to detail out what functionality should be implemented. Sometimes, however, important things remain unnoticed because they may seem trivial or they do not fit the set of epics. The following section describes the methodology of how *exploratory* user stories are used in this research.

All stakeholders are to be allowed to participate in exploratory user stories. The objective being not to get a full set of requirements or even a filled backlog, but to allow for broad participation and deepen the understanding of what interests are prevalent. It is not necessary that all user stories are compatible. Moreover, identification of conflicts in this early stage of platform development is advantageous. It is important to allow for all opinions to be voiced. Synthesis, streamlining and completion in order to have an actionable backlog follow in another step.

The main tool for the elicitation is a word template. It includes fields for a title, a user or role, an explicit, concrete and singular wish of this user and for a reason for the wish. Additionally, a test-case can be provided as well. Exemplary roles are presented in the template, but users are also allowed to add their own. All of this information is captured for each user story. The collected data is later transferred to a spreadsheet for more convenient handling, sorting and filtering.

In IntWertL three ways of collecting user stories are used. First, a broad survey is conducted. Therefore, the template and an explanation of its use is distributed among stakeholders, i.e. the research consortium. Individual interests of various stakeholders (customers, engineers, service providers, etc.) and their organisations are collected. This survey is completely free of restrictions. Any idea, might it even be over-engineered, not in the interest of the majority of the stakeholders or even unrealistic all together is included.

Further on, more user stories are collected from on *Customer Journey* maps. An initial workshop is conducted to identify the stakeholder groups of the platform. These are prioritized and the three most relevant are selected. In another workshop a characteristic, representing *persona* is created. In a third workshop the actual customer journey maps for each persona are created. Questions during the creation of such a journey include: 'Which steps does the persona go through on the platform?', 'Which actions are performed?', 'Which needs and pain points does she have?', 'With whom does she interact?', 'Which opportunities does the platform offer?', and 'Which feelings are associated with it?'. The result of this workshop are three Customer Journey maps, one for each persona from the highest ranked stakeholder groups. User stories are derived from the three customer journey maps for the three according roles.

Lastly, user stories are generated from the results of another workshop, that is aimed at unifying the mission statement of all consortium partners. In eight group discussions with three participants and a neutral host/moderator each, the vision for the platform is discussed. This workshop loosely followed the principals of the *Walt Disney Method* [9]. Therefore, the focus is the visions of the platform once it is fully up and running (some time after the research project). Each workshop participant is prompted to think big and dream of an ideal (future) platform, without being restricted by reason. The host is required to take notes during the discussion among all three participants and fosters a lively discussion through asking predefined follow-up questions. Some of the dreams are directly recorded as user stories and even more can be derived from the records of the discussion.

All of the user stories are thereafter compiled into one spreadsheet.

3.2   Synthesis

Following the design thinking approach the next step is about the synthesis of the collected information from the steps before. This section is divided into two thematic fields. The first subsection deals with the further processing of the collected user stories, while the second subsection details how all the input is unified into one PASS *Synthesis Model*, which builds upon the use-case capturing as well as the user stories.

Processing of the User Stories. The user stories are processed by neutral persons, that have no agenda in shaping the platform to better fit their own business model. The initial set of user stories is expanded, categorized and prioritized to identify commonalities and overarching themes. The categorization is one of the elementary foundations for the creation of the PASS model afterwards.

First, all user stories are expanded with a meaningful title describing the topic of the request and an unique ID number. Main roles are defined as clusters of the initially independently selected users and roles. This role definition is in close coordination with other activities within the research project. Each user story is connected to one of these standardized roles. Unclear user stories are completed with comments and duplicates are identified and eliminated.

The cleared up user stories are then categorized. Main topics, overarching themes (in SCRUM: epics) are identified. If applicable main categories can have subcategories for an even clearer categorization.

Lastly the user stories are prioritized. Here, two measures are taken into account: *importance* and *urgency*. Both measures have a four level ordinal scale as shown in Table 1. The *priority* of an user story is then indicated by the sum of both values. Initial values are proposed based on the understanding of the neutral researchers. Project partners can provide feedback on prioritization, if changes are desired they are made.

Table 1. Ordinal Scale applied to prioritizing user stories.

Value	Importance	Urgency
3	Absolutely necessary (MVP)	First release (1st year)
2	Extension of functionality	Second release (3 years)
1	Improved Usability	Grand Vision (5 years)
0	no importance	no urgency

Creating a PASS Synthesis Model. Ideas from the exploratory user stories and the use-case models are combined to build one uniform *Synthesis Model*.

Subject-orientation has been shown to be a suitable means to designing IT-systems, especially when a people-centric approach is considered important [1,5]. Therefore, the Synthesis Model is created with PASS as well. The focal point of interest for the Synthesis Model remains on the interaction possibilities with and on the digital platform and not the platform architecture or behavior. Therefore, only Subject Interaction Diagrams (SID) and no Subject Behavior Diagrams (SBD) are modeled. As the platform is designed to foster collaboration, the focus of the process model is not the interaction with the platform itself but rather the communication between stakeholders that is to be supported by the platform. Therefore, the subjects are tailored to mainly represent the main user groups of the platform. The starting point for these user groups are the identified main roles in the user stories.

Goal for the Synthesis Model is to create a common understanding among the research consortium about the main functionality of the platform. Neither system architecture, nor business models, nor workflows are directly depicted in the model. The model is not machine interpretable (due to the lack of SBDs) and (at this stage) only intended to aid discussions among humans.

3.3   Ideas

This section deals with the creation of new ideas, the next step in the design thinking approach. Individual user stories are mapped to the Synthesis Model in order to obtain a more detailed, comprehensive model. This model can become more tangible for the different parties and developers through such detailed examples, given in the user stories. Specifications from the user stories can further enrich the overall Synthesis Model for software development of specific features of the digital platform. For example, user stories can provide specifications for certain services that appear in the model only as an undefined subject. In order to use both approaches together, all high-priority user stories from the spreadsheet (see Sect. 3.2) are placed as boxes in appropriate positions in the Synthesis Model.

Generating new ideas opens up the solution space again, that has been narrowed down by means of the Synthesis Model. In order not to overload one model further, separate graphical representations are developed for each of the main areas of interest (i.e. the subjects and messages with the most user stories related to them). The aim is to present the wealth of information in a well-structured and categorized manner, as well as graphically edited. This new representations do not follow any specific scheme. The basis for the representations is the Synthesis Model. Visual aids, such as frames and colors are added for clustering purposes. However, the representations are not further evaluated. They are transferred to different parties, which will continue to work with them.

3.4   Prototyping and Testing

The following steps in the design thinking approach, prototyping and later testing, are planned for the future but exceed the boundaries of this report. The graphical representation of the order instance for example will be used as reference frame to develop a process model for a simple scenario of basic platform processes. The backlog for the first platform prototype is filled on basis of this scenario. The scenario process model will also yield as test-case and validation of the platform prototype functionality.

4   Results

This section deals with the different results of the previously discussed design thinking methodology. First, the results of the exploratory user stories will be reported. The Synthesis Model is presented thereafter and finally the graphical elaboration of the user stories on basis of the Synthesis Model is shown.

4.1   Exploratory User Stories

By following the approach detailed in Sect. 3.1 well over 200 user stories are collected. An extract of the resulting spreadsheet is shown in Fig. 2. Following the processing procedure four standardized roles are defined as: platform participant, customer, vendor, and platform developer/operator. Next, the user stories are categorized. The question of which topics are covered is answered. The user stories are divided into nine main categories, such as *marketplace* and *services*. Due to the large number of user stories in the main categories and the resulting lack of clarity, they are further divided into subcategories. For example, the main category *platform-general* is divided into 15 subcategories such as onboarding, home page, logout, etc. Afterwards the user stories are prioritized. The stories are ranked in descending importance and in descending urgency (see Table 1). The priority score of an user story is the sum of both values. Comments of many partners from the research consortium are taken into account for the prioritization of the user stories.

ID	Role	Title/topic	Wish/ What do I want	Who do I want	Oberkathegorie	Unterkathegorie	Priority	Comments to the wish	Importance	Dringlichkeit	Comments from partners
1 Vendor		sell products	sell products on the platform	buy products directly on the platform	marketplace	Sale/Order		6 from initial template	3	3 priority is correct
5 Vendor		sell extern products	sell new products on the platform	you can find everything on the platform	marketplace	Sale/Order		2 from initial template	1	1
6 Customer		Buy products	Einkauf von Produkten und Ressourcen (Teile, Material, Arbeitskraft) on-demand services (B2B services: for example: design, montage, tests,...	Produkte an Kunden außerhalb der Plattform weiter customer can find these and will pay for it	marketplace	Sale/Order		6 from initial template	3	3
7 Vendor		provide services			marketplace	Sale/Order		6 from initial template	3	3
8 Developer		Insight to the own capacities	Insight to the own capacities should be possible on the platform	for own controlling/moni toring	Services	Controlling/Monitor ing		2 own idea	1	1

Fig. 2. Extract from the spreadsheet of *User Stories* after the processing.

4.2   The Synthesis Model

This subsection deals with the description of the PASS Synthesis Model of the digital platform. First, a rough overview of the basic platform and all the actors on and around it is given, followed by a closer look at a special part of the platform, the so-called *order instance*.

Figure 3 shows the first SID of the model, which depicts the communication of all participants or involved systems to and on the *base platform*. All subjects are modeled as interface subjects. This means that their behavior is not defined more precisely in an SBD. The subjects are various participants of the process on the platform, which will be defined in more detail later. There are subjects that do not directly belong to the platform, such as the *customer* and other *external parties*. The base platform is modeled as a subject group and includes the following subjects: the *platform participants*, the *integrator*, the subject group *order instance*, and subjects representing IT systems: the *marketplace portal*, an *onboarding system*, and additional *services*. An order instance includes an *order management/controlling/monitoring* subject and one to many *order participants*.

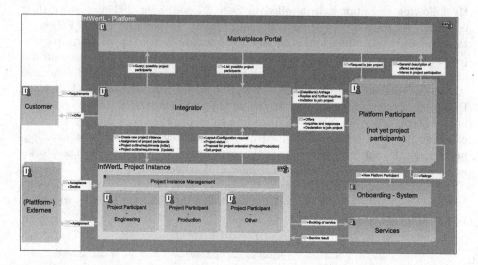

Fig. 3. SID of the digital platform.

The subjects are connected by message boxes. The succession of messages within the boxes is in logical order analogous to the process flow. The arrows show from which subject the messages originate and to which they are sent. The entire process is modeled to show how one order is processed on the platform. Once in operation the platform is going to handle many order instances at the same time.

All platform participants join the platform through a registration process in the onboarding system. Accordingly, this system flushes new platform participants onto the base platform. The customer however, does not mean customer of the platform and therefore isn't a platform participant but the end user (primary demand), who wants to buy a vehicle and approaches the integrator with his/her requirements. The integrator is a platform participant registered on the base platform. He/She is the link between customer and order participants and makes an offer to the customer in representation of the entire platform value network.

To find the right participants for the value network, the integrator uses the marketplace portal to search for order participants who can design and produce a vehicle with the given requirements. The search function for suitable partners is possible to be automated later with integration of artificial intelligence (AI). The marketplace portal is a kind of digital marketplace where suppliers can offer their products and services and integrators can find them. The portal sends a request to the platform participants to participate in the order, which is answered with interest in participation, if applicable. The integrator receives a list of potential partners from the marketplace portal and can contact them. Details about joining the order are clarified bilaterally, and an acceptance or rejection can finally be issued. The integrator is also responsible for organizing the order. He creates a so-called *order instance* on the base platform, a separate platform for handling each individual order. Within the order instance, the participants are divided by employment field into order participants of engineering, production and others. The integrator passes on the initial framework data and requirements of the customer as well as updates of these to the order instance. From the latter, he/she receives inquiries about designs and configurations, the order status, suggestions for project extensions and, if necessary, a notification in the event of an exit of an order participant from the order. These organizational tasks will later be at least partially automated by the platform. The base platform also includes so-called services. These are automated services that can be booked for an order and are directly integrated to the platform with a predefined interface. The services offered include instant quoting, a 3D viewer, a tool for life cycle assessment and many more. The diagram also shows participants external to the platform as not all value adding steps need to be performed by platform participants (in case the needed service is not available on the platform).

In the order instance (see Fig. 4) there are four subjects, the *order management/controlling/monitoring*, the *order participants* for engineering, for production and those for other services.

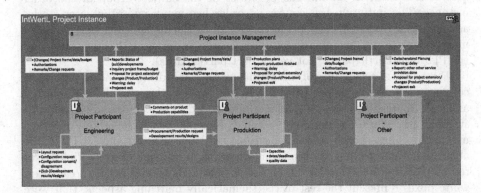

Fig. 4. Detailed SID of a Internal process System of an *order instance*. (Color figure online)

There is purposeful communication between order management and engineering participants. For example, the order management sends, among other things, general conditions/data/budget or changes to them. A feedback loop ensures the clarification of inquiries. Furthermore, the management gives approvals and comments on development results. On the part of the order participants, reports or interim reports are sent, as well as suggestions for project expansion. In case of problems in the order, warnings about the order status or even an exit from the order can also be communicated. Very similar messages are also exchanged between management and order participants in production. Engineering participants exchange messages with each other, by means of design requests, configuration requests and responses to them. Configuration commitments/contradictions are also shared. Development results/(sub)designs can also be shared among order participants.

Shared design of a vehicle also requires agreement between engineering and production order participants. Engineering can send requests for procurement and production in order to develop parts that are as suitable as possible. On the part of production, information about production capabilities is given for this purpose. Likewise, development results/(sub-)designs can later be sent to production with subsequent comments on the product as a feedback loop. The production participants also exchange information about their production capabilities with each other. Dates affecting the productions of, for example, linked parts are also coordinated. Quality information about the actual state of a product can be communicated as well.

4.3 Graphical Elaboration of User Stories

The topic of this subsection are the new graphical representations of two platform-processes. These two areas of interest are identified because most high-priority user stories are connected to them. The first cluster of many important user stories revolves around the processes of the subject group of the order instance. The initiation process for an order has many important user stories assigned to it, too. This process includes finding partners on the subject called marketplace portal and the dialog between the subjects of the integrator and the Platform Participants (not yet project participants).

For a greater acceptance of this results a graphical editing of the user stories is conducted. Here, the respective subjects from the synthesis model are depicted as larger topic boxes. New topics are also added. These boxes are filled with suitable user stories. They are presented as small boxes, separately for each user story. These boxes contain the topic of the user story and its ID, to be able to continue to find additional information in the spreadsheet. Pink boxes represent user stories that have been classified as high priority in the spreadsheet, white boxes represent the rest of the thematically matching aspects, that were mentioned in the user story elicitation.

Figure 5 shows a new representation of the order instance. It is based on Fig. 4. The respective subjects from the Synthesis Model are shown as larger topic boxes. Here the order management is shown as a gray box as well as the order participants as one yellow box. The administration/platform configuration and the technical implementation are shown as new blue boxes. The model shows all user stories, which suit the topic of the order instance. Frames with headings indicate thematic areas of the user stories in this context. In some cases, these frames are covering more than one colored box, as their topic extends into different responsibilities. Also in this representation, arrows indicate dependencies between specific topics. The communication between the order participants within the order instance, which was shown in the Synthesis Model, can be found here again under the topic *Communication*. Within the order instance, the features mentioned should not occur serially but in varying order and also in parallel, which is why no temporal component was included here.

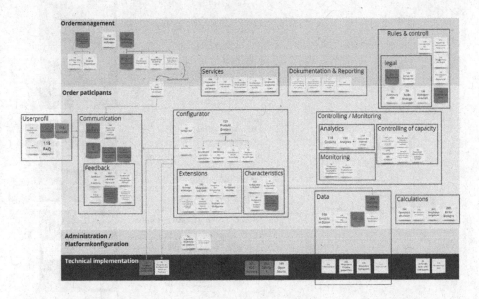

Fig. 5. Graphical elaboration of the user stories regarding the *order instance* and their context. (Color figure online)

For the initiation process a similar representation is shown in Fig. 6. Again, frames with headings indicate thematic areas of the user stories in this context. However, the only subject from the Synthesis Model, which can be found here, is the marketplace portal.

The aspects of what happens on the marketplace portal are framed by a pale blue box. Within this box, there are further thematic gray boxes. Topics are here once, the offer on the platform in the marketplace, the input of the customer requests, a configurator and a decision guidance for an offer. These topic boxes are connected by arrows, which describe the chronological sequence in the portal. For three topics, there are additional details on the technical implementation of the respective topic, summarized in dark blue boxes, again similar to Fig. 5. Below to the marketplace portal box, there are three gray boxes. The first box deals with the points to be considered for possible cooperation.

The communication from the Synthesis Model between integrator and platform participants that are not yet in the order (cf. Fig. 3) is also addressed here. This topic is followed by the user stories for placing orders and for ordering and payment.

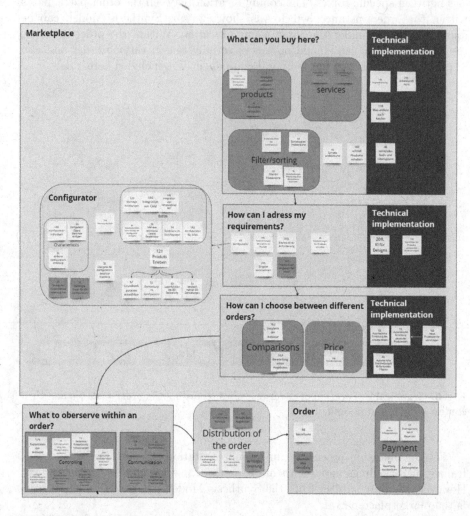

Fig. 6. Graphical elaboration of the user stories regarding the *initiation process* and their context.

5   Discussion

This paper presents a design thinking approach to create a common understanding of a new digital platform for SME collaboration, which has to be developed.

In this development a lot of different parties are involved, which makes common approaches not very easy to use. In this section the most relevant findings of the research are discussed. First, a discussion, why the common approaches are not sufficient, is given. The reasons and the benefits of the design thinking approach are discussed afterwards. Last, the most crucial realizations regarding the platform design are highlighted and the intended further use of the created means is described.

5.1   Reasons for Insufficiency of Common Approaches

The environment of digital platform development can be described as VUCA - volatile, uncertain, complex, ambiguous. Therefore, the reasoning for choosing the here presented Design Thinking approach (DTA) is discussed in context of these four problem fields.

Volatility. First, volatility of the problem at hand is related to the nature of research projects. At the beginning main changes in staff, initial discussions and even changes in the research consortium yield a difficult to handle research environment. By means of the exploratory user stories all stakeholders can be involved. Also, the long elicitation period (better part of three months) gives the possibility to create new user stories in accordance to the progress of the entire research project. The here presented approach combines the flexibility of agile with the general overview of plan-driven methods. Thereafter, the Synthesis Model serves as valuable tool to onboard new staff or even (associated) organisations.

Uncertainty. Main objective of the research project is to create a digital engineering and production platform for SMEs from the automotive sector. However, it is not exactly specified what such a platform entails. First, the Minimal Viable Product (MVP) needs to be designed and later further platform extensions. Partners from the research consortium need a common frame of reference to properly locate their own ideas and contributions in context of one another. Especially, since some partners provide access to their preexisting software components even though the MVP functionality is not set in stone, yet. On top of that the three use-cases for platform validation are still evolving in parallel withe the here presented works. The DTA allows for constant extension and growth of the observation. New ideas can then be easily put into context by means of the Synthesis Model.

Complexity. The problem at hand is complicated, complex and novel. Many partners and multiple use-cases lead to many different observations that need to be brought together. Even though the spreadsheet with user stories doesn't present a complete backlog, it is deemed to extensive to be readily understood. Therefore, to manage the complicatedness alone, a graphical elaboration is called for. Therefore, a good overview is given with the graphical representation of user stories. However, details are still available by looking up each user story in the spreadsheet by its ID. On top of that the models of the different use-cases need to be unified, since not three, but one platform is to be designed. This objective is achieved with the Synthesis Model as well. Complexity is induced through the diversity of stakeholders. Covering the end to end process of vehicle development is touching many domains. Especially, since passenger transportation and utility vehicles are represented in the use-cases. Adding IT-companies to that mix just diversifies further. Nevertheless, the detailed descriptions of very not intuitive aspects and the minute understanding of the peripheries of tasks in automotive production and digital platform development are the building blocks of success for this endeavor. Last, the novelty - no similar platform, even in separate domains exists - constitutes a lack of orientation. Common guidelines are obscured by too many details from other domains. Different views are required. The Synthesis Model and with it the inherit strength of PASS, i.e. to create context separation, helps to manage complexity.

Ambiguity. The diverse backgrounds among stakeholders lead to totally different understandings of seemingly the same concepts. A platform can be understood as digital platform or as vehicle platform, the customer can be a data consumer/provider on the platform or the user of a vehicle, and a console can be a part of the utility vehicle construction or the command-line interface; just to name a few ambiguous terms. On top of that SMEs are uniquely structured. Each has its own quirks and baseline. In the user stories this is taken into consideration by not only including narratives but also the reasoning behind it. The Synthesis Model then provides a common frame of reference, that might differ from ones original ideas, but is clearly communicated and well documented. With this in mind many misunderstandings can be prevented.

5.2 Discussion of the Design Thinking Approach

Overall, the here presented results turn out to be highly beneficial for the research consortium. They are used as baseline for shaping the platform architecture, the MVP scenario and additional platform processes. Both organisations from the automotive domain and from IT are relying on the generated frame of reference, especially the Synthesis Model, for communication. However, the difficulties resulting from the DTA approach detailed in Sect. 3 is valuable experience and discussed here as well.

The exploratory user stories are an effective tool to gather information from various stakeholders, spanning a broad range of topics. Nevertheless, very high effort is associated with performing the persona, customer journey and vision workshops. A lot of time was spent on evaluating all of the results of these. All of which yielded in user stories that still needed to be categorized, prioritized, etc. Additionally the capturing of the use-cases required time intensive interviews and a lot of post-processing. Therefore, only a small group of people were involved in these steps. The risk being, that these persons develop into 'experts' and only they share a common frame of reference, while the rest of the stakeholders do not partake in understanding and observing. Therefore, constant and efficient communication with all involved and interested partners is key. Also it showed that these 'experts' need to hold back and must not dictate backlogs, functionalities, etc. They rather need to be patient and involve the entire group in the decision making, e.g. the prioritization of user stories. However, through constant communication these risks could be mitigated. And going beyond that, having 'experts' helped to identify empty spaces, or gaps in the user stories, which meant they could be supplemented.

Creating the synthesis it was found, that doing the classification and prioritization of user stories and the modelling in PASS go hand in hand. The combination of use-case capturing and exploratory user stories fostered a deep understanding from different perspectives. Collaboration and overlap in the user story processing team and the PASS modeling team yielded beneficial synergies. Therefore, the resulting model really turned into a Synthesis Model by unifying the different concerns.

Adding the user stories back into the Synthesis Model generates a new mode of representation that complements the first. However, the level of detail of both modes of representations varies greatly. The initial User stories include a lot of detail. Especially because of the exploratory nature they are lacking in terms of overview of the overall system. The spreadsheet is too crowded and therefore incomprehensible. The Synthesis Model, on the other hand, shows fewer details, but makes it easy to get an overview of the overall system. Interrelationships are also directly shown. For clarity's sake the graphical elaborations cannot depict all user stories, but only those concerning one area of interest. Nevertheless, this provides valuable input for following tasks. The representation of the user stories regarding the order instance are used to create the initial backlog for the MVP and its architecture, while the second graphical elaboration user stories is used to define the onboarding process for the platform.

The idea of joining both, user stories and the Synthesis Model, in the new representations is beneficial to bring the different partners together and foster efficient communication. The concentration on specific processes in the new representations allows for more focus on one topic. Thereby, it is possible to have smaller working groups as interfaces are clear and detailed descriptions of requirements are provided. Participants of the discussions are now only persons, which are interested in the specific topic. By using the subjects of the Synthesis Model in the new representations, the mental integration into the overall picture is still given, despite individual user stories, which provide details. Following no specific scheme for the visualisation, made it easy for participants to quickly understand the main findings of each representation. The endless chunks of text from the user stories is outsourced to a lookup table and the formal requirements of PASS are abandoned (even though a viewpoint of subject-orientation prevails). The later becoming necessary because procedural and architectural concerns are combined into one representation.

Even though no formal validation or verification activities for the presented results are conducted the overall feedback from the research consortium was very positive. The Synthesis Model was presented at a general assembly of all consortium members and shared it in the internal newsletter. Which yielded no ill remarks from the otherwise very outspoken group. Moreover the constant use among all consortium partners and prevalence of the introduced terminology in many discussions and deliverables shows its usefulness. The choice of a PASS SID as modeling notation seems to have been good: Without any further introduction into the modeling language or even only the paradigm of subject-orientation an intuitive understanding was achieved.

5.3   Realizations Regarding the Platform Design

The Synthesis Model in combination with the additional layer of information in form of graphical representation of user stories and their context proved as vital for creating a common frame of reference among the research consortium. But not only the platform processes and architecture were better understood, also intangible assets were identified.

First and foremost among the intangibles is trust. Trust in the platform, but also in the platform participants. Therefore, common values need to be installed among the platform ecosystem. However, values alone are not sufficient for generating trust. Common rules and standards, governance structures and compliance measures are needed. Additionally, trust in the platform is strongly associated with the first impression: The user interface, the look and feel, the design of the platform. To comply with this requirement a design bureau is included in the conceptualization and realization of the digital platform from the get go.

Secondly, especially the Synthesis Model helps to clarify what AI can and can not automate in the platform processes. Reasonable discussion on possible applications for (semi-) automated services and smart platform modules become possible. The user stories explain wishes of various platform users and the data scientists can pull their use cases from this backlog.

Third and last the Synthesis Model provides the interface between designing the technical platform architecture and the formal platform processes. Both of which are created on basis of a specified scenario, which can be depicted as a derivation of the Synthesis Model. The graphical representations of user stories in specific contexts are used as input to following work packages and provide an initial building block for the backlog for code implementation.

6   Conclusion and Outlook

This work presents a Design Thinking approach to creating a common frame of reference for the design of digital platforms. A combined approach of exploratory elicitation of user stories (bottom-up) and capturing use-case processes (top-down) is used to foster understanding and observation. Building on this a unified

Synthesis Model is created with the formal modeling language PASS. An additional layer of more detailed information is added through graphical representation of user stories and their context in accordance to the Synthesis Model. This input will be used for further detailing of the platform architecture, especially the MVP, platform processes and additional functionality. Mainly the Synthesis Model, but also the graphical elaboration of user stories, is used to promote efficient communication between approximately 100 involved persons from about 25 organisations, but mainly SMEs.

All in all however, the Synthesis Model does provide much more than just the initial common frame of reference it was intended for. Valuable realizations for the platform design itself are made. Especially the value of trust within the emerging digital ecosystem is emphasized. Therefore, it is going to be an interesting task to adapt the European standards for data sovereignty and interoperability (GAIA-X) as well as their implementation in the first open and collaborative data ecosystem (Catena-X) to IntWertL.

Acknowledgements. Gefördert durch die Bundesrepublik Deutschland und die Europäische Union. Zuwendungsgeber: Bundesministerium für Wirtschaft und Klimaschutz aufgrund eines Beschlusses des deutschen Bundestages sowie die Europäische Union.

References

1. Bönsch, J., Elstermann, M., Kimmig, A., Ovtcharova, J.: A subject-oriented reference model for digital twins. Comput. Industr. Eng. **172**, 108556 (2022). https://doi.org/10.1016/j.cie.2022.108556, https://www.sciencedirect.com/science/article/pii/S0360835222005617
2. Büchi, G., Cugno, M., Castagnoli, R.: Economies of scale and network economies in industry 4.0. Symphonya. Emerg. Issues Manage. (2), 66–76 (2018). https://doi.org/10.4468/2018.2.06 buchi.cugno.castagnoli, https://symphonya.unicusano.it/article/view/12935
3. Dzwigol, H., Dzwigol-Barosz, M., Kwilinski, A.: Formation of global competitive enterprise environment based on industry 4.0 concept. Int. J. Entrepreneurship **24**(1), 1–5 (2020)
4. Elstermann, M.: Executing strategic product planning - a subject-oriented analysis and new referential process model for it-tool support and agile execution of strategic product planning. https://doi.org/10.5445/KSP/1000097859
5. Elstermann, M., Ovtcharova, J.: Subject-orientation as a means for business information system design-a theoretical analysis and summary. In: Abramowicz, W., Corchuelo, R. (eds.) Business Information Systems: 22nd International Conference, BIS 2019, Seville, Spain, 26–28 June 2019, Proceedings, Part I 22, pp. 325–336. Springer, Cham (2019). https://doi.org/10.1007/978-3-030-20485-3_25
6. Fleischmann, A., Oppl, S., Schmidt, W., Stary, C.: Ganzheitliche Digitalisierung von Prozessen: Perspektivenwechsel-Design Thinking-wertegeleitete Interaktion. Springer, Cham (2018). https://doi.org/10.1007/978-3-658-22648-0
7. Große-Dunker, F.: Die design thinking prozess phasen im Überblick. https://blog.thedarkhorse.de/design-thinking/die-design-thinking-prozess-phasen-im-ueberblick/

8. Liu, Z., et al.: The architectural design and implementation of a digital platform for industry 4.0 SME collaboration. Comput. Ind. **138**, 103623 (2022). https://doi.org/10.1016/j.compind.2022.103623, https://www.sciencedirect.com/science/article/pii/S0166361522000185

9. Schawel, C., Billing, F., Schawel, C., Billing, F.: Walt-disney-methode: (kreativitätstechniken). Top 100 Management Tools: Das wichtigste Buch eines Managers Von ABC-Analyse bis Zielvereinbarung, pp. 273–275 (2014)

10. Tremp, H. (ed.): Agile objektorientierte Anforderungsanalyse. Springer, Wiesbaden (2022). https://doi.org/10.1007/978-3-658-37194-4

11. Uebernickel, F., Brenner, W., Pukall, B., Naef, T., Schindlholzer, B.: Design Thinking: Das Handbuch. Frankfurter Allgemeine Buch (2015)

12. Veile, J.W., Schmidt, M.C., Voigt, K.I.: Toward a new era of cooperation: how industrial digital platforms transform business models in industry 4.0. J. Bus. Res. **143**, 387–405 (2022). https://doi.org/10.1016/j.jbusres.2021.11.062, https://www.sciencedirect.com/science/article/pii/S0148296321008699

13. Xie, X., Han, Y., Anderson, A., Ribeiro-Navarrete, S.: Digital platforms and SMEs' business model innovation: exploring the mediating mechanisms of capability reconfiguration. Int. J. Inf. Manage. **65**, 102513 (2022). https://doi.org/10.1016/j.ijinfomgt.2022.102513, https://www.sciencedirect.com/science/article/pii/S0268401222000470

14. Zahoor, N., Al-Tabbaa, O.: Inter-organizational collaboration and SMEs' innovation: a systematic review and future research directions. Scand. J. Manage. **36**(2), 101109 (2020). https://doi.org/10.1016/j.scaman.2020.101109, https://www.sciencedirect.com/science/article/pii/S095652211930096X

The Role of Stories in Software Development and Business-Process Modeling

Peter Forbrig[✉] [iD], Alexandru Umlauft, Mathias Kühn, and Anke Dittmar[iD]

University of Rostock, Chair of Software Engineering , Albert-Einstein-Str. 22,
Rostock 18055, Germany
{peter.forbrig,alexandru-nicolae.umlauft,mathias.kuehn,
anke.dittmar}@uni-rostock.de

Abstract. Scenarios and stories are widely used across different professional domains. The paper presents a case study on their use in a multidisciplinary project aimed at supporting therapies for patients after stroke. Existing training programs with patients and therapists served as starting point for exploring usage scenarios with the humanoid robot Pepper. Based on a set of envisaged scenarios, implementations for the robot's behavior in predefined "therapy workflows" were provided. Additionally, the domain-specific language TaskDSL4Pepper was developed that allows therapists to specify their own executable interaction models between the patient and the robot. The case study also reveals the need for involving various domain experts to create richer sets of stories with more alternatives.

Keywords: Group Stories · Domain-Specific Languages · Humanoid Robot Pepper

1 Introduction

Scenarios are stories about people (actors) carrying out activities [16] which are used in many domains to support knowledge sharing, sense-making and creativity. There are different understandings of scenarios depending on their intended use. For example, user stories in agile software development are one-sentence descriptions of user requirements which can be composed to epics and initiatives [2]. In the context of user-centered design, problem and activity scenarios help involved stakeholders to reflect on existing practices and possible solutions for identified problems. They can come e.g. in the form of narratives or storyboards and describe situated actions of one or more actors with personal motivations, knowledge, goals, and plans [16]. Such broader view on stories along with more detailed and complete descriptions of interactions between actors and systems can also be found in business-process modelling (e.g., [13]).

The paper describes the use of scenarios in a project on robot assistance in neurorehabilitation. The overall objective of the project was to support therapies for patients after stroke by a humanoid robot Pepper. Based on existing therapies, envisaged scenarios describing possible interactions between the patient and the robot were developed. These

M. Elstermann et al. (Eds.): S-BPM ONE 2023, CCIS 1867, pp. 83–90, 2023.
https://doi.org/10.1007/978-3-031-40213-5_6

scenarios informed not only the implementation but also the development of a domain-specific language which allows therapists to specify interaction models or "workflows" between the patient and the robot. Models of the robot's behavior are executable.

The paper is structured as follows. Section 2 discusses related work on the role of scenarios and stories in business-process modeling and software development. Section 3 describes the creation and use of scenarios in the case study. It also gives a glimpse of the domain-specific language by using a therapy example. A discussion follows that highlights successes and failures of our approach. The paper finishes with a summary and an outlook.

2   Related Work

Stories have been used since centuries to evoke the interest and participation of people in reflecting on current practices and envisioning the future. Katuscáková et al. [10] point out that storytelling helps to better keep in mind the meaning of some raw data. It also supports the development of a shared understanding: "if one tells a story of and someone else listens actively, their brains are actually starting to synchronize with one another" [10]. Hence, it is not surprising that stories or scenarios are also used in domains such as software development or business-process management.

As mentioned above, the terms story and scenario are used with different meanings and for different purposes. At the level of interaction scenarios and business processes, Forbrig and Dittmar [7] discuss the cross-pollination of personas, user stories, use cases and business-process models. Use cases consider scenarios to be sequences of actions. For Use Case Diagrams of UML 2.0 the concept of slices was introduced by Jacobsen et al. [9] to support iterative system development by selecting subsets of scenarios for each development cycle. This concept can be applied to stories for business processes as well. Additionally, it is shown at the example of use-case diagrams and S-BPM models how process specifications can be more expressive if the concept of stories is used to label elements of a model.

Erlach and Müller [3] take a broader view and argue even for 'narrative organizations' in which "the executives and employees… Fully realize and acknowledge that narrative structures, i.e., the basic components from which stories are built, lie at the core of nearly every process". The authors consider this new perspective as a "major step for any company to develop into a sustainable, future-oriented organization" [3]. Antunes et al. [1] mention that there is often a gap between official versions of processes documented by the organization and the live experience of end-users. They argue that process stories might help to bridge this gap. Similarly, Simões et al. [18] question traditional approaches to process elicitation and modeling rooted in the workflow paradigm. They suggest to use storyboards in collaborative process modelling and to empower end-users to model business processes themselves. Storyboards capture stories in a visual way by combining text with visual elements. Simões et al. [18] investigate in their study whether tool-supported storyboarding can 1) support the elicitation of meaningful business processes, 2) enable and incite users to externalize tacit knowledge and preserve contextualization, and 3) improve process modelling. The results suggest, for example, that some training is needed to include sufficient contextual information in the storyboards. Also, converged stories of teams were broader and more balanced than individual stories, and thus lead to better results. In [19], Simões et al. describe an approach that is consistent with the S-BPM perspective [5]: "It too is subject-oriented and regards process context as important to modeling. However, while S-BPM is mainly centered on control flows, we are mostly focused on the more diverse information brought by process stories." The authors also argue that process modeling should be left to the stakeholders, so they can describe business processes from diverse, complementary perspectives and without mediation from modeling experts.

Santoro et al. [14] discuss the advantages of storytelling in groups. They compare workflow models in BPMN that resulted from interviews with those from group stories and concluded that interviews are not as effective as stories. The reasons for that may lie in the limitations of interviews with stakeholders as described by Machado et al. [11]. Stakeholders may not describe their activities correctly because of low recall capabilities, lack of time, fear or because it is boring to specify routines and knowledge. Additionally, stakeholders may sometimes describe what they should do and not what they really do. Some information is not presented because stakeholders believe that it is not important. Storytelling in stakeholder groups may avoid some of these limitations by an increased engagement and an externalization of implicit knowledge in the stories.

Gonçalves et al. [8] provide a method for business-process elicitation and modeling based on collective stories. It consists of three phases and 6 steps: 1) tell stories (first phase: teams should recall important facts about daily work) 2) tokenizing, 3) morphologic and lexical analysis, 4) syntactic analysis (second phase: semi-automated mine stories), 5) domain analysis, 6) extract workflow alternatives, and 7) combine and validate model (third phase: generate a workflow model and reach consensus about it).

3   The Case Study

The case study is part of the E-BRAiN project (Evidence-Based Robot Assistance in Neurorehabilitation) [4], where collaborators from neurorehabilitation, psychology, sociology, software engineering and smart computing aimed to develop robotic-assistance rehabilitation therapies for stroke patients. This paper focuses on the role of scenarios in the development process.

Starting point were the training programs published in [14] and the idea to support therapists by humanoid robots. The neurorehabilitation expert in the project developed future therapy scenarios with the humanoid robot Pepper. The written scenarios are enriched by photographs and describe what the robot has to say and what has to be presented on its tablet, what the patient has to do and which tasks the therapist has to complete. Figure 1 captures the situation where Pepper presents the results of the performed exercises on its tablet.

All stories are told twice, once for patients having their handicap on the left-hand side and once for those with the handicap on the right-hand side. They are very detailed and include time information like: *The video starts on the tablet of the robot and after 10 s Pepper says: look in the mirror*. Sometimes the scenarios also include interactions with other devices such as additional tablets and a large interactive TV screen. Figure 2 shows example pictures that enrich a scenario to visualize how supporters need to help patients in certain training situations.

Fig. 1. The humanoid robot Pepper presenting results of exercises.

Fig. 2. Pictures that visualize the necessary activities of a patient and the supporting therapist.

The robot's behavior in the above described scenarios is implemented in Java and in Python. The implementation includes spoken dialogues and the presentation of linked pictures (see e.g. Fig. 2) and video material. They are intended to guide a patient and a supporter.

For some of the envisaged scenarios, the software engineering experts in the project specified the therapy processes as task models in the domain specific language CoTaL [6] to check correct understanding and to stimulate discussion about useful variations or alternative scenarios that could be supported by the humanoid robot. These models also informed the design and implementation of a textual domain specific language. TaskDSL4Pepper which is an extended version of CoTaL [6] can be used for prototyping approaches. It also provides the opportunity for end users such as therapists to define and implement alternative training scenarios.

Figure 3 gives an impression how patient-robot dialogues can be specified by hierarchical cooperative tasks. Let us first have a look at the activities the patient has to perform (see model fragment `role patient`). First, she or he greets and then listens to the instructions. Exercises are performed in an iteration (`performs_exercises{*}`). They can be performed correctly or wrong. The iteration ends when the patients finishes his or her exercises.

TaskDSL4Pepper provides a set of basic operations the robot can perform such as saying something (operation `say`), showing a picture (`show`), displaying a video (`play`) or waiting for a certain time (`wait`). In the example in Fig. 3, Pepper starts the therapy by greeting (task `greet` in model fragment `robot pepper`) that results in saying "Good morning" (see definition of text variable `greeting`). The subsequent

```
team coop {
  root training = greeting >> train{*} [> end_exercises
    task greeting = pepper.greet |=| patient.greet
    task end_exercises = pepper.end_exercises |=|
                         patient.finishes_exercises
}
role patient {
  root train = greet >> listens >>
                   perfoms_exercises{*} [> finishes_exercises
    task perfoms_exercises = perform_correctly [] perform_wrong
}
robot pepper {
  root armtraining= greet >> training{*} [> end_exercises
    task greet = say greeting
    task training = introduce >> train
      task introduce = say introduction ||| show startEndPict
      task train = play exerVid ||| say ten >> imagine
        task imagine = wait 8 >> say look >> say imagine
    task end_exercises = say bye
}
text greeting = "Good morning.";
text introduction = "Let us start to perform our second exercise";
image startEndPict = "st_pic_10_1.jpg"
video exerVid = "st_10_1.mp4"

text imagine = "Imagine it is your arm"
text look    = "Look in the mirror"
text ten     = "Train ten times"
text bye     = "Bye, till next time"
```

```
// *    Iteration
// >>   Enabling
// [>   Disabling
// |||  Interleaving
// []   Choice
// |=|  Order independence
```

Fig. 3. TaskDSL4Pepper model of a specific mirror therapy.

task `training` includes an introduction and the training itself. During the introduction the robot says the text stored in variable `introduction`, and in parallel, it shows the start and the end position of the arm as a picture on the tablet. During the task `train` the robot first displays a video of the exercise on the tablet and says in parallel "Train ten times" (see text variable `ten`). Afterwards the robot completes task `imagine` by waiting for eight seconds, then saying "look in the mirror" (see text variable `look`), and finally saying the text stored in variable `imagine`. Pepper closes the exercises by saying "Bye, till next time" (see text variable `bye`).

The model fragment `team coop` at the top of Fig. 3 describes general dependencies or the coordination between the patient and the robot in a similar way to the cooperative mode in CTTE [12]. During the `greeting` task both parties have to greet. This can be done in any order by patient and Pepper. The training task `train` is not further refined. Finally, Pepper has to perform task `end_exercises` and the patient has to complete `finishes_exercises`. Again, this can be done in any order. (The declaration of text, video and picture variables and the meaning of used temporal operators are to be seen at the bottom of at the bottom of Fig. 3.)

TaskDSL4Pepper comes with an editor and an animation tool. The editor was specified with the eclipse plugin Xtext [0]. The animation tool was programmed in Java. All pictures and videos which are available on the robot can easily be selected within the editor tool. The animation of TaskDSL4Pepper specifications also includes the execution of the basic operations by the robot.

4 Discussion

The detailed therapy scenarios with the humanoid robot were a valuable means for experts from medicine to express and for software developers to understand requirements in the project. In contrast to reported literature, the narrative descriptions were not enriched by sketches but by videos and photographs from existing therapies. The detailed scenarios guided the implementation of the robot's behavior and were used as resources for what the humanoid robot has to speak and show.

The neurorehabilitation expert had a dominant position as he created the therapy scenarios. Other members from the project team could suggest changes to envisaged scenarios with the robot but had not enough medical knowledge to counter statements of the domain expert such as "You are right. This might be true for healthy persons. However, patients after stroke need those repetitions in the explanations of the robot".

Santoro et al. [14] mentioned the advantages of storytelling in groups. For our project, a group of domain experts (including therapists that provide their opinion to professors) would have been necessary to develop team-based stories. We think that the quality of the scenarios could have been improved in this way. It turned out during the evaluation that the robot's applications could have been more flexible and support more variants of training scenarios. But group work in the project was restricted to formal aspects like forgotten texts or continuations in the scenarios.

It was only to a certain extent possible in the project to follow a participatory design approach. Patients are a vulnerable user group and their involvement has to be approved by an ethics committee. It is difficult to show that the patients' participation in a usability test brings some medical advancement as requested by the committee. Therefore, it took a long time to get approval. Our project lasted from 2019 till 2022 and the COVID-19 pandemic added to our problem to get in touch with patients. As a consequence, the application could be evaluated at the end of 2022 only and there was no feedback by patients in earlier development cycles.

Nevertheless, we were able to additionally develop a domain-specific language. It provides end users such as therapists with more flexibility by allowing them to specify a prototypical behavior of the humanoid robot Pepper. First experiments are promising. Therapists were able to change provided specifications and they said that they are confident to specify whole therapies after some training. For our experiment there was only an introduction to the language and corresponding tool support for about an hour. More empirical studies are needed here.

5 Summary and Outlook

The paper discusses the role of stories in software development and business-process modelling. It supports the idea of group stories by domain experts and end-users. A case study is presented where software was developed according to the stories that were provided by a domain expert. In the case of therapies, it does not make sense to include patients into the development of stories. They can provide their opinion during evaluations.

The idea of using stories worked quite well. However, it was not really possible to develop group stories because of the lack of experts. The group stories might have yielded to a better quality of the software.

A domain-specific language TaskDSL4Pepper was developed to specify stories of therapies on an abstract way that allows executions. A humanoid robot Pepper acts accordingly.

In the future it might be possible to mine sentences in natural language like Gonçalves et al. [8] and provide specifications in TaskDSL4Pepper.

Acknowledgement. This joint research project "E-BRAiN - Evidence-based Robot Assistance in Neurorehabilitation" is supported by the European Social Fund (ESF), reference: ESF/14-BM-A55–0001/19-A01, and the Ministry of Education, Science and Culture of Mecklenburg-Vorpommern, Germany. The sponsors had no role in the decision to publish or any content of the publication.

References

1. Antunes, P., Pino, J.A., Tate, M., Barros, A.: Eliciting process knowledge through process stories. Inf. Syst. Front. **22**(5), 1179–1201 (2019). https://doi.org/10.1007/s10796-019-099 22-0
2. Atlassian: Stories, epics, and initiatives - These simple structures help agile teams gracefully manage scope and structure work, [online], https://www.atlassian.com/agile/project-manage ment/epics-stories-themes. (Accessed 4 Jan 2023)
3. Erlach, C., Müller, M.: Narrative Organizations - Making Companies Future Proof by Working With Stories. Springer, Berlin Heidelberg (2020). https://doi.org/10.1007/978-3-662-61421-1
4. E-BRAiN Homepage. https://www.ebrain-science.de/en/home/. (Accessed 29 Jan 2023)
5. Fleischmann, A., Kannengiesser, U., Schmidt, W., Stary, C.: Subject-oriented modeling and execution of multi-agent business processes. In: IEEE/WIC/ACM international joint conferences on web intelligence (WI) and intelligent agent technologies (IAT), vol 2. IEEE, pp. 138–145 (2013)
6. Forbrig, P., Dittmar, A., Kühn, M.: A textual domain specific language for task models: generating code for CoTaL, CTTE, and HAMSTERS. In: EICS 2018 Conferences, Paris, France, pp. 5:1–5:6 (2018)
7. Forbrig, P., and Dittmar, A.: Cross-pollination of personas, user stories, use cases and business-process models. In: E. Babkin et al. (eds.) MOBA 2022. LNBIP, vol. 457, pp. 3–18 (2022). https://doi.org/10.1007/978-3-031-17728-6_1
8. Gonçalves, J., Santoro, F.M., Baião, F.A.: Business process mining from group stories. In: Proceedings of the 2009 13th International Conference on Computer Supported Cooperative Work in Design, pp.161–166 (2013)
9. Jacobson, I., Spence, I., Bittner, K.: Use Case 2.0: The Guide to Succeeding with Use Cases (2011). https://www.ivarjacobson.com/publications/white-papers/use-case-20-e-book. (Accessed 30 December 2022)
10. Katuscáková, M., Katuscák, M.: The effectiveness of storytelling in transferring different types of knowledge. In: Proceedings of 14th European Conference on Knowledge Management, Kaunas, Lithuania, 5–6 September 2013, vol. 1, pp. 341–348 (2013)

11. Machado, R.G., Borges, M.R.S., Gomes, J.O., Guerlain, S.: An observation model for the collaborative analysis of real workplaces. In: Proceedings of the 11th International Conference on Computer Supported Cooperative Work in Design, vol. 1, Melbourne, pp. 292–297. Swinburne Press, Australia (2007)

12. Mori, G., Paternò, F., Santoro, C.: CTTE: Support for developing and analyzing task models for interactive system design. IEEE Trans. Softw. Eng. **28**, 797–813 (2002)

13. Nguyen Hoang, T., Ai-Phuong, H., Nkhoma, M., Antunes, P.: Using process stories to foster process flexibility: the experts' Viewpoint. Australasian J. Inform. Syst. **26** (2022). https://doi.org/10.3127/ajis.v26i0.3479

14. Platz, T.: Impairment-oriented Training (IOT) – scientific concept and evidence-based treatment strategies. Restorative Neurol. Neurosci. **22**(3–5), 301–315 (2004). https://pubmed.ncbi.nlm.nih.gov/15502273/

15. Quesenbery, W., Brooks, K.: Storytelling for User Experience: Crafting Stories for Better Design. Rosenfeld Media (2010)

16. Rosson, M.B., John, M., Carroll, J.M.: Scenario-based design. The human-computer interaction handbook: fundamentals, evolving technologies and emerging applications, pp. 1032–1050. L. Erlbaum Associates Inc., USA (2002)

17. Santoro, F.M., Borges, M.R.S., Pino, J.A.: Acquiring knowledge on business processes from stakeholders' stories. Adv. Eng. Inform. **24**, 138–148 (2010)

18. Simões, D., Antunes, P., Cranefield, J.: Enriching knowledge in business process modelling: a storytelling approach. In: Razmerita, L., Phillips-Wren, G., Jain, L.C. (eds.) Innovations in Knowledge Management. ISRL, vol. 95, pp. 241–267. Springer, Heidelberg (2016). https://doi.org/10.1007/978-3-662-47827-1_10

19. Simões, D., Antunes, P., Carriço, L.: Eliciting and modeling business process stories. Bus. Inf. Syst. Eng. **60**(2), 115–132 (2017). https://doi.org/10.1007/s12599-017-0475-3

20. Stephens, G.J., Lauren, J.S., Hasson, U.: Speaker–listener neural coupling underlies successful communication. Proc. Natl. Acad. Sci. **107**(32), 14425–14430 (2010)

21. Xtext: Language Engineering for Everyone (2023). https://www.eclipse.org/Xtext/. (Accessed 26 Feb 2023)

Can a 'Metaverse by Design' Benefit from Digital Process Twins?

Christian Stary(⌧) (iD)

Business Informatics, Johannes Kepler University Linz, Linz, Austria
Christian.Stary@jku.at

Abstract. 'The Metaverse represents the next generation Internet' - this industry belief challenges the current understanding of Internet-based interaction, and the way it progresses towards a cyber-physical network. Will development techniques for the Internet-of-Things (IoT), Internet-of-Behaviors (IoB), and Internet of Everything (IoE) deliver what is the essence of Metaverse applications? In this reflection paper this question is tackled through the lens of Digital Process Twins (DPTs), as they are already an effective and efficient technology for Cyber-Physical System (CPS) development. The argumentation of industry for establishing the Metaverse as the next generation Internet allows the identification and specification of design requirements. In this contribution these requirements are derived from conceptual inputs on Metaverse developments. The requirements are used for analyzing subject-oriented Digital Process Twin capabilities on whether they can support design and implementation of Metaverse applications. Benefits that can be delivered by executable Digital Process Twins models do not only concern the design (process) when being supported by subject-oriented abstraction and representation overcoming interoperability barriers, but also by the validation of behavior models and their synchronization at runtime, in particular with physical components increasing the immersion capabilities of Metaverse applications.

Keywords: Metaverse · Digital (Process) Twin · Cyber-Physical System · Internet-of-Things · design-integrated engineering

1 Introduction

The Metaverse has been envisioned as single, immersive, and shared 3-dimensional virtual space where humans can experience situations in ways they could not do in the physical world. According to Ball [1], the Metaverse has to be understood as scaled network of interoperable, real-time rendered 3D virtual worlds that enables an unlimited number of users to experience these worlds synchronously, persistently, and effectively. Thereby, they feel an individual sense of presence along a continuity of information. This includes identity, history, entitlements, objects, communications, and business transactions like payments, manifesting what users should be provided with to make experiences similar to physical settings in their real life.

Since Metaverse applications are based on the Internet protocol for communication, the Metaverse is considered as 'inevitable evolution of the Internet' [2]. Due to

© The Author(s), under exclusive license to Springer Nature Switzerland AG 2023
M. Elstermann et al. (Eds.): S-BPM ONE 2023, CCIS 1867, pp. 91–110, 2023.
https://doi.org/10.1007/978-3-031-40213-5_7

the intensifying penetration of Metaverse applications to various ecosystems including healthcare, education, mobility, and production, providing immersive experience and digital commerce[1], a closer look to their structure and architecture helps better understand how existing development concepts can be used for organizing business operations and their transformation to immersive ecosystems.

Business operations in the Metaverse aim at virtual reality experiences, encounters, and social interactions while placing, selling, and operating products. Avatars of users can be assigned specific behavior and layouts in the immersive environment for operating elements, and digital goods can be offered for sale with Non-Fungible Tokens (NFTs). Consider an innovative service provider offering individualized home healthcare for clients that want to manage their health conditions with medical devices in an Internet-of-Things (IoT) home environment. For operating such a cyber-physical system including traditional web-based services and IoT systems, the Metaverse allows interactive experience in the virtual world as required in the physical world and beyond. For instance, when wearing binocular Augmented Reality (AR) glasses clients can step from the physical into the 3D world while being (re-)presented as an avatar. It helps through dual mode interaction for realistic training when handling medical devices, and configuring CPS features, e.g., adjusting IoT system elements mounted to the body to monitor the physical condition.

From a technological perspective, several domains have been identified as relevant for developing Metaverse applications that can be accessed by users via Augmented Reality (AR) or Virtual Reality (VR) devices (cf. [3, 4]):

- Internet of Things (IoT) to provide users immersive cyber-virtual experiences in mixed reality environments
- Responsible Artificial Intelligence (AI) as the practice of designing, developing, and deploying AI with the intention to empower users, developers, and organizations, and make transparent the impact of AI on customers and society, and finally, to engender trust in device intelligence
- High-speed data communications enabling high connectivity of devices and networked systems
- Cost-effective Mobile and Multi-access Edge Computing (MEC) to shorten the distance between data collections from wireless and IoT devices and processing their data for analysis in the cloud, and
- Digital Twins (DTs) as effective design and engineering representations

Digital Twins (DTs) cannot only serve as representations of physical counterparts in socio-technical settings, e.g., avatars representing human users, but also as development and runtime technique to address the convergence of physical and cyber worlds [5–7]. Since the Metaverse can be considered as a Cyber-Physical System (CPS), not only because of AR elements, but also because of including physical body language for interaction (cf. [2]), its development can be supported in principle by DTs.

In this contribution several design issues and requirements are studied that are considered relevant for Metaverse development from an application perspective, and that

---

[1] Cf. https://www.swoosh.nike/, https://vaultartspace.gucci.com/

can be addressed by Digital Process Twins (DPTs)[2]. This type of DTs does not only allow to focus on products or machinery-related components, but also includes their logical and/or temporal relations[3]. DPTs concern the 'macro level of magnification'[4]. They contain relations how systems work together to create a larger system.

Although the original DPT concept stems from production industry (e.g., [8]), it meets the objectives of developing and operating socio-technical CPS (e.g., [9]), that finally require socio-technical twin designs (cf. [10]). Design and implementation need to handle major development- and operation-relevant CPS properties including heterogeneity of components, autonomy, connectivity, and dynamic adaptation (cf. [11, 12]) and can be addressed from a behavior-centered perspective [7, 13]. Consequently, Metaverse application development and operation could be effectively and efficiently be supported by behavior-centered DTP models. This hypothesis is tested based on findings in Subject-oriented Business Process Management [14] from a CPS perspective in the following.

Section 2 identifies and describes design issues and requirements that need to be tackled by Digital Process Twins (DPTs) for Metaverse application development. They have been already identified from an application development perspective, and are put into the context of Metaverse development. Section 3 discusses in how far behavior-centered modeling of CPS and the development model of Subject-oriented Business Process Management could support DPT generation for Metaverse application development given the specified design requirements. Both, the open development cycle, and the subject-oriented development support capabilities are considered. Section 4 concludes the paper summarizing the findings and indicating further research.

2 Metaverse Design Requirements

In this section, Metaverse design issues are identified in terms of development requirements, enriching the scholarly work of Tucci et al. [2]. The design requirements are specified (*DES-REQ 1–8*) and referred to later on in Sect. 3 when discussing subject-oriented concepts for DPT modeling and generation.

According to the expectations of digital industries and research, the Metaverse will connect humans in a cyber-physical space (cf. [15]), including digital representation of users, and could change the way we interact in various business and private life contexts (cf. [16]). Since activities that humans can experience in the physical world will not only be replicated, but also enhanced in the virtual world and might represent self-contained processes, users are likely to switch continuously between the Metaverse and the physical world (cf. [17]).

So-called digital twin avatars will be rendered as AI-powered holograms or holographic images that are assigned tasks, thus enriching current personalization [18] and current human task capabilities [2]. Imagine a healthcare service agent, who activates its AI-powered hologram to engage with multiple clients at once in different service

---

[2] https://www.roi.de/unternehmensberatung/case-studies/digital-process-twin-prozessoptimier ung-durch-predictive-quality-und-predictive-production.

[3] https://info.microsoft.com/rs/157-GQE-382/images/Digital%20Twin%20Vision.pdf.

[4] https://www.ibm.com/topics/what-is-a-digital-twin.

cases. Instead of browsing, as clients are used to in web-based Internet applications, they need to act as avatars in collaborative interactive behavior that includes gestures and movements.

Virtual Reality (VR) technology simulates 3D environments to enable user interaction in a virtual reality approximating reality through human senses. Current access devices are VR headset for vision, gloves and body tracking suits for haptic interaction. Augmented reality (AR) as a less immersive alternative to VR adds digital overlays on top of the real world via a lens of some type. This type of access enables users still to interact with their real-world environment, e.g., through binocular glasses.

Since users as well as their access and interaction facility play a crucial in Metaverse applications, the first design requirement can be identified to that respect and specified as follows:

- *(DES-REQ 1) Immersion requires users and their interaction capabilities being represented as part of Digital Process Twin models, as well as respective execution capabilities to validate and support task-related behavior.*

According to Tucci et al. [2], 'rather than a single shared virtual space, the current version of the metaverse is shaping up as a multiverse' which means regarding technology and architecture, the metaverse is a digital ecosystem built on various kinds of 3D technology, real-time collaboration software, and blockchain-based decentralized tools. Hence, architecting and operating the Metaverse is a matter of aligning technological and technical capabilities for a business operation or set of tasks to be supported for users or their VR/AR representations [19]. Interfaces for data exchange and communication are required for seamless operation (cf. [20]).

With respect to the addressed Metaverse application in home healthcare, both, the provider, and the clients can enter it to configure and operate the devices in real-time 3D collaboration needed for monitoring the health status. It includes the digital twin of the sensor system that the client needs to wear in the physical world. Moreover, the provider can solve problems by reasoning alongside devices while they are in-operation, when they are operated at the client's remote location. In case sensitive medical data need to be collected and processed in a reliable way for medical diagnosis, blockchain technology can be applied to meet this objective.

The mutually adjusted use of various technologies and the integration of Metaverse application into socio-technical CPS architectures leads to the following design requirement:

- *(DES-REQ 2) A DPT model has to overcome interoperability problems, both, at design and runtime.*

A further design issue considers the level of maturity of involved technologies that provide access to the virtual world or are used in cyber-physical settings, including VR headsets and ambient intelligent objects. The level of maturity does not only concern the infrastructure for developing and operating Metaverse applications and CPS, but also domain-specific components or devices. In particular, in critical domains with complex facilities, such as healthcare, due to different paths of technological developments various levels of technological readiness have to be expected. They require adequate and adaptive modeling techniques to ensure accurate and timely representation and operation of heterogeneous systems:

- *(DES-REQ 3) Technology components need to be modelled on a level of abstraction that represents the required functionality and interaction capabilities, even when they are of different kinds and on different levels of technological readiness.*

Adaption is also required in case the application architecture changes, as the Metaverse is a dynamically evolving open space, much like Internet applications and CPS, however as digital 3D setting. This leads to the following design requirement:

- *(DES-REQ 4) Aside overcoming interoperability problems, a Metaverse DPT needs to be dynamically adaptable, i.e. in terms of adding and modifying components and functionality, at design and runtime.*

The design process is affected by the variety of technologies that can play distinct roles in the development of the Metaverse and thus, requires particular attention in the course of integrating (physical and digital) components[5]:

- Artificial Intelligence (AI) to create intelligent avatars or human representations, and support ad-hoc behavior, such as spontaneous conversations
- Internet-of-Things to seamlessly connect 3D virtual spaces with the real world
- Extended reality in the form of AR, VR, and Mixed Reality to virtualize and use data and behavior encapsulations in 3D
- Brain-computer interfaces for more direct user access and control
- 3D modeling and reconstruction to capture objects from the real world and provide corresponding 3D prototypes
- Spatial and edge computing to quickly respond to user actions that mimic reality
- Blockchain to decentralize the Metaverse, secure digital content, and avoid disruptive system behavior

The following design requirement aims to ensure the use of dedicated technologies in socio-technical development according to (domain-specific) stakeholder needs:

- *(DES-REQ 5) For DPT development and operation, each of these technologies needs to be checked, whether it affects user/work-related functionality, and thus, the design of Metaverse applications, or its implementation, and consequently, the Metaverse operational infrastructure.*

The Metaverse is designed for (work) collaboration. When organizations start to use Metaverse applications for more real-life experiences of their products and services, they lay ground to overall virtual sales and services processes (cf. [21]). This development includes setting up 3D rooms where users can collaborate, according to different roles

---

[5] See also https://cloudsolutions.academy/solution/what-is-the-technical-stack-for-metave rse/,https://www.bitkom.org/Themen/Technologien-Software/Metaverse, https://www.wef orum.org/agenda/2022/02/future-of-the-metaverse-vr-ar-and-brain-computer/, https://www. bitkom.org/sites/main/files/2023-01/230105LFMetaverseEN.pdf.

through dedicated avatars. Of particular interest are dual interactive experiences, e.g., configuring a device and training its operation while operating it in the physical world:

- *(DES-REQ 6) Collaboration requires the DPT capability to represent interaction mechanism between user-relevant roles and tasks, and to support interaction between human actors and/or their Metaverse (re)presentations.*

Finally, the Metaverse is expected to reshape business models and operation aside personalized interaction and collaboration. Non-Fungible Tokens (NFTs) are expected to be used for securing digital assets when buying and selling, based on some blockchain technology (cf. [22]). The Metaverse is becoming a trading place for digital goods, e.g., of temporal or permanent interest for business operations like novel product developments or service designs ('virtual spaces as Metaverse service') – see also Fernandez et al. [23]. Hence, DPTs need to be able to design business transactions exclusively performed in the virtual space. Customers served in the Metaverse need to trust that the goods they acquired in digital form remain accessible to them:

- *(DES-REQ 7) Business objects or valuables can be digital assets in the Metaverse that may have to be secured by digital means for trustworthy (business) operation. DPT should be able offer such mechanisms, regardless of the application context.*

Metaverse applications could significantly change business relations. Companies selling physical goods like Nike aim to offer creating and selling virtual sneakers and apparel [2]. Potential buyers can probe with avatars and connect with other stakeholders in Metaverse business applications in a focused way [24].

In addition, technology developers producing VR, AR, and MR technologies and ambient intelligent systems, like Meta and its partnering companies, will reframe their Metaverse applications with other (existing) applications like social media, and offer integrated or intertwined systems. Of particular interest will then be transition schemes for interfacing or embedding 2D systems like Microsoft Teams or Zoom into 3D applications, or some mesh-enabled immersive spaces to let users reconstruct and transmit high-quality 3D models of people (avatars) in real time (cf. [25, 26]).

Finally, once Metaverse applications are linked to physical bodies, both on the cognitive level, e.g., by brain-computer interfaces, and beyond, e.g., using wearables, the immersion of human users could be seamlessly enriched through Digital Twins and aesthetic interaction qualities (cf. DigiSense project[6] [27]). Such integration capabilities require special attention for Metaverse developments:

- *(DES-REQ 8) Integration of existing 2D applications with (cyber-)physical interaction modalities, such as bodily immersion and body language, based on DPTs should be facilitated to enrich Metaverse processes or interaction features for holistic human user engagement.*

Although most of the basic technologies required for Metaverse applications are already available, their interoperable entangling requires design and implementation effort. Digital Twin concepts and technologies aim to design, probe, and run Metaverse

---

[6] https://www.claudiaschnugg.com/projects/

applications. DPTs need to enable testing a set of possibilities with all required components and interactions in mutual context before putting an application to practical use.

3 Digital Process Twins Supporting Metaverse Developments

This section briefly reviews the subject-oriented life cycle enabling structured development based on DPT models. We discuss each development phase and bundle of activities with respect to the previously introduced design requirements (*DES-REQ 1–8*). In particular, separating modeling from validation and execution enables technologies to be considered from 2 perspectives, namely from the task/role-specific functionality required for a Metaverse application, and from an infrastructure perspective, namely to implement that functionality.

The second part of this section introduces Digital Process Twins modeling based on the experiences and findings from applying subject-oriented development principles and technologies. They are also analyzed with respect to meeting the design requirements (*DES-REQ 1–8*) introduced in the previous section. We exemplify essential activities and features referring to the already introduced home healthcare application.

3.1 Separation of Concerns for Design-Integrated DPT Engineering – Modeling and Validation, Organizational Implementation, and Technology Assignment

When looking at the open development cycle of subject-oriented development [14] the different activity bundles can be accessed based on the state of development affairs and according to design and implementations needs of the application at hand.

- *Analysis* leads to decomposing operational context and elaborating the rationale of DPT design. It considers in terms of an organization's strategy how to structure work and to use behavior modeling and to set other management activities (*DES-REQ 6*). Important (cross-cutting) concerns as addressed in (*DES-REQ 7*) also need to be considered here as they are relevant for successful operation. In the home healthcare case switching between Metaverse and (cyber-)physical elements for training how to handle medical equipment is important. Finally, analysis activities are also triggered by feedback from ongoing operation, thus stemming from another bundle of activities, especially monitoring, and require the identification of adaptation requirements like addressed in (*DES-REQ 4*). The same holds for integrating existing or novel developments as addressed in (*DES-REQ 8*). In home healthcare, adaptation is required when a novel generation of devices becomes available and features need to be considered in an integrative way, e.g., for intelligent medication.
- *Modeling* targets reducing the complexity through mapping it to DPT representations. Relevant design items need to be identified and abstracted from the observed physical reality or envisioned/experiences virtual reality. In subject-orientation modeling it is essentially a matter of representing which behavioral encapsulations or subjects perform which activities (tasks and functions) on which objects (information which is bound to specific carriers) using which tools (e.g., machinery, avatars, domain-specific systems, algorithms), and how they need to interact in a choreographic way to achieve

the desired process goals and outcomes. Initially, an abstract DPT is created, as this model is still independent of the specific actors or role carriers. These are then added in the course of the organizational and IT implementation of the DPT.

- It is this way of separating concerns and the message-based interaction that enable to identify a proper design abstraction from a functional *(DES-REQ 3, 4 and 6)* and use(r) perspective *(DES-REQ 1 and 8)* ensuring interoperability of components *(DES-REQ 2)*, and to specify a specific logic and infrastructure required for operation *(DES-REQ 5 and 7)*. Functional home healthcare elements are sensor system and device operations required to check the client's health condition. The devices need to be operated by users in a way reliable data can be delivered, and trigger further activities, such as informing medical experts to perform analyses.

- *Validation* means checking whether a process is effective, i.e., whether it leads to the expected output in the form of a product or service and outcome for concerned and involved stakeholders. The subject of validation is the behavior of a DPT. This activity bundle concerns a generic property and specific benefit of DPTs: probing before implementing a process or manufacturing a product. As such it requires an adequate level of abstraction for design and runtime operation *(DES-REQ 2 and 3)*. It enables following the flow of control and identifying gaps and potential for improvement. In home healthcare a routine medication process can be subject to validation, as well as irregular behavior of users and system functions.

- *Optimization* targets the efficiency of operating a process. It affects the consumption of resources and performance when a DPT and its subprocesses are adjusted to specific resources. Hence, it concerns the technology readiness of technological components, once it affects the Metaverse performance *(DES-REQ 2 and 3)*. Similar to validation, in home healthcare regular processes and handling of irregular behavior are subject to optimization.

- *Organization-specific implementation* addresses embedding a validated (and optimized) DPT in an existing or a novel organizational environment – user-specific details are handled at that stage *(DES-REQ 1 and 6)*. The allocation of tasks and roles either to humans or Metaverse technology is performed, leading to avatars and their organizational function in digital settings, e.g., for configuration support of home-healthcare appliances. Depending on the degree of automation, personal network connections need to be identified when operating the home healthcare application. If relevant, in case wearables and thus the human body can trigger behavior, this capability has to be specified at this stage of development *(DES-REQ 8)*. The same holds when 2D applications like social media support collaboration and have to be integrated according to their role into the Metaverse application *(DES-REQ 6, 8)*.

- *IT implementation* addresses operation and the technical introduction of the DPT into the processes of an organization, based on the technical components, systems, and the DPT workflow. The assignments concern the avatar(s) and their control facilities, the required business logic, and data handling, as all machinery, digital actors, and (business) objects are instantiated for operation *(DES-REQ 1,2,4–8)*. This step enables users to access the Metaverse through a proper device like AR-glasses, and to utilize the interaction features for physical and digital control based on the technical infrastructure.

- *Monitoring* completes implementation and targets the period after 'going live' of Metaverse applications. Along operation, DPT execution is evaluated to identify further needs of target groups and operation support. Home healthcare routines are experienced, and the generated information is then fed to analysis, modeling, or other bundles of activities, depending on the accuracy of monitoring. A Metaverse application may need to be adapted during runtime, e.g., home healthcare features adjusting to user requirements when becoming evident through operation *(DES-REQ 4)*.

Table 1 summarizes the findings according to the activity bundles and design requirements. Both, modeling, and IT implementation, concern most of the requirements and thus, significantly impact the use of DPTs in Metaverse development.

Table 1. Concerned design requirements in each of the activity bundles of DPT development

Design Requirement (DES-REQ) Activity Bundle	1	2	3	4	5	6	7	8
Analysis				x		x	x	x
Modeling	x	x	x	x	x	x	x	x
Validation		x	x					
Optimization		x	x					
Organization-specific Implementation	x					x		x
IT Implementation	x	x		x	x	x	x	x
Monitoring				x				

According to the open lifecycle concept, development and management activities are carried out along a feedback control cycle composed of the bundles mentioned above. Although they indicate a linear sequence, these activity bundles can be performed in different order. It is then triggered by events in the individual activity bundles leading to various paths of development. For instance, a technical optimization may lead to adaptation without monitoring. Hence, it is possible to skip steps, e.g., when a lack of resources can be handled providing another organizational or technical implementation of the DPT (by providing additional work force or devices) - the DPT itself does not have to be modified. Consequently, it depends on the activity that can be set in a specific situation of development or operation, which bundles of activities are executed (iteratively).

3.2   Design-Integrated Engineering Built on Architectures Integrating Functional Behavior and Interaction

This sub section introduces Digital Process Twins (DPTs) as a conceptual modeling construct and how it can be put to practice in the context of developing Metaverse applications. The presented experiences stem from findings when applying subject-oriented principles and technologies for the Internet-of Behavior [28] and Cyber-Physical System developments [7, 29]. They address.

- architecture concerns, including
- interoperability [30]
- autonomy of components and functionalities [31, 32])
- complex event processing [33]
- dedicated technologies including
- blockchain [33]
- (transport) robot systems [34]
- implementation of cross-cutting concerns including
- privacy and autonomy [35].

These findings are analyzed with respect to meeting the design requirements (*DES-REQ 1–8*) as introduced in Sect. 2. The starting point of utilizing subject-orientation for CPS developments was recognizing the integrative nature of the Internet-of-Behaviors (IoB) that finally would lead to a unifying Internet-of-Behavior that is built upon IoT (cf. [36]). It indicates a layer of abstraction that can be considered to address if not resolve interoperability issues. A further starting point was the socio-technical fit of value-based business transactions of subject-oriented modeling and its successful application in organizational transformations [37, 38]. These findings can be utilized as starting point for Metaverse developments. Hence, the first part of this section considers the organizational context of Metaverse applications and their development, defining stakeholder-centric networks that contain value transactions to meet common objectives. In the subsequent parts, the refinement of transactions to behavior sequences in terms of function and communication is addressed, and finally, the enrichments required for complex operations and adaptation of behavior.

3.2.1   The Starting Point: A Declarative Map of Interacting Behavior Entities

When DPTs are developed in the context of Metaverse applications, there needs to be some common ground or a baseline where the knowledge about the operational context comes from. It is based on understanding an organization as a set of interacting actors or components:

- Each node of a networked organization establishing the context and content of a Metaverse application encapsulates behavior and thus, represents a Behavior Entity BeE or subject, i.e. a professional or organization-relevant role of a Metaverse element.
- BeEs send and exchange deliverables to other BeEs. The direction in which deliverables are moving in the course of a specific transaction is complemented with a deliverable identifier or label.
- A deliverable can have some physical appearance, including tangible elements, e.g., product, manipulated objects of work, devices, or be of digital nature, such as service description or product sheet or a detailed request for information.

In the following we exemplify a BeE map that is represented as Subject Interaction Diagram [14] corresponding to the introduced home healthcare service provision case.

When clients are provided with services, devices, or technologies according to their specific healthcare needs, the Metaverse application could support them for informed utilization to make best use of the provided tools and related services through 3D collaboration.

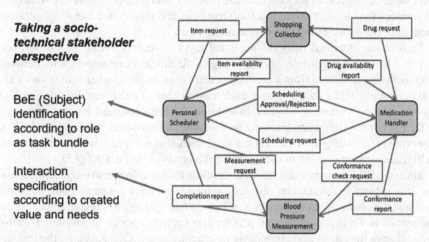

Fig. 1. Part of Subject-Interaction Diagram (SID – grey box = BeE/subject, rectangle = deliverable transmitted through transaction/message exchange) of a DPT for a home healthcare scenario

The goal in the considered home healthcare case is to support self-organized care taking. As shown in Fig. 1, medical devices like Blood Pressure Management are coupled with a Medication Handler and a Personal Scheduler, both for configuring and controlling timely caretaking activities and data collection for medical analysis. Regular and accurate drug taking is supported by a Shopping Collector designed for ensuring availability of medical goods and services for routine tasks.

A Metaverse application in home healthcare can be designed to help demonstrating in 3D how to track and collect a person's healthcare data, such as blood pressure and sugar level, sleeping patterns, or diet conventions with a corresponding set of devices. The application could also be used to set up a network of relevant stakeholders (including their avatars) to alert adverse situations and to suggest behavior modifications. Avatars of clients could simulate different situations and options to trigger behavior changes, in particular by demonstrating outcomes with respect to the client's health condition. Effects, such as reducing blood pressure through a different diet, or reducing the dose of pills for the sake of daytime agility, could be virtually experienced in a vivid and playful way in the Metaverse application. The required behavior model entities and interactions could initially only exist in the Metaverse application before adjusting the cyber-physical setting for operation according to the client's intention and abilities.

3.2.2 Setting the Stage for Choreographic Refinement

The first step designers need to consider in the DPT modeling process is the set of organizational tasks, roles, functional technology components, or systems that are considered of relevance for achieving an application's or organization's objective. These elements represent BeEs or subjects as they encapsulate behavior, and include the /device) functions and services for blood pressure measurement, diet and medication handling, personal scheduling, etc. as well as external medical services.

Each of the identified roles or functional tasks represents a node in the BeE network or SID which is partially shown in Fig. 1. At this level interoperability between components is considered from a conceptual and organizational rather than from a technical perspective *(DES-REQ 2)*, since each transmission of a deliverable is designed as message exchange between subjects. In addition, the organizational implementation of the DPT is left for later when focusing on available qualifications and functionalities to be provided *(DES-REQ 1,3)*. Setting the stage does also not reveal how much machine intelligence support is given to each of the BeEs or subjects *(DES-REQ 5)*.

Since the DPT design model serves as baseline for the subsequent engineering activities, it is subject to refinement. Subject-oriented refinement concerns both, the functional and the communication behavior of BeEs while utilizing a choreographic process representation. From an operational perspective, subjects operate in parallel. Thereby, they exchange messages asynchronously or synchronously. Consequently, the transactions forming value streams in organizations, leading to the exchange of deliverables as discussed above, can be interpreted as transmissions of messages between subjects.

(Metaverse) Applications specified as subject-oriented DPTs operate as autonomous encapsulated entities with concurrent behavior *(DES-REQ 7)*. Each entity (subject) is capable to performing (local) actions that do not involve interacting with other subjects, e.g., calculating a threshold value of blood pressure for an individual measurement service in home healthcare. Subjects also perform communicative actions that concern the transmission of messages to other subjects, namely sending and receiving messages, such as calling medical expert services in case of recognizing a blood pressure value above a certain threshold.

3.2.3 Refinement in Terms of Functions and Communication

Subjects as behavior encapsulations are detailed through Subject Behavior Diagrams (SBDs), introducing a refined level of behavior, whereas SIDs address a more abstract layer. SIDs denote behavior encapsulations and an accumulated view on message transmissions. Hence, refining the behavior of each subject of a SID reveals the sequence of sending and receiving messages as well as its local actions. These actions represent its functionality, as accumulated in Fig. 1 for the addressed use case:

- The Personal Scheduler subject coordinates all activities for a defined period in time (traditionally available on a mobile device).
- The Medication Handler subject takes care of providing the correct medication and is triggered by the Personal Scheduler subject for timely medication.
- The Blood Pressure Measurement subject enables sensing the blood pressure of the client and is also triggered by the Personal Scheduler subject.

- The Shopping Collector subject collects all items to be purchased, in order to ensure continuous availability of goods and services in home health care.

According to the Metaverse concept, the client as a Metaverse user needs to be present in the virtual 3D world as an avatar. Such an embedding requires modeling the avatar and the access device for user interaction (e.g., AR glasses) as subject(s) *(DES-REQ 1,8)* - it bundles the control of the Metaverse application from the client's Metaverse interaction perspective. This requirement is a special situation. The avatar exists in parallel to the physical person, and could perform actions, such as handling digital devices without physical correspondence.

In the addressed use case, depending on individual needs and according to the set of interactive interventions the client user handles the measurement device, and needs to know, when to activate it and whether further measurements need to be taken. The Shopping Collector receives requests from both, the Medication Handler when drugs are required from the pharmacy, physician, or hospital, and the Personal Scheduler, in case (further) medicine for the client is required *(DES-REQ 6)*.

Internal functions of subjects process received and generated data to implement the required functionality *(DES-REQ 3)*. In the sample case the subject Blood Pressure Measurement has a counter for each application. An internal maintenance function increases the counter by one when the client activates the device. The function can either end with the result "sufficient energy" or "change battery" to ensure the device's availability.

3.2.4 Getting Close to Operation: DPT Validation and Execution

Once a Subject Behavior Diagram, e.g., for the Blood Pressure Measurement subject is instantiated, it has to be decided (i) whether a human or a (digital) device (organizational implementation) and (ii) which actual device is assigned to the subject, acting as technological subject carrier (technical implementation). Validation of SBDs is sufficient for interactive process experience and testing task and process completion *(DES-REQ 1, 6–8)*. Thereby, the utility of features and additional requirements become evident *(DES-REQ 5)*.

Besides academic engines, e.g., Sisi [39], commercial solutions, such as Metasonic[7], Compunity[8] and actnconnect[9] can be used, both for DPT validation and execution. Since neither the message exchange protocol implementation nor the business object specification are part of the modeling notation, it depends on the modeling environment and runtime engine used for development, at which point in time and in which form data structures and the business logic determining the communication on the subject instance level are implemented.

3.2.5 DPT Adaptation: Integrating Intelligent Behavior

After refining SIDs from a function and communication behavior perspective, a runtime-valid version exists, that is likely to be subject to dynamic adaptation *(DES-REQ 4)*

---

[7] https://www.allgeier-inovar.de/de/produkte/metasonic.html.

[8] https://compunity.eu/

[9] http://actnconnect.de/index

according to the nature of cyber-physical environments, e.g., when a new generation of blood measurement devices with another level of technology readiness needs to become part of system operation *(DES-REQ 3)*. Dynamic adaptation in design-based engineering means modifying SIDs and/or subject refinements through Subject Behavior Diagrams (SBDs), and thus, allowing behavior modification(s). Due to the choreography approach, adaptation may be accomplished at runtime, when it only affects the internal behavior of a component (i.e. the SBD) that is subject to change. As long as an SBD follows the existing send- and receive patterns it can be replaced without modifying the SID, and thus, affecting the entire system architecture.

In order to handle adaptation in a generic way, we need to consider the trigger, such as a result from an analysis or a received sensor signal, which requires behavior changes. Triggers can be handled through an event processing scheme that captures variants of behavior at design time. Thereby, the trigger, e.g., "blood pressure above threshold", can carry some (context) data as payload *(DES-REQ 3,7)*. A data object represents a trigger and is structured to supported event processing: A header consists of meta-information about the trigger like name, arrival time, priorities, etc. The payload contains specific information about the triggering event.

With respect to operation and model execution, triggers are messages that carry data objects described above. At runtime - when a process instance is created and messages are sent, these messages become events. Instantaneous events can be handled by Message Guards. They are modeling constructs to represent behavior variants *(DES-REQ 4,8)* including the conditions when which variant is relevant and should be executed. For instance, the "blood pressure above threshold" message from the subject Blood Pressure Measurement can arrive at any time when handled by a Message Guard. It specifies the reaction, e.g., calling the emergency service. Message Guards are patterns included in the SBD of a DPT and reached by flagged behavior states (see also Fig. 2).

The design decision that has to be taken concerns the way how the adaptation occurs, either extending an existing behavior, or replacing it from a certain state on. In the home healthcare case, returning to the original sequence (regular SBD sequence) is given when the called emergency service in case of high blood pressure does not require any further intervention of medical experts. Replacement of the regular procedure is required, in case the Medication Handler subject, and as a follow-up, the Personal Scheduler subject (referring to the time of medication) has to be modified.

Figure 2 shows a Message Guard specification addressing the need for training how to handle the Blood Pressure Management device/services, e.g., when being provided with a novel device. This training could be supported by a Metaverse application, including a device avatar guiding a client avatar. Their behavior needs to be specified at design time. Further refinements, i.e. the allocation of Metaverse components and the technology assignments, take place in the course of organizational and technological implementation.

When cross-cutting concerns, e.g., management of client privacy, and specific types of users, e.g., customer service agents or quality managers, need to be supported, the basic SID pattern displayed in Fig. 3 needs to be applied. A subject is then defined as System-of-Systems. It can control the behavior of other subjects and thus, influence the entire system behavior *(DES-REQ 7)*. The example shown in the figure allows for

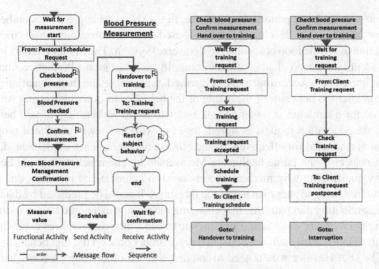

Fig. 2. Part of Blood Pressure Measurement subject behavior with Message Guard (flagged activities) for client training in home healthcare scenario

monitoring requested by an acting subject. It leads to collecting client behavior data and its evaluation for making decisions on future behavior, e.g., to call emergency services if required. Monitoring includes checking whether a complex event has occurred, e.g., several indications of non-expected behavior need to be handled. When including decision support to adapt the behavior of an acting subject, e.g., according to existing behavior variants (specified by Message Guards), available situation data are delivered to a corresponding System-of-Systems subject, and the Metaverse behavior can be adapted accordingly *(DES-REQ 4)*.

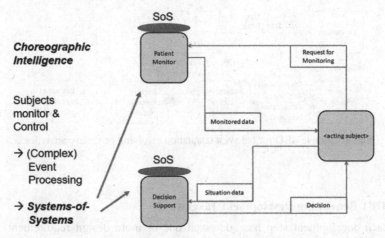

Fig. 3. System-of-Systems (SoS) subjects for Monitoring and Decision Support

In line with the basic pattern shown above, Fig. 4 shows an approach for embedding predictive analytics. The developed pattern is based on a Monitor subject that is triggered by a function in an idle loop observing a (Metaverse) system. The monitored data is evaluated to identify the need of adaptation. For intelligent adaptation a Predictive Analytics subject is introduced. According to the behavior data available and the calculation model to either predict the behavior of the acting or the behavior of other interacting subjects, a proposal for adaptation is generated. In order to avoid re-iterating certain behavior patterns, the adaptation request is stored, together with the newly generated proposal. The latter is evaluated for effectiveness and efficiency before being implemented.

With respect to the home healthcare Metaverse, the client behavior could be challenged by questioning why medical experts need to be contacted regularly due to the blood pressure being higher than a specific threshold. It could be predicted by data analysis (e.g., evaluating diet patterns) that changing the client's diet could help avoiding the triggering of emergency services. Implementing such a proposal requires extending the DPT with a Diet Handler subject that can deliver timely data on the diet behavior of the client. The Diet Handler would need to interact with all other subjects (as System-of-Systems), as its functional behavior to provide the requested data leads to novel patterns of interaction involving the existing system components (Medication Handler, Shopping Collector, etc.).

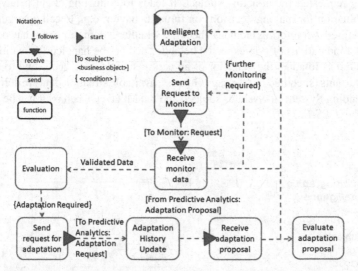

Fig. 4. Sample SBD for behavior adaptation involving predictive analytics

3.2.6 DPT Benefitting Development Takeaways

Since each development step has addressed one or more design requirements, and the addressed use case only reveals exemplary issues in Metaverse design-integrated engineering, Table 2 cross-checks the modeling and processing capabilities of subject-oriented DPT development support from a general perspective. For each characteristic subject-oriented DPT feature its relation to the design requirements is provided.

Table 2. Meeting design requirements by subject-oriented Digital Process Twin modeling and implementation capabilities

Design Requirement (DES-REQ) Subject-oriented DPT Modeling Capability	1	2	3	4	5	6	7	8
Behavior encapsulation	x	x	x	x	x	x	x	x
Choreography / message exchange	x	x	x	x	x	x	x	x
(Business) Object / data representation	x	x		x	x	x	x	
System-of-Systems architecting	x		x	x			x	x
Subject-oriented DPT Implementation Capability								
Validation	x			x	x	x	x	
Execution	x	x		x	x	x	x	x

As the table cell entries reveal, behavior encapsulation and the choreographic message interaction capability are considered major assets to meet the entire set of design requirements of DPTs of Metaverse applications. They do not only facilitate the concurrent operation of components and sub-systems, but also the dynamic adaptation of systems. The System-of-System capability is required for all features bundling control based on accumulating data and influencing system parts like operating in a specific Metaverse.

When operating a Metaverse application through a DPT, the data management is enabled through message exchanges with messages payloads ranging from complex (wrapped) business objects to event parameters triggering specific subject behavior. The validation serves for checking the semantic correctness of the Metaverse functionality depending on the role understanding and interaction for collaborative task accomplishment, whereas the execution of DPT facilitates checking and experiencing runtime behavior.

4   Conclusion

Given the variety of promises in the context of Metaverse, which may remind us to the propagation of the World Wide Web ('making the world a global village') renewed by Web3 conceptualizations (cf. [40]), its applications might further "shrink the world", but at the same time increase complexity in development and operation. When collaboration at work should be increased and organizational performance in the network economy should become more reliable and trustworthy with ubiquitous and concurrently operating Metaverse applications, existing development techniques need to be reframed.

In this paper we could identify and provide indicative evidence, that Digital Process Twin technology powered by Subject-oriented Business Process Management techniques and tools can support Metaverse application development effectively and efficiently. Effectively in this context means behavior-encapsulation and message-based interaction enable handling architecting including interoperability concerns when composing heterogeneous components. Efficiently in that context means using a design-integrated engineering approach that couples modeling with validation and execution of models, thus speeding up behavior-centered development and operation of cyber-physical Metaverse applications.

Our analysis is not exhaustive, as deriving design requirements and considering development facilities depend on the existing body of knowledge and applications in use. Currently, the latter cannot be provided to allow developing empirically valid evidence. We rather need to conclude at that stage of development: The more conceptual and development analyses are performed, the less exemplary will be the findings provided in this paper. However, methodologically, the road should be paved for further reflections of that kind.

References

1. Ball, M.: The metaverse: and how it will revolutionize everything. Liveright Publishing; W.W. Norton & Company, New York (2022)
2. Tucci, L., Needle, D.: What is the metaverse? An explanation and in-depth guide, WhatIs.com, downloaded, 26 February 2023 (2022). https://www.techtarget.com/whatis/feature/The-metaverse-explained-Everything-you-need-to-know?vgnextfmt=print
3. Bitkom: Augmented und Virtual Reality. Potenziale und praktische Anwendung immersiver Technologien. Bitkom, Berlin (2021)
4. Li, K., et al. When internet of things meets metaverse: convergence of physical and cyber worlds, Cornell University, 26 February 2023 (2022). https://arxiv.org/abs/2208.13501
5. Hamzaoui, M.A., Julien, N.: social cyber-physical systems and digital twins networks: a perspective about the future digital twin ecosystems. IFAC-PapersOnLine 55(8), 31–36 (2022)
6. Human, C., Basson, A.H., Kruger, K.: A design framework for a system of digital twins and services. Comput. Ind. 144, 103796 (2023)
7. Stary, C., Elstermann, M., Fleischmann, A., Schmidt, W.: Behavior-centered digital-twin design for dynamic cyber-physical system development. Complex Syst. Inf. Model. Q. (CSIMQ) 30, 31–52 (2022)
8. Caesar, B., Hänel, A., Wenkler, E., Corinth, C., Ihlenfeldt, S., Fay, A.: Information model of a digital process twin for machining processes. In: 25th International Conference on Emerging Technologies and Factory Automation (ETFA), vol. 1, pp. 1765–1772. IEEE (2020)
9. Barachini, F., Stary, C.: From Digital Twins to Digital Selves and Beyond: Engineering and Social Models for a Trans-humanist World. Springer Nature, Cham (2022).https://doi.org/10.1007/978-3-030-96412-2
10. Barn, B.S., Clark, T., Barat S., Kulkarni, V.: Towards the essence of specifying sociotechnical digital twins. In: Proceedings 16th Innovations in Software Engineering ISEC 2023, Article #18. ACM, New York (2023)
11. Darwish, A., Hassanien, A.E.: Cyber physical systems design, methodology, and integration: the current status and future outlook. J. Ambient. Intell. Humaniz. Comput. 9(5), 1541–1556 (2017). https://doi.org/10.1007/s12652-017-0575-4

12. Marwedel, P.: Embedded System Design: Embedded Systems Foundations of Cyber-Physical Systems, and the Internet of Things. Springer Nature, Cham (2021). https://doi.org/10.1007/978-3-030-60910-8
13. Bönsch, J., Elstermann, M., Kimmig, A., Ovtcharova, J.: A subject-oriented reference model for Digital Twins. Comput. Ind. Eng. **172**, 108556 (2022)
14. Fleischmann, A., Schmidt, W., Stary, C., Obermeier, S., Börger, E.: Subject-Oriented Business Process Management. Springer Nature, Cham (2012). https://doi.org/10.1007/978-3-642-32392-8
15. Guan, J., Irizawa, J., Morris, A.: Extended reality and internet of things for hyper-connected metaverse environments. In: Proceedings Conference on Virtual Reality and 3D User Interfaces Abstracts and Workshops, pp. 163–168. IEEE (2022)
16. George, A.H., Fernando, M., George, A.S., Baskar, T., Pandey, D.: Metaverse: the next stage of human culture and the Internet. Int. J. Adv. Res. Trends Eng. Technol. **8**(12), 1–10 (2021)
17. Bitkom: A guidebook to the Metaverse. Technological and legal basics, potential for business, relevance for society. Bitkom, Berlin (2022)
18. Mourtzis, D., Panopoulos, N., Angelopoulos, J., Wang, B., Wang, L.: Human centric platforms for personalized value creation in metaverse. J. Manuf. Syst. **65**, 653–659 (2022)
19. Bian, Y., Leng, J., Zhao, J.L.: Demystifying metaverse as a new paradigm of enterprise digitization. In: Proceedings Big Data–BigData 2021: 10th International Conference, pp. 109–119. Springer International Publishing, Cham (2022). https://doi.org/10.1007/978-3-030-96282-1_8
20. Dionisio, J.D.N., Iii, W.G.B., Gilbert, R.: 3D virtual worlds and the metaverse: current status and future possibilities. ACM Comput. Surv. (CSUR) **45**(3), 1–38 (2013)
21. Bennett, D.: Remote workforce, virtual team tasks, and employee engagement tools in a real-time interoperable decentralized metaverse. Psychosociol. Issues Hum. Resour. Manag. **10**(1), 78–91 (2022)
22. Yang, Q., Zhao, Y., Huang, H., Xiong, Z., Kang, J., Zheng, Z.: Fusing blockchain and AI with metaverse: a survey. IEEE Open J. Comput. Soc. **3**, 122–136 (2022)
23. Fernandez, C.B., Hui, P.: Life, the metaverse and everything: an overview of privacy, ethics, and governance in metaverse. In: Proceedings 42nd International Conference on Distributed Computing Systems Workshops, pp. 272–277. IEEE (2022)
24. Sayem, A.S.M.: Digital fashion innovations for the real world and metaverse. Int. J. Fashion Des. Technol. Educ. **15**(2), 139–141 (2022)
25. Rospigliosi, P.A.: Metaverse or Simulacra? Roblox, minecraft, Meta and the turn to virtual reality for education, socialisation and work. Interact. Learn. Environ. **30**(1), 1–3 (2022)
26. Zyda, M.: Let's rename everything "the Metaverse!" Computer **55**(3), 124–129 (2022)
27. Brill, D., Schnugg, C., Stary, C.: Makes digital sensemaking sense? - A roadmap for digital humanism in increasingly transhumanist settings. New Explorations **2**(3) (2022)
28. Stary, C.: The internet-of-behavior as organizational transformation space with choreographic intelligence. In: Proceedings 12th International Conference Subject-Oriented Business Process Management. The Digital Workplace–Nucleus of Transformation, S-BPM ONE 2020, pp. 113–132, Springer International Publishing, Cham (2020). https://doi.org/10.1007/978-3-030-64351-5_8
29. Stary, C.: Digital twin generation: re-conceptualizing agent systems for behavior-centered cyber-physical system development. Sensors **21**(4), 1096 (2021)
30. Weichhart, G., Stary, C.: Interoperable process design in production systems. In: Debruyne, C., Panetto, H., Weichhart, G., Bollen, P., Ciuciu, I., Vidal, M.-E., Meersman, R. (eds.) OTM 2017. LNCS, vol. 10697, pp. 26–35. Springer, Cham (2018). https://doi.org/10.1007/978-3-319-73805-5_3

31. Heininger, R., Stary, C.: Capturing autonomy in its multiple facets: a digital twin approach. In: Proceedings of the 2021 ACM Workshop on Secure and Trustworthy Cyber-Physical Systems, pp. 3–12. ACM, New York (2021)

32. Heininger, R., Jost, T.E., Stary, C.: Enriching socio-technical sustainability intelligence through sharing autonomy. Sustainability **15**(3), 2590 (2023)

33. Fleischmann, A., Stary, C.: Dependable data sharing in dynamic IoT-systems: subject-oriented process design, complex event processing, and blockchains. In: Proceedings of the 11th International Conference on Subject-Oriented Business Process Management, S-BPM ONE 2019, pp. 1–11. Springer International Publishing, Cham (2019)

34. Jost, T.E., Stary, C., Heininger, R.: Geo-spatial context provision for digital twin generation. Appl. Sci. **12**(21), 10988 (2022)

35. Stary, C., Heininger, R.: Privacy by sharing autonomy–a design-integrating engineering approach. In: Proceedings 13th International Conference on Subject-Oriented Business Process Management, S-BPM ONE 2022, pp. 3–22, Springer Nature, Cham (2022)

36. Javaid, M., Haleem, A., Singh, R.P., Rab, S., Suman, R.: Internet of behaviours (IoB) and its role in customer services. Sens. Int. **2**, 100122 (2021)

37. Stary, C.: Non-disruptive knowledge and business processing in knowledge life cycles–aligning value network analysis to process management. J. Knowl. Manag. **18**(4), 651–686 (2014)

38. Kaar, C., Stary, C.: Intelligent business transformation through market-specific value network analysis: Structured interventions and process bootstrapping in geomarketing. Knowl. Process. Manag. **26**(2), 163–181 (2019)

39. Elstermann, M., Ovtcharova, J.: SISI in the ALPS: a simple simulation and verification approach for PASS. In: Proceedings of the 10th International Conference on Subject-Oriented Business Process Management, pp. 1–9. ACM, New York (2018)

40. Kovacova, M., Horak, J., Higgins, M.: Behavioral analytics, immersive technologies, and machine vision algorithms in the Web3-powered metaverse world. Ling. Philos. Invest. **21**, 57–72 (2022)

Approach of Partial Front-Loading in Engineer to Order

Konrad Jagusch[1]([✉]), Jan Sender[1], David Jericho[1], and Wilko Flügge[2]

[1] Fraunhofer Institute for Large Structures in Production Engineering IGP,
Albert-Einstein-Str. 30, 18059 Rostock, Germany
konrad.jagusch@igp.fraunhofer.de

[2] Chair of Manufacturing Technology, University of Rostock, Albert-Einstein-Str. 2,
18059 Rostock, Germany

Abstract. Technical changes are an integral part of engineer to order product manufacturing. External as well as internal causes require these modifications throughout the entire product manufacturing process. Various factors prevent full front-loading, which provides for early implementation of the modifications. In this paper a method of partial front-loading is presented. Accordingly, the progression of the process is considered in the development of alternative solutions for change implementation. The data representation of the production processes, the digital shadow, is an essential part of the approach. This enables the filtering of alternatives based on the time progression. With the additional technical evaluation of the options, a two-stage validation is created. The necessary requirements for the extension of the existing engineering change management models are defined. A practical use case serves as a basis for the evaluation of the front-loading approach in engineer to order. In addition to the actual approximation of the front-loading target curve, the percentage of rejects is assessed.

Keywords: Engineer to order · engineering change management · front-loading

1 Introduction

The maritime industry with its products plays an essential role in the world-wide economy. In addition to maintaining global supply chains [1], they contribute to the desired energy transition [2]. Prominent representatives such as ships, offshore as well as onshore structures are thereby manufactured as engineer to order (ETO) products. A high degree of process parallelization to shorten lead times [3], an early customer decoupling point (CODP) [4] as well as changing political requirements [5] force engineering changes (EC) throughout the entire product development process [6]. The more advanced the process, the higher the negative impacts [7]. Efforts to implement all ECs before the actual start of production are not possible in ETO [8]. Despite more difficult conditions for the so-called front-loading, this paper discusses an approach for partial goal achievement. The focus of the considerations are results of practical application. In addition, challenges, and next steps for further optimizing the handling of ECs in the process are discussed.

© The Author(s), under exclusive license to Springer Nature Switzerland AG 2023
M. Elstermann et al. (Eds.): S-BPM ONE 2023, CCIS 1867, pp. 111–120, 2023.
https://doi.org/10.1007/978-3-031-40213-5_8

2 Current Status

2.1 Engineering Changes

In the following, the term EC is used to summarize the technical modifications described. "ECs are changes and/or modifications to released structure (fits, forms and dimensions, surfaces, materials, etc.), behavior (stability, strength, corrosion, etc.), function (speed, performance, efficiency, etc.), or the relations between functions and behavior (design principles), or behavior and structure (physical laws) of a technical artefact" [9].

Causes for EC are generally very diverse [10]. These include misinterpretation of customer requirements [11], snowballing changes involving a change in technical characteristics [12], or the motivation of cost savings [13]. In addition, there are political requirements [5] and the continuing customer influence within the ETO [6, 8].

Differences regarding the classification of EC exist furthermore in relation to the occurrence in the product life cycle [9]. In the definition after Wright [14] the changed product must be already in the realization and thus in the production phase. Whereas further specifications define an implementation over the entire life cycle as EC [15]. Therefore, according to Reidelbach [16], adaptations can be divided into early, late, or medium with respect to the occurrence during the holistic process flow.

Overall, ECs cause reactive and faulty performance [17]. Profit losses, disruptions in production planning and an increased use of resources are potential consequences [18]. In this paper, priority is given to ECs that take place after the production order has been released. These are considered necessary because they were initiated by the customer

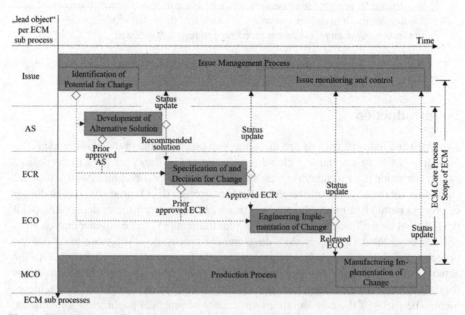

Fig. 1. Simplified overall picture of the dependencies of the phases of the SASIG change management reference-process [20].

or are driven by technical or political requirements. These must be minimized by taking appropriate measures.

2.2 Engineering Change Management

"Engineering change management (ECM) encompasses and shapes process and structure organization as well as strategies and measures for handling the lead time and execution of engineering changes as well as for cross-case change organization and prevention." [19] First, the potential for an EC is identified (issue). Then, alternative solutions (AS) are developed. In an engineering change request (ECR), a proposal is made for the EC and, if approved, is converted into an engineering change order (ECO). This is then implemented in production with a manufacturing change order (MCO). [20] The SASIG change management process summarizes the processes in a model (see Fig. 1). From the process shown, there are several challenges in applying it in the ETO.

3 Challenges in Engineer to Order

3.1 Engineering Changes in Engineer to Order

An early CODP and changing policy demands for large-scale maritime structures [5] force ECs throughout the product development process. Unlike in making to stock (MTS), ECs cannot be transferred to the upcoming product versions. Thus, necessary adaptations target already manufactured components or past procurement processes [6]. Therefore, ETO companies are confronted with adaptations during the ongoing production [21]. In addition to the external influences, the high degree of process overlaps [22] increases the risk of subsequent ECs. The start of manufacturing and assembly before the completion of design [23] require iteration loops and downstream modifications. The resulting steadily growing database [22] also has an impact on the planning processes. Own studies show that ECs are the second most frequent cause for subsequent planning changes in maritime ETO manufacturing [24].

Especially ECs occurring late in the process result in economic losses [7]. However, the timing of ECs is variable and, in most cases, cannot be influenced. Nevertheless, the negative consequences must be minimized by ECM methods.

3.2 Engineering Change Management in Engineer to Order

In addition to the ETO characteristics listed, other general conditions make the implementation of an optimal ECM more difficult. Examples include the complex product structure and various data silos and threads in the process levels [25]. Studies showed that for this reason, a strongly shortened ECM process is accepted by ETO companies [6]. Contrary to the model shown (see Fig. 1), no AS are developed. The issue is followed by impact assessment, customer approval and subsequent implementation. The goal of ECM must be to reduce the number of ECs by including all process levels such as the field level. To this end, rapid communication is required.

In general, the overall problem of ECs is the subject of acute research work. Especially in the ETO sector, however, this topic is treated deficiently from a scientific point of view [8].

Especially externally initiated ECs are bound to be implemented. Therefore, the challenge is to mitigate the associated disturbances for the ongoing manufacturing process. Deviating from the status quo, optional AS are to be developed. Based on the technical and temporal feasibility, an optimal implementation is to be defined. In contrast to current models (see Fig. 1), the shopfloor level is to be included in the AS-development process.

4   Approach to Engineering Change-Alignment

Figure 2 shows, in simplified form, the desired holistic process for minimizing change-related disturbances. In the following, the prerequisites and approaches are described in detail.

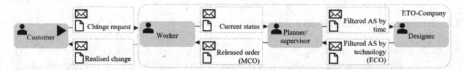

Fig. 2. Optimal process in subject-oriented business process management (S-BPM)

4.1   Inclusion of the Digital Shadow

In the current standards, the full inclusion of the shopfloor begins with the manufacturing implementation of change (see Fig. 1). However, due to the advancing production process in the ETO, this represents a lack of consideration of the production progress. If ECs are provided for components that have already been produced, faulty performance and a completely new production are unavoidable. The exception to this are ECs that can be implemented at a later stage by reworking the component subsequent. However, these are often associated with an enormous coordination effort and disruptions in the material flow and should therefore be avoided.

In the present approach, the technical feasibility of ECs is considered. Furthermore, the consideration of the process progress takes place through the collection of essential data points. A creation of transparency with the help of this approach is called digital shadow [26]. The resulting representation of the processes then forms a data-technical basis for decision-making. For this a sufficiently accurate represent is aimed at. This means that the respective beginning and the end of the physical processing steps of the components are recorded with time stamps. The paper therefore primarily discusses EC relating to the structure (fits, forms and dimensions, surfaces, materials, etc.).

4.2   Filtering Potential Alternative Solutions

In the present use case, first a set of technical convertibles AS must be generated. In the second step, these are to be filtered through the process progress. All components that have already gone through the processing step for the implementation of the EC must then be excluded. The result is a two-stage process for the development of AS (see Fig. 3).

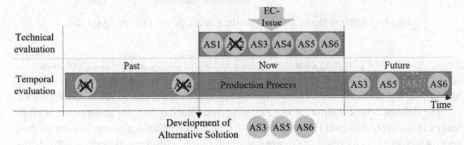

Fig. 3. Filtering of Alternative Solution (AS) based on technical and time aspects

This approach in turn presupposes specific requirements:

- In principle, there is more than one AS for the implementation of an EC-Issue.
- The technical features (fits, forms and dimensions, surfaces, materials, etc.) of the EC implementation can be traced using the digital shadow.
- Throughout ECM, all necessary data is available to all ECM responsible parties in sufficient quality and quantity.

The requirements in turn presuppose a continuous flow of information and synchronization of the process levels. If these requirements are met, a set of potential ASs are available after the evaluation (see Fig. 2). Via this filtering, a kind of front-loading is made possible.

4.3   Front-Loading in Engineer to Order

The primary goal of front-loading is to minimize defects by implementing ECs at an early stage [27]. To this end, EC should be reduced to zero before the start of production of a new series [28]. This is a situation that cannot be realized in ETO.

The timing of the issues is sometimes externally determined. In addition, neither a prototype implementation nor a zero series exist in the ETO. Figure 4 shows the course of the target curve, which is aimed at with front-loading. Furthermore, exemplary times of occurring EC-issues are added. This clearly shows that the target curve for the whole product cannot be achieved by definition in the ETO.

Despite the present circumstances, a kind of front-loading is aimed at. After filtering possible ASs, the recommended solution should target a component that is still early in the product development phase. Blind and mis-performances are then avoided. The result is the alignment of the target curve for individual components of assemblies. A

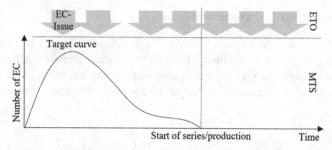

Fig. 4. Technical changes during product development (according to) [29]

further increase of planning changes by ECs are accordingly accepted and/or aimed at. Adjustments in the design, planning and control phases, are preferable to ECs during manufacturing and assembly. Economic consequences are much lower in these phases.

The defined requirements for investigating and filtering ASs are understood as challenges in the ETO context. The consistency of the data is often not given. In view of this, approaches exist to increase the degree of digitization within the shopfloor [30]. If the necessary transparency is given, implementation of the front-loading approach in this form is basically possible in practical application.

5 Application in Practice

5.1 Use Case

The following evaluations refer to a production area of a maritime ETO company. First, the defined prerequisites were met so that the process progress within the production system can be traced in terms of data. The digital shadow is therefore available as a basis for decision-making for the second stage of the temporal AS alignment. In addition, all relevant data relating to the ECM is made available via a department-wide digitization. This is followed by a less time-consuming evaluation of the technical aspects by the specialist personnel. The processes within the ECM run across the levels and are synchronized as far as possible. Together with the digital shadow, the two-stage validation of the ASs is guaranteed.

Over a period of 12 months, approximately 8000 assembly orders were processed in the production system. These represent low-order assemblies with permanent joints. Depending on the EC content, subsequent implementation is often accompanied by destruction or immediate re-production. This must be avoided.

In the investigation period, around 9% of all orders were subject to ECs. These have already been approved by the design department. As a result, these are late ECs that are being handled. For the analysis, documentation functions were implemented to describe the ECM processes. The available database allows well-founded statements to be made about the time of the MCO release. The process phase of the component affected by the ECs can be clearly determined. In contrast, the time of issue identification is not known. The target achievement of the front-loading can still be derived.

5.2 Frontloading in Practice

Further, the phases are split into four sections after construction:

- Planning/control phase,
- Manufacturing/assembly phase,
- Transport phase,
- Construction site phase.

The transport phase describes the section after completion of the assembly orders. During this time, the lower-order assemblies can pass through further processing stations and steps in other areas. However, these are not recorded in a differentiated manner. This is followed by the delivery of the construction site production.

In 51% of the cases, the subsequent EC is aimed at a component within the planning/control phase. Even though the design has already been approved, this can again be categorized as early in this context. In this respect, no intervention in the production process is required. In contrast, 7% relate to the manufacturing/assembly phase. Potential rejects and failures due to irreversible processing steps are the possible consequences. A further investigation of the reject rate is required in this respect.

12% of the EC concern assemblies during the transport phase. 30%, on the other hand, are at the construction site. A more detailed specification is still required, especially for the construction site. Assembly orders that have already been finally assembled cause higher expenses for ECs than installation processes that are still outstanding. The practical investigations also show that, despite the permanent connection, MCO on the construction site are dissolved by the on-site implementations. It is also clear, however, that these require a high degree of coordination between the different departments. Figure 5 (left) illustrates the course of the MCO.

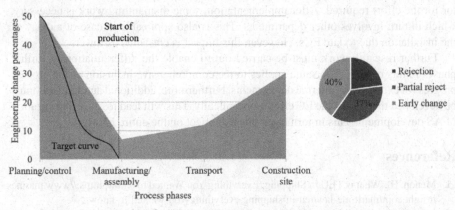

Fig. 5. Front-loading in practice (left); Rejection rate after front-loading (right)

It becomes visible that front-loading is achieved to a certain extent. Because of the variable issue timing, however, the occurrence of MCO after the start of production cannot be completely avoided. Nevertheless, the shifts to the early phases are evident.

This fact is due to the knowledge about the process progress. A targeted determination of ASs supports the optimized choice of the later MCO.

5.3 Rejection Rate

Despite the improved database and the consideration of the process progress, MCOs cannot be excluded after the start of production of the components. This resulted in 23% of the changed assembly orders being classified as rejects. A new production with inclusion of the ECs was the respective consequence. In 37% of the cases, only individual components had to be remanufactured. The remaining components were adapted at an early stage or could be reused without ECs. In contrast, 40% of the assemblies did not experience any negative consequences due to an EC after release. Only further cycles of planning and the design processes as such increased the effort, which means that the objective was achieved. Figure 5 (right) shows the allocation of the categories.

6 Conclusion and Outlook

As a result of the general conditions, full achievement of the front-loading approach in the ETO is not guaranteed. External influences prevent the ECs from being affected. Nevertheless, there is the potential to influence the alignment of the MCO of individual components. A profound data base on production progress as well as involvement are considered prerequisites. In addition, the two-stage validation of ASs must be ensured.

It is shown that the approach offers added value in terms of the rejection rate. Despite this, the target curve is not fully achieved. The investigations showed that MCO implementation on the construction site is an effective method. In future, a distinction must be made here as to whether the component or assembly in question has already been finally installed or whether an adjustment made beforehand is possible. This is the decisive factor for the effort required. After implementation, some dismantling work is necessary, which in turn involves other departments. This is also applicable in case of a delay of the installation due to late ECs. However, this impact is classified as lower.

Further research work must be carried out to enable the differentiation of further phases in this respect. The same applies to the comprehensive inclusion of the process progress of external and internal departments. Furthermore, additional automatisms must be developed that derive the EC efforts systemically. This will lead to other optimization of AS development. This in turn has a positive effect on the entire ECM.

References

1. Menon, H.: What is TEU in Shipping: Everything You Wanted to Know. https://www.marine insight.com/maritime-law/teu-in-shipping-everything-you-wanted-to-know
2. International Energy Agency. Offshore Wind Outlook 2019: World Energy Outlook Special Report, p. 1 (2019)
3. Hiekata, K., Grau, M.: Case studies for concurrent engineering concept in shipbuilding industry. In: Moving Integrated Product Development to Service Clouds in the Global Economy: Proceedings of the 21st ISPE Inc. International Conference on Concurrent Engineering, 8–11 September 2014; [Held at the Beijing Jiaotong University, China; CE2014, IOS Press, Amsterdam, p. 102 (2014)

4. Olhager, J.: The role of the customer order decoupling point in production and supply chain management. Comput. Ind. **61**, 863 (2010)
5. Foo, J.: Digitalisation driving change in shipbuilding. https://www.lr.org/en/insights/articles/digitalisation-driving-change-in-shipbuilding/
6. Iakymenko, N., Romsdal, A., Semini, M., Strandhagen, J.O.: Managing engineering changes in the engineer-to-order environment: challenges and research needs. IFAC-PapersOnLine **51**, 144 (2018)
7. Fricke, E., Gebhard, B., Negele, H., Igenbergs, E.: Coping with changes: causes, findings, and strategies. Syst. Eng. **3**, 169 (2000)
8. Iakymenko, N., Brett, P.O., Alfnes, E., Strandhagen, J.O.: Analyzing the factors affecting engineering change implementation performance in the engineer-to-order production environment: case studies from a Norwegian shipbuilding group. Prod. Plann. Control **33**, 957 (2022)
9. Hamraz, B., Caldwell, N.H.M., Clarkson, P.J.: A holistic categorization framework for literature on engineering change management. Syst. Eng. **16**, 473 (2013)
10. Lee, H.J., Ahn, H.J., Kim, J.W., Park, S.J.: Capturing and reusing knowledge in engineering change management: a case of automobile development. Inf. Syst. Front. **8**, 375 (2007)
11. Pikosz, P., Malmqvist, J.: A comparative study of engineering change management in three Swedish engineering companies. In: 1998 ASME Design Engineering Technical Conferences: DETC 1998; 13–16 September 1998, p. 78. Atlanta, Georgia, American Society of Mechanical Engineers, New York, NY (1998)
12. Huang, G., Mak, K.: Computer aids for engineering change control. J. Mater. Process. Technol. **76**, 187 (1998)
13. Clark, K.B., Fujimoto, T.: Product Development Performance: Strategy, Organization, and Management in the World Auto Industry. Harvard Business School Press, Boston (2005)
14. Wright, I.C.: A review of research into engineering change management: implications for product design. Des. Stud. **18**, 33 (1997)
15. Huang, G.Q., Mak, K.L.: Current practices of engineering change management in UK manufacturing industries. Int. J. Oper. Prod. Manage. **19**, 21 (1999)
16. Reidelbach, M.A.: Engineering change management for long-lead-time production, p. 84 (1991)
17. Jarratt, T.A.W., Eckert, C.M., Caldwell, N.H.M., Clarkson, P.J.: Engineering change: an overview and perspective on the literature. Res. Eng. Des. **22**, 103 (2011)
18. Jarratt, T., Clarkson, J., Eckert, C.: Engineering Change, in Design Process Improvement: A Review of Current Practice, p. 262. Springer, London (2005). https://doi.org/10.1007/978-1-84628-061-0
19. Langer, S.: Änderungsmanagement, in Handbuch Produktentwicklung, p. 513. Carl Hanser Verlag GmbH & Co KG, München (2016)
20. Verband der Automobilindustrie. Engineering Change Managment Reference Process: covering ECM Recommendation V2.0 (2009)
21. Semini, M., Haartveit, D.E.G., Alfnes, E., Arica, E., et al.: Strategies for customized shipbuilding with different customer order decoupling points. Proc. Inst. Mech. Eng. Part M: J. Eng. Maritime Environ. **228**, 362 (2014)
22. Gruß, R.: Schlanke Unikatfertigung: Zweistufiges Taktphasenmodell zur Steigerung der Prozesseffizienz in der Unikatfertigung auf Basis der Lean Production, 1st edn. Gabler Verlag, s.l. (2010)
23. Nam, S., Shen, H., Ryu, C., Shin, J.G.: SCP-Matrix based shipyard APS design: application to long-term production plan. Int. J. Naval Archit. Ocean Eng. **10**, 741 (2018)
24. Jericho, D., Jagusch, K., Sender, J., Flügge, W.: Herausforderungen in der durchgängigen Produktionsplanung bei ETO-Produkten. ZWF Zeitschrift fuer Wirtschaftlichen Fabrikbetrieb **115**, 890 (2020)

25. Jagusch, K., Sender, J., Jericho, D., Flügge, W.: Digital thread in shipbuilding as a prerequisite for the digital twin. Procedia CIRP **104**, 318 (2021)
26. Bergs, T., Gierlings, S., Auerbach, T., Klink, A., et al.: The concept of digital twin and digital shadow in manufacturing. Procedia CIRP **101**, 81 (2021)
27. Lodgaard, E., Ringen, G., Larsson, C.E.: Viewing the engineering change process from a lean product development and a business. Perspective **9**, 1374 (2018)
28. Tavčar, J., Demšar, I., Duhovnik, J.: Engineering change management maturity assessment model with lean criteria for automotive supply chain, vol. 29, p. 235 (2018)
29. Dombrowski, U., Ebentreich, D., Krenkel, P., Meyer, D., et al.: Gestaltungsprinzipien. In: Lean Development, p. 21. Springer, Heidelberg (2015). https://doi.org/10.1007/978-3-662-47421-1_2
30. Jagusch, K., Sender, J., Flügge, W.: Databased product adjustments during manufacturing based on agile production and digital representation in shipbuilding prefabrication. Procedia CIRP **93**, 789 (2020)

Addressing the Data Challenge in Manufacturing SMEs: A Comparative Study of Data Analytics Applications with a Simplified Reference Model

Stefan Rösl[✉], Thomas Auer, and Christian Schieder

Technical University of Applied Sciences Amberg-Weiden, Hetzenrichter Weg 15, 92637 Weiden, Germany
{s.roesl,t.auer,c.schieder}@oth-aw.de

Abstract. Digital transformation and Industry 4.0 pose challenges for all industries. Small and medium-sized enterprises (SMEs) are particularly affected due to cost pressure and the shortage of skilled workers. Adequate process models are needed to manage data analytics projects (DAP) efficiently and effectively in the face of a steadily growing amount of data. However, existing methodologies in the literature are not widely used in SMEs mainly because they are not addressing their specific needs. In this paper we present a Simplified Reference Model (SRM) for early-stage DAPs and compare it to the well-known Cross-Industry Standard Process for Data Mining (CRISP-DM). Three practical scenarios were used to evaluate the applicability of the SRM and identify weaknesses in the execution of DAPs in manufacturing SMEs. Based on our exploration, the main issues are data availability, insufficient data consistency, and inability to understand complex technical environments. Additionally, the paper highlights the need to develop SME-specific operational guidelines and identify potential barriers to the adaption of advanced technologies.

Keywords: SME · CRISP-DM · Process Model · Data Mining · Industry 4.0

1 Introduction

In recent years, there has been a significant increase in the volume and potential value of manufacturing-related data [1]. Technologies have developed alongside the expanding technical possibilities of Industry 4.0, such as the Internet of Things (IoT) [2]. They offer enhanced monitoring and networking capabilities throughout production processes, allowing for the extensive collection of real-time data on process resources [3]. As a result, the possibilities of analyzing data and deriving valuable information are growing. Various buzzwords are used to describe data analytics activities. Terms like *Business Intelligence* or *Business Analytics* are frequently used in this context [4]. Data mining is a central element of data analytics, which utilizes statistics and machine learning techniques to extract structures, correlations, or trends from datasets [5].

© The Author(s), under exclusive license to Springer Nature Switzerland AG 2023
M. Elstermann et al. (Eds.): S-BPM ONE 2023, CCIS 1867, pp. 121–130, 2023.
https://doi.org/10.1007/978-3-031-40213-5_9

To standardize data mining processes, several process models have been proposed. One widely known model is the Cross-Industry Standard Process for Data Mining (CRISP-DM) [6]. Successful applications of existing process models in data analytics projects (DAP) often require cross-disciplinary cooperation among domain experts, including data scientists, process engineers, and control engineers [7]. SMEs often cannot afford the necessary human recourses as qualified experts are in high demand. SMEs' limitations in terms of resources and their limited knowledge of existing technology can hinder rather than facilitate the implementation of such resource-intensive process models [8]. This paper introduces the SRM – Simplified Reference Model for early-stage DAPs – to simplify existing methodologies. Within this paper, an early-stage DAP is characterized by one or more of the following aspects: (1) a lack of well-defined organizational processes, (2) an inadequate understanding of pertinent technologies, or (3) a deficit in the corresponding skills of employees. The lean structured SRM ensures a goal-oriented and resource-saving execution of early-stage DAPs.

This paper is structured as follows: Sect. 2 presents existing process models and describes the established CRISP-DM. Section 3 introduces the SRM and its artifact. Furthermore, we will compare the characteristics between CRISP-DM and SRM. In Sect. 4, the developed SRM is demonstrated by three practical scenarios to evaluate the practicality of the SRM. Finally, Sect. 5 concludes and addresses future work.

2   State-of-the-Art Methodologies for Data Mining

Process models already exist for a standardized approach to DAPs. The Knowledge Discovery in Database (KDD) process was one of the first methodologies to be introduced. Years later, international companies designed the CRISP-DM [9]. The CRISP-DM reference model was published in 2000 and is considered as a central approach in the evolution of these methodologies [10]. Other process models have been developed based on the KDD and CRISP-DM [10]. The CRISP-DM, SEMMA (Sample, Explore, Modify, Model, Assess), and DMAIC (Define, Measure, Analyze, Improve, Control) are commonly used in the industry, while the KDD process assists in academics [11].

Surveys of leading online platforms for data science show that CRISP-DM is the leader in the practical usage of data mining methodologies. More than 40% of the respondents are constantly operating with the CRISP-DM. Over time, CRISP-DM has become the prevailing process model while individual approaches are declining and new generalized methods like SCRUM and Kanban are emerging [12, 13].

Considering these aspects, the CRISP-DM is the established standard. The results of a systematic literature review support this statement. Here, the *de facto standard status* of the CRISP-DM crystallizes as the primary decision-making reason in its favor [14].

2.1   CRISP-DM

The CRISP-DM methodology contains a cyclical process and comprises six phases that guide the planning and management of data analysis tasks. Figure 1 shows a schematic diagram of the CRISP-DM process. Each process phase, like Business Understanding,

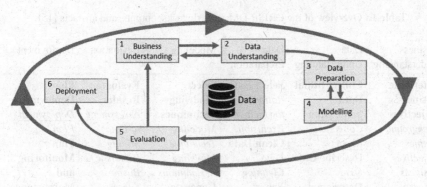

Fig. 1. Schematic diagram of the CRISP-DM process [15].

contains other sub-stages or tasks and comprises at least one output. All together is provided in the user guide, which describes a list of activities for each output [15].

For a better overview of the CRISP-DM, Table 1 provides the phases with the corresponding generic tasks (**bold**) and the required outputs (*italic*). The CRISP-DM covers 25 tasks and contains more than 40 outputs. In four phases (Business Understanding, Data Preparation, Modeling, and Evaluation), a report is prepared to summarize the results. These four reports represent the artifacts of each phase. Additional artifacts are created as outputs in the Data Understanding and Deployment. Such special outputs are also marked in Table 1 (*italic and underlined*). In total, the CRISP-DM generates eleven artifacts in the form of written reports or plans [15].

3 Simplified Reference Model

Despite existing methodologies, processing industrial data into usable information is usually a complex task. Due to limited project resources within the SME environment, practicality and simplicity are essential [8]. We designed a Simplified Reference Model (SRM) to address this problem in the early stage of realizing DAPs. The SRM has a sequential workflow divided into four phases, including an optional one. Figure 2 shows the schematic concept of the SRM.

The SRM artifact is a template and serves as both a user guide for the process steps and a working document to record various activities and results of each step. The template consists of predesigned spreadsheets, allowing targeted documentation. It is independent of tools or technologies, making it easy to integrate into DAPs. As evident from the concept (see Fig. 2), there is an optional phase 3A called *Data Analytics*, which entails the application of machine learning algorithms for data analytics tasks. The SRM approach does not necessarily require a data mining aspect, it can also be applied to DAPs in general. Table 2 provides the details of the SRM. Each phase is related to its tasks and its individual *Idea Space*. The Idea Space is suitable for recording contingencies, such as assumptions or delimitations, newly gained insights, and recommendations for action. All this is summarized and documented in the SRM artifact.

Table 1. Overview of the CRISP-DM: generic tasks, outputs, and artifacts [15].

Business Understanding	Data Understanding	Data Preparation	Modeling	Evaluation	Deployment
Determine Business Objectives	**Collect Initial Data**	**Select Data**	**Select Modeling Techniques**	**Evaluate Results**	**Plan Deployment**
Background	*Initial Data Collection Report*	*Rationale for Inclusion Exclusion*	*Modeling Technique*	*Assessment of Data Mining Results w.r.t*	*Deployment Plan*
Business Objectives	**Describe Data**	**Clean Data**	*Modeling Assumptions*	*Business Success Criteria*	**Plan Monitoring and Maintenance**
Business Success Criteria	*Data Description Report*	*Data Cleaning Report*	**Generate Test Design**	*Approved Models*	*Monitoring and Maintenance Plan*
Assess Situation	**Explore Data**	**Construct Data**	*Test Design*	**Review Process**	**Produce Final Report**
Inventory of Resources	*Data Exploration Report*	*Derived Attributes Generated Records*	**Build Model**	*Review of Process*	*Final Report Final Presentation*
Requirements, Assumptions, and Constraints	**Verify Data Quality**	**Integrate Data**	*Parameter Settings Models Model Descriptions*	**Determine Next Steps**	**Review Project**
Risks and Contingencies	*Data Quality Report*	*Merged Data*	**Assess Model**	*List of Possible Actions*	*Experience Documentation*
Terminology		**Format Data**	*Model Assessment*	*Decision*	
Costs and Benefits		*Reformatted Data Dataset*	*Revised Parameter Settings*		
Determine Data Mining Goals		*Dataset Description*			
Data Mining Goals					
Data Mining Success Criteria					
Produce Project Plan					
Project Plan Initial Assessment of Tools and Techniques					
Artifact: Business Understanding Report	**Artifact:** *Outputs* above (see *underline*)	**Artifact:** Data Preparation Report	**Artifact:** Modeling Report	**Artifact:** Evaluation Report	**Artifact:** *Outputs* above (see *underline*)

Fig. 2. Schematic concept of the Simplified Reference Model.

Table 2. Overview of the SRM: tasks, outputs, and artifact.

1: Definition	2: Data Situation	3: Transformation	3A: Data Analytics	4: Solution Container
• Basic Information • Problem, Solution, Goal • **Idea Space** • Evaluation & Approval	• Data Preprocessing & Profile • Data Exploration & Quality • Evaluation & Approval • **Idea Space**	• Data Selection & Preparation • Data Creation • Evaluation & **Idea Space**	• Technology Selection • Modeling • **Idea Space**	• Evaluation & Visualization of the results • Lessons Learned • **Idea Space**, To-Do & Outlook
Artifact: Template as guideline and working document				

The primary goal of the SRM is to improve transparency and feasibility, as well as provide answers to questions and recommendations for further actions and next steps. The SRM intentionally uses a simple sequential flow. Considering the usage for early-stage DAPs, a simple flow makes it easy to get started. A new SRM instance should be started if a DAP is operated repeatedly. These restarts may increase the dropout rate of DAPs, but it minimizes the resources needed to keep long-term DAPs running. To demonstrate the simplicity of the SRM and its associated application in the SME environment, we compare some of the characteristics to those of the CRISP-DM. We conducted a research workshop to discuss the meta-levels and individual characteristics. The results are presented in Table 3.

Comparing the flow within the models (see Fig. 1 and Fig. 2), it becomes transparent that in the CRISP-DM, almost every phase has more than one option to continue. Classical sequential flows (cf. Data Understanding to Data Preparation) and back-and-forward loops (e.g., between Data Preparation and Modeling) exist. We can also see a jumping step from phase 5 (Evaluation) to phase 1 (Business Understanding). Such a mixed flow increases the model's complexity and promotes the DAP participants' restraint. The SRM provides a continually sequential. Phase 3A (Data Analytics) is the only one that can be skipped without data mining context. This straightforwardness increases the acceptance among the DAP participants. The SRM has fewer phases, tasks, outputs, and artifacts. This issue also supports acceptance in the SME environment and reduces the effort and associated costs for a DAP.

Table 3. Comparison of meta-level characteristics

Meta-level characteristic	CRISP-DM [15]	SRM (incl. Data Analytics)
Number of phases	6	4 (5)
General process flow	Cyclical	Sequential
Flow between phases	Mixed (sequential, back- & forward, jumping)	Sequential
Total tasks	25	14 (17)
Total outputs	41	4 (5)
Total artifacts	11	1
Artifact file type	Not defined	Spreadsheets
Artifact type	Reports and plans	Fulfilled templates

The CRISP-DM has eleven artifacts in the form of reports or plans. Guidance is provided on the possible content of the artifacts, but no specific instructions are given on their layout or configuration. Therefore, each artifact is individually dependent on the DAP participants, and there is a possibility that individual DAP become neither transparent nor repeatable. The SRM represents only one artifact which is already configured as a predefined template. This blueprint must only be filled during the DAP and provide a standardized artifact structure. As a result, it is possible to compare individual applications, even if different people participate in the DAP. Due to the simplification approach, the SRM has advantages over the CRISP-DM regarding the resource-saving application. This feature is essential for SMEs, especially in the early-stage DAPs.

4 Demonstration and Evaluation of the SRM

As proof of the practicality of the SRM, implementation takes place in the following three use cases in manufacturing SMEs:

1. Machine Park: correlation between produced scrap and ambient temperature
2. Cleanroom: correlation between the number of incidents in the cleanroom per day and the environmental conditions on the previous day
3. Recycling: throughput-based wear indication in the crusher

The listed use cases are early-stage DAPs and serve as proof of concepts for the applicability of the SRM. They are comparable due to similar conditions of the participant's know-how and specific manufacturing environment. The simplified approach (see Fig. 2) is a guideline for conducting these DAPs. The following sections describe the scenarios, focusing on their unique features and practical challenges when using the SRM.

4.1 Machine Park

In a medium-sized medical company, an elevated scrap rate in metal-cutting production is observed on warm or hot days. Despite the associated costs, there is insufficient justification for installing additional hall air conditioning. The analysis aims to examine the correlations and provide evidence for further actions. Therefore, the daily amount of scrap is analyzed concerning environmental conditions, particularly the temperature.

Initially, the main problem was the unavailability of environmental data. To compensate the lack of on-site weather data, we obtained information from the closest weather station operated by the Bavarian State Research Center for Agriculture, which allows free access to its data. During the data situation phase, it was discovered that the rejected dataset was not directly suitable for processing, and the desired key figure was unavailable. During the *Data Preprocessing* the key figure (scrap per day) was calculated. In addition, the weather station dataset was examined during data exploration to ensure credibility and plausibility. Within the third phase, the key figure is divided into classes (*No scrap - Low - Medium - High*) to classify the amount of scrap per day with a decision tree algorithm. After first tests, the performance of the machine learning model was limited, making it impossible to create valid predictions. Due to these circumstances, we conducted a further analysis using all available data to train the model and present the findings. The results support the assumption that increased temperatures lead to higher scrap rates, but the analysis also revealed a similar trend on very cold days with temperatures below -2.5 °C. Recording ambient conditions in the machine environment are recommended to conduct more meaningful analyses.

4.2 Cleanroom

The same company has cleanrooms for finishing medical products, where pressure, temperature, and relative humidity must be monitored to prevent production stoppages. Each cleanroom has its own air conditioning system and control unit. However, *Cleanroom 2* experiences more breakdowns after hot or humid days, while *Cleanroom 1* performs consistently due to its modernized air conditioning system. The DAP aims to investigate the correlation between the number of breakdowns per day and the environmental conditions of the previous day.

The analysis excluded the pressure parameter since fluctuations in the clean room significantly impact this value. Like in the previous case, environment data are unavailable, and data from the nearest weather station are used, including the relative humidity. It is specified that only a descriptive analysis should be conducted to understand past behavior. A document with 2178 pages is available as the data basis of the cleanroom. To make the document suitable for further analysis, it needs to undergo *preprocessing*, as only a small part of it is relevant to this application. Therefore, the breakdown events are limited to only 29 days in a period from 01.01.2018 to 31.05.2021. Within the data transformation the classes of days (*No Event - OK - NOK*) are defined and the weather station dataset is shifted forward by one day to associate the disturbance events with the previous day. The result shows a slight risk of breakdowns at higher temperatures (>33.25 °C) and high humidity ($>99.35\%$).

Further analysis or expert input can provide a more precise understanding of the clean room's behavior, enabling investigation hourly rather than daily. The weather station dataset should be qualified carefully. Installing measuring instruments in the halls is recommended to obtain data directly from the cleanroom environment. Sensor data from existing facilities can also be used if necessary.

4.3 Recycling

The third application is conducted within the recycling industry, in a wood processing plant. Wood materials such as beams and doors are disposed of, shredded, and sorted into different quality grades for further usage. The crusher module is the core element and leads to high maintenance costs because of its costly wear parts. Depending on the supervisor's intuition, these wear parts are replaced every six to eight shifts. The manual inspection before replacing the wear parts requires a significant investment of time and resources, making it economically unfeasible to delay the replacement regardless of the actual wear state. The DAP aims to create a throughput-based indicator to support the supervisor in deciding if the wear parts should be replaced before the next shift starts.

At the beginning, detailed information about the application were provided to ensure that all participants had a common understanding of the recycling process. The modules around the crusher are belts and one screen. Belts are used for transportation, and the screen differentiates the crushed material. The *good grain* is processed further, while *oversize grain* (wood pieces that are still too large) is sent back to the crusher and shredded again. This *oversize grain* is an essential criterion for evaluating the wear condition of the *flails* mounted in the crusher (the more wear, the more oversize). Figure 3 shows on the right the flails mounted in the crusher, there is slight wear visible at the flail pairs. Despite the minimal wear, a significant difference in the outer contour compared to a new spare part (Fig. 3, left side) can already be observed.

The use case was based on an Excel file containing data that was spread across multiple worksheets. In addition, *Data Preprocessing* was carried out to rate the data's quality and transform the existing worksheets into one dataset. All available data were mapped to the relevant machines. The mapping showed that the wood processing plant relied on a single scale to measure the throughput value. The scale was located at the end of the production line and not close to the crusher. Moreover, the available data for the crusher was limited to runtime and energy values. Due to the lack of data or inadequate data availability, the DAP was terminated at this point.

Fig. 3. New flail as a spare part (left) and flail pairs mounted in the crusher (right).

The recommendation is to retrofit two scales directly before and after the crusher, record new mass data as well as spare part exchange events, and evaluate the data availability. Vibration analysis during a no-load run in regular operation is also an option for condition monitoring of the flails' wear condition.

5 Conclusion

The widely known CRISP-DM approach is too extensive for efficient implementation in early-stage DAPs of SMEs. The presented SRM is more compact with fewer elements and allows flexibility depending on specific DAPs needs. It can be used independently or in combination with other process models. The model was evaluated through three use cases in a manufacturing SMEs. The lean design of the SRM ensures efficient usage of resources and targeted implementation. It consists of a single artifact that already serves as a template and minimizes the need for additional documentation. In contrast, CRISP-DM requires the creation of eleven new artifacts without existing templates.

Considering the use cases, we found overlapping challenges. *Data preprocessing* was mandatory in each use case. This indicates that the existing data often do not have the required consistency for further use. Due to insufficient data availability, alternative data sources were utilized in two cases. In the recycling application, the same issue even caused the termination. Additional sensors or connecting existing machine controls are needed in all presented DAPs to obtain the required data.

Examining the overall data situation at manufacturing SMEs, we identified a problem space that needs to be counteracted. IoT technologies are gaining new data and improving the existing data infrastructure. Through their usage, data availability can be enhanced. The specified issue cannot be solved within the data mining framework. Instead, it requires broader considerations in the expanded domain of Industry 4.0.

Overall, there is a need for actionable recommendations to assist SMEs in their transition toward Industry 4.0. In the literature, there is a lack of SME-specific guidelines for implementing IoT technologies and the associated application of Artificial Intelligence (AI). One approach to address explicit guidelines is to develop individual artifacts for each key area. On the other hand, we need to reduce the complexity of procedures, as the SRM in this paper shows [16].

The SRM presented in this paper offers an initial approach for developing data mining guidelines in the SME environment and justifies various other specific operational guidelines tailored to the needs of SMEs. With appropriate guidelines and individual artifacts, SMEs can successfully transition toward Industry 4.0. However, it is essential to consider both technological and organizational factors. Further research can explore these factors and help to develop more comprehensive guidelines for SMEs adopting IoT and AI technologies.

References

1. Fasel, D., Meier, A.: Was versteht man unter Big Data und NoSQL? In: Fasel, D., Meier, A. (eds.) Big Data. EH, pp. 3–16. Springer, Wiesbaden (2016). https://doi.org/10.1007/978-3-658-11589-0_1

2. Xu, L., He, W., Li, S.: Internet of things in industries: a survey. IEEE Trans. Industr. Inform. **10**, 2233–2243 (2014). https://doi.org/10.1109/TII.2014.2300753
3. Huber, S., Seiger, R., Kühnert, A., Theodorou, V., Schlegel, T.: Goal-based semantic queries for dynamic processes in the Internet of Things. Int. J. Semant. Comput. **10**, 269–293 (2016). https://doi.org/10.1142/S1793351X16400109
4. Seiter, M.: Business Analytics. Vahlen, München (2019). https://doi.org/10.15358/978380 0658725
5. Gluchowski, P., Schieder, C., Chamoni, P.: Methoden des data mining für big data analytics. In: D'Onofrio, S., Meier, A. (eds.) Big Data Analytics. EH, pp. 25–48. Springer, Wiesbaden (2021). https://doi.org/10.1007/978-3-658-32236-6_2
6. Wirth, R., Hipp, J.: CRISP-DM: towards a standard process model for data mining. In: Proceedings of the Fourth International Conference on the Practical Application of Knowledge Discovery and Data Mining, pp. 29–40 (2000)
7. Choudhary, A.K., Harding, J.A., Popplewell, K.: Knowledge discovery for moderating collaborative projects. In: 2006 4th IEEE International Conference on Industrial Informatics, pp. 519–524. IEEE Computer Society, Singapore (2006). https://doi.org/10.1109/INDIN. 2006.275610
8. Masood, T., Sonntag, P.: Industry 4.0: adoption challenges and benefits for SMEs. Comput. Ind. **121** (2020). https://doi.org/10.1016/J.COMPIND.2020.103261
9. Otte, R., Wippermann, B., Otte, V.: Das theoretische und mathematische Konzept der technischen Datenauswertung. In: Otte, W. et al. (ed.) Von Data Mining bis Big Data, pp. 33–190. Carl Hanser Verlag GmbH & Co. KG, München (2020). https://doi.org/10.3139/978344645 7171.003
10. Mariscal, G., Marbán, Ó., Fernández, C.: A survey of data mining and knowledge discovery process models and methodologies. Knowl. Eng. Rev. **25**, 137–166 (2010). https://doi.org/ 10.1017/S0269888910000032
11. Atzmüller, M., et al.: Implementierung und Betrieb von Big-Data-Anwendungen in der produzierenden Industrie (2022). https://www.vdi.de/richtlinien/details/vdivde-3714-blatt-1-implementierung-und-betrieb-von-big-data-anwendungen-in-der-produzierenden-indust rie-durchfuehrung-von-big-data-projekten
12. Saltz, J.: CRISP-DM is Still the Most Popular Framework for Executing Data Science Projects - Data Science Process Alliance. https://www.datascience-pm.com/crisp-dm-still-most-pop ular/. Accessed 17 Feb 2023
13. Piatetsky, G.: CRISP-DM, still the top methodology for analytics, data mining, or data science projects – Kdnuggets. https://www.kdnuggets.com/2014/10/crisp-dm-top-methodology-ana lytics-data-mining-data-science-projects.html. Accessed 23 Feb 2023
14. Schröer, C., Kruse, F., Gómez, J.M.: A systematic literature review on applying CRISP-DM process model. Procedia Comput. Sci. **181**, 526–534 (2021). https://doi.org/10.1016/J. PROCS.2021.01.199
15. Chapman, P., et al.: CRISP-DM 1.0: Step-by-step data mining guide (2000). https://www. kde.cs.uni-kassel.de/wp-content/uploads/lehre/ws2016-17/kdd/files/CRISPWP-0800.pdf
16. Leineweber, S., Wienbruch, T., Kuhlenkötter, B.: Konzept zur Unterstützung der Digitalen Transformation von Kleinen und Mittelständischen Unternehmen. In: KMU 4.0 - Digitale Transformation in kleinen und mittelständischen Unternehmen, pp. 20–39. GITO Verlag (2018). https://doi.org/10.30844/WGAB_2018_02

Improving Interoperability in the Exchange of Digital Twin Data Within Engineering Processes

Constantin Liepert[1]([⊠]) [ID], Christian Stary[2] [ID], Axel Lamprecht[4], and Dennis Zügn[3]

[1] Siemens Industry Software GmbH, Otto-Hahn-Ring 6, 81739 Munich, Germany
constantin.liepert@siemens.com
[2] Johannes Kepler University Linz, Altenberger Straße 69, 4040 Linz, Austria
[3] Siemens Industry Software GmbH, Schwieberdinger Street 95-97, 70435 Stuttgart, Germany
[4] Steinbeis Hochschule, Gottlieb-Manz-Street 12, 70794 Filderstadt, Germany

Abstract. In the context of digital transformation, digital twin data is increasingly being exchanged across company boundaries. As this data exchange is little or not at all standardized today, this results in major interoperability problems. Consequently, inefficiencies in the transfer of data occur, leading to high efforts in identification, structuring and completion as well as a lack of quality of the digital twin data especially within the engineering phase. Looking at the requirements from industrial experts to solve interoperability in the exchange of digital twin data, the concept of the asset administration shell (AAS) presented by Industry 4.0 offers possible solutions, which have not yet been implemented and validated in practice across organizations. For this purpose, a new, standardized, and cross-company data exchange and collaboration model as well as a prototype implementation in the context of the interoperable digital twin is under development to also analyze the benefits and potentials of the standardization approach. This paper presents the motivation and research problem of the project, and how expert knowledge and relevant existing work can be utilized to develop a solution based on empirical evidence and AAS capabilities.

Keywords: Digital twin · interoperability · product lifecycle management · supplier collaboration · asset administration shell

1 Introduction

Across different industries numerous players are often involved until a final product is completed. Not only raw materials and physical products are exchanged via extensive supplier structures all the way, e.g., to the manufacturer of a machine or production line, but increasingly also information in digital form in the context of digital transformation [1, 2]. This mostly involves data of the digital twin [3–5], which is of central importance for the development, engineering, and manufacturing process as well as for the subsequent operation. In this respect, the efficient creation, synchronization, integration, and use of cross-company digital twin data throughout the entire lifecycle are taking on

M. Elstermann et al. (Eds.): S-BPM ONE 2023, CCIS 1867, pp. 131–150, 2023.
https://doi.org/10.1007/978-3-031-40213-5_10

an increasingly important role [6–11]. As digital twins have emerged from the field of Product Lifecycle Management (PLM) [12], "they aim to create value via managing the information flow along the entire life-cycle from imagination until retirement or disposal of an asset" [13]. In accordance with these characteristics, the research project initially focuses on the early phases of the product life cycle shown in Fig. 1 with particular attention to the engineering phase, when mainly digital models (e.g., computer-aided design (CAD) models, simulations model, etc.) are created and exchanged. As stated in Fig. 1, these digital models – which are also referred to as pre-twin or digital twin data in the following – are of high relevance for the subsequent lifecycle phases.

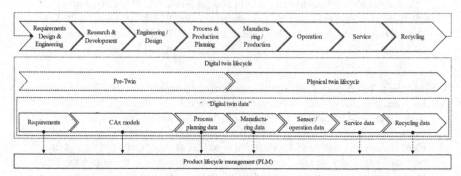

Fig. 1. Digital twin and Product Lifecycle Management, adapted from Adamenko et al. [14]

The necessity of developing these pre-twins already in the early phases of the product lifecycle is also described by the common model-based systems engineering (MBSE) approach. Therefore, the digital models, which do not necessarily have to be connected to the physical counterpart, are the prerequisite when following the multidisciplinary MBSE process along the entire lifecycle [15].

As outlined in Fig. 1, the PLM framework supports the creation of the digital twin, as a pre-twin from the beginning. After the production phase, the physical twin with the characteristics of the pre-twin is initially built. Since the pre-twin is crucial for the functionality and quality of the physical twin, combining the system-supported PLM approach with the digital twin lifecycle is particularly value-adding [14].

For many years, there have been established product data management (PDM) / PLM solutions from various software providers, like Siemens, PTC, Dassault Systems, SAP, Aras, etc., that already enable the management of a significant share of the static digital twin data [15]. As indicated by the continuous arrows in Fig. 1, these systems today mainly hold data from the product development processes, i.e. from the early phases of the product lifecycle. In addition, digital twin data is also built up and managed in the PLM systems in the further lifecycle phases (e.g. manufacturing/service bill of material, manufacturing/service bill of process, etc.) - although other systems often also have a significant function in this respect. Data generated in operations is often managed by other systems such as industrial internet of things platforms, manufacturing execution systems, enterprise resource planning, etc., hence no arrow has been drawn in Fig. 1.

However, as this data exchange is little to not standardized today and often based on proprietary and industry-specific approaches, interoperability across companies is a major challenge [8]. As a result, the creation, exchange and reuse of the digital twin data is associated with additional time, cost and quality expenditure throughout the entire value-added process, i.e. from the extraction of raw materials to the end product. At the same time, the implementation of a universal standard for the seamless reusability and interoperability of this data offers competitive advantages and economic potential. Concepts established in the field of business engineering, such as the asset administration shell (AAS), offer comprehensive and standardized solutions in this regard and seem to be the perfect fit for solving the problem as well as meeting the defined requirements.

The AAS has several engineering challenges, as it'wraps' around each (intelligent) element of a machine, and is supposed to explain its identity and functional core in its application context and architecture. As a result, it should speed up the design of complex machinery and enhance the effectiveness of machine operation along its lifecycle (see Sect. 3 for further specification and definition).

Moving from the physical asset management to information management when using AAS, the design process of interoperable components progresses from a single asset to a sub-system. The AAS as digital descriptor grows and integrates the sum of all relevant parts for engineering. The resulting digital model can be accessed throughout the lifecycle of machines, ranging from their introduction to configuration, operation, adaptation, maintenance, and suspension. As such, the AAS can be considered as an enabler of digital twins/digital twin data and their shared use [16].

However, the AAS concept have not yet been implemented and validated in a cross-company context and established PLM software solutions [12]. Consequently, the following design problem will be addressed in our research, applying the design problem formulation suggested in [17]:

Improve the interoperability in the cross-company exchange of digital twin data by establishing a standardized data exchange and collaboration concept that reduces effort in completing, providing, identifying, structuring, and integrating data, in order to increase data quality and to speed up engineering processes.

To provide a deeper understanding of the design problem and targeted solution, Sect. 2 explains the requirements and measurement criteria when developing a roadmap towards a solution. This knowledge has been elicited from experts in industry. It forms the empirical basis to review related work and lays ground to establish a solution space. Section 3 discusses related work and identifies the research gap. Section 4 addresses the methodological approach, namely applying the design science methodology, and its benefits to tackle complex development problems. This section also details the initial design science cycle, in order to demonstrate the effectiveness of the selected methodological approach. In addition, the scientific contribution of the approach, first results and further steps are provided in Sect. 4 and 5. Section 6 concludes the paper.

2 Developing Deeper Understanding of the Research Problem Based on Expert Knowledge

When addressing the research problem outlined above, several elements will be part of the solution. According to industry needs, a standardized data exchange and collaboration concept as well as a prototype implementation for reference scenarios must be developed when applying and validating the AAS across company boundaries. The latter enables the demonstration of an artefact that needs to be evaluated for a set of requirements when sharing digital twin data [18].

Initial requirements, abbreviated with R in the following list, have been identified within an industrial working group, consisting of around 30 engineering and digital twin experts from eight companies, both, from component, and software suppliers. The requirements were recorded in an online-moderated brainstorming session with 20 participants on the 24th of November 2022 led by one of the authors. The participants of that session were experts and managers, most of them with more than ten years of professional experience in the field of digital twins, PLM, engineering, digitalization, innovation, and new technologies. They are predominantly working for large international component manufacturers of automation technology and machine parts as well as for software providers.

The focus of this brainstorming session was on the digital twin data of a product, especially within the engineering phase. The results of the brainstorming session were consolidated by the moderator, presented, discussed and approved within the working group in an online follow-up meeting one week after the first session. The requirements that have been identified are listed below:

- R1: Establish interoperability when exchanging digital twin data across companies especially within the engineering phase
- R2: Include the following information/data as part of the digital twin:

  - R2.1: general meta data about the asset
  - R2.2: mechanical CAD data
  - R2.3: electrical CAD data
  - R2.4: simulation/behavioral models

- R3: Enable the PLM platform, to provide standardized digital twin data
- R4: Ensure openness of the data standard without having vendor lock-in effects or proprietary formats
- R5: Ensure high relevance of the standard for the industry
- R6: Establish central availability of and access to the digital twin data
- R7: Enable new business models regarding digital twin data provision
- R8: Ensure trustworthiness and validity of the data

The following qualitative and quantitative evaluation items (abbreviated with C) have also been defined in the course of the working group meeting. They refer to the first prototype implementation as part of the first design science cycle (see Sect. 4):

- C1: From a technical perspective the prototype realization ...

  - C1.1: ... offers functionality to provide the data from the PLM platform according to a digital twin standard
  - C1.2: ... enables the mapping of PLM data towards a digital twin standard
  - C1.3: ... provides the standardized digital twin on an accessible digital twin data hosting server

- C2: Time reduction due to less effort for ...

  - C2.1: ... exchanging digital twin data
  - C2.2: ... searching and identifying the correct digital twin data
  - C2.3: ... structuring and completing the digital twin data

- C3: Increased digital twin data quality due to ...

  - C3.1: ... less formatting
  - C3.2: ... a universal digital twin standard

Besides the prototype implementation the envisioned concept will consider information technology (IT) architecture models, business processes, and data exchange scenarios from the perspective of different roles. The roles include component manufacturers and integrators as well as industrial software vendors, as it is assumed, that with these roles, the cross-company exchange of digital twin data can be validated. The Business Process Model and Notation (BPMN) will be used as standardized tool for documenting and mapping the actual and target state. In addition, the cross-company exchange of data of the digital twin will be realized as a prototype with the help of a PLM system and the AAS standard and evaluated regarding the measurement criteria stated before. The focus of the development of the planned artifacts is the solution of the problem, in accordance with the scientific methodology explained in Sect. 4.

3   Related Work

The related work considered relevant for addressing the objectives of this work, comprises five research areas: digital twins, shared digital twins, AAS, interoperability and PLM. They are briefly described below, recognizing that due to space limits only part of the related work can be presented.

The origin of the **digital twin** is attributed to Michael Grieves, who worked with John Vickers from the NASA and used the term in the context of PLM [12, 19]. According to the Industrial Internet Consortium, a digital twin is defined as the digital representation - typically of an asset, process, or system - that is sufficient to meet the requirements of specific use cases [4]. Due to the large number of existing and evolving definitions of the term digital twin, several publications, such as [5, 7, 20–22], are devoted to it in the context of systematic literature reviews and case studies to characterize the term, as there is no universal or standard definition. Since the terms digital twin, digital shadow, and digital model are often used as synonyms, there is an established distinction according to [21, 23], based on the level of data integration between the physical and digital object:

- The *digital model* is defined as a digital representation of a physical object, that is planned or already exists. These digital models do not include any automated data integration or exchange mechanism. For that reason, changes in the state of the physical world do not affect the digital object as long as no manual changes are made.
- Through the *digital shadow*, the digital model is extended by an automated one-way data flow from the physical object towards the digital counterpart.
- The *digital twin* realizes a fully automated data flow integration in both directions, meaning that changing the state of the physical object directly affects its digital counterpart and vice versa.

Sharing digital twins is on one hand being triggered by coalition in production and engineering, either on the company level (cf. Siemens or General Electrics) or managed by government agencies or academic institutions (cf. OpenVertebrate platform funded by the US National Science Foundation), but on the other hand hindered by open issues on data ownership and openness. Platforms for sharing digital twins of this kind would allow researchers from industry to utilize not only existing digital twin data and models, but also to share those for innovation and distribution purposes. In particular, considerable potential lies in cross-company networks extending application boundaries of digital twins [24].

However, to become effective in business cases and distributed system environments, shared digital twins require "greater consideration of interoperability and data security aspects" [10]. When striving for sharing resources, transparency, openness, and scalability [10] design principles help for implementation. They are based on several key requirements of shared digital twins – see Table 1.

In addition, shared digital twins have five mandatory characteristics, namely ownership, data quality, data source, cybersecurity, and identification, when the following design principles are applied - cited from Haße et al. [10]:

- Design Principle 1 (Data Link): Provide the digital twin with bi-directional data connection capabilities to allow users to have concurrent data flow between the digital twin and its counterpart, as the digital twin is for inter-enterprise and multi-lateral data exchange.
- Design Principle 2 (Purpose): Provide the digital twin with customized functionalities to allow users to process, transfer and store data, as the digital twin is for inter-enterprise and multi-lateral data exchange.
- Design Principle 3 (Interface): Provide the digital twin with Interfaces to allow users to interact with the digital twin on the one hand, and on the other hand, for direct and human-independent communication between distributed systems, given that the digital twin should enable cross-company and multilateral data sharing.
- Design Principle 4 (Synchronization): Provide the digital twin with convenient synchronization functionalities to allow users to receive both a continuous real-time

Table 1. Key requirements of shared digital twins, according to Haße et al. [10]

	Key Requirements (KR)	Short description
Data link	Bi-directional data link (KR 1)	Refers to the communication between the physical and the virtual part and describes a simultaneous data flow between them
Purpose	Data processing (KR 2)	Refers to the functionality of a digital twin to further process-incoming data sets, allowing for more detailed information regarding the counterpart
	Data repository (KR 3)	Refers to the capability to use the digital twin as a repository for the entire lifecycle
	Data transfer (KR 4)	Refers to the ability to transfer data from the digital twin to other systems or databases. This includes the data transfer from one digital twin to another
Interface	M2M (KR 5)	Refers to the direct communication between the digital twin and other devices in order to exchange data without any human interaction
	HMI (KR 6)	Refers to the capability of human interaction for monitoring purposes or system intervention
Synchronization	On-demand data synchronization (KR 7)	Refers to the update of the digital twin being either in real time or non-real time
Data input	Raw data (KR 8)	Refers to the ability of a digital twin to capture and store unprocessed raw data such as sensor data
	Processed data (KR 9)	Refers to the ability of a digital twin to capture and store processed data
Data acquisition	Automated (KR 10)	Refers to a fully automated data input without any human intervention
	Semi-manual (KR 11)	Refers to a partially automated data input, which also includes human intervention
	Manual (KR 12)	Refers to a fully manual data input without any automated processes

(continued)

Table 1. (*continued*)

	Key Requirements (KR)	Short description
Interoperability	Interoperable via interface (KR 13)	Refers to digital twins which semantic models differ and where the input data is translated via the interface
	Entirely interoperable (KR 14)	Refers to digital twins which semantic models are completely identical without the need for any translation
Data security	Usage control (KR 15)	Refers to multi-sided platforms allowing for sovereign data sharing in distributed networks, by adding policies to the data being shared

update of incoming data and on demand also as a non-real-time data update, given that the digital twin is developed to enable cross-company and multilateral data sharing.

- Design Principle 5 (Data Input): Feature the digital twin with capabilities to process both raw data and processed data to provide a complete data set of its counterpart, given that the digital twin should enable cross-company and multilateral data sharing.
- Design Principle 6 (Data Acquisition): Provide the digital twin with functionalities to obtain a semi-automated data acquisition to allow users to still enter data manually, if necessary, since the digital twin should enable cross-company and multilateral data sharing.
- Design Principle 7 (Interoperability): Provide the digital twin with interfaces that allow for a semantic translation of the various data sets if distributed digital twins are not fully interoperable to allow users to share completely interpretable and logical data sets, when the digital twin is used for cross-company and multilateral data sharing.
- Design Principle 8 (Data Security): Provide the digital twin with security concepts that allow for the application of usage control policies to enable users to retain sovereignty over their data being shared, given that the digital twin operates cross-company and can share multilateral data.

For sharing digital twins, interoperability and data security issues require higher development effort than traditional digital twins [10].

Another concept for shared digital twins replaces human goal-driven behavior in production processes by digital twins: They automatically compose the corresponding physical processes, similar to web service composition. Digital twins thereby expose services to execute certain operations and produce data describing their activities. These data are stored in a factory data space as a polystore, for sharing purposes [25]. The concept considers digital twins as wrapper of physical entities (manufacturing machines or human operators) involved in a process. The web API of digital twins provides (a)synchronous access and querying facilities. Synchronous access addresses the control of physical entities, whereas asynchronous access enables subscription by others. Querying allows for retrieving (status) information [25].

Such approaches become increasingly important in the context of servitization, as not only the creation of virtual models is complex, but also data fusion and analysis. Digital models and data should be shared through digital twins that provide the representation capability to abstract from underlying heterogeneous components [26]. As a result, services capsulate digital twin components that can be addressed by non-native users via sharing platforms. They can be used in various contexts, and further developed in smart applications. In particular, real-time control of resources could be shared in digital twin-enabled information-sharing systems with cyber-physical visibility and traceability, and thus, facilitate business and production processes [27].

The concept of **AAS,** developed by the German Platform Industry 4.0, is defined as the digital representation of an asset that includes at least one sub-model and also exists over one or more lifecycle phases [28]. In some cases, AAS and digital twin are used synonymously. Wagner et al. [29] justifies that by stating that the terms converge with each other and in the future, a fully developed digital twin will be equal to the AAS. Moreover, the AAS is seen as a key concept for the technical implementation of the digital twin to ensure interoperability across companies and systems [30]. The AAS realizes interoperability through a standardized data model (metamodel) as well as standardized data access [31]. Due to the distinction between types and instances, it is possible to exchange asset type information via the AAS, even when the production of the asset has not begun [32]. This aspect is of special interest when focusing on the first lifecycle phases, such as engineering.

In the IT environment, the term **interoperability** basically refers to the ability of different systems to successfully work together and exchange information [33]. In the context of enterprise architecture, interoperability is further defined as the ability of an enterprise to interact with other enterprises in terms of informational, organizational, and semantic aspects [34].

The concept of **PLM** refers to the systematic management of all product-related information throughout the entire product lifecycle. In this context, the product life cycle encompasses various phases, from the initial idea, requirements management, product planning and development throughout to production, operation, maintenance and recycling [35].

Several findings will contribute to improving the interoperability in digital twin data exchange in PLM. In an initial step, they have been analyzed through indicative evaluation. In Tab. 2, a five-stage evaluation system is used according to a Likert scale [36] in combination with a visualization by the Harvey Ball method [37] to check and visualize the extent to which the publications solve the problem and requirements presented in Sect. 1 and 2.

As listed in Table 2, Deuter and Imort [38] present and apply a first concept with limited functionality for providing AAS-relevant data from a PLM system. In order to realistically present the potential of AAS, the publication emphasizes that further work is needed in this regard. Inigo, Miguel et al. [39] state interoperability and standardization as a key success factor for the realization of digitalization initiatives and therefore rely on the AAS standard for the implementation of real world manufacturing use cases. The authors have validated the AAS and proven the feasibility of the use case within the operations and manufacturing lifecycle phase. Sakowski, Dangelmaier et al. [16] address

Table 2. Indicative evaluation of existing approaches

Source	Type	Focus (concept/format)	Evaluation*
Deuter & Imort 2021 [38]	Case Study	Product lifecycle management with the AAS (PLM, digital twin & AAS)	◑
Inigo, Miguel et al. 2020 [39]	Case Study	A use case for interoperability and standardization in Industry 4.0 (AAS)	◔
Sakowski, Dangelmaier et al. 2019 [16]	Case Study	Bidirectional Interoperability of Product Engineering and Manu-facturing (AAS)	◔
Lim, Zheng et al. 2020 [7]	Review	State-of-the-art - digital twin: technology, PLM and business perspective (digital twin & PLM)	◔
Wei, Sun et al. 2019 [40]	Review	AAS research progress and challenges: interoperability, modeling & application (AAS)	◑
Smirnov, Shilov et al. 2019 [41]	Case Study	Creation of ontologies for semantic interoperability in PLM (PLM)	◔
Platenius-Mohr, Malakuti et al. 2020. [42]	Case Study	Interoperability of digital twins through model transformation in the IIoT environment (AAS & IIoT)	◔
Guqi & Zhong 2020 [9]	Case Study	Exchange of digital twins despite existing heterogeneity (digital twin & AML)	◔
Lehner, Sint et al. 2021 [43]	Case Study	AutomationML for digital twins (digital twin & AML)	◔
Binder, Cala et al. 2021 [44]	Case Study	Automatic model transformation for digital twin modeling (digital twin & AML)	◔

Evaluation: Rating ranges from 'complete' to 'no fulfillment' w.r.t. the stated requirements using the Harvey Ball gradations ●, ◕, ◑, ◔ and ○

the necessity of bi-directional interoperability to enable mass customization. However, the presented technical approaches using the AAS still need to be implemented and tested in a real-world environment, in order to be able to evaluate the feasibility and benefits of the envisioned solutions.

To reflect the development and application status of digital twins for academia and practice, Lim, Zheng et al. [7] explore these aspects in a systematic review. Wei, Sun et al. [40] present the research progress as well as the challenges of the AAS in terms of interoperability, among others, in a review. Furthermore, Smirnov, Shilov et al. [41] address existing interoperability issues across the different phases of the product lifecycle and address it by developing an ontology.

Platenius-Mohr, Malakuti et al. [42] address the requirements and solution of inter-operable digital twins through the use of the AAS in an industrial Internet-of-Things case study. Using the AutomationML standard, Guqi & Zhong [9] research on sharing digital twins and develop a simple example of how digital twins can be exchanged despite heterogeneous data. The case study by Lehner, Sint et al. [43] further demonstrates the advantages of developing and maintaining digital twins based on AutomationML models. Binder, Cala et al. [44] make also use of the AutomationML standard. However, Binder, Cala et al. [44] use it for modeling a digital twin based on functional architecture requirements.

Although the studies initially analyzed as listed in Table 2 address the research problem, they only deal partially with the presented requirements and meet them to a very limited extent. In particular, the aspect of implementation, validation, and potential analysis of the solution concepts in a cross-company context is not in the focus of most of the presented works. Therefore, the analysis does not allow a valid assessment regarding the added value, especially in terms of time savings, of the AAS for the efficient and standardized digital twin data exchange within the engineering phase.

Furthermore, the focus of the currently available publications, that address interoperability in the digital twin context, is often on the interoperability of the digital twin data in operation and less on engineering. However, since the interoperability of engineering data is the prerequisite for further phases of the product life cycle, like commissioning, operation, maintenance, and recycling, the analysis provides an important basis for interoperable digital twin data exchanges.

4 The Solution-Oriented Iterative Research Design

Agility and flexibility are needed to solve the research problem as the set of requirements will evolve throughout the research and due to the fact that the design problem cannot be solved in one iteration. Therefore, the design science research methodology is used as the central research paradigm of this research project. According to the design science paradigm, based on a real-world problem, new knowledge and understanding are achieved through the development and application of innovative artifacts [45]. The problem-solving approach is used not only in the domain of information systems but also in other areas such as engineering, business, IT, etc. [46]. In the context of this research in the field of information systems, the specific design science research methodology for information systems by Peffers et al. [18], which is well established in science and practice, is used. This design science research process consists of six steps, that can be seen in Fig. 2 [18, 46, 47]:

1. **Identify problem and motivate**: The aim of this first activity is to define and understand the research problem and to present the importance and added value of the envisioned solution.
2. **Define objectives of a solution**: In the second step of the process, quantitative and qualitative measurement criteria or goals are defined based on the first activity.

3. **Design and development**: The third phase focus on the development of the artifact. According to Hevner et al. [46] an artifact can basically be any designed object that makes a research contribution in the design.
4. **Demonstration**: In this step, the designed artifact is applied through experiments, case studies, simulations, etc. The benefit of the artifact for solving one or more aspects of the problem can be demonstrated. Thereby, the generated benefit of the artifact for solving one or more aspects of the problem can be shown.
5. **Evaluation**: The evaluation phase is used to check and measure the extent to which the artifact solves the problem. Once this process is complete, either another iteration in the design science cycle follows to improve the effectiveness of the artifact, or the final step of communication begins.
6. **Communication**: The final phase involves publishing and disseminating the results, including the problem statement and developed artifacts, to relevant stakeholders.

As shown in Fig. 2, the design science research methodology adapted from Peffers et al. 2007 [18] has been complemented with the concrete research procedure planned for the first design science cycle (DC1) illustrated in green color as well as essential steps for the second design science cycle (DC2) depicted in blue color. Throughout the research project, it is assumed that, especially in the context of the prototype development, several design science cycles will be performed to gradually add and validate further functions to fulfill the problem definition and measurement criteria in the sense of agile software development. The existing problem formulated in Sect. 1 is used as the initial research entry point, so the design science process begins with step 1. Thus, the planning of the first design cycle of prototype development consists of the following:

1. **Identify problem and motivate**: The motivation and problem identification are covered in Sect. 1, especially by the formulated design problem.
2. **Define objectives of a solution**: Initial requirements and quantitative as well as qualitative measurement criteria have already been defined by experts from industrial companies within a working group as presented in Sect. 2. An extension and/or modification of the requirements is expected to take place through further design science cycles.
3. **Design and development**: The focus of this step is on the development of a prototype for the exchange of an AAS using one of the leading PLM systems - Siemens Team-center [48] - as such a platform already covers a large percentage of the static digital twin data. Therefore, the prototype aims towards the provision of digital twin data from a PLM system towards an AAS server/repository utilizing the AAS standard with engineering relevant sub-models. BPMN process models and feature lists are planned as artifacts.
4. **Demonstration:** The demonstration phase is realized with the help of a case study in which the AAS-specific PLM functions are tested and analyzed on a cloud environment. In addition, presentation material as well as videos and a concept description will support the documentation und demonstration process.
5. **Evaluation:** A qualitative approach in the form of semi-structured interviews with relevant stakeholders, such as technical experts from industrial companies, will be taken for the evaluation of the prototype. Additionally, technical tests with the prototype on the cloud environment will be performed addressing the functional requirements as

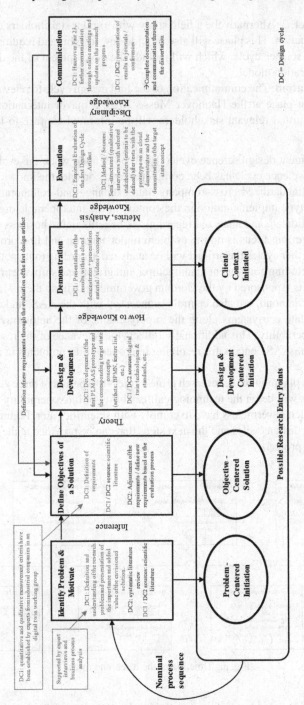

Fig. 2. Design science research methodology including the instantiation for the first design cycle, adapted from Peffers et al. [18].

stated in Sect. 2. Alternatively, a field study with similar stakeholders could be used for the evaluation. This phase will also provide new insights and requirements for the next design science cycle, which will include the development of the data exchange and collaboration model.

6. **Communication**: The communication of the first design cycle to relevant stakeholders will take place at the Hannover Messe 2023, a mayor international industrial trade fair. Further relevant stakeholders will be informed via face-to-face or online meetings.

The subsequent design science cycle(s) will be defined when the evaluation of the current design science cycle has been completed, and consider the knowledge gained.

Finally, a standardized cross-company data exchange and collaboration model as well as a prototype implementation in the context of the interoperable digital twin will be realized, validated, and analyzed regarding its benefits in the business environment. Although the current focus is on the problem understanding and first problem solving steps, in the further cycles the artifact will be analyzed according to its potential for different roles, including component manufacturer, integrator, and software provider. Large research projects (sponsored by the German government), among them Manufacturing-X, Catena-X, Diamond, are also centrally concerned with the AAS, and consider it as a standard in data ecosystems along the supply chains of the automotive industry to achieve interoperability. This additionally reflects the relevance of the research and the suitability of the AAS concept for resolving interoperability problems in a digital twin environment.

The current planning of the research project refers to a period of three years, whereby the initial focus will be on the technological feasibility of interoperability concepts and prototypes, which nevertheless have to comply with scientific rigor. Figure 3 shows the planning of the design cycles and the next steps that can be provided at the current stage of the research project.

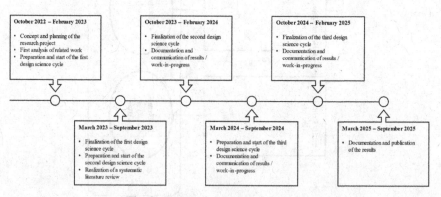

Fig. 3. Timeline of the research project

The upcoming steps are to focus on the implementation of the first design science cycle and finalizing it. Based on the results and existing requirements, a systematic literature review will be conducted. The further steps can be seen in Fig. 3, as far as they can be identified given the current state of affairs. To provide more insight into the first design science cycle, the following section presents first results of the development effort so far.

5   First Results

As part of the design and development phase of the first design science cycle and based on the requirements listed in Sect. 2, the following user story has been defined, according to the widespread user story format [49, 50]: As a [user], I want to [goal], so that [reason/benefit].

> *"As a component manufacturer, I want to provide the digital twin data of my asset (item revision) from Siemens Teamcenter (PLM) in the form of an AAS on an AAS server/repository via a button so that the interoperable exchange of the digital twin data is enabled in accordance with the AAS standard."*

After consultation with the experts that have been involved in the brainstorming and recording of the requirements (see Sect. 2), the following submodels were identified as part of the AAS for implementing the user story, taking into account that not all of these submodels are already standardized by the central AAS standardization organization (Industrial Digital Twin Association):

- **Digital Nameplate**: standardized provision of asset nameplate information
- **Technical Data**: standardized provision of technical data of an asset and related conformities to product classifications
- **Handover Documentation**: standardized format for asset specific information and documentation exchange
- **MCAD**: standardized mechanical CAD data exchange
- **ECAD**: standardized electrical CAD data exchange
- **Simulation**: standardized simulation model file exchange

The reason for choosing not only the meta data (nameplate and technical data), handover documentation, and the mechanical CAD sub-models, but also the electrical CAD and simulation sub-models was, that it is expected to realize even greater potentials within engineering when exchanging cross-domain/discipline digital twin data.

As shown in Fig. 4, some of the AAS sub-model elements are identified through ECLASS identifiers, called international registration data identifier (IRDI) and therefore also rely on semantic descriptions coming from the ECLASS, which is a cross-industry ISO/IEC-compliant standard for the classification of product and services and provides a large taxonomy [51]. Since the Siemens Teamcenter software can manage classification data according to the ECLASS standard, a mapping between the AAS sub-model elements and the specific Teamcenter data model can be realized via the IRDIs.

Files, like CAD data, as part of the AAS are usually stored as attachments of an ItemRevision within the PLM system. An ItemRevision allows the user to control and track changes of an Item, which is a fundamental object for managing data within Teamcenter. For the mapping towards the AAS the details of the attachment, including the data format and relation to the ItemRevision among others, need to be considered.

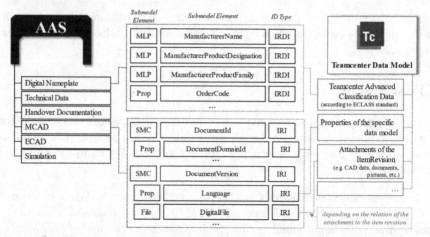

Fig. 4. Simplified mapping between the AAS and the Teamcenter data model, abbreviations: International Registration Data Identifier (IRDI), Internationalized Resource Identifiers (IRI), MultiLanguageProperty (MLP), Property (Prop) and SubmodelElementCollection (SMC)

By implementing a first minimal viable product (MVP) with the support of Siemens PLM experts, data from Teamcenter could already be provided to an AAS server/repository in the form of an AAS. Nevertheless, the development still requires further elaboration for a consistent mapping of the relevant data.

6 Conclusion

First steps for a standardized digital twin data exchange and collaboration have been detailed in this paper. The developed concepts and initial prototype within engineering processes will be evaluated with respect to the achieved benefits and potentials of further improving the interoperability in the cross-company exchange of digital twins.

Sharing digital twins across company borders requires design science cycles that will be successively defined taking up the results of the previous ones. They will not only take into account practical knowledge gained from the developed and evaluated demonstrators, but include existing timely research findings concerning sharing digital twins in other engineering contexts.

Since the current focus is on the alignment of data structures, the consideration of different roles, such as component manufacturer, integrator, and software provider, is likely to require a behavior perspective on interoperability. Such a shift enables recognizing information flows that represent relevant context of shared digital twins, and can be captured by business process models.

References

1. Piromalis, D., Kantaros, A.: Digital twins in the automotive industry: the road toward physical-digital convergence. Appli. Syst. Innovat, **5**, 65 (2022). https://doi.org/10.3390/asi5040065
2. Bhatti, G., Mohan, H., Raja Singh, R.: Towards the future of smart electric vehicles: Digital twin technology. Renew. Sustain. Energy Rev. **141**, 110801 (2021). https://doi.org/10.1016/j.rser.2021.110801
3. Eigner, M., Detzner, A., Schmidt, P.H., Tharma, R.: Definition des Digital Twin im Produktlebenszyklus. Zeitschrift für wirtschaftlichen Fabrikbetrieb **114**, 345–350 (2019). https://doi.org/10.3139/104.112107
4. Baudoin, C., Bournival, E., Buchheit, M., Guerrero, R.: The Industrial Internet of Things Vocabulary. An Industrial Internet Consortium Framework Publication (2020), https://www.iiconsortium.org/pdf/Vocabulary-Report-2.3.pdf, (Accessed 10 Feb 2023)
5. VanDerHorn, E., Mahadevan, S.: digital twin: generalization, characterization and implementation. Decis. Support Syst. **145**, 113524 (2021). https://doi.org/10.1016/j.dss.2021.113524
6. Botín-Sanabria, D.M.: Digital twin technology challenges and applications: a comprehensive review. Remote Sensing 14, **1335** (2022). doi: https://doi.org/10.3390/rs14061335
7. Lim, K.Y.H., Zheng, P., Chen, C.-H.: A state-of-the-art survey of Digital Twin: techniques, engineering product lifecycle management and business innovation perspectives. J. Intell. Manuf. **31**(6), 1313–1337 (2019). https://doi.org/10.1007/s10845-019-01512-w
8. Piroumian, V.: Digital twins: universal interoperability for the digital age. Computer **54**, 61–69 (2021). https://doi.org/10.1109/MC.2020.3032148
9. Guqi, P., Hongen, Z.: Research and Implementation of Digital Twin Heterogeneous Data Exchange System. J. Phys.: Conf. Ser., vol. 1617, 12063 (2020). doi: https://doi.org/10.1088/1742-6596/1617/1/012063
10. Haße, H., van der Valk, H., Möller, F., Otto, B.: Design principles for shared digital twins in distributed systems. Bus. Inf. Syst. Eng. **64**, 751–772 (2022). https://doi.org/10.1007/s12599-022-00751-1
11. Barnstedt, E., Lin, S.-W., Boss, B., Malakuti, S., Martins, T.W.: Open Source Drives Digital Twin Adoption (2021)
12. Grieves, M.: Digital Twin: Manufacturing excellence through virtual factory replication. Digital Twin White Paper **1**, 1–7 (2014)
13. Bönsch, J., Elstermann, M., Kimmig, A., Ovtcharova, J.: A subject-oriented reference model for Digital Twins. Comput. Ind. Eng. **172**, 108556 (2022). https://doi.org/10.1016/j.cie.2022.108556
14. Adamenko, D., Kunnen, S., Nagarajah, A.: Digital twin and product lifecycle management: what is the difference? In: Nyffenegger, F., Ríos, J., Rivest, L., Bouras, A. (eds.) PLM 2020. IAICT, vol. 594, pp. 150–162. Springer, Cham (2020). https://doi.org/10.1007/978-3-030-62807-9_13
15. Eigner, M.: System Lifecycle Management. Springer, Berlin (2021) https://doi.org/10.1007/978-3-662-45937-9_29
16. Sakowski, A., Dangelmaier, M., Hertwig, M., Spath, D.: Bidirectional interoperability of product engineering and manufacturing enhancing mass customization. Procedia Manufacturing **39**, 81–89 (2019). https://doi.org/10.1016/j.promfg.2020.01.231
17. Wieringa, R.J.: Design Science Methodology for Information Systems and Software Engineering. Springer, Berlin (2014). https://doi.org/10.1007/978-3-662-43839-8
18. Peffers, K., Tuunanen, T., Rothenberger, M.A., Chatterjee, S.: A design science research methodology for information systems research. J. Manag. Inf. Syst. **24**, 45–77 (2007). https://doi.org/10.2753/MIS0742-1222240302

19. Grieves, M., Vickers, J.: Digital twin: mitigating unpredictable, undesirable emergent behavior in complex systems. In: Kahlen, F.-J., Flumerfelt, S., Alves, A. (eds.) Transdisciplinary Perspectives on Complex Systems, pp. 85–113. Springer, Cham (2017). https://doi.org/10.1007/978-3-319-38756-7_4

20. Trauer, J., Schweigert-Recksiek, S., Engel, C., Spreitzer, K., Zimmermann, M.: What is a digital twin? – Definitions and insights from an industrial case study in technical product development. In: Proceedings of the Design Society: Design Conference, vol. 1, pp. 757–766 (2020). https://doi.org/10.1017/dsd.2020.15

21. Kritzinger, W., Karner, M., Traar, G., Henjes, J., Sihn, W.: Digital Twin in manufacturing: A categorical literature review and classification. IFAC-PapersOnLine **51**, 1016–1022 (2018). https://doi.org/10.1016/j.ifacol.2018.08.474

22. Jones, D., Snider, C., Nassehi, A., Yon, J., Hicks, B.: Characterising the digital twin: a systematic literature review. CIRP J. Manuf. Sci. Technol. **29**, 36–52 (2020). https://doi.org/10.1016/j.cirpj.2020.02.002

23. Rabe, M., Kilic, E.: Concept of a Business-Process-related digital twin based on systems theory and operational excellence. In: 2022 IEEE 28th International Conference on Engineering, Technology and Innovation (ICE/ITMC) & 31st International Association For Management of Technology (IAMOT) Joint Conference, pp. 1–9. IEEE (2022). doi: https://doi.org/10.1109/ICE/ITMC-IAMOT55089.2022.10033175

24. Chen, Z., Huang, L.: Digital twins for information-sharing in remanufacturing supply chain: A review. Energy **220**, 119712 (2021). https://doi.org/10.1016/j.energy.2020.119712

25. Catarci, T., Firmani, D., Leotta, F., Mandreoli, F., Mecella, M., Sapio, F.: a conceptual architecture and model for smart manufacturing relying on service-based digital twins. In: 2019 IEEE International Conference on Web Services (ICWS), pp. 229–236. IEEE (2019). doi: https://doi.org/10.1109/ICWS.2019.00047

26. Qi, Q., et al.: Enabling technologies and tools for digital twin. J. Manuf. Syst. **58**, 3–21 (2021). https://doi.org/10.1016/j.jmsy.2019.10.001

27. Jiang, Y., Li, M., Guo, D., Wu, W., Zhong, R.Y., Huang, G.Q.: Digital twin-enabled smart modular integrated construction system for on-site assembly. Comput. Ind. **136**, 103594 (2022). https://doi.org/10.1016/j.compind.2021.103594

28. VDI/VDE GMA: Industry 4.0 Begriffe / Terms and definitions. VDI-Statusreport (2022). https://www.vdi.de/ueber-uns/presse/publikationen/details/industrie-40-begriffe-terms-and-definitions, (Accessed 10 Feb 2023)

29. Wagner, C., et al.: The role of the Industry 4.0 asset administration shell and the digital twin during the life cycle of a plant. In: 2017 22nd IEEE International Conference on Emerging Technologies and Factory Automation (ETFA), pp. 1–8. IEEE (2017). doi: https://doi.org/10.1109/ETFA.2017.8247583

30. Plattform Industrie 4.0: The Asset Administration Shell: Implementing digital twins for use in Industrie 4.0 (2019). https://www.plattform-i40.de/IP/Redaktion/EN/Downloads/Publikation/VWSiD%20V2.0.html, (Accessed 10 Feb 2023)

31. Gerhard, D., Wolf, M., Huxoll, J., Vogt, O.: Digital Twin representations of concrete modules in an interdisciplinary context of construction and manufacturing industry. In: Nyffenegger, F., Ríos, J., Rivest, L., Bouras, A. (eds.) PLM 2020. IAICT, vol. 594, pp. 101–115. Springer, Cham (2020). https://doi.org/10.1007/978-3-030-62807-9_9

32. Plattform Industrie 4.0: Details of the Asset Administration Shell. Part 1 - The exchange of information between partners in the value chain of Industrie 4.0 (Version 3.0RC02). https://industrialdigitaltwin.org/wp-content/uploads/2022/06/DetailsOfThe AssetAdministrationShell_Part1_V3.0RC02_Final1.pdf, (Accessed 10 Feb 2023)

33. Eloff, J., Eloff, M.M., Dlamini, M.T., Ngassam, E., Ras, D.: Interoperability as a catalyst for business innovation. In: Zelm, M., van Sinderen, M.J., Ferraira Pires, L., Doumeingts, G.

(eds.) Enterprise interoperability. Research and applications in the service-oriented ecosystem: proceedings of the 5th International IFIP Working Conference IWEI 2013, pp. 33–46. ISTE Ltd; John Wiley & Sons, Inc, London (2013). doi: https://doi.org/10.1002/978111884 6995.ch4

34. Bernus, P., Doumeingts, G., Fox, M.: Enterprise Architecture, Integration and Interoperability: IFIP TC 5 International Conference, EAI2N 2010, Held as Part of WCC 2010, Brisbane, Australia, September 20–23, 2010. Proceedings. Scholars Portal, Berlin, Heidelberg (2010)

35. Eigner, M., Stelzer, R.: Product lifecycle Management. Ein Leitfaden für Product Development und Life Cycle Management. Springer, Berlin (2009)

36. Likert, R.: A technique for the measurement of attitudes **22**, 1–55 (1932)

37. Katz, J.: Designing information. Perception, human factors, and common sense. Wiley, Hoboken (2012)

38. Deuter, A., Imort, S.: Product lifecycle management with the asset administration shell. Computers **10**, 84 (2021). https://doi.org/10.3390/computers10070084

39. Inigo, M.A., Porto, A., Kremer, B., Perez, A., Larrinaga, F., Cuenca, J.: Towards an Asset Administration Shell scenario: a use case for interoperability and standardization in Industry 4.0. In: NOMS 2020 - 2020 IEEE/IFIP Network Operations and Management Symposium, pp. 1–6. IEEE, [S.l.] (2020). doi: https://doi.org/10.1109/NOMS47738.2020.9110410

40. Wei, K., Sun, J.Z., Liu, R.J.: A review of asset administration shell. In: 2019 IEEE International Conference on Industrial Engineering and Engineering Management (IEEM), pp. 1460–1465. IEEE (2019). doi: https://doi.org/10.1109/IEEM44572.2019.8978536

41. Smirnov, A., Shilov, N., Parfenov, V.: Building a multi-aspect ontology for semantic interoperability in PLM. In: Fortin, C., Rivest, L., Bernard, A., Bouras, A. (eds.) PLM 2019. IAICT, vol. 565, pp. 107–115. Springer, Cham (2019). https://doi.org/10.1007/978-3-030-42250-9_10

42. Platenius-Mohr, M., Malakuti, S., Grüner, S., Schmitt, J., Goldschmidt, T.: File- and API-based interoperability of digital twins by model transformation: An IIoT case study using asset administration shell. Futur. Gener. Comput. Syst. **113**, 94–105 (2020). https://doi.org/10.1016/j.future.2020.07.004

43. Lehner, D., Sint, S., Vierhauser, M., Narzt, W., Wimmer, M.: AML4DT: A model-driven framework for developing and maintaining digital twins with automationML. In: 2021 26th IEEE International Conference on Emerging Technologies and Factory Automation (ETFA), pp. 1–8. IEEE (2021). doi: https://doi.org/10.1109/ETFA45728.2021.9613376

44. Binder, C., Cala, A., Vollmar, J., Neureiter, C., Luder, A.: Automated model transformation in modeling digital twins of industrial internet-of-things applications utilizing automationML. In: 2021 26th IEEE International Conference on Emerging Technologies and Factory Automation (ETFA), pp. 1–6. IEEE (2021). doi: https://doi.org/10.1109/ETFA45728.2021.9613172

45. Hevner, A.R., March, S.T., Park, J., Ram, S.: Design science in information systems research. Manag. Inf. Syst. Q. **28**, 75–105 (2004)

46. vom Brocke, J., Hevner, A., Maedche, A.: Introduction to design science research. In: vom, J., Hevner, A., Maedche, A. (eds.) Design Science Research. Cases. PI, pp. 1–13. Springer, Cham (2020). https://doi.org/10.1007/978-3-030-46781-4_1

47. Peffers, K., et al.: Design Science Research Process: A Model for Producing and Presenting Information Systems Research, arXiv preprint arXiv:2006.02763 (2020)

48. Lawrie, G.: The Forrester Wave™: Product lifecycle management for discrete manufacturers, Q1 2021. The seven providers that matter most and how they stack up (2021). https://www.forrester.com/report/the-forrester-wave-product-lifecycle-management-for-discrete-manufacturers-q1-2021/RES161531, (Accessed 10 Feb 2023)

49. Lucassen, G., Dalpiaz, F., Werf, J.M.E.M.V.D., Brinkkemper, S.: The use and effectiveness of user stories in practice. In: Daneva, M., Pastor, O. (eds.) REFSQ 2016. LNCS, vol. 9619, pp. 205–222. Springer, Cham (2016). https://doi.org/10.1007/978-3-319-30282-9_14

50. Cohn, M.: User stories applied: For agile software development. Addison-Wesley, Boston (2004)

51. Gönül, S., Çavdaroğlu, D., Kabak, Y., Glachs, D., Gigante, F., Deng, Q.: A B2B marketplace ecommerce platform approach integrating purchasing and transport processes. In: Archimède, B., Ducq, Y., Young, B., Karray, H. (eds.) Enterprise Interoperability IX. Interoperability in the Era of Artificial Intelligence. Proceedings of the I-ESA Conferences, vol. 10, pp. 105–121. Springer, Cham (2023). doi: https://doi.org/10.1007/978-3-030-90387-9_10

Credit to Machine Learning – Performance of Credit Card Fraud Detection Models

Andreas Widenhorn[1][✉] and Paramvir Singh Gaawar[2]

[1] International School of Management, Karlstraße 35, 80333 Munich, Germany
andreas.widenhorn@ism.de
[2] Experteer, Lenbachpl. 3, 80333 Munich, Germany

Abstract. "Efficiency is doing better what is already being done" – When economist Peter Drucker came up with this quote, the world was largely unaffected by machine learning (ML) techniques and the way modern artificial intelligence (AI) can facilitate processes. Yet, fraud detection methods had already evolved from manual to data-matching systems in the late 90s. Thereafter, individual risk profiles helped in better understanding the potential roots and causes of fraud. Nowadays, modern AI and ML methods look promising, with applications gaining importance and popularity in various fields. However, the performance, efficiency and ease of implementation may vary substantially for different specifications of fraud detection endeavors. Relating to a general process of customer orders and prompt shipment, ML-supported assessments on fraudulent orders can accelerate transactions. When trying to identify irregular credit card payment, this article highlights the usefulness and limitations of popular ML fraud detection methods in relating them to more traditional approaches. Considering different alternative models, we also assess the volatility in some of the most common modifications in modern ML fraud detection techniques.

Keywords: Fraud Detection · Machine Learning · BPM

1 Introduction

1.1 Credit Card Fraud Categories

Fraudulent credit card use has been a considerable financial problem for the past decades. In the U.S., credit cards have recently accounted for the most fraud reports by payment method (Bankrate, 2023). Illegal credit card transaction can broadly be classified as either online or offline (Laleh & Azgomi, 2009), with the vast majority of 92% in credit card fraud happening online (Statista, 2021). While some forms such as stolen and lost credit card fraud can be checked via additional authentication requirements, others such as phishing remain to be a threat (European Central Bank, 2018).

M. Elstermann et al. (Eds.): S-BPM ONE 2023, CCIS 1867, pp. 151–159, 2023.
https://doi.org/10.1007/978-3-031-40213-5_11

1.2 Business Processes Connected to Credit Card Fraud

Credit card fraud can affect virtually any business process involving external customers' payments (Tekkali, Natarajan 2023). A very general subject-oriented perspective considers order handling as a straightforward subject affected by efficiency gains in detecting fraudulent orderings:

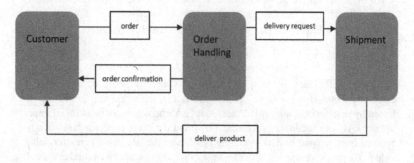

Internal behavior for Order Handling can be depicted as follows:

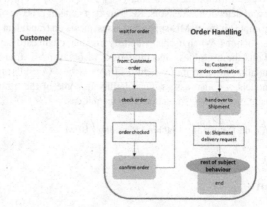

Fig. 1. Generic example of a business process including customers' order handling Source: Kurz et al. (2013)

As illustrated in Fig. 1, efficient checking of an order requires a customer input. In order to validate whether this input is legitimate or fraudulent, several approaches exist.

1.3 Popular Processes in Credit Card Fraud Detection

A popular means of detecting fraud is depicted in Fig. 2, in which a human element is present when experts carry out manual inspections of possibly fraudulent transactions (Pozzolo, 2015). These inspections are initiated when the ML algorithm identifies a suspicious pattern.

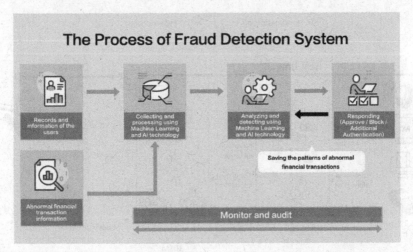

Fig. 2. Example of a fraud detection process with human experts included. Source: Penta Security (2021)

Other than the process illustrated in Fig. 2, multi-factor authentication approaches or processes based on past behavior patterns, biometrics, shared information among merchants or expert systems represent alternatives. Aiming for an efficient detection of fraud, some of these concepts include real-time methods (Fig. 3), which do not necessitate high levels of human intervention in the classification procedure (Jurgovsky, 2019).

When comparing real-time methods to more manual ones, it seems natural to assume that the two will yield different rates of wrongfully accepted or rejected credit card transactions. Besides the concern over undetected fraud, customer satisfaction deserves top priority for card issuers. Hence, avoiding wrongfully rejected credit card transactions need to be kept at an absolute minimum, in particular when no human supervision is included in real-time processes. It is certainly challenging to determine a threshold of first- and second- degree errors for which either process logic turns superior. The aim of this paper is to shed some light on the potential of ML advancements successfully shifting fraud detection towards self-learning techniques with little human intervention needed.

As illustrated in Figs. 2 and 3, the question of an ideal fraud detection process strongly relates to precision in predictive modeling. In order to investigate the potential of creating an efficient ML fraud detection process, information on individuals and aggregated inputs are combined and tested for several ML approaches. As a result, various predictors are joined, performance of various methods is assessed and conclusions regarding efficient processes are drawn.

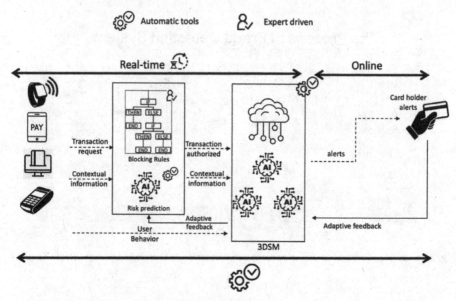

Fig. 3. Example of a real-time fraud detection process. Source: Cherif et al. (2023)

2 Methodology

2.1 Machine Learning (ML) Techniques Applied in Fraud Detection

A commonly found definition of machine learning (ML) sees ML as a form of artificial intelligence (AI) giving an operation the ability to get knowledge from its own experiences automatically and independently of human intervention (Mainali et al., 2021).

Contrary to more traditional approaches, calculation and problem-solving are less important than processing raw data inputs to utmost precise forecasts in ML. Generally, there are the three ML sub-divisions of supervised, unsupervised and reinforcement learning.

This article will focus on supervised learning and compare its performance in fraud detection to that of traditional models, including several external predictors. To this end, fraudulent activities are classified in a binary way (Jurgovsky, 2019). Binary machine learning approaches have been applied in a number of studies, such as in Maes et al. (2002) or Yeh & Lien (2009) with neural networks, Pozzolo et al. (2014) or Zareapoor & Shamsolmoali (2015) with support vector machines, and applications of decision trees in Mahmoudi & Duman (2015) or random forests in Bhattacharyya et al. (2011). Building on these findings, we analyze the variation in prediction quality when various parameters are altered and the set of predictors is extended to include more external information.

2.2 Performance Measures and Challenges

One of the most prominent obstacles in fraud detection are imbalanced classes. When classification categories are not approximately equally represented, this typically leads to varying levels of sample bias and a poor fit in regions in which minority-class instances appear side-by-side with instances of the majority class (Jurgovsky, 2019). Potential remedies include undersampling, in which the majority class of non-fraudulent cases is reduced, or oversampling, artificially increasing the minority class of fraud cases.

This article applies various resampling and adjustment techniques as well as data augmentation approaches in order to improve precision. Model performance is eventually measured using confusion matrix metrics such as precision and recall rate, as well as their relation for different probabilities applying ROC curves (Shakya, 2018).

The confusion matrix is summarized in Fig. 4:

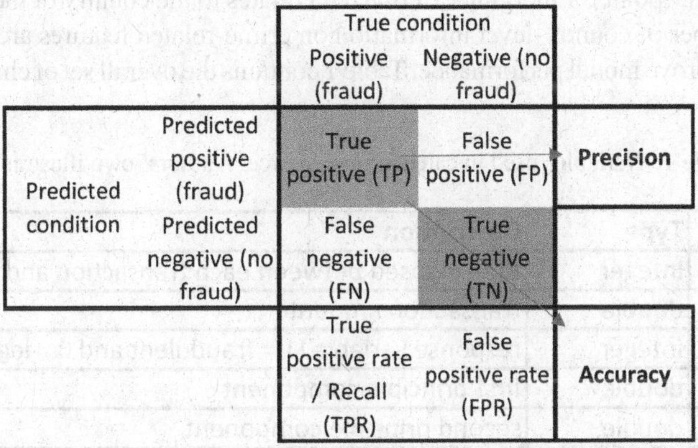

Fig. 4. Confusion matrix. Source: Authors' own illustration

Several measures such as accuracy, precision and F1 scores are commonly used as evaluation metrics in fraud detection models (Shakya, 2018).

Beyond these, true positive rates (TPR or recall) can be insightful. TPR include both precision and type 1 error elements. The latter is relevant as it refers to undetected cases of fraud. TPR is calculated as follows:

$$TPR = \frac{TP}{TP + FN}$$

Furthermore, popular metrics considering probability thresholds include areas under the Receiver Operator Curve (ROC) and Precision Recall (PR).

All the above-mentioned performance measures can yield values between 0 and 1, with higher values indication better performance.

3   Data

Main data source for our calculations is a publicly available dataset from a research project (Pozzolo et al., 2015) conducted by Worldline along with the Machine Learning Group of ULB. In order to meet confidentiality requirements, characteristics on an individual level have been provided in the form of principal components. As a result, 28 grouped features serve as explanatory variables, alongside transactional information on time and value, plus a binary response variable indicating fraud. The binary representation of the class label serves as an indication of the legitimacy of a transaction. The label was bestowed upon the card holder by human investigators following a discussion with the card bearer. In the vast majority of instances, the value 0 is assigned to the label. The label is set to 1 only if it is determined that the transaction was issued by someone other than the user. This occurs only when it has been determined that a transaction was issued by a third party.

In addition, a set of external features has been included on an aggregated level. Connecting features on an individual to a more aggregated level is impeded in our case, as the only entry point for merging external data relates to the country of the cardholder. Hence a number of country-level information on crime-related features are added in an attempt to improve model performance. Table 1 contains the overall set of characteristics:

Table 1. Variables used in calculations. Source: Authors' own illustration

Variable	Type	Description
time	integer	time elapsed between each transaction and the first
amount	double	transaction amount
class	integer	response variable (1 = fraudulent and 0 = legitimate)
v1	double	first principle component
v2	double	second principle component
...	...	...
v28	double	last principal component
country	char	card holder, country
population	integer	population of the country
crime index	integer	survey-based perceived crime rate from 0 to 100
GDP	integer	gross domestic product of the country
CPI	integer	Consumer Price Index
QoL	integer	survey-based quality of life index from 0 to 100
corruption	integer	survey-based corruption index from 0 to 100

Overall, cardholders were located in Europe, with transactions covering the course of two days in September 2013. The number of transactions is 284,807, only 492 of which were fraudulent.

4   Results

When applying different models in estimation, it turns out that machine learning-based approaches Random Forest (RF) and XGBoost tend to outperform the traditional logistic regression (LR) model. In terms of precision, best performance was achieved by using the random forest – random oversampling approach. Precision in this case reached 97%, which is roughly in line with findings of e.g. Bin Sulaiman et al. (2022) who compared several fraud detection approaches.

Results in precision generally indicate the potential to accelerate processes such as the one illustrated in Fig. 1 by relying more strongly on ML models and less on human intervention. Interestingly, the results vary not only depending on choice of methods, but also considerably for different sampling techniques. While methods of XGBoost and Logistic Regression (LR) achieve the highest precision without resampling, random forest (RF) precision is highest for random oversampling. However, RF and random undersampling exhibits precision values as low as 5%. Besides accuracy and precision, which most studies consider the key performance indicators, false negatives may also be of interest especially for fraud detection processes involving little or no human interference, such as real-time systems. Here, the TPR (recall) values turn more important, as they directly relate cases of detected fraud to those where fraudulent transactions remain undetected. In this regard, the more traditional logistic regression yields very good results in 6 out of 8 specifications. However, random forest and XGBoost produced better results on average, regarding all five measures of performance. This holds

Table 2. Results overview. Source: Authors' own calculations

Model	Technique	TPR (recall)	Precision	ROC	PR	F1 Score
LR	No resampling	0.53	0.68	0.852	0.454	0.59
	Random undersampling	0.91	0.09	0.973	0.729	0.16
	Tomek links removal	0.53	0.67	0.854	0.455	0.59
	Random oversampling	0.9	0.07	0.971	0.726	0.13
	SMOTE	0.88	0.09	0.967	0.726	0.17
	SMOTE + TLR	0.91	0.08	0.973	0.727	0.15
	(arithmetic) mean	0.78	0.28	0.93	0.64	0.3
	coefficient of variation	0.25	1.09	0.07	0.22	0.75
Random Forest	No resampling	0.79	0.96	0.966	0.869	0.87
	Random undersampling	0.92	0.05	0.978	0.774	0.09
	Tomek links removal	0.78	0.92	0.959	0.853	0.84
	Random oversampling	0.77	0.97	0.966	0.871	0.86
	SMOTE	0.87	0.68	0.979	0.847	0.76
	SMOTE + TLR	0.84	0.84	0.977	0.87	0.84
	(arithmetic) mean	0.83	0.74	0.97	0.85	0.71
	coefficient of variation	0.07	0.48	0.01	0.04	0.43
XG Boost	No resampling	0.74	0.93	0.925	0.824	0.82
	Random undersampling	0.89	0.04	0.96	0.676	0.08
	Tomek links removal	0.71	0.87	0.925	0.826	0.78
	Random oversampling	0.84	0.8	0.954	0.824	0.82
	SMOTE	0.88	0.53	0.987	0.855	0.66
	SMOTE + TLR	0.88	0.22	0.98	0.565	0.35
	(arithmetic) mean	0.82	0.57	0.96	0.76	0.59
	coefficient of variation	0.1	0.65	0.03	0.15	0.52

true for both higher mean values and lower relative spread of values, as indicated by the coefficients of variation in Table 2.

5 Discussion and Outlook

Given the variation in results, the extent to which a business process can benefit from ML-based fraud detection clearly depends on the ability to optimize modeling techniques. This also suggests that constant model evaluations and reinforcement approaches could turn beneficial. Our perspective does not cover the full variety of methods available. Hence, adding to the scope of methods by e.g. considering various deep-learning techniques would be a straightforward extension (Vimal et al. 2021).

While ML techniques were found to yield better results on average, a generalized statement relating to more traditional methods would also be too bold at this point. However, our findings indicate some support for promoting automated ML systems, as precision and recall (TPR) rates were partly improved by using ML techniques, which in turn require less human supervision.

Trying to improve processes via automatically detected fraudulent credit card use, data protection certainly plays a role beyond the mere methodology. In light of the importance of personal buyers' history, data privacy laws and regulations could boost ML methods' results even further. While the broader country-level perspective did not substantially improve results, the picture is likely to look very different if more personal identifiable information (PII) on behavioral patterns of the past was available. As an example, the General Data Protection Regulation (GDPR) in Europe and the Chinese Personal Information Protection Law (PIPL) support different interpretations of sensitive and identifiable parts of personal information (dataguidance, 2023). Adding to card-related usage information, social and criminal affinities might have the potential to improve fraud detection processes substantially.

Results have been presented with regard to several measures of performance. The importance of each measure largely depends on the associated costs of e.g. mistakenly rejecting credit card transaction, i.e. on costs of false positives or negatives. This aspect deserves further investigation regarding the likeliness and costs of increased churn probabilities when type 1 and 2 errors are incurred. In the U.S., overall costs of fraudulent credit card activities will total \$165.1 billion over the next 10 years, according to a Nielsen report in December 2022 (Bankrate, 2023). Yet the opportunity costs of higher rejection rates e.g. through changed thresholds in ML approaches or stronger human supervision remain to be quantified.

References

1. Bankrate.   https://www.bankrate.com/finance/credit-cards/credit-card-fraud-statistics/. Accessed 06 Feb 2023
2. Bhattacharyya, S., Jha, S., Tharakunnel, K., Westland, J.C.: Data mining for credit card fraud: a comparative study. In: Decision Support Systems, pp. 602–613 (2011)
3. Bin Sulaiman, R., Schetinin, V., Sant, P.: Review of machine learning approach on credit card fraud detection. Hum.-Centr. Intell. Syst. **2**, 55–68 (2022). Springer

4. Cherif, A., Badhib, A., Ammar, H., Alshehri, S. Kalkatawi, M., Imine, A.: Credit card fraud detection in the era of disruptive technologies. J. King Saud Univ. Comput. Inf. Sci. **35**(1), 145–174 (2023)
5. dataguidance.   https://www.dataguidance.com/resource/comparing-privacy-laws-gdpr-v-pipl. Accessed 06 Feb 2023
6. European Central Bank. Fifth report on card fraud (2018)
7. Jurgovsky, J.: Context-Aware Credit Card Fraud Detection. Dissertation at University of Passau (2019)
8. Kurz, M., Fleischmann, A., Lederer, M., Huber, S.: Planning for the unexpected: exception handling and BPM. In: Fischer, H., Schneeberger, J. (eds.) S-BPM ONE 2013. CCIS, vol. 360, pp. 123–149. Springer, Heidelberg (2013). https://doi.org/10.1007/978-3-642-36754-0_8
9. Laleh, N., Abdollahi Azgomi, M.: A taxonomy of frauds and fraud detection techniques. In: Prasad, S.K., Routray, S., Khurana, R., Sahni, S. (eds.) ICISTM 2009. CCIS, vol. 31, pp. 256–267. Springer, Heidelberg (2009). https://doi.org/10.1007/978-3-642-00405-6_28
10. Mainali, S., Darsie, M.E., Smetana, K.S.: Machine Learning in Action: Stroke Diagnosis and Outcome Prediction. National Library of Medicine (2021)
11. Maes, S., Tuyls, K., Vanschoenwinkel, B., Manderick, B.: Credit card fraud detection using bayesian and neural networks. In: Proceedings of the First International NAISO Congress on Neuro Fuzzy Technologies, 16–19 January 2002 (Havana, Cuba) (2002)
12. Penta Security Homepage: Fraud Detection System (FDS) with AI Technology (2021). https://www.pentasecurity.com/blog/fraud-detection-system-fds-with-ai-technology/. Accessed 06 Feb 2023
13. Pozzolo, A.: Adaptive Machine Learning for Credit Card Fraud Detection. Dissertation at Université Libre de Bruxelles (2015)
14. Pozzolo, A., Caelen, O., Borgne, Y.-A., Waterschoot, S., Bontempi, G.: Lessons learned in credit card fraud detection. Expert Syst. Appl. **41**(10), 4915–4928 (2014)
15. Pozzolo, A.D., Caelen, O., Johnson, R.A., Bontempi, G.: Calibrating probability with under-sampling for unbalanced classification. In: 2015 IEEE Symposium Series on Computational Intelligence (2015)
16. Shakya, R.: Application of Machine Learning Techniques in Credit Card Fraud Detection. UNLV Theses, Dissertations, Professional Papers, and Capstones 3454 (2018)
17. Statista. Most frequently reported types of cyber crime (2021). https://www.statista.com/statistics/184083/commonly-reported-types-of-cyber-crime/. Accessed 06 Feb 2023
18. Tekkali, C.G., Natarajan, K.: RDQN: ensemble of deep neural network with reinforcement learning in classification based on rough set theory for digital transactional fraud detection. Complex Intell. Syst. (2023)
19. Vimal, S., Kayathwal, K., Wadhwa, H., Dhama, G.: Application of Deep Reinforcement Learning to Payment Fraud. arXiv preprint, arXiv:2112.04236 (2021)
20. Yeh, I.-C., Lien, C.: The comparisons of data mining techniques for the predictive accuracy of probability of default of credit card clients. Exp. Syst. Appl. **36**(2), Part 1, 2473–2480 (2009)
21. Zareapoor, M., Shamsolmoali, P.: Application of credit card fraud detection: Based on bagging ensemble classifier. In: Procedia Computer Science - International Conference on Computer, Communication and Convergence (ICCC 2015) (2015)

(S-)BPM Modeling, Technology and Infrastructure

Comparing BPMN 2.0 and PASS: A Review and Analysis of Previous Research

Christoph Piller[✉]

Bitpanda GmbH, Stella-Klein-Löw Weg 17, 1020 Vienna, Austria
christoph.piller@bitpanda.com, chpiller@live.com

Abstract. Business Process Management is a discipline characterized by a variety of activities and tasks. The process notation BPMN 2.0 is also an activity-and task-oriented modeling language. In this paper, we examine whether PASS, a subject-oriented modeling language, can support today's requirements for modeling processes. We have gathered relevant research and provided a qualitative evaluation of their results by applying them on a real production use case. The research is showing that the use of PASS as a common modeling language provides a better understanding and overview of complex processes than BPMN 2.0. Additionally, the analysis shows that the modeling of processes via PASS can be simpler. Nevertheless, as our research is providing only a qualitative evaluation more verification is needed for evaluating our results.

Keywords: BPMN 2.0 · PASS · subject-orientation · activity-orientation · S-BPM · BPM

1 Introduction

One of the central goals of the Business Process Management (BPM) discipline in general and the modeling of business processes specifically is providing an overview and understanding for all activities which are necessary to create a company's product or provide their services. Such an overview usually includes core activities, such as production or sales, as well as support activities, e.g., recruiting or production planning. BPM provides structure for these activities and process models provide a visual overview for these. This ensures an understanding of their (inter-)connections among each other and makes the collaboration among different stakeholders as well as tasks of decision-making, error-finding and improvement-realizations more efficient (see [10,11]).

Additionally, the requirements to companies as well as to BPM have seen a notable shift toward more connections and interactions between different process participants. Consequently, communication between process participants, clarification of overlapping process ownership, as well as collaboration across team and company borders is becoming increasingly important (see [1]).

To master these BPM challenges, BPM needs to represent business processes visually via models. The present study aims to investigate the extent to which

M. Elstermann et al. (Eds.): S-BPM ONE 2023, CCIS 1867, pp. 163–179, 2023.
https://doi.org/10.1007/978-3-031-40213-5_12

Business Process Model and Notation 2.0 (BPMN 2.0), the predominant modeling language, satisfies the existing modeling requirements. Alternatively, we aim to assess whether the more recent and subject-oriented modeling approach, Parallel Activity Specification Schema (PASS), more effectively addresses the identified modeling needs. To address this inquiry, we have synthesized current research pertaining to the utilization of PASS in comparison to BPMN 2.0, and subsequently present our findings herein.

1.1   Requirements for Modeling Processes

In order to effectively tackle the above mentioned BPM hurdles, it is imperative that BPM adequately models business processes with their interdependencies, activities, and execution constraints between them. This leads to several requirements that especially business process models must fulfill, to ensure a collective understanding company-wide as well as an efficient way of finding process improvements. The following explicit requirements for business process models in a BPM context were identified by Kannengiesser [6] and Becker [1]:

- **Using a common modeling language, to provide an understandable overview:** To have a collective understanding of the ongoing processes in a company and discuss them in an effective and efficient way, a common modeling language must be used for all models within a BPM effort. This language should also be used in a correct way, so that every stakeholder is able to understand it.
- **Simple and fast approach for modeling:** In order to avoid spending too much time and money on modeling business processes, one feature of a modeling language is that it is easy and fast to use. Therefore, more time can be spent for analyzing and improving a process.
- **Flexibility in modeling a process:** Especially within the concept of Continuous Process Improvement and the increasing complexity of businesses, a given flexibility of modeling and improving business processes is an important goal. On one side, it is important to be able to change models incrementally in an efficient way. On the other side, the possibility of a distributed modeling approach is advantageous since not all involved stakeholders are available at the same time or at the same location and the modeling of a complex business model should nevertheless be done in the most efficient way possible.
- **Usage of created models for IT systems requirements engineering:** As more business processes are digitized and the change of a business process often leads to changes in the IT system environment of an organization, a business process model should also serve as requirements list for the IT department as it defines the processes that should be supported by the system.

Although there are different notations for modeling business processes, BPMN 2.0 is the current standard notation (ISO/IEC 19510:2013). So, why introducing a different process notation, when BPMN 2.0 has already been identified as standard 10 years ago? The change of requirements for companies towards more visibility of connections and interactions between different stakeholders the last years have led to the detection of some BPMN 2.0 deficits, as it is an activity- and task-oriented modeling approach[1]. This activity-oriented perspective of modeling processes is also called Orchestration. Such an orchestration implies that there is a central control system which manages the execution of the defined process steps. As mentioned above, the focus of connections and interactions between different participants has increased, BPMN 2.0 introduced two additional types of diagrams, the choreography and the conversation diagram. Those diagram perspectives are called choreography and are explained in 2.1 Orchestration vs. Choreography. Contrary to PASS, which is a subject oriented modeling approach. Therefore, PASS is only using the choreography perspective, but nevertheless using two types of diagram, Subject Interaction and Subject Behaviour Diagram. As PASS is following a totally different description paradigm and both notations claim to be able to meet the BPM requirements, we have decided to compare both notations in the context of a real-life application use-case. Therefore, we will use findings and conclusions of related works.

2   Starting Point of the Comparison

Before we are going to present the articles, which are used in the paper, we must describe the difference between the modeling perspectives of orchestration and choreography. After that we are giving and overview of the articles, which have been released about these topics in the last years. As all of these related works only cover a specific aspect of BPMN 2.0 or PASS, we tried to gather them, in order to give an overview about the deficits and advantages of both notations compared to each other[2].

2.1   Orchestration Vs. Choreography

Fleischmann [4] presented an overview about two process modeling perspectives, called orchestration and choreography, especially for BPMN 2.0. A prior but more detailed explanation of the two perspectives can be found in Weske [11].

"An orchestration[3]"represents a single, centralized, executable business process that defines an allowed sequence of operations or interactions. In service orchestration, there is a central control system which manages the execution of the defined process steps. This control system invokes the execution of all parties involved in the business process according to the allowed sequence specified in

---

[1] In this paper, by task and activity we mean the same thing, a modeled step of a process.

[2] In this paper we assume that the basics of BPMN 2.0 and PASS are known. For a detailed explanation of both languages we refer to [11] for BPMN 2.0 and [5] for PASS.

[3] In the sense that it is the result in the form of a process model that is the result of the activity of orchestrating.

the model. Orchestration does not support modeling of decentralized business processes.

When using a pool with at least one swim lane in BPMN 2.0, we are talking about orchestration. Every step has a defined input and output and there is no exchange with parties outside of the pool. This also ensures that there is only one control system, which orchestrates the execution of this business process. As the requirements to companies have seen a notable change toward more connections and interactions between different stakeholders respectively process participants, we will focus in this paper mainly on choreographies. We can assume that the requirements for more connection and interaction requires exchange with parties across pools.

A service choreography is a global description of all parties and services involved in a process. The exchange of information between participants is essential in choreography. There is no central instance that controls process execution.

BPMN 2.0 is offering different options for modeling a process with the choreography perspective. With the so-called conversation diagram the communication between participants can be modeled. Then there is the so-called choreography diagram. Instead of the conversation diagram every exchanging message between sender and receiver is modeled. Finally, also the collaboration diagram is defined as choreography. Here, several pools relate to each other via the messages they must exchange to keep the process running.

The PASS modeling language must also be seen as tool for choreography definitions, as you define the interaction between the involved subjects via an Subject Interaction Diagram (SID) and specify the behavior of each subject separately. Additionally, the activities of each in the SID defined subjects is modeled via a Subject Behavior Diagram (SBD).

So as stated and to emphasis: the collaboration diagram of BPMN 2.0 as well as the SBD of PASS can be partially seen as orchestration definitions, as at least the behavior of the defined subject respectively pool must have one control system, which manages the execution of their process.

In the next section, we give an overview about the relevant work, which is covering different aspects of our initial question.

2.2 Related Works

Moser [9] are examining the PASS approach by using it for manufacturing processes. The article examines whether PASS can support digitization in manufacturing processes by analyzing three digital transformation projects in the industry. It specifically looks at the above-mentioned process modelling requirements and includes the analysis and improvement of value streams across departments, the introduction of Automated Guided Vehicles, and the specification of a new Manufacturing Execution System. One of the used manufacturing processes of this article will serve as the main use case in this paper.

Fleischmann [4] are examining the use of BPMN 2.0 for describing cross-organizational business processes, known as choreographies, which involve interactions and coordination through message exchange.

Elstermann [2] are describing a method for modeling business process systems within an organization, which involve interconnected and related activities that form a large network or ecosystem. In this article they introduce the concept of structuring in PASS and demonstrate how it can be applied in BPMN models as well.

Elstermann [3] are reporting about a study done in an industry context to evaluate three different tools for modeling, simulating, and evaluating business processes as part of business process management and robot process automation effort. The report gives insight on pros and cons of each tool for different given circumstances in order for the reader to be able to select which tool is meeting which requirements.

Moattar [8] are providing a comparison between two approaches to business process modeling, the traditional control flow approach with BPMN 2.0 and the more recent approach of Subject-oriented Business Process Management (S-BPM) which focus on communication between process participants. The study aims to provide insights on their suitability for novice modelers.

We will investigate the findings of these use cases and studies, and try to match them with the goals of business process modeling identified before in order to conclude which modeling language fulfills them. To ensure an easy understanding of the findings, we will use one manufacturing use case as example from Moser [9].

In the next sections, we will evaluate the different modeling approaches within the context of a use case of a production facility in order to find out, which modeling approach fulfills our defined goals. We will therefore use the different choreography modeling options, conversation diagram, choreography diagram, collaboration diagram, SID and SBD.

3   Comparison via a Production Use Case

In Moser [9] 3 use-cases about using PASS for process analysis in the manufacturing and planning area domain can be found. We have chosen one of these examples as our main use case for this paper. This use case serves as our template for this paper. The use case, which was modeled by Moser [9] using PASS, is used by experienced BPMN 2.0 modelers to model it using the different BPMN 2.0 notations. Based on this, we want to contrast, review and present the findings of the existing papers with our findings.

In Moser [9] a project is described undertaken by the company ENGEL in 2016, to decrease the lead time of major components for injection molding machines by at least 30% without increasing production costs. The aim of the project was part of a larger goal to decrease overall delivery times by improving processes and utilizing existing digital solutions more efficiently. This was a complex project as the production of the main component was a cross-company process that spanned two production plants in different countries with different languages, several departments, dozens of process actors, and an IT environment. The company's digitalization strategy was to utilize existing software solutions

as efficiently as possible and keep changes within the possibilities of the organizational structure. An initial analysis revealed that approximately 95% of all
orders sent between the factories arrived too late and could not be processed
automatically, resulting in an internal delivery reliability of only 39%.

The only available description of this manufacturing process at the beginning
of the project was following:

"The main component is assembled using three sub-components (Product 1,
Product 2, and Product 3), which are produced in two production plants and
[...] the process is coordinated through production orders sent between these
plants. Incoming orders are registered in the ERP of the respective plant and
the resulting internal demand creates a production order with a corresponding
delivery date. In case that the registration process takes longer than 2 working
days (due to several varied factors), the production order will not arrive in
production on time, which in turn results in a delay of the delivery of the final
component." [9], p.5f

In the next chapter, we will look at Moser [9]'s results. As he has used PASS,
we will compare his results with the given BPMN 2.0 options by modeling this
manufacturing process with the very same.

3.1   PASS Diagrams

Moser [9] tried to improve the ordering and production process by analyzing
the communication flow via an SID as well as the activities for the process
participants via an SBD.

As we can see in this SID representing a real-life process, the interaction
between the different subjects for producing a product is already quite complex.
Nevertheless, the different stakeholders were given only a brief introduction to
PASS for process evaluation and discussions. Everyone was able to understand,
interpret, modify and verify the process models on their own. They even used
PASS as their project language, not only for their requirements but also for
IT requirements. They also mentioned that the changes of the process could
be done incrementally, as every subject is responsible for its own behavior and
knows which input and output is necessary to create.

Another advantage was the fact that they didn't have to create SBDs for all
subjects as they only looked into the behaviors of those subjects, which have
been relevant for their improvement goals. This saved a lot of time and money.
The authors showed in total 3 similar use cases, which have all shown comparable
results.

To compare PASS with BPMN 2.0, we modeled the given use case with the
usage of the conversation diagram. ·

3.2   BPMN 2.0 Conversation Diagram

On first glance, it looks like the conversation diagram can provide a better
overview of the process. But this is mainly due it simply containing much less

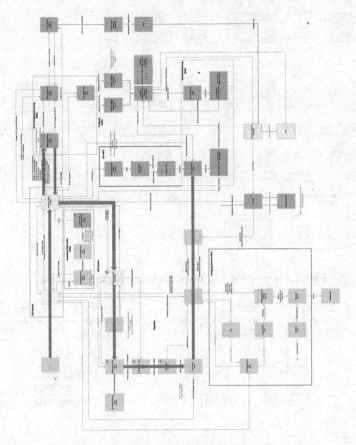

Fig. 1. Production Use Case from [9]

information. When taking a deeper look this has some drawbacks. First, we cannot see the messages which are included in the several communication packages which are defined in the original PASS model. We also cannot see the direction or number of communications which are included. Another critical point, which is mentioned in Elstermann [2], is the difficulty to recognize a hierarchical structure. Without deeper knowledge about the process itself, it would be impossible to gain a structural process overview when looking at this conversation diagram.

As we have mentioned above, one goal of Moser [9] was improving the delivery time between factories in order to increase the delivery reliability. In the SID (see Fig. 1., Christoph Moser already could mark the critical material path (see thick, blue arrows) and the entire project team was able to analyze the behavior of the involved subjects. This has not only saved time, as not every behavior of every subject had to be analyzed, but it served already the cause, by doing only

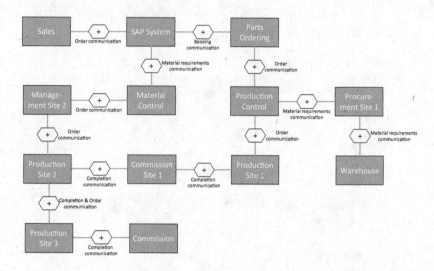

Fig. 2. Production Use Case via Conversation Diagram

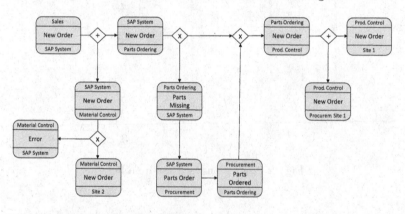

Fig. 3. Production Use Case via Choreography Diagram

one workshop together. With a conversation diagram, we would have an easy-to-understand overview without having the necessary information for planning the next steps.

Next, we tried to model the production process with the choreography diagram, as we can see in Fig. 3.

3.3   BPMN 2.0 Choreography Diagram

In contrast to the conversation diagram, where indeed the active entities are at the center, in this type of diagram it is the "processes" that are at the center with the "active entities" being only on the side of the processes.

This type of diagram provides us with more detail regarding the direction and the type of message. Nevertheless, the structure becomes more complex the more subjects are involved. As you must always define sender and receiver of a message, messages cannot be just sent back but a new shape must be created. When you compare Fig. 3 with 1 you can see that only the very first part of the process was modeled, as it already becomes almost impossible to keep the model structured.

Furthermore, as mentioned in Fleischmann [4], this type of model is also not Turing complete. This means that we can get in a situation, which cannot be solved by a computer. Let us imagine that Sales have already sent n orders, SAP has sent n-x orders to Parts Ordering and n-y orders to Material Control and Material Control have sent n-z orders. As the number of messages cannot be counted or stored, nobody knows what has been ordered and what has already been sent as soon as a new process instance is starting. This means such a model becomes very difficult to implement, when handing it over to developers as IT requirement for digitizing the information flow.

As we can see, the usage of the conversation diagram as well as the choreography diagram has some drawbacks. That is why we also created a collaboration diagram.

3.4   BPMN 2.0 Collaboration Diagram

As you can see, we have now included all information about communication and activities. Nevertheless, I only have started with a rough description of the first 6 "subjects" or rather respectively single-lane pools. The message and information flows, displayed with the dotted arrows, are already quite complex and hard to follow and messages are not named so no data is given in regards to what kind of information is actually being transmitted. As it was quite hard modeling this manufacturing process with the collaboration diagram (that is why we only modeled the behavior of the first 6 subjects), we provide in Fig. 5 a collaboration diagram of the so-called infrastructural On boarding of a medium-sized manufacturing company with approximately 12,000 employees. Therefore, we want to make sure that the only partly drawn collaboration diagram of the production use case leads to wrong conclusions.

Entire BPMN 2.0 Collaboration Diagram of a Process. With infrastructural on boarding, this company is talking about making sure that all the equipment and software accesses new employees need, is available for them on their first working day. The process starts with having the signed contract and

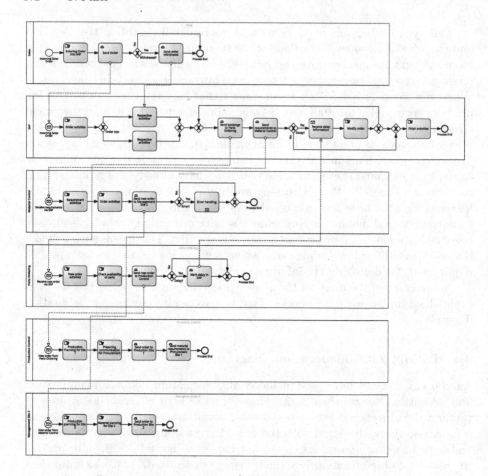

Fig. 4. Production Use Case via Collaboration Diagram

necessary information about the employee available and ends (ideally) on the first working day of the employee. As you can see, although this process is only a sub-process of the end-to-end onboarding process and only consists of 6 swim-lanes, the different message flows can only be followed when looking at it in detail. Besides that, it is not mentioned which message is actually sent. This must be assumed by reading the activity of the sender as well as receiver. That is why we conclude that it is quite difficult getting a quick overview about the process as well as following the message flow. Additionally, no exceptions are considered in this model, as the handling of exceptions with BPMN 2.0 has its drawbacks.

Exception Handling in BPMN 2.0 Collaboration Diagrams. The handling of exceptions is not done perfect. For example, if we know that inside Material Control, an error could happen, but we cannot say which impact does

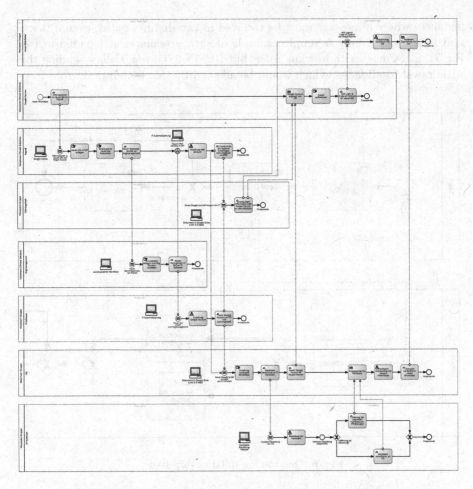

Fig. 5. Infrastructural Onboarding via Collaboration Diagram

such an error has for the other pools. Therefore, interviews with all relevant stakeholders should be done and the diagram must be changed accordingly. As all three types of diagrams in BPMN 2.0 are missing relevant information about the activities and message flows when considered on their own, we could use all three diagrams together to analyze such exceptions. This would also mean that we have to model the same process three times, which also means that we must interview all relevant stakeholders thoroughly and invest a lot of time.

Besides that, a multitude of exceptions can occur in our process system, such as the need to change a spare part order or postpone a previously agreed-upon appointment. To accurately represent these situations, it is essential to receive an event in several states. However, BPMN 2.0 enforces a one-to-one relationship between send and receive events. Consequently, a message sent in a process can only be received in one path of the receiving process. Nevertheless, there are instances where a message must be received in two distinct paths, even if it was sent in a single event. A simple example of such a scenario is depicted in (see Fig. 7). Sales must withdraw an order, but BPMN 2.0 doesn't allow sending this withdrawal to all lanes, which would be affected by this withdrawal.

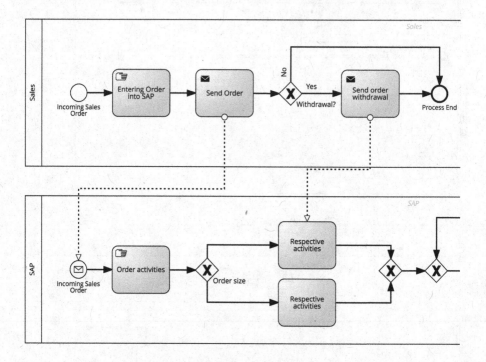

Fig. 6. One-to-One Relationship Issue

The only solution in BPMN 2.0 is creating an own order store, from which such activities, which may arrive (or not) can be handled correctly. Therefore, you must create a separate message path. This path is distributing the messages to the respective lane, when needed. This would lead to a more complex model, which makes the overview of the entire process more unclear (for a detailed analysis see [4]). One might say that we could ignore this one-to-one relationship rule and model the message flow to every affected path. But then we also must say, we don't follow the BPMN 2.0 rules or even must ask, why this rule is even in place.

3.5   Describing and Understanding the Activities in a Process

In Elstermann [3] they compared process simulation tools which are using BPMN 2.0 and PASS for modeling processes. In this use case, the management recognized that the duration of a process is much clearer, if the necessary steps are always divided to send, receive and doing something. In the classical BPMN 2.0 pool approach (one pool with several swim lanes) the duration of a process with different subjects is not always clear.

For example, if the wrong subject receives a message, they are just forwarding it to the correct subject. As we can see in Fig. 7, Sales just receives a withdrawal of an order and is forwarding the message to SAP. Sales must not only receive the withdrawal, but read and understand the withdrawal, check if the withdrawal is legally valid, look for the correct order and prepare everything for SAP, to make sure that the necessary actions in SAP and for every other stakeholder can be done correctly (see Fig. 8).

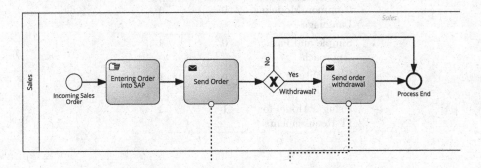

Fig. 7. Order Withdrawal via BPMN 2.0

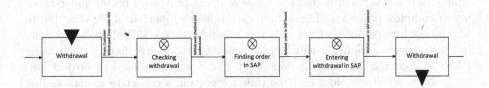

Fig. 8. Order Withdrawal via an SBD

The way of modeling behaviors always with the three activities sending, receiving and doing seems to be a more realistic. Where it must be added that also in a collaboration diagram you can model that way and this conclusion is only based on results in one paper.

After we have modeled the manufacturing with all types of BPMN 2.0 choreography models and PASS as well as analyzed the pros and cons, we are going to compare those findings with the requirements of process models in the next chapter.

4   Comparing the Findings with the BPMN Requirements

For the comparison, we created a simple table in which we used a binary system for fulfilling the specific requirement, 1, or not fulfilling it, 0. If we cannot answer this question for a specific requirement, we just us the common abbreviation n/a (not applicable). The results of our comparisons are explained in detail below the Table 1.

Table 1. Comparison Results

	BPMN 2.0	PASS
Common Modeling Language	0	1
Simple and Fast Approach	0	1
Flexibility in Modeling	n/a	n/a
Using a Model for IT Requirements	1	1

Now, let us take a look at the first goal, **using a common modeling language, to provide an understandable overview**.

Which modeling language a company is using, is their own choice. What was figured out in this paper is that the usage of PASS provides a better understanding of complex processes. These findings are also supported in Moattar [8], in which they figured out that not only is it possible to save 40% of modeling time, but also ensure a higher semantic and syntactic modeling quality, when using PASS as common language. In Moser [9], PASS was even used as project language by every stakeholder and the time for getting a collective understanding of the process has been reduced to a minimum.

This leads directly to the next goal, **a simple and fast approach for modeling**. Regarding paper [8] over 80% of all modeled processes with BPMN 2.0 are semantically and syntactically incorrect. Furthermore, there is a lot of knowledge and experience necessary, if BPMN 2.0 is the chosen modeling language. Not only can you choose between three different model types, Communication Diagram, Choreography Diagram and Collaboration Diagram, you also should know more than 100 different shapes. On the contrary, standard PASS uses only 5 different shapes and in [9] the authors mentioned that the introduction of PASS took only 10 min. In [8] the study was done with people without a BPM background. So, people with the same time of introduction to PASS and BPMN 2.0 were faster and created more correct models when using PASS.

It seems that the strict separation of interactions and behaviors and at the same time having a fixed semantic connection between SID and SBD in PASS seems to be a solution for gaining an overview about a complex process without losing important details. BPMN 2.0 tries to solve this challenge, with using only one type of diagram (collaboration diagram) for displaying interactions and behaviors. The conversation and choreography diagrams are not mandatory to use or linked to collaboration diagram. That makes them useless, as they are only showing a tiny part of the entire process. Additionally, the Turing-completeness issue of BPMN collaboration diagrams and one-to-one send to receive relationship does not occur when using PASS and makes several use cases therefore easier to model.

The next goal, **flexibility in modeling a process**, is especially important when it comes to changes and modifications of an existing model. In this case, very few papers about the handling of such circumstances when using BPMN 2.0 or PASS were found. Although the authors mentioned in [9], that for their projects, changes could be done "on-fly" and an incremental approach of process changes has been done. As such statements have not been found in other papers, a verification is still missing. Logically having the concepts of only loosely coupled subjects should make it easier when punctual changes are required as only selected SBDs or only individual 1:1 subject interactions need to be modified instead of a whole singular model.

Using a Process Model for IT Requirements Analysis and Conveying, on the other side, is simply possible with PASS. Not only are there no occurring Turing-completeness issues, but also several use cases have proven, that with PASS the necessary IT requirements could be specified. Nevertheless, also BPMN 2.0 is a valid process language for defining IT requirements, as it has not only been used for many years by many people, but also defines Input, Output, necessary activities, and objects. Related to this requirement, a survey was conducted on LinkedIn (see [7]). In this survey, 60% out of 114 of the participants mentioned that they are using a simplified BPMN 2.0 notation for modeling processes. If we assume that every process modeler has their own simplified BPMN 2.0 version, it would be even harder using it for IT requirements, as a variety of different models would be used to specify the same requirements. This makes the use of BPMN 2.0 a little bit more complex as a modeler would need to know a lot of different varieties or"dialects" of the same process notation. Contrary to this, PASS has only its five different base shapes and doesn't need any simplification.

5   Summary and Conclusion

In this paper we gathered relevant research and provided a qualitative evaluation about using an activity-oriented approach for modeling processes, BPMN 2.0, versus a subject-oriented approach, PASS. We used the findings of several papers in a cross literature study to compare them with the presented requirements for process models; provide an understandable overview, simple and fast modeling approach, flexibility in modeling a process and usage for IT system requirements. With this approach we came to following conclusions.

The research is showing that the use of PASS as a common modeling language provides a better understanding of complex processes than BPMN 2.0. Furthermore, the analysis shows clearly that processes can be modeled simpler and faster by using PASS as modeling language compared to BPMN 2.0. This conclusion leads us to following hypothesis: The use of PASS as a common modeling language results in a better understanding of complex processes, as well as a reduction in modeling time and an increase in semantic and syntactic modeling quality. Although, especially Moser [9] and Moattar [8] are supporting this hypothesis. However, we think more data is necessary to further establish this.

Additionally, we have found that PASS is better suited for specifying IT requirements, but also acknowledge that BPMN 2.0 can be used for that purpose. We also suggest that there is limited research on the flexibility of modeling processes with PASS and BPMN 2.0 and that more verification is needed. As we could not find any concrete data for the other two process modeling requirements which is fulfilled better with BPMN 2.0 or PASS, we only can recommend investigating further.

In total, we think that PASS has proven to meet the present modeling requirements better than BPMN 2.0. We even suppose that this is due to the fact that PASS is following a totally different description paradigm which makes it possible to have a strict separation of interactions and behaviors and at the same time a formal connection between them. This seems to be a solution for gaining an overview about a complex process without losing important details, compared to the three BPMN 2.0 diagram types with only informal relationships between them.

References

1. Becker, J., Kugeler, M., Rosemann, M.: Prozessmanagement. Ein Leitfaden zur prozessorientierten Organisationsgestaltung (2012)
2. Elstermann, M., Fleischmann, A.: Modeling Complex Process Systems with Subject-oriented Means. In: Proceedings of the 11th International Conference on Subject-Oriented Business Process Management, pp. 1–10 (2019)
3. Elstermann, M., Piller, C.: A Comparative Study of Simulation Tools for Business Processes. In: Subject-Oriented Business Process Management. Dynamic Digital Design of Everything-Designing or being designed? 13th International Conference on Subject-Oriented Business Process Management, S-BPM ONE 2022, Karlsruhe, Germany, June 29-July 1, 2022, Proceedings, pp. 61–78. Springer (2022)
4. Fleischmann, A.: Limitations of choreography specifications with BPMN. In: Freitag, M., Kinra, A., Kotzab, H., Kreowski, H.-J., Thoben, K.-D. (eds.) S-BPM ONE 2020. CCIS, vol. 1278, pp. 203–216. Springer, Cham (2020). https://doi.org/10.1007/978-3-030-64351-5_14
5. Fleischmann, A., Schmidt, W., Stary, C.: Subject-oriented Business Process Management. Handbook on Business Process Management 2: Strategic Alignment, Governance, People and Culture, pp. 601–621 (2015)
6. Kannengiesser, U., Müller, H.: Industry 4.0 Standardisation: Where Does S-BPM Fit? In: Proceedings of the 10th International Conference on Subject-Oriented Business Process Management, pp. 1–8 (2018)

7. Kloppenburg, M.: Are you modeling processes by using the full bpmn 2.0 notation with all its gateways, events, and artifacts etc.? https://www.linkedin.com/posts/mirkokloppenburg_bpm-bpmn-processmodeling-activity-7013565412588036096-1PbI (2023). Accessed 24 Jan 2023, Published: 2023-01-03

8. Moattar, H., Bandara, W., Kannengiesser, U., Rosemann, M.: Control flow versus communication: comparing two approaches to process modelling. Bus. Process Manage. J. **28**(2), 372–397 (2022)

9. Moser, C., Kannengiesser, U., Elstermann, M.: Examining the PASS approach to process modelling for digitalised manufacturing: results from three industry case studies. Enterprise Modell. Inform. Syst. Architect. (EMISAJ) **17**, 1–24 (2022)

10. Schmelzer, H.J., Sesselmann, W.: Geschäftsprozessmanagement in der Praxis: Kunden zufrieden stellen-Produktivität steigern-Wert erhöhen. Carl Hanser Verlag GmbH Co KG (2020)

11. Weske, Mathias: Business process management architectures. In: Business Process Management, pp. 351–384. Springer, Heidelberg (2019). https://doi.org/10.1007/978-3-662-59432-2_8

Modelability of Agile Development Projects - An Assessment of the Opportunities and Limitations of BPMN and S-BPM

Matthias Lederer[1]([✉]), Stefanie Betz[2,5], Werner Schmidt[3],
and Matthes Elstermann[4]

[1] OTH, Amberg-Weiden, Germany
ma.lederer@oth-aw.de
[2] Hochschule Furtwangen, Furtwangen, Germany
besi@hs-furtwangen.de
[3] TH Ingolstadt, Ingolstadt, Germany
werner.schmidt@thi.de
[4] Karlsruhe Institute of Technology, Karlsruhe, Germany
matthes.elstermann@kit.de
[5] Lappeenranta-Lahti University of Technology LUT, Lappeenranta, Finland
stefanie.betz@lut.fi

Abstract. Modelability of processes is a recognized and important characteristic of any modeling language. Nevertheless, it is not always purposeful or easy to create process models for every kind of workflow. This article discusses the opportunities and limitations of modeling agile development projects with SCRUM as an example. For this purpose, a BPMN and an S-BPM model for SCRUM are presented. The discussion along recognized rules for good process models shows that both notations provide possible and accurate insights into the process of SCRUM on the one hand. On the other hand, the models raise questions of necessity, added value, and relevance in practice. Practitioners can use the developed models to technically implement agile project management, while researchers benefit from a discourse on opportunities and limitations of modeling agility.

Keywords: S-BPM · Subject Orientation · BPMN · Business Process Model

1 Motivation

The basic idea behind any kind of process model is to convey information about the execution of a set of tasks and events following certain rules to achieve a particular goal. A process model is always an abstraction of reality. What makes a model a high quality model? There are some quality attributes that are usually

© The Author(s), under exclusive license to Springer Nature Switzerland AG 2023
M. Elstermann et al. (Eds.): S-BPM ONE 2023, CCIS 1867, pp. 180–186, 2023.
https://doi.org/10.1007/978-3-031-40213-5_13

applied, but sometimes difficult to asses such as: consistency of the model, completeness, non-redundancy, the model should be changeable and corresponding to the original ("valid"), it can be displayed at different levels of accuracy and it can be presented from different perspectives. However, the quality attributes differ and have a different weighting depending on the purpose of the model and the chosen modeling notation, e.g. if the process model is to be automated, accuracy is more important than that the ability to present aspects from different perspectives.

Now, the preceding paragraph sets the premise of this work, where we investigate of how process models differ conceptually depending on a chosen modeling language but given the same particular purpose (process models for agile projects). Additionally, we investigate whether the effort of creating detailed, formal industrial process models for agile projects is worth the efforts in comparison to the already existing process models that are complemented by textual descriptions (see figure for example 1).

2   Describing SCRUM

The scenario that we have chosen for this comparison is the domain of *Agile Development* processes with the relatively well known agile development methodology of SCRUM based on the works of Schwaber and Sutherland [5].

As part of this research, we created and compared two different process models depicting of this agile development process. Next to the classical depiction or approach to describing SCRUM, we used the industry standard of the Business Process Model and Notation (BPMN) and the subject-oriented process modeling language Parallel Activity Specification Schema (PASS). The reason for the latter is its subject-oriented modeling paradigm. Thus, the resulting model is quite different from the BPMN model (that serves as a stand-in for all "similar" classical modeling approaches).

2.1   The Classical Idea of SCRUM

The SCRUM concept provides three basic roles: The *Product Owner* represents the stakeholders/the customers. The product owner translates their needs and requirements into a definition of goals and deliverables that are held in a *product backlog.* He later on evaluates delivered increments and thus takes responsibility that the product creates value for the target group. The *Development Team* does the actual work and develops the product in iterative sprints where at the end a deliverables should be ready. The *SCRUM Master* guides the development team as a facilitator, assures that the team adheres to the agile framework and helps overcoming obstacles. Her or his responsibility includes moderating sprint planning (backlog) and stand-up meetings, conducting retrospectives etc. Neither Product Owner nor Scrum Master have the same role as a classical project manager.

Their interaction and the overall SCRUM process is classical depicted in a manner similar to Fig. 1.

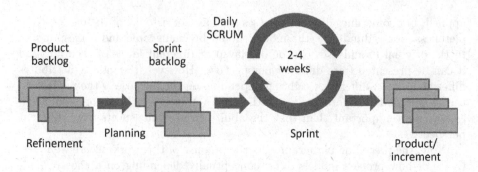

Fig. 1. Standard SCRUM process depiction (informal) - based on [5]

2.2   A BPMN Model of SCRUM

As discussed, the first model to be discussed was realized with BPMN. The starting point was the three basic SCRUM roles, each forming a swim lane. At the
highest level of abstraction (see Fig. 2), each SCRUM event fundamentally represents an activity. The description of goals (e.g. as a backlog) is then followed
by the actual development, which is repeated several times in sprints. This is
described by grouping the three central tasks of (1) sprint planning, (2) realization and (3) review with retrospective in the model. Within the activities, which
are carried out until a marketable product has been created or the customer's
budget has been used up, there are of course manifold tasks to be done. This
concerns, for example, the assignment of tasks or the configuration and actual
coding.

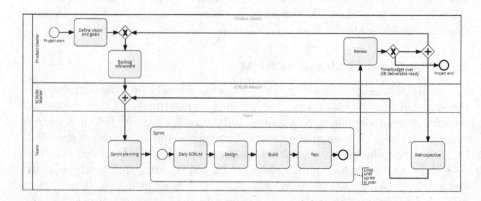

Fig. 2. BPMN Diagram (control flow-oriented)

It is noticeable in the model that not every essential role has an assigned
activity in the control flow. The SCRIM Master causes some difficulties in the
process models because the role's task is to ensure the Scrum framework (e.g.,

support in the rules and practices) and ensure and promote the other activities (e.g., remove obstacles, resolve conflicts within the team). Exactly here one sees the problem of the meaningful modelability of SCRUM: This phased work of the SCRUM Master accompanies the other tasks, but is not on the control flow in the sense of the BPMN model. One possibility would be to map the tasks as variants in the process. However, this would mainly concern exceptions or complicate the model too blatantly. The SCRUM master thus remains without an explicitly modeled task - a realization that shows the limits of BPMN.

2.3 A PASS Model for SCRUM

Figure 3 shows a so-called subject interaction diagram (SID) of a subject-oriented process description for SCRUM. It defines all active roles in the process (the subjects) and what kind of messages they exchange (objects), but not in what order the exchange takes place. Due to the limits of this format, the corresponding subject behavior diagrams (SBDs) belonging to the individual subject are not shown.

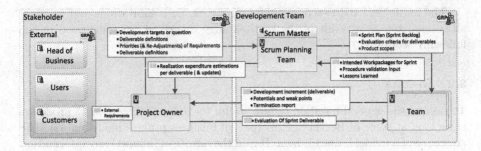

Fig. 3. PASS Interaction Diagram (subject-oriented)

What can be seen is that especially the role of SCRUM Master actually has no project-related interaction with the others. Officially his or her role is to facilitate that joint planning and other SCRUM rituals take place and that the general rules of interaction are adhered to[1]. But the actual activities are conducted jointly by the persons filling out the Product Owner role and the people that comprise the actual Development Team. This joint activity is done by a SCRUM Planning Team subject witch is a pass concept to model e.g. trilateral communication. All typical meetings are between the team and project owner and they have to come to an agreement on how to proceed for the next sprint.

---

[1] the Product Owner is not in the position to *demand* certain steps.

3   Challenges for Describing and Understanding

3.1   Method

To reach an interpretation of the value of the two models, a triangulation in the specific form of an investigator triangulation was performed [1,3,4]. In this method, several researchers investigate the same artifact in different profile analysis and compare their results in a discussion. This discussion was guided by the accepted "principles of proper modeling" by [3] because they are (a) recognized in the BPM discipline and (b) represent a wise balance between formal and practical orientation, which fits to the purpose of the paper. Furthermore, (c) these rules are open enough to be discussed in principle, but concrete enough to focus on the value of the models (see introduction). In this contribution, four experienced (S-)BPM researchers first openly discussed the two models. Second, each model was first interpreted textually by an expert based on the discussion and his/her analytical profile. Third, the preliminary considerations were presented in turn to each of the other three experts and, after a revised interpretation, were refined step by step until there were no major discrepancies in the textual evaluation.

The findings of the two modeling approaches, their limitations and an overall comparison as a result of the methodology described is summarized in the following section.

3.2   Results

To discuss the general question of how useful formal modeling of agile processes is we look at some of Becker's 'Principles of business process modeling' [3]. The *relevance* of a model is one of them. It is in the nature of (almost) any information model that full completeness cannot be achieved. Omitting, simplifying, generalizing or summarizing aspects of reality provides understanding and increases the relevance of the model. According to this principle, models are to be designed in such a way that only facts are modeled that are useful for the purpose. For the BPMN modeling of the agile approach, the relevance is mainly a question of the importance of the model contents in a certain context: (1) If one summarizes the agile approach (see Fig. 1) as a few activities in a very rough way, the contents with phases, events, roles and tasks are correct, but at the same time trivial. There is no significant advantage to general SCRUM diagrams, as they can be found en masse in books or on the web. The relevance of this representation must therefore be denied, because these models are not very suitable for training or demonstrating the procedure. (2) If, on the other hand, all contents (phases, events, roles and tasks) are represented in a more fine-grained way, many activities result (or even sub-tasks, just think of the various steps of testing as little part of the developer tasks). Such a detailed level of process modeling meets the requirement of the principle as the model depicts what actually occurs in the original flow. However, according to the agile manifesto, the focus is on people and not on rigid and detailed processes - therefore, stakeholders do not need detailed models. Unfortunately, the aspect of executability of detailed BPMN models does not lead to any further relevant advantage, because human processes are in focus. This is true in agile development even if parts of the process are certainly further automated.

At the bottom line the main criticism regarding relevance in BPMN models is that no suitable level of granularity can be found. This is mainly due to the fact that the activity-based view on models allows a too coarse or too detailed view of SCRUM. The presented subject-oriented diagram as communication-based alternative focuses on the roles defined according to the standard as subjects and describes their interaction. (1) If one takes a human-centered view, the behavior of the subjects is encapsulated. Thus, depending on the need for support, detailing within the subjects is possible as long as it serves relevance. Too coarse and too fine granular models are avoided. Instead of being passive elements as in the BPMN model, roles become active entities as subjects that synchronize their tasks. This corresponds to the agile manifesto with focus on people instead of following a rigid process. In the last consequence this holistic synchronization of tasks done by different actors (e.g. in the Daily SCRUMs) follows the flexible working in a self-organized team via communication. (2) From a technical point of view, the detailed BPMN model has the advantage of many events available to monitor and learn (think of project mining). This drives the relevance of the model to increase maturity. However, the communication-oriented view of the S-BPM model can also provide this data set. In addition, the advantage arises that instead of the sequential process, which probably corresponds little to reality in SCRUM, now many parallel works become possible and basically measurable. Both views combined, the S-BPM model does better adhered to the principle of relevance than its brother model in BPMN due to its fundamental adaptability to reality.

To discuss the question of whether formal procedural models generate added value for agile software development, we draw on *economic efficiency* as another principle of proper modeling according to [3]. The principle of economic efficiency in business process modeling aims at the optimal use of resources. According to the minimum principle, the desired purpose of the modeling should be achieved with minimal effort. The modeling purpose can include documentation, creation of transparency and communication basis for process (re-)design and implementation of IT-supported workflows. The level of detail required for modeling depends on the purpose. More detail typically requires more effort to collect, document, and further use information about the objects and issues being mapped. The effort involved is only justified if it is necessary to achieve the modeling purpose. This means that the marginal benefits of (additional) modeling activities must exceed their marginal costs. With this in mind, let us consider the modeling purposes mentioned above. The visualization of agile procedures is not very complex. Experiences from practice and university teaching show that simple overview images, such as those for SCRUM being available on the Internet, are sufficient for explanation and understanding (see 1). No formal notation is necessary for the representation of elements, artifacts, course of action and the roles involved. The question remains whether the purpose of implementing existing frameworks for agile software development as a workflow justifies formal modeling. Communication and collaboration tools support project participants in the application and design of frameworks such as SCRUM or Kanban in practice. The combination of Confluence and Jira from Atlassian can serve as an example [2]. Agile projects can be efficiently managed there, for example with templates for SCRUM and Kanban and the automation of steps. The 'on-board tools' of the software with constructs for specifying processes in a no-code environment are sufficient for this. Users can implement agile procedures relatively easy and without in-depth knowledge of methods and notation. Formal process models written in a process description language such as BPMN, which are then executed by a workflow engine, are not required for this.

Summoning the presented thoughts on the principle of economic efficiency, formal modeling of agile procedures does not generate added value. It would rather be economically inefficient. Hence, here the question of which formal modeling language or paradigm suits better is not relevant.

4   Summary and Outlook

In this paper we have investigated if an industrial process depicted by a (semi-) formal process model is "useful". We did so by comparing a models in PASS and one BPMN 2.0 and discussing their relevance and added value. Overall, we deducted that in both cases and even with different description paradigms behind them, developing such a model might not be worth it as it does not really add value, especially in comparison to existing models. However, if a company thinks it is worth it, e.g. for benchmarking or better reuse, then we recommend to use PASS as the modeling language as it enables the modeler to better adapt to reality. However, the presented work is only a theoretical comparison based on two models with their own deficiencies. Therefore, further research is needed. For example, an evaluation of the models and their impact on understanding in the field.

References

1. Archibald, M.M.: Investigator triangulation: a collaborative strategy with potential for mixed methods research. J. Mixed Methods Res. **10**(3) (2015)
2. Atlassian: https://www.atlassian.com/de/agile/tutorials/how-to-do-scrum-with-jira-software Accessed 3 Feb 2023
3. Becker, J., Rosemann, M., von Uthmann, C.: Guidelines of business process modeling. In: van der Aalst, W., Desel, J., Oberweis, A. (eds.) Business Process Management. LNCS, vol. 1806, pp. 30–49. Springer, Heidelberg (2000). https://doi.org/10.1007/3-540-45594-9_3
4. Denzin, N.K.: The research act. Routledge (Jul 2017)
5. Schwaber, K., Sutherland, J.: The scrum guide. Scrum Alliance **21**(1), 1–38 (2011)

Proposal for a Recursive Interpreter Specification for PASS in PASS

Matthes Elstermann[✉]

Karlsruhe Institute of Technology, Karlsruhe, Germany
matthes.elstermann@kit.edu

Abstract. While there does exist a formal interpreter specification for the subject-oriented process modeling language that is the Parallel Activity Specification Schema (PASS), the existing spec is somewhat out-of-date and does not cover every aspect of current PASS. This work analyzes the shortcomings of the existing specification and furthermore contains a new interpreter specification that does fill the gaps. This new interpreter model is written in PASS itself thus forming a recursive definition upon itself (using PASS to specify PASS). Next to covering the gaps, the main benefit of this approach is its much more easy accessibility and understandability.

Keywords: S-BPM · Subject-Orientation · PASS · interpreter specification

1 Motivation

The Parallel Activity Specification Schema (PASS), as conceptualized by Fleischmann [15,16], is currently still the sole explicitly subject-oriented[1] process modeling language in existence.

The claims regarding PASS are, that it is a formal and executable language. For that regard, over the last decade several specifications have been created in combination to form the formal basis for PASS as detailed in [10] and [12].

One of those is a structural description using the Web Ontology Language (OWL) to define the syntactical rules of PASS models with the main goal of having an formal exchange standard for PASS. It is based one the works of [4] and [5] and has been optimized by a community effort over the last years (e.g. [11]. It is available in its current version at [17].

The second specification uses the Abstract State Machines (ASM) formalism[2] to define an interpreting machine for a single Subject Behavior Diagram (SBD) of standard PASS. It was created by Egon Börger and published

---

[1] Note that for this work the reader is required to have a sufficient understanding of the subject-oriented paradigm as well as the fundamentals of the various elements of PASS with its SIDs and SBDs. If that knowledge is not available, we would kindly refer the reader to sources such as the aforementioned [16] or [13] for prior reading.

© The Author(s), under exclusive license to Springer Nature Switzerland AG 2023
M. Elstermann et al. (Eds.): S-BPM ONE 2023, CCIS 1867, pp. 187–201, 2023.
https://doi.org/10.1007/978-3-031-40213-5_14

in [14] over a decade ago. This specification has remained the official definition for the execution semantics of PASS and is also the basis for a reference implementation by Wolski [18].

However, this Börger-Interpreter is limited in several regards and not necessarily up to-date, as will be discussed in the following Sect. 2. From those limitations stems the need and thus the motivation for an updated interpreter specification that is defining all aspects for the execution of modern PASS.

2   Analysis of the Börger ASM Interpreter Spec

As stated in the previous section, the main disadvantage of the original Börger interpreter is that it is not up to date with current development in wording and conceptualization of research in Subject-Orientation and the Parallel Activity Specification Schema (PASS)—the main reason for that being obviously that the Börger interpreter was created in 2011 and was based on the proprietary PASS concept of the Metasonic AG, while the current official PASS standard with OWL specification was defined starting in 2018 with the need of modelers in mind.

The following sub-sections detail what is missing:

Multiple Behaviors: First and foremost, the Börger Interpreter considers only the interpretation of single behavior graphs (single SBDs) for each subject. While that is sufficient for simple PASS models, the current understanding of PASS considers models where subjects can be linked to multiple behaviors at once. Next to "simple" *Extension Behaviors* , there are *Macro* and **Guard** Behaviors. While especially the last two concepts existed already in 2012, their explicit existence as separate model elements did not.

Now Extensions and Macros could actually be handled via graph-substitution (integrating or merging their graphs into the *Base Behavior*). However, a specification for such a mechanism, defining how or when that would take place, does not exist.

Even more diverging are *Guard Behaviors*. The Börger spec contains a so called *Interrupt* handling mechanism that seems to work outside the definitions of a PASS model that is supposedly being interpreted. The interrupt (now guard) is not a mechanism that is defined in a PASS model but something that the interpreter needs to know beforehand. How this is related to specified Guard Behaviors is unclear. This is even more the case, when, instead of going to a specific state, an interrupt behavior defines that, after the interrupt behavior has finished, normal behavior execution should resume where left before the interrupt was triggered.

In any case, an interpreter for models with multi-behavior subjects is needed.

Unspecified Elements: The next aspect that the Börger Interpreter does not embrace are certain advanced PASS model elements that exist in the OWL spec. Those are: *Time-out Transitions, Timer-Transitions, Sending-Failed transition,*

User-Cancel Transitions and especially the *Choice Segment* with its variable *Choice Segment Paths*.

Some of these could be somewhat substituted. E.g. in time-out transitions originating from receive states the time-out can be interpreted as another message arriving from an implicitly defined timer-subject. However, Time-out originating from Do-States, or Send-States with Sending-Failed or User-Cancel-transition do not posses equally simple PASS substitutions that would run on the Börger Interpreter.

And the concepts of Timer-Transitions, that allows to specify and iteration interval or general calendar-based time events, did not even exist when the Börger Spec was created and therefore could not be covered.

Finally, the Choice-Segment, especially with choice segment paths with more than one state is the hardest element to be handled. The Börger interpreter would only be able to cope with it, if a choice segment was to be transformed into a sequence of path-sections where after executing all states in one section, the user could choose how to continue. However, such a substitution approach would not enable the handling of choice segments that is actually envisioned, where an external user can switch between all path-behaviors individually at all times, no matter how much the execution of each path behavior has progressed.

Interaction with the Environment: This aspect is somewhat debatable, depending how much the ASM approach of the Börger Interpreter is embraced. Being completely abstract and function oriented, the ASM interpreter kind of leaves out many aspects of relevance that would play a major role in an implementation. Some of these omissions are justified, but some also could be argued to be crucial for the execution of PASS. The, already-mentioned, handling of multi-behavior models by the execution entity is one of those. Furthermore, finding corresponding subject instances, especially if those instances are hosted on distributed engines, and aspects like routing, new subject-instantiation, or address resolving also belong to this category of limitations to the Börger Interpreter.

Function Calls: The next consideration and somewhat linked to the previous one is that of external function calls. PASS models allow for each state to specify a function call outside of the interpreter engine. This maybe the case, e.g., if a Do-State requires a web-service call or some operating system setting to change. For the ASM approach this simply is another function execution to be specified in a refinement model and a model may contain such refinements. However this is a little bit more complex since, as stated, a function call is directed to the outside of the jurisdiction of the workflow engine and may not only take a few millisecond, but potentially could last minuets or hours. Depending on the implementing technology and software-nature of the called function, its behavior might vary vastly, especially in interaction with the interpreter engine. For this work, four different principle *function call modes* have been identified (that are not covered by the Börger spec):

- "blocking": a call that basically stops the execution of the interpreter until the function returns something
- "fire-and-forget": the function call does not impact the behavior execution
- "cancel only": the interpreter engine is allowed to, but also supposed to stop a function call if the calling state is left due to interrupts or time-outs
- "interruptable": The interpreter can not only terminate the external function execution but also interrupt and resume it later if necessary—thus tightly binding this type of function call to the execution of the interpreter spec.

Nice to Have: Being very abstract, the Börger spec is not per-se incompatible with a few further aspects that, however, have not been defined clearly.

One aspect that would be nice to have, is the ability for an interpreter to allow ad-hoc model extensions during the interpretation of a model, thus giving greater flexibility upon execution. This is necessary for cases where a process instance may be executed not for minuets or hours, but months or even years and the underlying model would need the change to cope with external events, without the need to restart or reset the process instance. The PASS OWL specification knows the concept of *"Extension Behaviors"*. However as previously discussed, with the Börger Interpreter they could only be incorporated if the extension behavior is merged with the original model's base behavior, thus implying the requirement that a new, merged model would need to replace the original model during executing (for which no mechanism is defined).

Vocabulary: Finally, as already discussed in [10], the wording used in the Börger ASM spec is outdated as it was created before standardization and uses older variants of terms and naming.

To quote: [10] speaks of an *"indiscriminate and somewhat erroneous usage of the term S-BPM throughout the whole specification without any explicit mentioning of the actual term PASS"* and that there are names and a few other examples for older terms such as *"Function-State"* (now *"Do-State"*) or *"External Subject"* (now *"Interface Subject"*). Other terms like *"Guards"* (most likely interrupts), or the already mentioned time-based transitions also do not appear.

This aspect does not have impact on the correctness or functionality of the interpreter, but somewhat hinders comprehension and understanding and an updated specification that is more in-tune with the current wording would be very useful.

3   Methods and Concepts

The previous section derived a need for at least an updated interpreter specification for the execution of PASS. The following work is the result of an effort to remedy that situation. However, the presented interpreter specification diverges conceptually from the original ASM approach. The following sections highlight and discusses the most important aspects necessary to understand the model.

3.1   Using PASS for PASS

The Parallel Activity Specification Schema is explicitly intended to describe, well, parallel activities of *Distributed Systems* [15]. With its formal nature and its potential advantages for the conceptualization of information systems (see [8]), it is a seemingly an obvious conclusion to use PASS for the specification of an interpreter for PASS itself. As is demonstrated by the later model, such a description is much easier to comprehend as it is much less abstract. Also, following the general idea of subject-orientation, it should be much simpler to understanding a PASS interpreter as set of different interacting, active entities, instead of the more abstract mathematical understanding of intertwined functions when using something like the ASM approach.

3.2   The Arbitrator Pattern

As stated in Sect. 2, modern PASS models may contain subjects with multiple behavior graphs (SBDs) of different types. Instead of proposing a merging mechanism for multiple behaviors, the approach followed for this work is explicitly intend to handle multiple behaviors.

The so-called *Arbitrator Pattern* was first sketched out and explored for the execution of PASS in [9]. The base idea implored is that of an arbitrating instance (the Arbitrator) that evaluates the priority of multiple behaviors and (arbitrarily) gives control to one of them at a given moment. In order to gain execution rights, a behavior must be eligible to be executed and needs to have the highest execution priority. The concept stems from robotics research in the late 1980s s and 90s and its original author advised against using it anywhere else but robotics[1]. However, as described in [9], it is actually quite fitting for multi-behavior subject interpretation, where the executed behavior does not gain control over some sensors or motors as it would be the case for robots, but rather control over the sending and receive functions of its subject-instance. This mechanism allows for great flexibility during execution and enables previously mentioned concept such as Macro-calls, Guard-interrupts, Choice-Segment handling, and also ad-hoc extensions, as will be seen in the actual model.

The right part of Fig. 1 sketches the concept of multiple behavior layers within a subject instance with different execution priorities that are part of a *"stack of behaviors"*. Additionally, a subject instance possesses the facilities to send and receive messages (e.g. the input pool) as well as data storage capacities.

A behavior is supposed to be executable if the official current state is defined in its SBD-graph and/or if certain other conditions are met—e.g. if the interrupt message that is received in a guard receive state is in the inbox. Conceptually, this implicates that it may be the case that more than one behavior could be executed at a given moment so the arbitrator has to choose one.

3.3   Complex State Concept

Ideally, a subject is in exactly one state at one time. For a simple PASS model with single SBDs per subject this is always the case. However, there are several concepts in modern, multi-behavior PASS that require a more complex notion. Namely the concept of the "Return to Origin" reference that could appear in Guards or Macros. This is made even more complex with Choice Segment Paths and how to handle them.

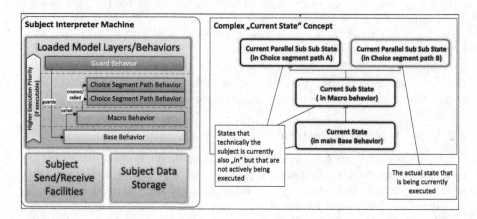

Fig. 1. Sketches for Multi-Behavior Priority Execution (Left) and Complex State (right) Concepts

The scenario indicated in Fig. 1 illustrates that point: The idea is that there is Macro Behavior that was called from one state of the base behavior. However, the Macro Behavior contains a Choice Segment with two paths of which only one contains the state that is actually being executed.

Now with a simple notion of state, if an interrupt message would be received and the question would be whether the Guard that guards the Base Behaviors should be triggered, the answer would be 'no' as the we are currently in a state that is not a part of the guarded base behavior. With a more complex concept, indicated by the tree structure, the answer would be 'yes' since a subject is 'in' all depicted states or 'sub states' at the same time—while only one state is actually being executed.

This concept is also important for the "Return to Origin" reference in Guards or Macros where there needs to be some note of which state was active before a Macro call or especially before a Guard was triggered and execution "jumped". With the more complex state concept depicted here, that is no problem.

4   The Recursive PASS Interpreter Specification

Note: With PASS being first and foremost a graphical modeling language and its execution being non-trivial, the resulting model is rather extensive. As consequence of that and the limits of a paper format, the presented figures (after reh bibliography) are not intended to be read in a printed version of this work.

In a digital version of this paper, the presentation still may not be ideal, but the figures should be zoomable. For reference the model itself is also published and available at [3].

Second Note: Also for printing reasons, base behaviors are shown seemingly integrated with their guard behavior(s) without a clear distinction between. In the actual model, the guard behaviors are not directly part of the same graph.

4.1   Subject Interaction

The interpreter specification's subject interaction diagram of Fig. 5 shows all active entities necessary for executing one subject instance with multiple behaviors. In addition to the central "Arbitrator" subject and the stack of multiple

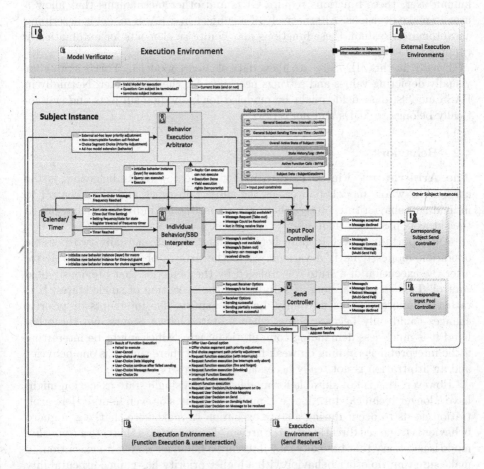

Fig. 2. SBD for the Arbitrator Subject from Fig. 5 - Shown is the base behavior and three Guard Behaviors

behaviors interpreters, there is a calendar subject to handle function in regards to time-out and timer transitions, as well as separate subjects for send and receive functionalities.

The central group interacts with several entities that are all part of the technical execution environment in which such a subject interpreter necessarily will be running.

It was decided to separate the execution environment into three different sub-task areas to better differentiate the various technical functions that the execution environment needs to provide to a subject instance. Next to the general control functions, these are support for finding a target subject instance for sending messages to (possibly existing within a separate execution environment) and secondly functions that are necessary to interact with a *subject carrier* or to handle external function calls. As can be seen from the number of messages to and from it, especially the last aspect is rather important. In a case of a human user, these functions require GUIs and other mechanisms that allow a user to make decisions. Alternatively, if a subject in a PASS model is describing an automated system, these functions may comprise elements for automatically running the subject.

Finally, in this SID there are a few data elements modeled. This is simply for visually depicting values and settings necessary for the interpreter. Normally in PASS models, data fields might be modeled for individual subjects and syntactically belongs to SBDs and not on SIDs.

4.2   Behaviors

The Arbitrator - Fig. 2: The Arbitrator subject with its behaviors is the core of the whole model. It oversees the subject instance and gives control to individual behavior interpreters that are responsible for individual behaviors (if the subjects has more than one).

An important aspect to note here is, that there are actually two possible operation modes. One is a variant where the arbitrator only becomes active after the execution of a state was finished by the behavior that previously held control. This *step-wise* mode is suitable for the execution of single states. It is rather atomic and lacks flexibility, because aspects like interrupts or priority changes could only become active when a state change occurs. On the other hand it is much less demanding computational wise which might be interesting if the interpreter is running on weak hardware or if there simply is one behavior and an arbitration is not really necessary (no guards or macros).

However, this is not suitable for models where a single state execution might have a longer technical duration (e.g. multiple minuets or even hours). Here arbitration needs to occur during a state execution to make sure that, e.g. a guard behavior is triggered directly after the arrival of a message. In this case a *time-slice* mode is necessary that basically may interrupt a behavior mid-state-execution, to make sure that no other behavior with a higher priority has gained executability in the mean time. The duration of a time slice depends on an environment setting and may vary depending on the given hardware and use-case.

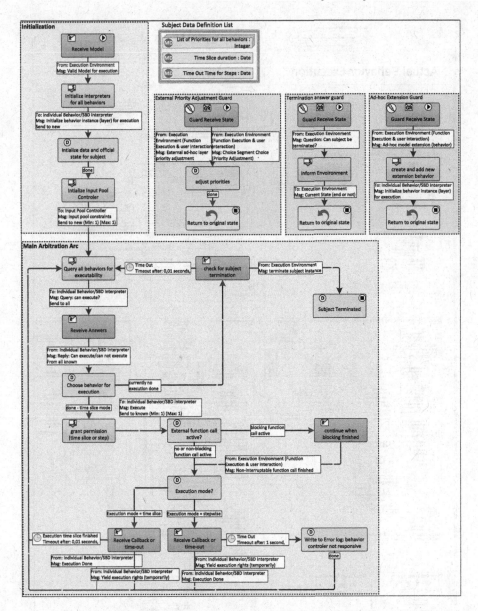

Fig. 3. SBDs for the SBD Interpreter Subject from Fig. 5 - Shown is the base behavior and four Guard Behaviors. (Zoom in digital version)

Individual Behavior Interpreter - Fig. 3: This subject is the actual PASS SBD interpreter. As shown in the SID (Fig. 5) the Individual Behavior Interpreter is a multi-subject, meaning that each behavior-graph has its individual instance of this behavior. Interactions with the arbitrator are outsourced to

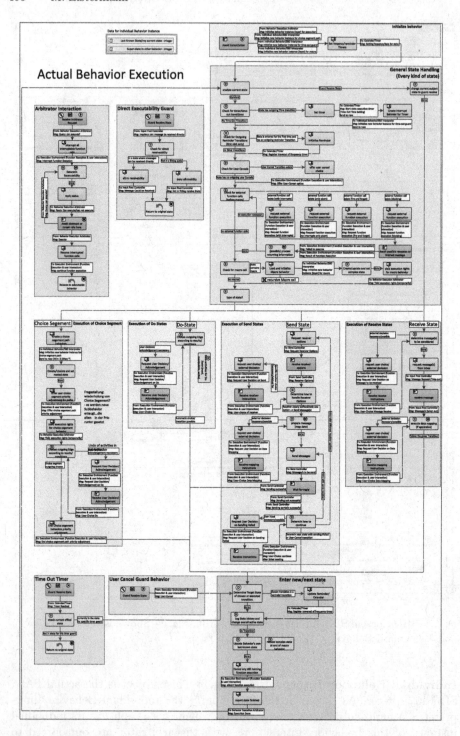

Fig. 4. Additional Macro Behavior called in *Determine Excitability*-State in one of the Guard Behaviors of Fig. 3

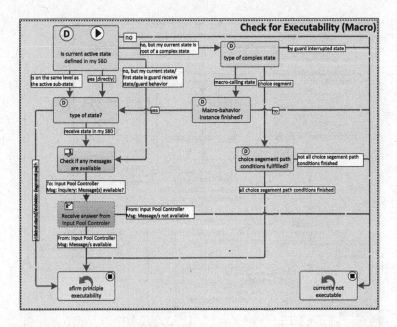

Fig. 5. SID of Recursive PASS Interpreter Spec defining all activate elements active as part of a Subject Instance executing on model

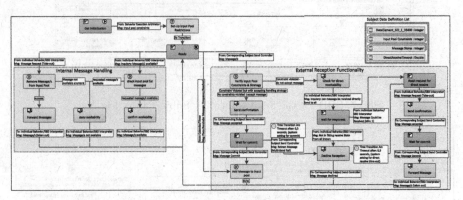

Fig. 6. SBD for the Input Pool Controller Subject from Fig. 5

Guard Behaviors (the upper right including a macro call that contains the actual check for executability shown in Fig. 4). Consequently, the actual main behavioral loop is expected to run continuously, differing in the middle between the type of state including a special consideration of the choice segment.

Input Pool Controller - Fig. 6: The Input Pool Controller serves two different purposes. The function loop depicted on the left side is about the interaction with the individual behavior interpreter instances and informing them about the

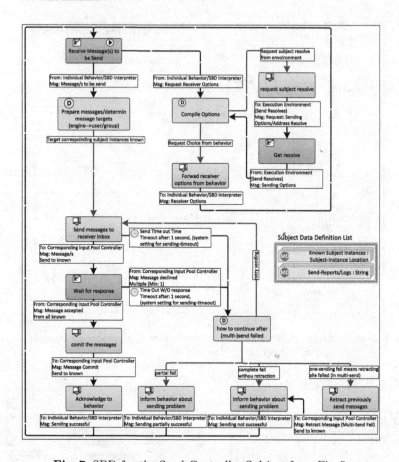

Fig. 7. SBD for the Send Controller Subject from Fig. 5

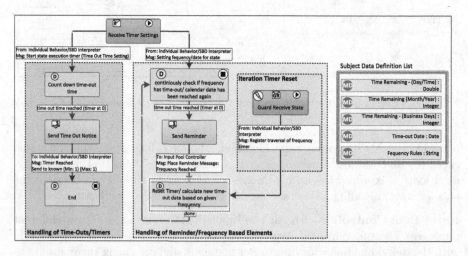

Fig. 8. SBD for the Calendar/Timer Subject from Fig. 5 + one Guard Behavior

availability of messages or, upon request, removing message from the input pool and forwarding them to the requesting behavior.

The second purpose on the right is to interact with an external sending subject and facilitate the actual reception or possible decline of messages, including the evaluation of the input pool constraints and execution of according handling rules.

Send Controller - Fig. 7: The Send Controller is one of the simplest subjects in this model and does not even contain a guard behavior. It simply describes the activities necessary to interact with the Input Pool Controller of another subject. The only complication in this behavior stems from the concept of sending messages to multi-subjects, where there may be the case that not all message are accepted and consequently, depending on the send setting, may require to retract the messages from the subjects that already received their message version.

Calendar/Timer - Fig. 8: The timer or calendar subject is also kept relatively simple. Its main feature is the two different strands of possible activities that actually are quite different. The left one is straight forward and depicts simple time-outs. Instance of behaviors going down this path are created whenever the execution of a state with a time-out transition is started and requires time to wait and send an according time-out message at the correct time. The right path is more complex and describes the handling of Timer-transitions that may be repeating.

5   Verification/Validation

Due to this nature of this work, there are limits to its verification or validation.

The model was created based on all available material on PASS execution machines as well as extensive experience on the topic as well es exchange over the previous years with other experts on the topic.

The formal method was to use the Simple Simulation (SiSi) tool for PASS [7] built into the editor, to systematically verify the syntactical coherency during creation, which was successful and the model is syntactically sound.

6   Conclusion and Outlook

The presented model was created due to identified gaps left by previous formal specifications for PASS that predate the standardization efforts of the last years. The model is syntactical coherent and does cover all relevant aspects of the only subject-oriented process modeling language in existence.

However, to further test and evaluate the model, the next step would be to use it as a basis of a development effort for the creation of an actual PASS program/work-flow engine that is actually able to execute PASS models.

Until then, this work, at very least, serves as a supplement to the original Börger specification that should be much more accessible due to being written in

PASS itself and therefor can help interested parties to understand this execution concept behind PASS much more easily.

Furthermore, this is only an interpreter specification for imperative PASS, where imperative-style process modeling is a rather rigid, classical approach to describing processes. The alternative to that is an abstract or declarative style, that offers much more flexibility, especially for execution. With the Abstract Layered PASS (ALPS) [6] concept, this style of process description does exist in the domain of PASS and subject-orientation. ALPS is a declarative modeling concept with two different usage scenarios. The first is its usage as a mechanisms that allows to define standard PASS models to implement or adhere to the declarative specification ALPS process model. Here tools exist. However, the second usage scenarios is that of direct execution of the declarative, and thereby less restricted or incomplete process models. For other, non-subject-oriented declarative modeling approaches this direct execution is actually the norm. For ALPS no such interpreter exist and also the model in this work can merely serve as the basis for an interpreter specification that also encompasses ALPS.

References

1. Arkin, R.C.: Behavior-Based Robotics. MIT Press (1998)
2. Börger, E., Stärk, R.: Abstract state machines: a method for high-level system design and analysis; with 19 tables. Springer, Berlin (2003)
3. Elstermann, M.: Reference-execution-model-for-PASS. https://github.com/MatthesElstermann/Reference-Execution-Model-for-PASS. Accessed 24 Jan 2023
4. Elstermann, M.: Proposal for using semantic technologies as a means to store and exchange subject-oriented process models. In: Proceedings of the 9th Conference on Subject-Oriented Business Process Management, pp. 1–9 (2017)
5. Elstermann, M., Krenn, F.: The semantic exchange standard for subject-oriented process models. In: Proceedings of the 10th International Conference on Subject-Oriented Business Process Management, pp. 1–8 (2018)
6. Elstermann, M., Ovtcharova, J.: Abstract layers in PASS – a concept draft. In: Zehbold, C. (ed.) S-BPM ONE 2014. CCIS, vol. 422, pp. 125–136. Springer, Cham (2014). https://doi.org/10.1007/978-3-319-06191-7_8
7. Elstermann, M., Ovtcharova, J.: SiSi in the ALPS: a simple simulation and verification approach for PASS. In: Proceedings of the 10th International Conference on Subject-Oriented Business Process Management, pp. 1–9 (2018)
8. Elstermann, M., Ovtcharova, J.: Subject-orientation as a means for business information system design – a theoretical analysis and summary. In: Abramowicz, W., Corchuelo, R. (eds.) BIS 2019. LNBIP, vol. 353, pp. 325–336. Springer, Cham (2019). https://doi.org/10.1007/978-3-030-20485-3_25
9. Elstermann, M., Seese, D., Fleischmann, A.: Using the arbitrator pattern for dynamic process-instance extension in a work-flow management system. In: Derrick, J., et al. (eds.) ABZ 2012. LNCS, vol. 7316, pp. 323–326. Springer, Heidelberg (2012). https://doi.org/10.1007/978-3-642-30885-7_23
10. Elstermann, M., Wolski, A.: Mapping execution and model semantics for subject-oriented process models. In: Freitag, M., Kinra, A., Kotzab, H., Kreowski, H.-J., Thoben, K.-D. (eds.) S-BPM ONE 2020. CCIS, vol. 1278, pp. 46–59. Springer, Cham (2020). https://doi.org/10.1007/978-3-030-64351-5_4

11. Elstermann, M., Wolski, A.: Performance investigation and proposal for updates on the exchange standard for PASS. In: Freitag, M., Kinra, A., Kotzab, H., Kreowski, H.-J., Thoben, K.-D. (eds.) S-BPM ONE 2020. CCIS, vol. 1278, pp. 33–45. Springer, Cham (2020). https://doi.org/10.1007/978-3-030-64351-5_3

12. Elstermann, M., Wolski, A., Fleischmann, A., Stary, C., Borgert, S.: The combined use of the web ontology language (OWL) and abstract state machines (ASM) for the definition of a specification language for business processes. In: Raschke, A., Riccobene, E., Schewe, K.-D. (eds.) Logic, Computation and Rigorous Methods. LNCS, vol. 12750, pp. 283–300. Springer, Cham (2021). https://doi.org/10.1007/978-3-030-76020-5_16

13. Elstermann, M.: Executing Strategic Product Planning - A Subject-Oriented Analysis and New Referential Process Model for IT-Tool Support and Agile Execution of Strategic Product Planning. https://doi.org/10.5445/KSP/1000097859

14. Fleischmann, A., Schmidt, W., Stary, C., Obermeier, S., Börger, E.: Organization-specific implementation of subject-oriented processes. In: Subject-Oriented Business Process Management, pp. 173–188. Springer, Heidelberg (2012). https://doi.org/10.1007/978-3-642-32392-8_9

15. Fleischmann, A.: Distributed Systems: Software Design and Implementation. Springer, Heidelberg (1994). https://doi.org/10.1007/978-3-642-78612-9

16. Fleischmann, A.: Subjektorientiertes Prozessmanagement: Mitarbeiter einbinden, Motivation und Prozessakzeptanz steigern. Hanser Verlag, München (2011). https://doi.org/10.3139/9783446429697. https://www.hanser-elibrary.com/doi/book/10.3139/9783446429697

17. I2PM: OWL standard document for PASS. https://github.com/I2PM/Standard-PASS-Ontology. Accessed 24 Jan 2023

18. Wolski, A., Borgert, S., Heuser, L.: A CoreASM based reference implementation for subject-oriented business process management execution semantics. In: Proceedings of the 11th International Conference on Subject-Oriented Business Process Management, pp. 1–15 (2019)

Handling Cross-Cutting Concerns in Subject-Oriented Modeling: Exploration of Capabilities and an Aspect-Oriented Enrichment

Thomas Ernst Jost[✉][iD], Christian Stary[iD], and Richard Heininger[iD]

Institute of Business Informatics - Communications Engineering, Business School,
Johannes Kepler University Linz, Linz 4040, Austria
{thomas.jost,christian.stary,richard.heininger}@jku.at

Abstract. Subject-oriented modeling has recently found increased application for the modeling of processes in Cyber-Physical Systems (CPS). While models are generally used as a means of dealing with the complexity of such systems, modeling languages are challenged by various cross-cutting concerns that are inherently difficult to depict in an efficient manner. Common examples include regular logging mechanisms, authentication procedures, and the like. If not appropriately supported by the used language, modeling such concerns can result in duplicated model elements that are scattered across the same or different models. They furthermore become tangled with the core functionality needed to realize a business case. This negatively impacts qualities such as model understandability, reusability, maintainability, and evolution. Aspect-oriented programming and modeling concepts have been applied in different contexts to address such issues. In this contribution, we examine subject-oriented modeling with regard to its capabilities for supporting modularity and separation of concerns using the running example of a logistics CPS. Certain limitations are present that could be addressed by an aspect-oriented enrichment. We outline an initial proposal and discuss related considerations and challenges.

Keywords: Subject-Oriented Business Process Management ·
Subject-Oriented Modeling · Aspect-Oriented Modeling ·
Aspect-Oriented Programming · Cross-Cutting Concerns ·
Cyber-Physical Systems

1 Introduction

Cyber-Physical Systems (CPS), characterized by the integration of physical processes with computation [17], are increasingly gaining importance in many different fields. Some of their common application contexts include Industry 4.0 [19] and Logistics 4.0 [25]. However, developing and operating such systems comes with a number of challenges. One of the most prominent challenges concerns

M. Elstermann et al. (Eds.): S-BPM ONE 2023, CCIS 1867, pp. 202–222, 2023.
https://doi.org/10.1007/978-3-031-40213-5_15

handling the complexity and heterogeneity of CPS, generally requiring multi-disciplinary approaches. To help alleviate complexity-related issues, the use of models, e.g., in the context of model-driven engineering, has become a possible solution that has received much research attention [20].

In this context, the employment of modeling techniques from Subject-Oriented Business Process Management (S-BPM) [9,10] has been explored in recent research (see [11,14,21,23]). Specifically, the subject-oriented modeling notation has been selected due to its ability to depict parallel behavior synchronized through communication with a minimal number of notational elements. It can be used to depict processes that are enacted by a CPS at various levels of abstraction, by encapsulating behavior into subjects that interact with each other through message exchanges.

However, CPS as complex systems require the need to address various concerns in their associated models that are hard to capture in an efficient manner. We consider a system that was outlined in a previous work [14]. It concerns a logistics CPS, where a mobile robot is used to fetch a package from an input location, to put it in a smart transport container that is equipped with different sensors depending on the requirements of the payload, and to transport it to an output location. The surrounding environment is also enriched with different sensors and a digital twin system receives information from CPS components to monitor the status. This requires the components to send the required information throughout the process. Such a concern is cross-cutting in nature, making it difficult to model in an efficient manner, i.e., by avoiding duplicated model elements scattered across models and intermixed with model elements addressing the actual core functionality - the functionality related directly to the business case. These inefficiencies that arise when depicting cross-cutting concerns also negatively impact understandability, re-use, and maintenance of models. Not modeling cross-cutting concerns is often not an option, especially, if executable models need to become the basis for operating the system (see [21]).

Therefore, the question is raised, whether the inherent encapsulation properties and constructs of subject-oriented modeling are sufficient to achieve the desired quality of efficiently handling various concerns, while also representing the core functionality. To prevent a "tangling of concerns", in the field of software development, Aspect-Oriented Programming (AOP) has been proposed as a possible solution [15]. The underlying principles were subsequently transferred to the field of modeling and were also studied in the context of business process modeling (see [5,12]). Due to its history of enhancing existing languages to deal with cross-cutting concern in a more efficient manner, the transfer of aspect-oriented modeling concepts to enrich subject-oriented modeling is of interest, specifically with the application in CPS in mind.

Therefore, the first contribution of this work is to examine subject-oriented modeling with regard to its capabilities for the modularization and separation of concerns. For this purpose, we use the case from Ref. [14] that was outlined above to illustrate our considerations. The goal is to determine the potential that an enrichment with aspect-oriented principles could bring to subject-oriented modeling, while retaining the unchanged language core to specify functionality (to keep the burden for a new modeler to learn additional constructs to a minimum). As basis for a potential realization, we also examine related work addressing aspect-oriented modeling in the context of CPS and business process management. We use the identified potential and the insights from the related work to outline an initial proposal and discuss related considerations and challenges, representing the second contribution of this work.

The rest of this paper is structured as follows: Sect. 2 introduces the core concepts of AOP. Furthermore, aspect-oriented modeling is covered, with a specific focus on research in the areas of business process management and CPS. Then, Sect. 3 briefly introduces the core ideas behind S-BPM and outlines its modeling approach and notation. Based on these conceptual foundations, Sect. 4 examines subject-oriented modeling in depth with regard to its capabilities for dealing with certain concerns. It explores the extent to which subject-oriented modeling can support modularization and separation, using the case outlined here in the introduction as a running example. Based on this examination, the value of an enrichment with aspect-oriented principles is identified. In Sect. 5, first ideas for such an enrichment are presented, based on insights gained from the related work. The running example is used to showcase the application of the modeling approach. Finally, Sect. 6 summarizes the work and discusses possibilities for future research.

2   Aspect-Oriented Programming and Modeling

In this section, we first outline the principal ideas of Aspect-Oriented Programming (AOP), as they provide the basis for the remainder of this work. Subsequently, we examine the application of aspect-oriented principles in the context of modeling. We review existing research on aspect-oriented modeling in the fields of Business Process Management (BPM) and CPS in particular. This provides the conceptual basis for discussing the capabilities of subject-oriented modeling and a potential aspect-oriented enrichment.

2.1   Aspect-Oriented Programming

AOP was developed in response to the limitations of existing programming paradigms (e.g., procedural and object-oriented programming) when dealing with specific concerns for which related code would become dispersed across a program and intermixed with core functionality [15]. This would lead to similar problems as the ones outlined in the introduction. AOP aims to handle aspects - things that cannot be cleanly encapsulated using the existing language constructs - enabling "...appropriate isolation, composition and reuse of the aspect code" [15, p. 221]. The core components required for creating aspect-oriented programs were listed as the following [15]: a language to write the core program, one or multiple languages to write aspect programs, and an aspect weaver to build a combined program.

Since the outline of the core ideas of AOP, more research and development has followed. Existing general purpose programming languages were extended with the concepts of AOP. Examples include AspectJ[1] for Java and Aspect C++[2] for C/C++. A variety of different terms are used in the context of AOP to denote concepts needed for its realization. They have slightly different meanings and connotations depending on the concrete approach and context. In the following, we will introduce a few common terms and give a rather general description of what they refer to (to the extent required for the discussion of the related work and the proposed enrichment).

Four important concepts used in realizations of AOP (such as, e.g., AspectJ) are *joinpoints*, *pointcuts*, *advice*, and *aspects*. Aspect-orientation is built around the idea of separating cross-cutting concerns from core functionality during programming, while later weaving them back together in preparation for execution. This requires means to designate the required connections. *Joinpoints* are certain points in a program, where it is generally possible to add functionality related to cross-cutting concerns. Pieces of *advice* refer to program code that implements certain cross-cutting functionality. A *pointcut* specifies the concrete *joinpoints* for which certain *advice* code should be executed. *Aspects* are used to group *pointcuts* and pieces of *advice* together. There can be different modalities governing how to insert *advice* in relation to the *joinpoint*. Common designations are *before*, *around*, and *after*. In AspectJ, *before*-advice is executed before the joinpoint, *after*-advice is executed after the joinpoint, and *around*-advice is executed in the joinpoint's stead (the execution of advice code of the type *around* can be further configured using *proceed(...)*, which can be used to execute the code of the original joinpoint[3]).

2.2 Aspect-Oriented Modeling

The aspect-oriented ideas that were originally developed and applied in the context of programming were subsequently also adopted for modeling languages to realize the corresponding benefits. Aspect-oriented modeling was explored in the context of Software Engineering (e.g., for the Unified Modeling Language - UML - see [24]) and also in the domain of business process modeling. More recent research has looked at utilizing the concepts in the context of CPS. In the following, we discuss aspect-oriented approaches in the business process modeling context, due to the closeness with subject-oriented modeling. We specifically focus on the realization of the potential of aspect-orientation for each modeling language and/or modeling approach and how the enrichment/integration was achieved. We also give a short overview with regard to current applications of aspect-orientation in CPS.

---

[1] see https://www.eclipse.org/aspectj/.

[2] see https://www.aspectc.org/.

[3] see   https://www.eclipse.org/aspectj/doc/next/progguide/semantics-advice.html, retrieved 30.01.2023.

Aspect-Oriented Approaches in the Domain of Business Process Management: An aspect-oriented extension to the Business Process Model and Notation (BPMN) was proposed in Ref. [5]. The authors listed the insufficient capabilities of BPMN to modularize relevant concerns, such as auditing and compliance, as their main motivation. Both a light-weight (re-using existing artifacts and elements for visual representation of aspect-oriented concepts) and a heavy-weight syntax (introducing new elements) were provided for the proposed language. The presented extension uses flow objects as joinpoints (activities, gateways, ...). The authors list three possible options for the definition of pointcuts (which were, following BPMN extension mechanisms, realized as a new artifact): Visually connecting a pointcut to joinpoints via associations, using a textual model query language to select joinpoints, or using annotations that are connected to joinpoints. Pieces of advice were realized as sub-processes that implement cross-cutting functionality, with a special *proceed*-activity to configure execution order with respect to the joinpoint. Finally, an aspect consists of multiple pointcuts and associated pieces of advice. The authors used multiple examples to showcase the use of their language extension. These also illustrate how the extension achieves its goals (increased re-usability, understandability, and maintainability), by encapsulating concerns that otherwise would be strewn about models and breaking up the complex and monolithic models that result from the tangling of concerns [5].

In a follow-up work [26], the original approach of Ref. [5] was extended further. Specifically, the authors adjusted it to conform to BPMN 2.0 and proposed a dedicated pointcut language and a weaving mechanism built on model-to-model transformations. Dynamic weaving was covered in Ref. [13].

A light-weight approach to aspect-oriented modeling in BPMN (contrasted with heavy-weight approaches that require modifications of the language meta-models and tools) was presented in Ref. [12]. The authors provide a BPMN language profile, extending the existing meta-model and re-using existing elements of the notation for expressing the required aspect-oriented concepts. This is accomplished through the stereotyping of existing meta-classes. Pools are, e.g., used to represent aspects and contain sub-processes to represent pieces of advice and data objects to represent pointcuts. Advice is associated with pointcuts. The authors also provide a dedicated pointcut language, developed as a Domain-Specific Language (DSL) using XText[4]. Expressions written in this language are used to provide the details of a pointcut by adding them to the data association of the pointcut data object. The authors also outlined related implementation concerns by discussing the architecture of an aspect-oriented modeling tool for BPMN. One of the main motivations listed in Ref. [12] were limitations of existing light-weight approaches with regard to expressiveness, e.g., when modeling concepts such as pointcuts. The developed DSL can provide an expressive tool for this purpose.

In Ref. [2], a meta language for aspect-oriented process modeling was proposed. It is independent of the concrete modeling language used to depict busi-

---

[4] see https://www.eclipse.org/Xtext/, retrieved 30.01.2023.

ness processes. The authors utilized a BPMN example to showcase the instantiation for a concrete language. They used adapted modeling constructs to represent cross-cutting concerns (dotted rectangles - activities - for cross-cutting processes in a dedicated lane and dotted flows for cross-cutting relationships that link the cross-cutting processes to joinpoints, e.g., activities). The presented example shows the positive impact on understandability, reusability, and maintainability of the model (through reduction of duplicate elements and clearer separation). However, the approach taken by the authors for visual representation (cross-cutting concerns, core functionality, and connections between the two in the same model) is not ideal with regard to its scalability. If the number of concerns and relationships that apply to the core process increases, the complexity of the model will also increase. Since a concern is handled in a new swimlane, concerns that effect multiple process models would require modeling new lanes in each of them. Despite being able to extend any business process modeling language in principle, a solution tailored to a specific modeling language could better capture and account for its peculiarities.

In a follow-up work [3], the authors further examined the application of aspect-oriented techniques in business process modeling. They also proposed to model cross-cutting concerns in their own respective swimlanes that contain model elements connected to the core process via cross-cutting relationships. They considered multiple different types of model elements that might be used in a cross-cutting concern swimlane (e.g., activities, data elements). Both a visual and a textual representation of cross-cutting concerns were outlined. The authors provided a DSL for specifying pointcuts and pieces of advice as part of the textual representation. They also extended an existing editor to support the required modeling constructs for depicting cross-cutting concerns in an aspect-oriented way. Overall, the presented approach achieves an increase in modularity and offers more expressiveness than the one in Ref. [2], due to considering more elements to represent cross-cutting concerns. The textual representation using the pointcut language can be easier to understand compared to the visual representation, especially when models increase in complexity. Another follow-up work [4] outlined an updated graphical notation, with changes that were specifically aimed at improving the visual representation with regard to scalability and understandability (e.g., pointcuts are now denoted by circles containing numbers - as reference to aspects - that are attached to the control flow in the core process model).

Some of the key take-aways from the related work for designing aspect-oriented enrichments to existing languages are the following:

– Most of the examined approaches aim to utilize as many of the existing modeling constructs and concepts of the language that they extend as possible to represent cross-cutting concerns. In the case that additional constructs are required, they are based on existing elements of the language. Such a strategy may facilitate the adoption of the extended language by modelers, especially if they are already familiar with the basic language.

– Increased modularity of cross-cutting concerns was achieved through the aspect-oriented extensions, supporting qualities such as maintenance, re-use, and evolution of models. Modeling examples were provided to illustrate some of these improvements. However, there were differences with regard to the expressiveness of the proposed approaches, depending, e.g., on the available options for defining pointcuts and advice.
– A visual representation of a model that includes the core process, the aspects that depict the cross-cutting concerns, as well as the connections between the two, might run into scalability issues. Textual representations or different model types for core processes and aspects are among the possible alternatives.
– Weaving of models can occur during run-time (e.g., through execution engines) or during design-time (through transforming models).
– The specification of various aspect-oriented concepts (e.g., pointcuts) during modeling can be supported through dedicated languages.

Aspect-Oriented Approaches in the Domain of Cyber-Physical Systems: A few proposed applications of aspect-oriented ideas exist in the context of modeling CPS. We will give a short overview over some of these approaches and the types of concerns that were considered.

In Ref. [1], the authors presented the employment of aspect-oriented concepts for enriching actor-oriented models (these models consider concurrent actors that communicate through messages). They highlighted various CPS-related concerns of a non-functional nature that could be encapsulated using aspects (communication, execution time, fault/error handling, logging, verification, . . .). Furthermore, multiple examples were provided to illustrate the modeling approach and its prototype implementation, as well as the benefits of increased modularity (e.g., understandability, domain experts being able to focus on their respective concerns, the ability to explore the design space). A robot swarm scenario was modeled with different concerns, such as communication/networking and robot dynamics, as aspects.

In a similar vein, the authors of Ref. [22] used aspect-oriented ideas to link attack models to an actor-oriented model of a CPS and its components for the purpose of security analysis during design. They specifically considered the examination of the behavior of the system in case of attacks through executable models and provided a case study concerning an adaptive cruise control system. A key advantage of the proposed approach is that it promotes the independent development of different models (attack models, system models).

An aspect-oriented modeling method for the Quality-of-Service (QoS) of CPS was outlined by Ref. [18], specifically considering real-time systems. The authors used the UML and Real-Time Logic (RTL) as basis for their approach, thus considering both semi-formal and formal specification means. They provided the case of a fire alarm system to illustrate their approach. The main advantages that were highlighted concern the ability to configure QoS requirements without needing to change the models with the core functionality.

These examples show some of the benefits that the application of aspect-oriented concepts can bring in the context of CPS. The models considered by the authors in Ref. [1] and [22] show similarities to subject-oriented modeling (see Sect. 3), e.g., they consider parallel behavior and are executable. However, they address the behavior of the system on a low level of abstraction (focusing on technical and physical details). The approach presented in [18] takes a different perspective by utilizing the UML. These existing approaches could be complemented by a higher-level business process view provided by subject-oriented modeling.

3 Subject-Oriented Modeling

In this section, we briefly introduce key concepts from Subject-Oriented Business Process Management (S-BPM) [9,10]. We mostly focus on the associated modeling approach. This provides the basis for the deeper examination provided in the following section.

One of the core underlying ideas of S-BPM is to focus on active entities or elements of processes, which are referred to as "subjects". These can be seen as analogous to subjects in the grammar of natural languages; the structure of natural languages (subject, object, predicate) was also one building block for the subject-oriented modeling approach. Subjects encapsulate a certain set of behavior that occurs as part of the process, which can be assigned to concrete actors (human or technological) during process execution.

The language used for creating subject-oriented models, the Parallel Activity Specification Scheme (PASS), uses two different types of diagrams [9,10]: A Subject-Interaction Diagram (SID) is used to show the possible communications between subjects as part of a process. To this end, it contains subjects and message exchanges between them. Message exchanges synchronize the individual behavior of different subjects. The behavior of these subjects is specified using a dedicated diagram type. These Subject-Behavior Diagrams (SBDs) can contain three types of states: do-states are used to represent the performing of actions, send-states to represent transmitting messages to other subjects, and receive-states to represent obtaining messages from other subjects (send- and receive-states of subjects need to correspond to message exchanges in the SID). States are connected via transitions (labels provide additional details). In the remainder of this work, we use yellow rectangles to designate do-states, red rectangles to designate send-states, and green rectangles to designate receive-states. We provide transition labels only for send- and receive-states. Due to limited space, we present an SID together with the SBDs of its subjects in a singular graphic, despite them being different models.

4 Subject-Oriented Modeling Principles and Constructs - Possibilities and Limitations

In this section, subject-oriented modeling is examined in more depth with respect to how the separation of different concerns can be supported and modularity can be achieved. We use different scenarios derived from the case outlined in the introduction to discuss how subject-oriented modeling constructs can deal with certain concerns - and to identify potential shortcomings. Based on these insights, the potential benefits that an enrichment with aspect-oriented concepts might bring are highlighted. This examination and the take-aways from the related work lay the ground for the following section.

A key feature of subject orientation is that it is built around the idea of encapsulating different behavior into different subjects, according to some set of criteria. In subject-oriented modeling, behavior related to a certain concern can be modeled as its own subject, with other subjects calling it through a message exchange whenever its behavior needs to be executed. Figure 1 illustrates this approach for a fragment of the illustration case. The core functionality, i.e., the behavior of a subject that is directly related to the handling of packages, is contained in the subject on the left. The concern of handling potential errors that might occur during the movement of the robot was encapsulated into its own subject. Whenever handling of movement errors is needed, another subject can call the subject containing this specific concern. As one can observe, send-states in the calling subject behavior are required (and potentially also receive-states; both lead to message exchanges in the SID). Therefore, some behavior related to the error handling concern remains in the SBD - only the number of states related to this concern was reduced.

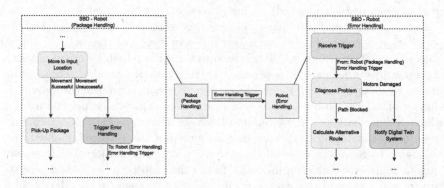

Fig. 1. SID and SBDs depicting the extent to which separation of the error handling concern from core functionality can be achieved through encapsulation of concern-specific behavior into a separate subject.

There are also scenarios, where the encapsulation of concern behavior into separate subjects brings no benefits. Assume the process depicted in Fig. 2. The three subjects on the right depict components of the overall CPS - the robot, the room, and a shelf. A digital twin system provides a digital representation of the whole system for the purpose of process monitoring. To realize synchronization with the twin, the CPS components need to regularly send their status information, so that the package handling process can be logged. As the SBD fragment for the robot subject depicts, after each state, the needed status information is sent. The same pattern is relevant for the other two subjects. Creating a new subject for this logging behavior has no benefit with regard to reducing the number of states related to the logging concern that are present in the SBD of the core package handling functionality, since only a single send-state is required at each point. Another drawback of this separation approach is its scalability. As models get bigger and bigger, they also become increasingly harder for a human to understand. For sizeable business processes, with many different concerns and related behavior, the number of subjects and message exchanges would quickly get out of hand. This can somewhat be alleviated through splitting up larger process models through the use of external subjects, to create connected processes (see [9], also cf. the other listed methods for defining complex processes).

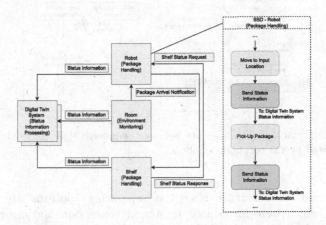

Fig. 2. SID depicting a scenario where encapsulation of logging-related behavior of the three subjects on the right would bring no benefit with regard to modularity.

Besides this inherent property of the subject-oriented approach that can be used for the separation of concerns, dedicated language constructs have been proposed that provide further means.

First, so-called "macros" [9] can be used to encapsulate sequences of behavior that are used at multiple points in a process model, be that within the same subject or across different subjects. Figure 3 illustrates the usage of a macro for a part of the illustration scenario. The macro on the left side contains behavior associated with the robot using an attached arm unit to interact with different objects as part of the packaging process. This behavior is needed whenever the robot needs to manipulate something. First, the needed commands are issued to the arm unit, and its response is received, indicating either a successful or an unsuccessful execution of the movement. In case of unsuccessful execution, the DT system is notified. Otherwise, the robot-internal status information concerning the carried object is updated. While macros can be used to contain such behavior required at multiple points in a process, they still need to be called in the behavior definition of the subjects that use them, like any other state. This can be seen in Fig. 3, with the macro being called in the SBD on the right side. Similar to the previously discussed option of using subjects for encapsulation, a certain part of the concern-specific behavior remains, albeit in a more compact manner.

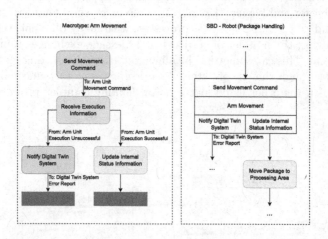

Fig. 3. Usage of macros to encapsulate behavior sequences that are used at multiple points, indicated by the rectangle symbols.

Second, another construct aimed at separating concerns are "message guards" [9], which were introduced to simplify exception and error handling and separate the associated behavior from what is referred to as the "happy path". The underlying idea behind this construct is that for certain business cases, it might be necessary to react to messages during multiple states of a subject's behavior. Examples are cancellation or error message. To support this task, a subject can have multiple message guards. Figure 4 shows an example from the introduced CPS case: the SBD on the left depicts the behavior of the robot subject as part of the package handling process. The message guard on the right is triggered during the listed states, if an error message from the scanner unit subject (another add-on to the robot system) is received. Following the receipt of the error message, the robot notifies the DT system that it cannot continue with its task. It then requests manual repairs of the defective add-on and returns to the initial location (in this example it is assumed that the robot can still navigate there successfully, even without the scanner unit).

Message guards can be used to separate the specific associated behavior, such as error handling, from the other behavior of the subject. From the set of discussed constructs, message guards are close to aspect-oriented mechanisms in the respect that the associated behavior is completely removed from the core behavior of the subject. However, there are limits to the types of scenarios that they can deal with, as they require a message to react to. Thus, they can only be used to deal with specific concerns. Furthermore, a message guard belongs to a single subject. In case the same guard behavior would be needed by n different subjects, then n message guards need to be defined.

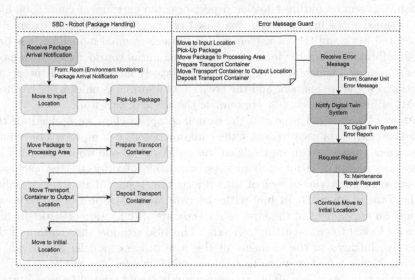

Fig. 4. Application of message guards to react to specific messages that can occur during multiple states of the subject.

Despite the present options in subject-oriented modeling, the examples in this section have shown that there are certain shortcomings with regard to modularity and separation when cross-cutting concerns are addressed. As a consequence, subject-oriented modeling cannot handle certain complexities of the underlying processes in an efficient manner. When modeling certain concerns, these limitations lead to an increase in model complexity, which manifests itself in duplicated model elements (within and across SIDs and SBDs), models where the core functionality is mixed with behavior and structure linked to cross-cutting concerns, and a high number of subjects and message exchanges. By separating concern-related behavior from the core process models in a stronger fashion, re-usability of this behavior and overall maintainability of the process specification can be improved further. Modeling efficiency can also be increased, since it is no longer necessary to model the same behavior needed at different points multiple times. Furthermore, the modeling of core functionality and different concerns can be split between different people. Modelers working on the core functionality can concentrate on what is directly relevant to the business case, without needing to worry about dealing with various other concerns. These are some of the potential benefits that an enrichment with aspect-oriented concepts can bring.

5 An Aspect-Oriented Enrichment for Subject-Oriented Modeling

Following the analysis of subject-oriented modeling presented in the previous section, this section outlines how an aspect-oriented enrichment could look like. The outlined modeling approach was based on insights gained from examining the related work and the basic elements of subject-oriented modeling. It is presented informally, since the focus is on discussing initial considerations in a more general manner - which are also meant to be largely independent of the actual notation. Further refinement and the creation of a formal definition are required as part of future research, but are outside the scope of this work.

As was the case with most of the examined approaches, we decided for the modeling constructs used to depict the core functionality of a process to remain unchanged. Processes can be modeled the same way as one would normally do it, by creating an SID for each process, consisting of subjects that exchange messages. The behavior of each of the subjects that is part of an SID is specified in the form of an SBD. In line with the core ideas of aspect-orientation, we propose an enrichment in the form of the separate specification of structure and behavior linked to cross-cutting concerns. This also requires the creation of the respective linkages to the elements of the core process models, which can be resolved during aspect weaving to create a unified model.

For the purpose of specifying structure and behavior related to cross-cutting concerns, it comes naturally to also employ the core constructs of subject-oriented modeling. We make use of the terms and concepts introduced in Sect. 2 and organize these constructs in the form of pieces of *advice*. Each piece of *advice* has one associated SID, again consisting of message-exchanging subjects with their SBDs. *Aspects* are used to group together pieces of *advice* that are related to a common cross-cutting concern. The linkage to the elements of the core process models where *advice* should be inserted is realized through the specification of the related *pointcuts*. These *pointcuts* are also grouped according to the corresponding *aspects* and select the respective elements from the process models containing the core functionality. In subject-oriented modeling, we propose to use the states of SBDs as *joinpoints*.

With regard to the definition of *pointcuts*, we find the three options listed by Ref. [5] for their extension of BPMN to also be valid candidates for subject-oriented modeling. The first option, visually connecting *joinpoints* to *pointcuts*, would run into similar problems as some of the present options for the modular modeling of concern-related behavior discussed in the previous section. Although no additional states would be necessary in the SBDs, if there is a large number of visual connections, readability and interpretability of the models would likely be impaired. Furthermore, the distributed nature of the behavior specification of a process across different subjects needs to be considered as well. Therefore, this option was deemed to not be optimal. Considering one of the other listed options, it would be possible to attach annotations to *joinpoints* that declare the *pointcuts* and related information. A possibility would be the modality of *advice* execution, with the common options of *before*, *around*, and *after*. This was sketched in Fig. 5. However, the associated drawback listed in Ref. [5], the weakening of the obliviousness property (i.e., the property that a programmer, or in this case a modeler, that works on core functionality should not expend any additional effort towards realizing aspect-oriented mechanisms [8]), has to be kept in mind.

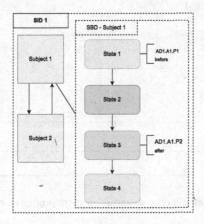

Fig. 5. Using annotations to specify joinpoints in SBDs.

The remaining option suggested by the related work is the usage of a dedicated language to support the creation of *pointcut* definitions. Such a language can support the definition of all or selected details of a *pointcut* specification, such as the desired *joinpoints*, the related piece(s) of *advice*, and the modalities of *advice* execution. To realize *joinpoint* specification, it can enable the querying and selection of the desired model elements. In the context of the proposed enrichment of subject-oriented modeling, this would mean the selection of states after certain criteria, e.g., their type (do, send, receive), their name, and their position in relation to other states. In terms of expressiveness, and under consideration of the listed limitations of the other options, the creation of such a language seems like a desirable solution to be researched further. As the exploration and discussion of weaving-related aspects in the following section will show, there is also the potential need to deal with certain peculiarities of the subject-oriented approach as part of the specification of *pointcuts*.

Figure 6 shows how the resulting organisation of the discussed elements could look like in the form of a diagram. It is intended to give the reader an idea of the general workings of the proposed enrichment. Further work is required to create an appropriate visual representation to depict the type of model needed to express cross-cutting concerns, once the underlying elements have been fully specified and formalized.

5.1 Considerations for the Weaving of Models

With regard to aspect weaving, the process of creating a unified model, the related work indicates two possible solutions: either dynamically at run-time or

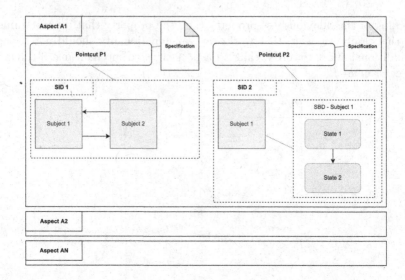

Fig. 6. Outline of the general structure of modeling cross-cutting concerns.

statically at design-time. Different subject-oriented execution engines have been proposed, both from the commercial[5] and the academic sector [7,16], which could be extended to support the aspect-oriented extensions proposed and dynamically weave models. The use of, e.g., model-to-model transformations to create a unified model, would allow the potential execution of this model with subject-oriented engines that do not support the aspect-oriented elements (as long as the format of the created model is supported). In the following, we sketch an initial simple approach for creating a unified model and discuss some of the associated considerations and challenges.

For all defined *aspects*, the associated *pointcut* specifications need to be checked against the core process models to identify the respective applicable *joinpoints*. For each selected *joinpoint*, the elements of the SID related to the advice of the selecting *pointcut* are taken and inserted into the SID that contains the subject with the SBD containing the *joinpoint* (if the elements of the same SID were already inserted for a previous *joinpoint*, they are not inserted again). Following that, depending on the defined execution modality (*before*, *around*, *after*), send- and receive-states are inserted into the SBD with the *joinpoint*. If *before* was specified, one send-state dispatching a message to the first (in terms of execution order) inserted subject and one receive-state receiving a message from the last inserted subject are needed to integrate the advice-related behavior. This description only covers the simplest case, where there is only one inserted subject that can be last in execution order. In case that multiple subjects could be the last, different strategies are required for behavior integration. Depending

---

[5] Metasonic, see https://www.metasonic.de/en/, retrieved 21.02.2023.
   Compunity, see https://compunity.eu/, retrieved 21.02.2023.

on whether the behavior of inserted subjects that could be last in execution order can occur exclusively or inclusively, options could include the insertion of multiple receive-states into the behavior, or of one receive-state waiting for messages from multiple inserted subjects. These considerations are also valid for the following modalities of *after* and *around*. If *after* was specified, the send-state and the receive-state are inserted after the *joinpoint* state. If *around* was specified, the transformations become a bit more complicated. In the simplest case, the behavior of the *joinpoint* state(s) is replaced by that of the inserted subjects. This can be done by replacing them with a send- and receive-state to call the behavior of the inserted subjects. An existing approach like in Ref. [5] uses a specialized *proceed*-activity for *advice* with the modality *after* (similar to AspectJ). This could be adapted by allowing the use of a *proceed*-state in SBDs related to *advice* and then inserting states appropriately when weaving the models together.

Finally, the SBDs of the inserted subjects also need to be modified to link the flow of behavior between them and the subjects with the *joinpoints*. A receive-state (specifying the subject with the *joinpoint*) needs to be included at the beginning of the SBD of the inserted subject that is executed first (if such a state was already inserted for a previous *joinpoint*, it needs to be modified to list the potentially new subject with the *joinpoint*). Furthermore, a send-state (specifying the subject with the *joinpoint*) is required at the end of the behavior of the inserted subject(s) that could be executed last (if already inserted previously, some modification may be required in case of a new subject). These insertions of states also require the designation of new start- and end-states. The message exchanges that were included through the modifications of the SBDs of subjects also need to be added in the SID.

It should also be noted that since the behavior of subjects is executed in a parallel manner, there should also exist an option to allow for the asynchronous execution of *advice*-related behavior. A possible option includes the insertion of a send-state before a *joinpoint* state and of the corresponding receive-state after the *joinpoint* state, so that the *advice*-related behavior is executed in parallel to the *joinpoint*. Synchronization with advice-related behavior is realized through the receive-state inserted in the core process model. It would also be possible to completely omit the receive-state when weaving the models together, so that the *advice*-related behavior is called and then the regular flow of behavior in the core process model continues, without waiting for any response from the *advice*-related subjects. Such features with regard to the execution of *advice*-related behavior require appropriate configuration options when defining *point-cuts*. Strategies need to be considered for dealing with situations, where multiple different pieces of *advice* apply to the same *joinpoint*, to determine the appropriate order in which inserted subjects should be integrated through message exchanges. With regard to the sharing of data between the subjects of the core model and the inserted subjects, the exchanged messages can be used to transfer business objects (see [9]).

5.2   Illustration Using a Cyber-Physical Systems Case

Considering the outlined use case, we return to one of the examples given in Sect. 4 and show how it would be handled with an enriched modeling approach. This serves to illustrate the discussed enrichment and to give an idea about the benefits. We consider the logging example. To recount, the robot, after finishing each of the steps needed for preparing the package, sends status information (current step of the process, sensor information, ...) to a supervisory digital twin system for the purpose of logging and monitoring the process, e.g., to detect potential anomalies. As was discussed previously, modeling this behavior would necessitate including the required send-states for the logging functionality into the subject encapsulating the robot's package handling behavior. When employing an aspect-oriented approach to model the same behavior, the robot subject only needs to contain the required core functionality, as seen in Fig. 7.

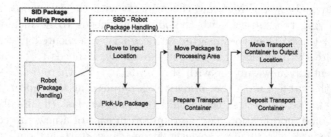

Fig. 7. SID and associated SBD showing the behavior of the robot during package handling. Only the core functionality was modeled.

Figure 8 shows the newly introduced logging aspect. The behavior needed for sending and processing the status information was moved into a separate SID with two subjects. The corresponding *pointcut* specification is responsible for selecting the desired *joinpoints* in the model of Fig. 7.

Finally, Fig. 9 shows how a combined model could look like. The considerations discussed in Sub-sect. 5.1 were applied to the example. The subjects from Fig. 8 were copied into the SID of the core process and the inserted SBDs, as well as the SBD with the *joinpoint* state, were adapted as previously described. One can observe that while the model might be syntactically correct, semantic factors need to be considered as well. In this case, it might not be desirable for the robot subject encapsulating package handling to wait for the confirmation that *advice*-related behavior was executed before continuing. Therefore, the receive-states waiting for a message from the inserted subject might need to be omitted. This again serves to highlight the importance of respecting the characteristics of the modeling approach, which is required to ensure that weaved models can correctly capture the behavior intended by the modeler.

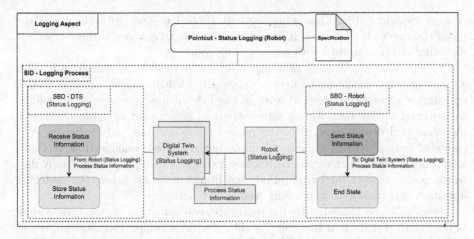

Fig. 8. SID and SBDs that are part of a pointcut definition, grouped under the aspect of logging.

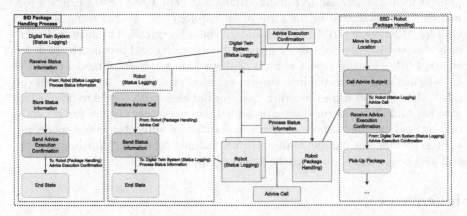

Fig. 9. Outline of a composed model, including both the behavior from the main process model and the relevant advice behavior inserted at the required points.

6 Summary and Outlook

In this work, we examined subject-oriented modeling with respect to its capabilities to modularize and separate different concerns. The case of a Cyber-Physical System, a rising application area of subject-orientation, was used as basis for this discussion. We identified certain limitations of its present language constructs that result in deficiencies when handling cross-cutting concerns. For instance, existing options require certain modeling constructs related to the separated concerns to remain in the models with the core functionality (macros, subject encapsulation), or encapsulate only certain specific concerns for a singular subject (message guards). This negatively impacts maintainability of models, reusability of concern-related behavior specifications, and the overall efficiency of process modeling. Since modeling is often applied to deal with the complexity of the modeled system(s), it would be desirable to enhance subject-oriented modeling's ability to deal with cross-cutting concerns.

To this end, we argued that aspect-oriented techniques can complement subject-oriented modeling to help alleviate the identified shortcomings. Based on insights gained from related work in the field of business process modeling, we outlined initial ideas for an aspect-oriented enrichment of subject-oriented modeling and discussed some of the related considerations and challenges. We provided examples using the case to illustrate the related benefits. However, this work only presents first steps towards integrating the two paradigms. Many different points require further detailing and implementation before the sketched approach can actually become fully usable in practice.

Specifically, as indicated by the literature, the definition of pointcuts would benefit from a dedicated language to allow for fine-grained specification, separated from the core process models. The creation of a DSL for this purpose is one possible option. The proposed enrichment also needs to be formalized and applied to a concrete subject-oriented language. For PASS, there exists a formal exchange standard in the form of an ontology [6], created using the Web Ontology Language (OWL). This standard could be extended to include the discussed aspect-oriented concepts. Such a formalization could become the basis for subsequently creating aspect weavers that work on the basis of model-to-model transformations. Down the line, subject-oriented run-time engines could also be adapted to support aspect weaving. Some initial ideas with regard to how aspect weaving could be performed were presented, however, they require further elaboration and testing. Especially the peculiarities of subject-oriented modeling, such as its inherent parallel nature, require tailored solutions. Modeling support will also be needed to support the practical application.

References

1. Akkaya, I., Derler, P., Emoto, S., Lee, E.A.: Systems engineering for industrial cyber-physical systems using aspects. Proc. IEEE **104**(5), 997–1012 (2016). https://doi.org/10.1109/JPROC.2015.2512265
2. Cappelli, C., Leite, J.C., Batista, T., Silva, L.: An aspect-oriented approach to business process modeling. In: Proceedings of the 15th workshop on Early aspects - EA 2009, p. 7. ACM Press, Charlottesville, Virginia, USA (2009). https://doi.org/10.1145/1509825.1509828
3. Cappelli, C., et al.: Reflections on the modularity of business process models: The case for introducing the aspect-oriented paradigm. Bus. Process. Manag. J. **16**(4), 662–687 (2010). https://doi.org/10.1108/14637151011065955
4. Carvalho, L.P., Cappelli, C., Santoro, F.M.: AO-BPM 2.0: aspect oriented business process modeling. In: Teniente, E., Weidlich, M. (eds.) BPM 2017. LNBIP, vol. 308, pp. 719–731. Springer, Cham (2018). https://doi.org/10.1007/978-3-319-74030-0_57
5. Charfi, A., Müller, H., Mezini, M.: Aspect-oriented business process modeling with AO4BPMN. In: Kühne, T., Selic, B., Gervais, M.-P., Terrier, F. (eds.) ECMFA 2010. LNCS, vol. 6138, pp. 48–61. Springer, Heidelberg (2010). https://doi.org/10.1007/978-3-642-13595-8_6

6. Elstermann, M., Krenn, F.: The semantic exchange standard for subject-oriented process models. In: Proceedings of the 10th International Conference on Subject-Oriented Business Process Management - S-BPM One 2018, pp. 1–8. ACM Press, Linz, Austria (2018). https://doi.org/10.1145/3178248.3178257

7. Elstermann, M., Ovtcharova, J.: Sisi in the ALPS: a simple simulation and verification approach for PASS. In: 10th International Conference on Subject-Oriented Business Process Management - S-BPM One 2018, pp. 1–9. ACM Press, Linz, Austria (2018). https://doi.org/10.1145/3178248.3178262

8. Filman, R.E., Friedman, D.P.: Aspect-oriented programming is quantification and obliviousness. In: Proceedings of the Workshop on Advanced Separation of Concerns in conjunction with OOPSLA, October 2000 (2000)

9. Fleischmann, A.: What is S-BPM? In: Buchwald, H., Fleischmann, A., Seese, D., Stary, C. (eds.) S-BPM ONE 2009. CCIS, vol. 85, pp. 85–106. Springer, Heidelberg (2010). https://doi.org/10.1007/978-3-642-15915-2_7

10. Fleischmann, A., Schmidt, W., Stary, C., Obermeier, S., Börger, E.: Subject-Oriented Business Process Management. Springer, Heidelberg (2012). https://doi.org/10.1007/978-3-642-32392-8

11. Heininger, R., Jost, T.E., Stary, C.: Enriching socio-technical sustainability intelligence through sharing autonomy. Sustainability 15(3), 2590 (2023). https://doi.org/10.3390/su15032590

12. Jabeen, A., Tariq, S., Farooq, Q.u.a., Malik, Z.I.: A lightweight aspect modelling approach for BPMN. In: 2011 IEEE 14th International Multitopic Conference, pp. 255–260. IEEE, Karachi, Pakistan (Dec 2011). https://doi.org/10.1109/INMIC.2011.6151484

13. Jalali, A., Wohed, P., Ouyang, C., Johannesson, P.: Dynamic weaving in aspect oriented business process management. In: Meersman, R., et al. (eds.) OTM 2013. LNCS, vol. 8185, pp. 2–20. Springer, Heidelberg (2013). https://doi.org/10.1007/978-3-642-41030-7_2

14. Jost, T.E., Stary, C., Heininger, R.: Geo-spatial context provision for digital twin generation. Appl. Sci. 12(21), 10988 (2022). https://doi.org/10.3390/app122110988

15. Kiczales, G., Lamping, J., Mendhekar, A., Maeda, C., Lopes, C., Loingtier, J.-M., Irwin, J.: Aspect-oriented programming. In: Akşit, M., Matsuoka, S. (eds.) ECOOP 1997. LNCS, vol. 1241, pp. 220–242. Springer, Heidelberg (1997). https://doi.org/10.1007/BFb0053381

16. Krenn, F., Stary, C.: Exploring the potential of dynamic perspective taking on business processes. Complex Syst. Inform. Modeling Q. 8, 15–27 (2016). https://doi.org/10.7250/csimq.2016-8.02

17. Lee, E.A.: Cyber physical systems: Design challenges. In: 2008 11th IEEE International Symposium on Object and Component-Oriented Real-Time Distributed Computing (ISORC), pp. 363–369. IEEE, Orlando, FL, USA (May 2008). https://doi.org/10.1109/ISORC.2008.25

18. Liu, J., Zhang, L.: QoS modeling for cyber-physical systems using aspect-oriented approach. In: 2011 Second International Conference on Networking and Distributed Computing, pp. 154–158. IEEE, Beijing, China (Sep 2011). https://doi.org/10.1109/ICNDC.2011.38

19. Lu, Y.: Industry 4.0: A survey on technologies, applications and open research issues. J. Industrial Inform. Integrat. 6, 1–10 (2017)

20. Mohamed, M.A., Challenger, M., Kardas, G.: Applications of model-driven engineering in cyber-physical systems: A systematic mapping study. J. Comput. Lang. 59, 100972 (2020). https://doi.org/10.1016/j.cola.2020.100972

21. Stary, C., Elstermann, M., Fleischmann, A., Schmidt, W.: Behavior-centered digital-twin design for dynamic cyber-physical system development. Complex Syst. Inform. Model. Q. **30**, 31–52 (2022). https://doi.org/10.7250/csimq.2022-30.02

22. Wasicek, A., Derler, P., Lee, E.A.: Aspect-oriented modeling of attacks in automotive cyber-physical systems. In: Proceedings of the The 51st Annual Design Automation Conference on Design Automation Conference - DAC 2014, pp. 1–6. ACM Press, San Francisco, CA, USA (2014). https://doi.org/10.1145/2593069.2593095

23. Weichhart, G., Reiser, M., Stary, C.: Task-based design of cyber-physical systems – meeting representational requirements with S-BPM. In: Freitag, M., Kinra, A., Kotzab, H., Kreowski, H.-J., Thoben, K.-D. (eds.) S-BPM ONE 2020. CCIS, vol. 1278, pp. 63–73. Springer, Cham (2020). https://doi.org/10.1007/978-3-030-64351-5_5

24. Wimmer, M., Schauerhuber, A., Kappel, G., Retschitzegger, W., Schwinger, W., Kapsammer, E.: A survey on UML-based aspect-oriented design modeling. ACM Comput. Surv. **43**(4), 1–33 (2011). https://doi.org/10.1145/1978802.1978807

25. Winkelhaus, S., Grosse, E.H.: Logistics 4.0: a systematic review towards a new logistics system. Int. J. Production Res. **58**, 18–43 (2020)

26. Witteborg, H., Charfi, A., Colomer Collell, D., Mezini, M.: Weaving aspects and business processes through model transformation. In: Villari, M., Zimmermann, W., Lau, K.-K. (eds.) ESOCC 2014. LNCS, vol. 8745, pp. 47–61. Springer, Heidelberg (2014). https://doi.org/10.1007/978-3-662-44879-3_4

Autonomy as Shared Asset of CPS Architectures

Richard Heininger[✉][iD], Thomas Ernst Jost[iD], and Christian Stary[iD]

Institute of Business Informatics - Communications Engineering, Business School, Johannes Kepler University Linz, 4040 Linz, Austria
{richard.heininger,thomas.jost,christian.stary}@jku.at

Abstract. Autonomous cyber-physical systems (CPS) will influence our daily lives more and more. Collaboration between intelligent machines and humans will become commonplace and negotiation of the autonomy of the actors involved may be required. The concept of shared autonomy is used to address this situation. An implementation of a subject-oriented architecture for shared autonomy is implemented in the context of a use case in smart logistics. Based on this use case, we present the generic concept and aim at its technical feasibility.

Keywords: shared autonomy · subject orientation · cyber-physical systems · PASS · system behavior

1 Introduction

The concept of autonomy is key to the CPS vision promising increasing integration of heterogeneous components and services maximizing their autonomy and minimizing adaptation to the situation of use. This vision challenges developer capabilities to build complex while autonomous systems [21,24]. In the journal Sustainability [14], we have introduced an architectural framework for sharing autonomy among functional components in CPS systems. It is based on various patterns that can evolve in the course of CPS evolvement given specific functional building blocks that themselves can be composed of sub-systems. Sharing autonomy of functionalities as a design issue requires not only architectural but operational support, i.e., some process knowledge how to handle autonomy [2,9,17].

Autonomous functionality involves components and data exchanges coordinated in some common environment in a way that their collective behavior meets the objectives of developing a CPS. In this contribution, we propose to implement a system architecture model for sharing autonomy through a subject-oriented executable process model. The architecture model already allows the expression of (re)configurable arrangements and coordination between functionality components including human control [2,9]. The subject-oriented process model consists of interacting components implementing each pattern based one characteristic features of sharing autonomy: Recognizing, exploring, arrangement, and

M. Elstermann et al. (Eds.): S-BPM ONE 2023, CCIS 1867, pp. 223–239, 2023.
https://doi.org/10.1007/978-3-031-40213-5_16

adaptation. These features establish an operational concept of sharing autonomy between CPS functionalities to develop and run dynamically adaptable autonomous systems - when sharing autonomy itself is a kind of moving target [7]. A CPS that enables sharing of functionalities as an autonomous system must have business logic that enables sharing of CPS functionalities and adaptive response to environmental changes when sharing autonomy [2].

Our work is structured as follows: We sum up related work in Sect. 2. Section 3 summarizes and presents our previous work. Section 4 discusses issues we encountered in implementing the architecture while designing a CPS. Finally, Sect. 5 briefly illustrates the implementation of the proposed architecture as an executable model and Sect. 6 concludes the contribution.

2   Related Work

Shared autonomy is an emerging concept that refers to the collaboration between human operators and autonomous systems in a shared control environment. This paradigm shift in the way humans interact with machines is a response to the growing complexity of tasks that require both human expertise and machine precision. In shared autonomy, the human operator and the machine work together as a team, with each contributing their strengths to achieve a common goal. The concept of shared autonomy has wide-ranging applications, including in healthcare, transportation, and defense. Moreover, the underlying concept of autonomy has already been taken up in many different scientific disciplines (e.g., see [7,18,19,21]). As such, there is a need to review the existing literature on (shared) autonomy to identify existing findings. The goal of this review is to provide a basic understanding of the research landscape on shared autonomy to inform our own research.

We conducted our literature review based on the following four research questions:

RQ1 What are the architectural concepts for autonomy as a design element?
RQ2 To what extent is autonomy presented/used as a design element?
RQ3 From which domain/discipline does the contribution/the autonomy concept originate?
RQ4 How can the design and implementation of autonomy be supported and considered in an integrated way?

Literature was searched with a keyword/forward/backward search using Scopus and Google Scholar. We derived the keywords from the research questions and identified 24 contributions to include in our review.

Regarding the first research question, we can confirm the statement we found in the course of our literature search, namely "that many designs only consider autonomy implicitly" [15, p. 159]. Some approaches provide design elements of architectural concepts for autonomy as a kind of layers or tiers [3,5,10–12,17] and others as a kind of agents [15,16,21]. At an abstract level, autonomous functionality was introduced as a property of parts of a system [24]. We can summarize that autonomy or shared autonomy has been rarely and variously incorporated into architectures as a dedicated design element.

The second research question relates to the manifestation of autonomy as a design element. Again, we identified agents [4,16,21] and levels [9]. Autonomy also manifests itself in terms of the architecture or property of architectures [5,6,13,17,20,22,24]. In addition, we found reference to the system itself [19], refined self-organization [7], and self-adaptation [8]. Others use autonomy in relation to requirements [18,23], or concerning the operational domain [1], but also for properties such as transparency [2], or cooperating team members in human-autonomy teams [25]. Autonomy manifests itself lastly in modeling: as independent model elements [11], in task modeling [12], as a meta-model [15], and in an ontology [3]. In summary, autonomy as a design element is used at many different levels of abstraction and has multifaceted implications.

Autonomy as a philosophical concept has been around at least since the ancient Greeks. Accordingly, this concept can be seen broadly, and with the third research question we wanted to find out from which field or discipline the found contribution originates. Mainly we found contributions from Systems Engineering [1,5,8,24,25] and related domains like cyber-physical production systems, industrial CPS, or smart manufacturing [3,4,16,20,22]. In addition, we found contributions in areas and disciplines such as agent theory [15,21], autonomic computing [19], software engineering [18,23], philosophy [7], neuro-robotics [2], chip manufacturing [17], and artificial intelligence [13]. Autonomous driving and autonomous vehicles are another area with many contributions [9, 11,12]. In conclusion, our research can be informed by many different domains spanning the entire spectrum of sociotechnical systems.

The fourth research question relates to the integrated approach to autonomy design and implementation. Table 1 summarizes our findings. Many approaches discuss a design that includes a concept and an implementation [3,6,12,19,21, 22]. We can conclude that these take a design-integrated engineering approach. Others point out the crucial role of design with respect to the integrated perspective [5,9,13,18,24] and furthermore (system) architectures are also mentioned as a possible approach [8,23]. In addition, we have highlighted the impact of artificial intelligence [17] and the importance of modeling [11,15]. All these contributions show that autonomy is a multi-faceted aspect that can be approached in many different ways. The literature analyzed suggests that design-integrated engineering (concept with associated implementation), modeling, and system architectures are valid approaches for incorporating autonomy.

In this section, we have summarized related work to our research project. We found that autonomy is a multi-faceted issue that can be addressed with a design-integrated engineering approach. System architectures and modeling also appear to be supportive. In the next sections, we will incorporate these findings on a conceptual basis before proceeding to the actual implementation of a use case.

Table 1. Contributions from related work relevant for design and implementation of autonomy in an integrated way

Ref.	Contribution
[21]	has concept and implementation
[19]	has concept and implementation
[6]	compares concepts and implementations
[18]	design adaptive implementations
[7]	–
[23]	generic mechanism based on domain architecture
[9]	multifaceted design task when human-centered
[1]	awareness of operational sphere
[24]	by design
[5]	design controller
[2]	transparency at the user interface
[17]	AI-algorithms for runtime
[16]	through collective intelligence
[13]	by design
[10,11]	has model-based approach and validation
[20]	two-stage consensus algorithm
[8]	system architecture
[22]	has concept and implementation
[25]	–
[4]	has concept
[12]	has concept and implementation
[15]	modeling
[3]	has concept and implementation

3   CPS Architecture for Shared Autonomy

In this section, we summarize the results of our previous work in [14]. We introduce the architecture based on the system structure of CPS and the components used to flexibly support shared autonomy. We focus on the behavior of the CPS components in the system structure and refer to them as functionalities. Thus, a CPS consists of multiple functionalities at the behavioral level. The sharing of autonomy is handled at this level. Figure 1 depicts the system structure.

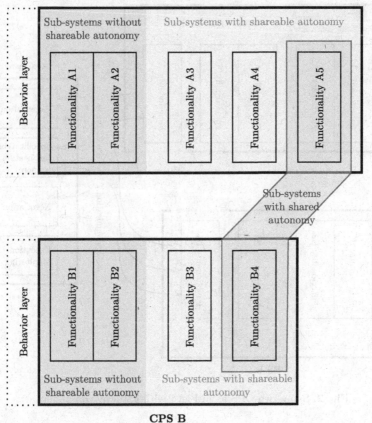

Fig. 1. Behavior level of two autonomous CPS with their respective sub-systems with and without shared autonomy

Figure 1 shows the schematic structure of autonomous CPS. Next, we present an architecture for this abstract concept that shows how shared capabilities work. It is essentially based on the system-of-systems concept and introduces a gateway component that serves as an intermediate control unit. This gateway component has codified the purpose of sharing and is able to negotiate before executing and monitoring a particular CPS. Figure 2 outlines the concept including the gateway, the two self-controlling CPS, and the required communication or message channels between the CPS and the gateway. The socio-technical context requires that the concept also work with human actors.

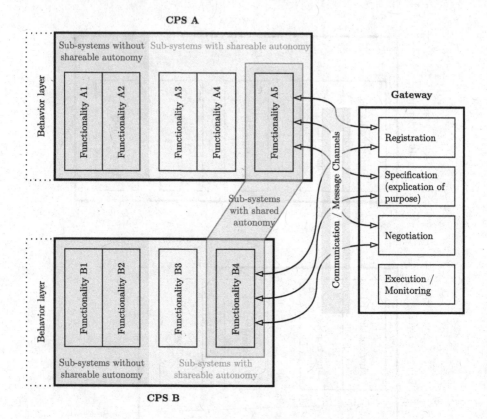

Fig. 2. Same two CPS as in Fig. 1 with gateway component

The gateway component manages the process of sharing autonomy as well as the operation of a CPS with components that share their autonomy:

Registration: each CPS component must be registered to share autonomy with other components in the system. It provides the basis for mechanisms to optimize or balance the functional and operational implementation of requirements.

Specification: sharing autonomy requires an explanation of the purpose of sharing autonomy. Specifying a rationale for sharing is the basis for devising ways to improve the functionality of the CPS.

Negotiation: it may be necessary to deal with different options to ensure technical operation or improvements of the CPS.

Execution/Monitoring: operation of a system requires control of whether the technical design meets the requirements of the CPS.

We have already conceptually illustrated the architecture on an intelligent logistics use case. The next challenge is to model and validate executable models with respect to shared autonomy using our architecture. This is the starting point for the following Sect. 4.

4 The Concept and Its Implementation

Autonomy is a key concept stemming from IoT application development that aims for integrating autonomously operating sensors and actuators through smart service designs to achieve overarching goals such as ensuring cooling quality of goods. From IoT architecting, autonomous systems consist of components of predefined element types, as the defined CPS functionalities, sharing some common environment. They need to be coordinated in a way their collective behavior of the components meets goals. The behavior affects system states that are changed through component behavior.

The components are considered active elements. They have the ability to monitor behavior and act on their state, either alone or in some coordinated manner as part of a CPS functionality. Each functionality implements meets a specific set of requirements that may dynamically change with respect to the autonomy of the components depending on the state of the CPS environment [23].

The CPS needs to provide some infrastructure and mechanisms implementing coordination rules that govern the interaction between functionalities, components, and the sharing of their autonomy. Both determine the connectivity between components and functionalities, and as a consequence, the sharing capability. Hence, the design of autonomous CPS needs to aim to adapt the behavior of each component and functionality of a CPS that it can act independently from each other to an extent that the overall CPS objectives are met through collective behavior.

The operational frame to implement autonomy-sharing CPS requires several phases: Recognizing, exploring, arranging, and adapting. They address the coordination requirements and their realization to achieve autonomous behavior for each of the involved components, since each CPS component is expected to perform some specific, goal-driven tasks [21,23]. CPS components and functionalities interact with their environment through message exchanges capturing physical/business object-relevant data. All components can interaction with others and change accordingly the state of the CPS and its environment.

According to the internal behavior capabilities components and functionalities can receive inputs and produce outputs when interacting with others.

For instance, the environment of a smart shelf is a room and a transport robot. Its behavior can be triggered by the arrival of a transport robot and its state to grab a good from the shelf. For the transport robot, the environment is more involved as it includes moving objects and obstacles in its way as well as robot arm control and communication capabilities.

CPS components and functionalities control their acting based on available environment data including other components and functionalities.to accomplish their specific tasks. They follow their internal business logic if not sharing autonomy request are recognized. When autonomy is the capacity of a component or functionality to achieve a set of coordinated goals according to its internal behavior specification, sharing autonomy enriches overall capabilities but requires complementary functions: Recognizing, exploring, arranging, and adapting [6,18,19].

- Recognizing a sharing request is achieved through receiving inputs, interpreting them and determining relevant information on how to proceed with respect to the own operation and the sharing request.
- Exploring through choosing among possible opportunities to meet the sharing request and to select the most appropriate ones for the given CPS configuration.
- Arranging the sharing of components or functionality, including negotiating on how to achieve the goal of sharing.
- Adaptation, i.e., the implementation of consensual result for the involved components or functionalities. It results in adjusted behavior specifications that can be executed.

These four stages incorporate situational analysis, solution space generation, decision preparation and implementation. An autonomous CPS needs to some extent to support each one of these stages. In case of human intervention in terms of implementing some functionality or making decision its behavior could be encapsulated to capture the interaction patterns required to achieve the CPS objectives [9].

Some design principles to implementing sharing autonomy on the basis of behavior-oriented functionality (i.e., a system (SID) of CPS component) specifications:

- Sharing autonomy is described as a transition relation between configurations. A configuration is the set of the sharing states of its functionalities and components Configurations change when events occur as the result of functionality or component coordination: by execution of interactions rules or of configuration rules.
- Each sharing requirement has to translate in one of these rules: interaction or configuration rule.
- An interaction concerns one or more state changes when synchronizing functionalities or components in the course of sharing their autonomy [5]. The rule involves state variables of the synchronizing components and may require a sequence of operations on their states. For instance, a rule can specify when two components or functionalities are close enough to each other to exchange their data. The robot transportation system could exchange transport good data timely when approaching a shelf. Then the shelf waits for specific input for delivering transport equipment.
- Configuration rules refer to the structure of a CPS. Typical effects expressed by this type of rules are complementing components or functionalities to the CPS and their removal. For instance, a new sensor is added in case of enriching functionality affecting the existing sensor configuration. A transport box is enriched with a temperature sensor to become part of a cooling chain. This type of rules could cumulate or reduce components as part of functionalities, or affect one or more type of component across functionalities. They express conditions on state variables of components or functionalities and contain sequences of specific reconfiguration operations.

A gateway coordinating sharing autonomy requests requires knowledge on [1]

- all relevant (types of) functionalities or components and their correspond- ing behavioral specification including interaction types and reconfiguration capabilities
- coordination patterns for functional achievement of CPS objectives
- constraints, such as critical properties that require that a particular condition never be violated, including the effectiveness of communication and use of components/functionality
- run-time behavior, including monitoring and analysis techniques

Sharing autonomy can be designed in a flavor of self-organization, namely as non-intrinsic property of autonomous systems. Even a CPS structured accord- ing to its functionalities it has to be initially considered as ordinary distributed system involving components with explicit sharing autonomy control compo- nents. Once autonomy should be handled in a dynamic way, as requirements for sharing 'pop-up', timely situational knowledge becomes crucial [5,23]. In case of human involvement, the barrier to be overcome is that low-level information or raw data, e.g., as collected by sensors or commands of actuators, needs to understood by humans. Thereby, the recognition process needs to analyzed to that respect [9].

In order to handle sharing autonomy during CPS runtime, is to identify and apply rules that fit to the situation. A semantic CPS model can help to test and further development of interaction and configuration rules. And most important for developing intelligence, to consider never encountered situations for adapting existing functionalities and their relations to achieve system objectives. Overall, sharing autonomy should primarily be associated with the (core) functionality as this focus allows to judge whether a CPS can operate to achieve its objectives [1].

5   Use Case

We have attempted to implement the proposed architecture based on the use case shown in Fig. 3. In this scenario, there are two robot arms: a fixed industrial robot arm mounted on a smart shelf and a robot arm mounted on a mobile robot. They should share their autonomy with respect to the overall goal of the CPS, which is to provide smart transport boxes. The smart shelf is used to store these boxes. The overall goal of the CPS is now to select and move an intelligent transport box from this same shelf to an assembly table. We called this functionality *grasp and place*.

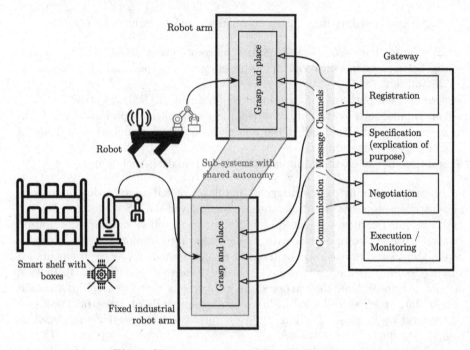

Fig. 3. Use case scenario with two robot arms

We used Metasonic Suite 5.4.1 to model the scenario. Figure 4 displays the subject interaction diagram of the use case. The starting subject is the subject *Smart room*, which communicates with a sensor to detect the placement of incoming parcels (subject *Parcel drop-off detection sensor*). The smart room activates the sensor through the message *Activation*, and once the smart room receives the message *Incoming parcel detected*, it notifies the mobile robot (subject *robot*).

Figures 5, 6, 7 and 8 show the behavior diagrams for the use case. The behaviors of the defined event handlers for dynamic negotiation of shared autonomy are not included because we modeled them without intelligence, i.e., only for receiving and forwarding messages.

When the mobile robot receives the notification (message *Incoming parcel detected*), it has to walk across the room to fetch the parcel. The behavior of the robot at this moment is linear (see Fig. 5), since the order of the parcel transport is strictly given and the robot does not have to make any decisions. The function states related to the robot's movement invoke a web service that controls the robot's movement. After each movement, the robot communicates with its gripper (subject *Mobile arm with gripper*) and sends it its position depending on the progress of the process.

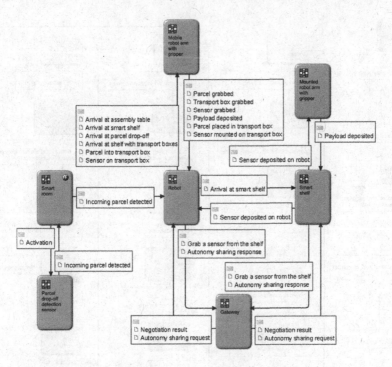

Fig. 4. Subject interacted diagram of scenario with two robot arms

We have modeled the gripper in a way that it knows what to do based on the message indicating the robot's position (see Fig. 6). However, these position messages are basically just instructions from the robot and the gripper executes them. The gripper/robot arm currently has no other intelligence.

Once the robot arrives at the smart shelf, we incorporated sharing autonomy into the model. This starts with the robot checking if it is able to reach the sensor needed to be placed on the smart transport box. The result of the check is stored and the negotiation of which subject will grab and place the sensor is initiated. Therefore, we modeled messages that are sent to the subject *gateway* that coordinates the negotiation.

The subject behavior diagram of the subject *Smart shelf* is shown in Fig. 7. It stores the sensors and controls the robotic arm mounted on the shelf. Therefore, it handles requests for shared autonomy as the mobile robot does with its robotic arm. When the robot arrives at the smart shelf and intends to grasp a sensor, it notifies the smart shelf by sending the message *Arrival at smart shelf*. This informs the smart shelf that the robot intends to grasp a sensor. The smart shelf can now check if it is able to reach the sensor with its own mounted robot arm, or it can also check if the robot can reach the sensor. Once all capacities are known, the smart shelf also participates in the negotiation by communicating with the gateway.

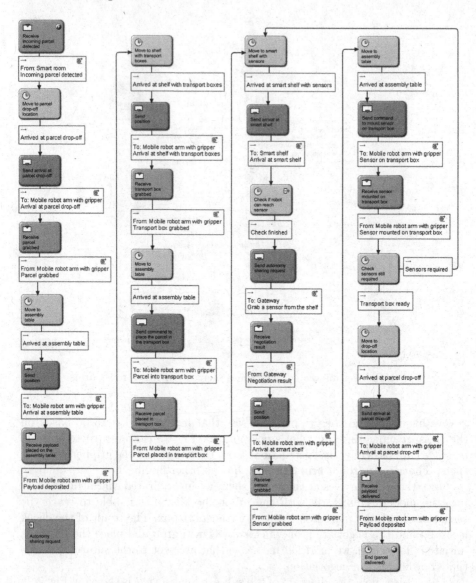

Fig. 5. Subject behavior diagram of mobile robot

Figure 8 represents the behavior of the gateway component. In principle, the gateway could be modeled in an abstract way considering all requests regarding an sharing autonomy request. We used labels pointing at the specific functionality of grasping the sensor. Once the subject receives an sharing request it

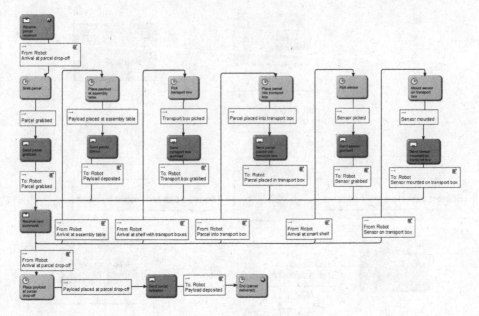

Fig. 6. Subject behavior diagram of robot arm mounted on mobile robot

handles the request according to our proposed architecture [14]. However, the subject behavior diagram reveals a problem regarding clarity with the modeling tool. Messages and subjects are closely related. Therefore, messages must be modeled for each subject. The architecture provides for equal treatment of messages, which is possible in principle with the Metasonic Suite, but the modeling becomes confusing.

The defined event handlers in subjects *Robot* and *Smart shelf* currently handle the shared autonomy requests. For example, if the robot arm mounted on the mobile robot is unable to reach a specific sensor, the other robot arm is notified to take over this task. This could also happen in reverse. For example, the intelligent shelf could detect that the mobile robot is unable to reach a particular sensor and proactively initiate a shared autonomy request.

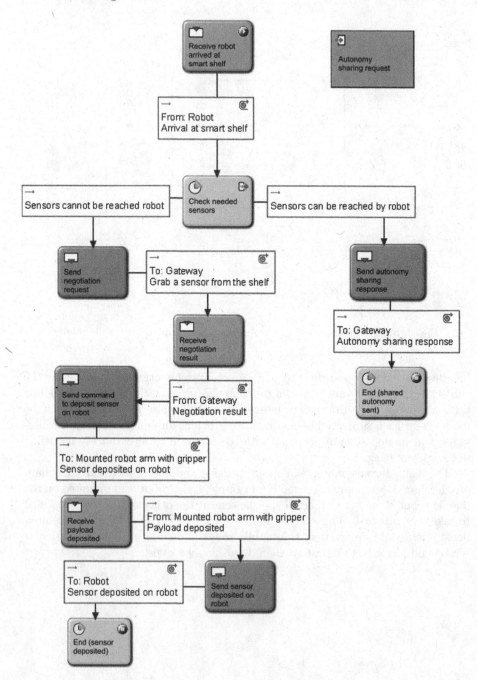

Fig. 7. Subject behavior diagram of smart shelf

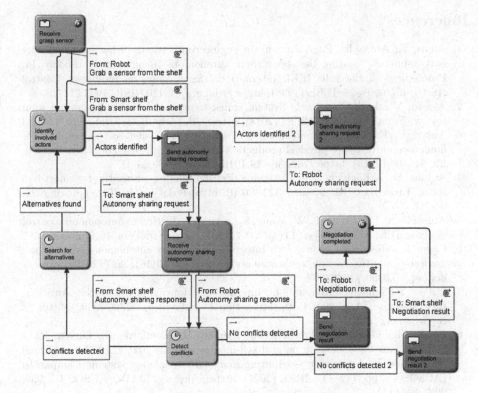

Fig. 8. Subject behavior diagram of gateway component

6   Conclusion

Our goal was to design an executable model with respect to our architecture for sharing autonomy. To achieve this, we discussed the requirements for such an artifact and created a subject-oriented model in Metasonic Suite as a proof of concept. The tool used has some limitations and we would like to work with the Compunity ToolSuite in our future work. This subject-oriented ToolSuite uses a component-skill-concept that fits better with our architecture and allows a looser coupling of messages and subjects.

We began modeling with the intention of following two principles for distributing the gateway functionality. First, we wanted to model the gateway component as a separate component within a federated system architecture. Second, the goal was to view the gateway as an integrative part of each component that must be able to share its autonomy within the federated system. However, when we completed the first version of the model and moved to the second perspective, we immediately realized that we would be modeling the same subject-oriented model. This points to an advantage of using subject-oriented modeling of cyber-physical systems. The level of abstraction taken allows for multiple possibilities of implementation at the component level (implementation of the subjects). We will further explore this aspect in our future research.

References

1. Albus, J., Antsaklis, P.: Autonomy in engineering systems: what is it and why is it important? setting the stage: some autonomous thoughts on autonomy. In: Proceedings of the 1998 IEEE International Symposium on Intelligent Control (ISIC), pp. 520–521. IEEE (1998). https://doi.org/10.1109/ISIC.1998.713716
2. Alonso, V., de la Puente, P.: System transparency in shared autonomy: a mini review. Front. Neurorob. **12**, 83 (2018). https://doi.org/10.3389/fnbot.2018.00083
3. Ansari, F., Khobreh, M., Seidenberg, U., Sihn, W.: A problem-solving ontology for human-centered cyber physical production systems. CIRP J. Manuf. Sci. Technol. **22**, 91–106 (2018). https://doi.org/10.1016/j.cirpj.2018.06.002
4. Antons, O., Arlinghaus, J.C.: Designing decision-making authorities for smart factories. Procedia CIRP **93**, 316–322 (2020). https://doi.org/10.1016/j.procir.2020.04.047
5. Antsaklis, P.J., Passino, K.M., Wang, S.J.: An introduction to autonomous control systems. IEEE Control Syst. **11**(4), 5–13 (1991). https://doi.org/10.1109/37.88585
6. Chen, J., Abbod, M., Shieh, J.S.: Integrations between autonomous systems and modern computing techniques: a mini review. Sensors **19**(18), 3897 (2019). https://doi.org/10.3390/s19183897
7. Collier, J.: What is autonomy? In: International Journal of Computing Anticipatory Systems: CASY 2001-Fifth International Conference, vol. 20 (2002). https://cogprints.org/2289/
8. Esterle, L., Gomes, C., Frasheri, M., Ejersbo, H., Tomforde, S., Larsen, P.G.: Digital twins for collaboration and self-integration. In: 2021 IEEE International Conference on Autonomic Computing and Self-Organizing Systems Companion (ACSOS-C), pp. 172–177. IEEE (2021). https://doi.org/10.1109/ACSOS-C52956.2021.00040
9. Fridman, L.: Human-centered autonomous vehicle systems: principles of effective shared autonomy (2018). https://doi.org/10.48550/arXiv.1810.01835
10. Gharib, M., Lollini, P., Ceccarelli, A., Bondavalli, A.: Governance & autonomy: towards a governance-based analysis of autonomy in cyber-physical systems-of-systems. In: 2020 IEEE 15th International Conference of System of Systems Engineering (SoSE), pp. 000217–000222. IEEE (2020). https://doi.org/10.1109/SoSE50414.2020.9130527
11. Gharib, M., Dias da Silva, L., Ceccarelli, A.: A model to discipline autonomy in cyber-physical systems-of-systems and its application. J. Softw. Evol. Process **33**(9), e2328 (2021). https://doi.org/10.1002/smr.2328
12. Gil, M., Albert, M., Fons, J., Pelechano, V.: Designing human-in-the-loop autonomous Cyber-Physical Systems. Int. J. Hum.-Comput. Stud. **130**, 21–39 (2019). https://doi.org/10.1016/j.ijhcs.2019.04.006
13. Gillespie, T.: Building trust and responsibility into autonomous human-machine teams. Front. Phys. **10** (2022). https://doi.org/10.3389/fphy.2022.942245
14. Heininger, R., Jost, T.E., Stary, C.: Enriching socio-technical sustainability intelligence through sharing autonomy. Sustainability **15**(3), 2590 (2023). https://doi.org/10.3390/SU15032590
15. Janiesch, C., Fischer, M., Winkelmann, A., Nentwich, V.: Specifying autonomy in the Internet of Things: the autonomy model and notation. Inf. Syst. e-Bus. Manag. **17**(1), 159–194 (2018). https://doi.org/10.1007/s10257-018-0379-x
16. Leitão, P., Queiroz, J., Sakurada, L.: Collective intelligence in self-organized industrial cyber-physical systems. Electronics **11**(19), 3213 (2022). https://doi.org/10.3390/electronics11193213

17. Leng, J., Chen, Z., Sha, W., Ye, S., Liu, Q., Chen, X.: Cloud-edge orchestration-based bi-level autonomous process control for mass individualization of rapid printed circuit boards prototyping services. J. Manuf. Syst. **63**, 143–161 (2022). https://doi.org/10.1016/J.JMSY.2022.03.008

18. Neema, S., Parikh, R., Jagannathan, S.: Building resource adaptive software systems. IEEE Softw. **36**(2), 103–109 (2019). https://doi.org/10.1109/MS.2018.2886831

19. Nordstrom, S.G., Shetty, S.S., Neema, S.K., Bapty, T.A.: Modeling reflex-healing autonomy for large-scale embedded systems. IEEE Trans. Syst. Man Cybern. Part C: Appl. Rev. **36**(3), 292–303 (2006). https://doi.org/10.1109/TSMCC.2006.871597

20. Prenzel, L., Steinhorst, S.: Decentralized autonomous architecture for resilient cyber-physical production systems. In: 2021 Design, Automation & Test in Europe Conference & Exhibition (DATE), vol. 2021-February, pp. 1300–1303. IEEE (2021). https://doi.org/10.23919/DATE51398.2021.9473954

21. Sifakis, J.: Autonomous systems – an architectural characterization. In: Boreale, M., Corradini, F., Loreti, M., Pugliese, R. (eds.) Models, Languages, and Tools for Concurrent and Distributed Programming. LNCS, vol. 11665, pp. 388–410. Springer, Cham (2019). https://doi.org/10.1007/978-3-030-21485-2_21

22. Stock, D., Bauernhansl, T., Weyrich, M., Feurer, M., Wutzke, R.: System architectures for cyber-physical production systems enabling self-x and autonomy. In: 2020 25th IEEE International Conference on Emerging Technologies and Factory Automation (ETFA), vol. 2020-September, pp. 148–155. IEEE (2020). https://doi.org/10.1109/ETFA46521.2020.9212182

23. Vassev, E., Hinchey, M.: Autonomy requirements engineering. In: Autonomy Requirements Engineering for Space Missions. NMSSE, pp. 105–172. Springer, Cham (2014). https://doi.org/10.1007/978-3-319-09816-6_3

24. Williams, A.P.: Defining autonomy in systems: challenges and solutions. In: Williams, A.P., Scharre, P.D. (eds.) Autonomous Systems: Issues for Defence Policymakers, Chap. 2, pp. 27–62. NATO Communications and Information Agency, The Hague (2015). https://apps.dtic.mil/sti/citations/AD1010077

25. Yaxley, K.J., Joiner, K.F., Bogais, J., Abbass, H.A.: Life learning of smart autonomous systems for meaningful human-autonomy teaming. In: A Framework of Human Systems Engineering, pp. 43–61. Wiley (2020). https://doi.org/10.1002/9781119698821.ch4

Using OPC UA for Integrating and Tracing Data Flows in the Insurance Industry

Udo Kannengiesser[1]([⊠]), Florian Krenn[2], and Harald Müller[2]

[1] Institute of Business Informatics – Communications Engineering, Johannes Kepler University, Linz, Austria
udo.kannengiesser@jku.at
[2] Compunity GmbH, Linz, Austria
{florian.krenn,harald.mueller}@compunity.eu

Abstract. Process compliance is a major concern in the financial services industry. Today there is no standard approach for ensuring the traceability of data transfers, requiring development and maintenance of customized solutions. This paper shows how one of the key technologies for integrating production systems, the OPC Unified Architecture (OPC UA, IEC 62541), can be used for addressing this issue. OPC UA provides a number of out-of-the-box functionalities including history management and data validation, which are generic and applicable to any type of data. However, to date there are hardly any known applications of this standard outside the manufacturing domain. The paper presents the architecture and implementation of a prototype incorporating an OPC UA communication interface, and illustrates its application in the context of insurance processing. This work provides the potential not only for enhanced data traceability within the financial services industry but also for a more enterprise-wide use of OPC UA leading to cross-domain system integration such as envisioned for Industry 4.0.

Keywords: OPC UA · Compliance · Business processes · Enterprise integration · Traceability

1 Introduction

Compliance is concerned with ensuring that business processes adhere to a defined set of legal or regulatory requirements [1]. It is an important issue in many companies, especially in heavily regulated industries such as the financial services industry. Various compliance demands need to be monitored and controlled, ranging from basic transactional security requirements to more complex frameworks such as Sarbanes-Oxley and Basel III. Strategies have been developed for design-time, runtime or ex-post (i.e., auditing) compliance checking, focusing on different process aspects including control-flow structure, temporal information, data- and resource-related norms [2].

As enterprise operations are more and more digitalised, often across heterogenous system landscapes, compliance increasingly becomes an issue for the IT organisation. All data transfers between enterprise systems need to be traceable, and dedicated logging systems need to be put in place. Some of them, such as the open-source platform ELK [3], provide service-oriented interfaces to facilitate this integration.

Traceability has also been addressed in other domains and industries. In production automation, an IEC standard – namely, IEC 62541 [4], commonly known as OPC Unified Architecture (OPC UA) – has emerged that specifies an integrated architecture for information exchange with built-in extensions for data traceability. Although it was designed for integrating automated manufacturing systems, e.g. Programmable Logic Controllers (PLCs), its basic concepts are generic and likely to be applicable to any kind of components and data, not just shopfloor data. However, silo thinking seems to have prevented researchers and practitioners from exploring OPC UA as an established, standardized approach addressing traceability independently of the particular domain. This paper presents the results of a project that investigates whether OPC UA could be used for integrating and tracing data in the financial industry, by means of a prototype implementation for handling household insurance applications.

The paper is organised as follows: Sect. 2 presents the case of an insurance company and the typical compliance questions it needs to answer. Section 3 presents the fundamental characteristics of OPC UA that are relevant regarding these challenges. Section 4 describes an integration solution using OPC UA, focusing on the basic architecture and a failover concept. Section 5 shows the application of a prototype solution to the online processing of household insurance applications. Section 6 concludes with a summary of benefits, limitations and future research potential.

2 Case Description

The financial services industry including insurance services is heavily regulated [5, 6]. Surveys show that compliance is a major concern in this industry [7]. In this Section, we briefly outline some of the specific compliance challenges faced by an Austrian insurance company, here called Company A, which offers a variety of insurance products for businesses and individuals. For realising the processes involved in providing these products, the company's IT department needs to integrate a combination of third-party applications and own developments, in the areas of data processing, logging, monitoring and process management. The integration of these applications is based on service-oriented architecture (SOA) and message bus.

In regular audits, Company A needs to be able to demonstrate compliance of its digitalised solutions with various legal and other regulatory requirements. For example, some of the questions that need to be answered by the company include:

Q1: Were all data transfers successful and complete? What was the error rate? Did any data changes occur during the transfer?
Q2: Were all calculations (e.g. of insurance premiums) made on the basis of the most current datasets?
Q3: Where does a data item come from: directly from the customer, a customer advisor or a backend system?

Q4: Which actions were triggered when the value of a data item exceeded a given threshold (e.g. the insurance sum exceeding the authorised amount to conclude the contract)?

Answering such questions accurately and efficiently is critical for the company, as there are important litigation and reputation risks that may potentially lead to the cancellation of claims, complaints or underwriting authority. The required traceability issues are currently addressed based on customized log management systems.

A project was initiated by Company A to develop a prototypical integration and traceability solution based on OPC UA. The choice of OPC UA was primarily driven by previous experience and research interest of one of the authors of this paper who at that time was the Head of Company A's IT department. He supervised the implementation of the prototype, which took 4 months and was carried out by an IT developer with no prior experience in OPC UA. At the time of the project, it was not intended to write a scientific paper on its outcomes; therefore, no particular case study methods (e.g., for data collection) were used. The results reported in this paper are based entirely on the artefacts produced in terms of the implemented software.

3   OPC Unified Architecture

OPC UA is a platform-independent standard for exchanging data between automated industrial systems [8], including manufacturing systems, building automation systems and smart devices. It has been adopted as the international standard IEC 62541 [4] and is widely regarded as a key technology for Industry 4.0 – the digitalisation and decentralisation of production operations [9, 10].

The meta-model of OPC UA follows the object-oriented paradigm including type hierarchies and inheritance [8, 11, 12]. Information is represented in the OPC UA address space [13] that defines a graph structure allowing multiple hierarchies and pathways to access the same data item. Both types and instances are represented as nodes in the address space. Nodes are identified by a unique NodeId and are connected by references. In addition, every node has a number of mandatory and optional attributes. Common data types (e.g. Boolean, String, Double) are provided for these attributes.

OPC UA uses a client-server approach for data exchange. Information models are always stored on an OPC UA server. They can be accessed and updated from an OPC UA client. Clients can be notified of data value changes based on a publish-subscribe model.

A number of extensions are defined on top of this OPC UA base model, to provide information models relevant for automation systems including for data monitoring and traceability. Examples include extensions for events (alarms) and condition monitoring (Alarms & Conditions; IEC 62541-9) and for accessing historical data (Historical Access; IEC 62541-11). Further extensions are defined in so-called companion specifications. These are domain-specific information models included in other organisations and standardisation bodies, such as PLCopen for exchanging control programmes for PLCs. In addition, extensions for specific vendors and devices can be defined, building on top of all other architectural layers of OPC UA.

While OPC UA has shown to provide effective and reliable data communication in many automated system applications, there has hardly been any uptake beyond the domain of automation [14]. A number of OPC UA-based approaches have been developed for the vertical integration of shopfloor level and the enterprise level of the automation pyramid [15–18]. However, for the horizontal integration between IT systems on the enterprise level there is no known application of OPC UA.

4   Integration Solution Based on OPC UA

The existing integration solution developed by Company A has been extended to provide the ability to create and persist OPC UA data models as well as to exchange them within a client-server architecture. In addition, a failover concept was realised based on clustering multiple OPC UA servers, in order to reduce the impact of individual server failures.

The overall architecture of the resulting prototype is shown in Fig. 1. The existing solution used by Company A is termed Storage Manager (SM). It is used for creating, storing and exchanging business objects across the company's IT systems. Using the SM-SDK, an export functionality was developed that transforms (hierarchically organised) business objects into OPC UA graph structures. These structures are represented in XML according to the UANodeSet schema (http://opcfoundation.org/UA/2011/03/UAN odeSet.xsd) and are cached in a central Redis database (https://redis.io/), from which instances of OPC servers can load the data. OPC UA clients can access the server instances via the web to allow manipulation of the data using Read, Write and Update operations. The allocation of server instances to clients is hardcoded. For productive use, more dynamic allocation mechanisms based on load balancing would be needed. OPC UA clients can interact with the model transformation component to modify existing business object types.

The central Redis database allows keeping the OPC UA data structures consistent across arbitrary numbers of server instances. A publish/subscribe model is used as the basis of a clustering concept, where server instances can reload the most current data from the Redis cache. This allows adding and removing server instances dynamically without affecting the running business process.

The publish/subscribe model is shown in Fig. 2. The *EntryPoint* of an OPC UA graph references a set of unique *SessionIds* representing a customer's online sessions used when applying for an insurance. Every *SessionId* references a set of *InstanceIds* representing different states in the evolution of a business object (e.g., the insurance application) as the customer creates, modifies or deletes individual data items. Every *InstanceId* references a *Model* representing the type or version of the business object definition used when the respective instance was created. As OPC UA server instances need to know only the *EntryPoint* of the graph, the remaining data can be loaded dynamically using this set of references. The unique identifiers of the nodes in the graph are identical with the names of the subscription channels in the Redis database. Any change of a data item is published on the corresponding channel, so that all subscribed server instances receive the new value.

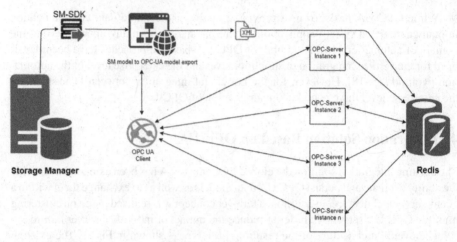

Fig. 1. System architecture.

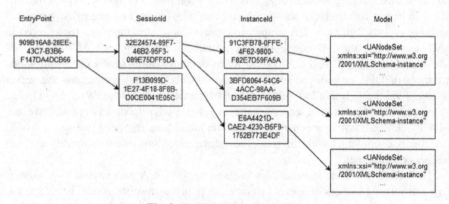

Fig. 2. Publish/Subscribe model.

5 Application

A prototype was implemented using the concepts presented in Sect. 4, and applied to a case of insurance processing. In particular, the prototype implements 'Part 8: Data Access' (IEC 62541-8) and 'Part 11: Historical Access' (IEC 62541-11) of the OPC UA standard. In this Section, we present how it is able to address some of the traceability issues outlined at the beginning of this paper.

One of the insurance products that can be applied for on Company A's website is household insurance. Applicants need to fill out an online form with details of their household, as shown in Fig. 3. (As Company A targets the Austrian market, the website is available only in German. We annotated a few English translations for non-German speaking readers of this paper.) The OPC UA data structure generated from this form is shown on the lower righthand side of Fig. 3, provided as a screenshot of the OPC UA client (https://www.unified-automation.com/products/development-tools/uaexpert.html) used for developing the prototype. The data structure is consistent with the publish/subscribe model in Fig. 2.

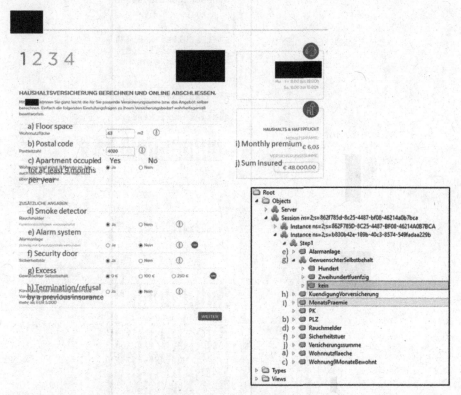

Fig. 3. "Step 1" in a 4-step process of applying for a household insurance: Online form to be filled out by a customer. On the lower righthand side is the OPC UA data model generated from the online form. Any information revealing the company's identity has been blackened.

The data access view of the OPC UA client is shown in Fig. 4, highlighting the standardised description of some of the data items provided by the insurance applicant. Every data item is identified with a unique Node Id. Status codes indicate whether the transfer between client and server was successful, thus providing a basis for answering question Q1 in Sect. 2. Both the data creation by the insurance applicant on the online form and the data transfer to the OPC UA server instance are timestamped. As shown in Fig. 4, the difference between the two timestamps is smaller than 1 ms. This allows simultaneous access to the data by multiple clients, which may be used for enhanced customer support. For example, Company A's customer service representatives may use their OPC UA clients to monitor data entries in real time while answering the customers' questions on the phone. A representative may also enter new data directly, in which case the changes can be immediately viewed on the customer's online form.

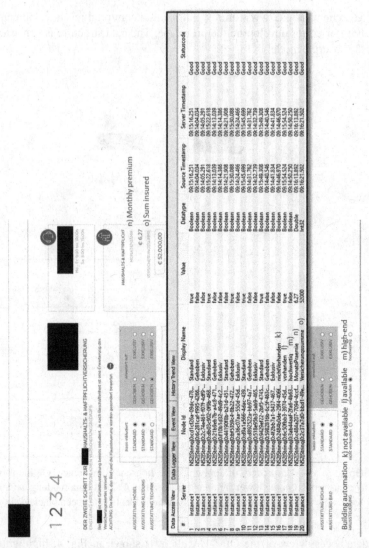

Fig. 4. Data access view of the OPC UA model instance generated from "Step 2" of the online application process. Any information revealing the company's identity has been blackened.

All data entries, including their provenance from the customer or a service representative, are recorded using the historical access functionalities provided by OPC UA. A screenshot of the historical view of a particular data item in a OPC UA client is shown in Fig. 5, displaying all timestamped value changes (basis for answering Q2 and, to some extent, Q4). An extended logging feature was implemented that also records the particular person or system effecting a change (basis for answering Q3). This history is stored in an SQL database.

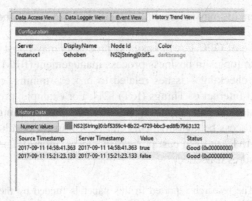

Fig. 5. Historical access to a data item provided by the OPC UA client.

6 Conclusion

The project reported in this paper has explored an OPC UA-based solution for the issue of traceable data transfers for compliance purposes in an insurance company, as one of the first known implementations of OPC UA outside manufacturing. While for business reasons the prototype was not turned into a productively used solution, it has shown its support for answering the types of questions commonly posed by auditors. Using OPC UA's standard mechanisms has advantages over custom-built solutions. This includes the availability of information models and service architectures that are normed, proven in practice, and supported by existing tools. OPC UA also provides additional capabilities that are novel for enterprise integration beyond the shopfloor and may lead to innovation in business operations. An example was described in Sect. 5 that includes the possibility to provide customer support simultaneously online and on the phone, based on the real-time capabilities of OPC UA data transfers.

The benefits of OPC UA-based integration come with limitations that mainly act as entry barriers. The first issue is the knowledge gap. OPC UA is a relatively domain-specific technology, and most IT professionals – especially those working in the financial services domain – are not familiar with it. Even for developers in the automation domain the learning curve for using the OPC UA standard appears to be quite steep [19]. Other issues include the high risk involved in migrating from existing integration solutions, and the high investment cost incurred by acquiring OPC UA development licences and training personnel.

It can be expected that these entry barriers will impede the adoption of OPC UA in the financial services industry. Yet, momentum may arise from emerging business models involving cross-domain enterprise integration. Many Industry 4.0 business models are based on the integration of production and business processes from shopfloor to office floor and across company networks [20]. This aims to provide greater flexibility, enabling the individualisation of products and services to different customers. For example, hybrid service bundles may combine products with data-driven services, such as production machines provided in combination with usage-based (predictive) maintenance services. OPC UA, as an important Industry 4.0 standard, can enable such a business model. In turn, the expected benefits may increase the adoption of OPC UA in the financial services domain.

A possible uptake of OPC UA in business processes may boost a number of other data-centred research topics in business process management (BPM), which include – besides compliance checking – issues related to process mining, context awareness, predictive BPM, and Internet of Things (IoT) [21]. For example, predictive BPM may benefit from the historical data captured via OPC UA by obtaining rich datasets for forecasting future process behaviours. This can be useful for developing digital twins that have the ability to learn from past process instances, monitor current instances and take corrective measures if needed.

Acknowledgments. The research reported in this paper is funded by the Austrian Research Promotion Agency (FFG) via project no. 862143.

References

1. Governatori, G., Sadiq, S.: The journey to business process compliance. In: Cardoso, J., van der Aalst, W. (eds.) Handbook of Research on Business Process Modeling, pp. 426–454. IGI Global (2009)
2. Hashmi, M., Governatori, G., Lam, H.-P., Wynn, M.T.: Are we done with business process compliance: state of the art and challenges ahead. Knowl. Inf. Syst. **57**(1), 79–133 (2018). https://doi.org/10.1007/s10115-017-1142-1
3. Ahmed, F., Jahangir, U., Rahim, H., Ali, K., Agha, D-e-S.: Centralized log management using Elasticsearch, Logstash and Kibana. In: 2020 International Conference on Information Science and Communication Technology. Karachi, Pakistan, pp. 1–7 (2020)
4. IEC: OPC Unified Architecture Part 1: Overview and Concepts (IEC/TR 62541-1:2010). International Electrotechnical Commission, Geneva (2010)
5. Gozman, D., Currie, W.: Managing governance, risk, and compliance for post-crisis regulatory change: A model of IS capabilities for financial organizations. In: 2015 48th Hawaii International Conference on System Sciences (HICSS), Kauai, HI (2015)
6. Kshetri, N.: Regulatory technology and supervisory technology: current status, facilitators, and barriers. Computer **56**(1), 64–75 (2023)
7. Forbes. https://www.forbes.com/sites/servicenow/2021/10/21/the-creeping-cost-of-compliance/?sh=4339140556cc. Accessed 03 Apr 2023
8. Mahnke, W., Leitner, S.-H., Damm, M.: OPC Unified Architecture. Springer, Heidelberg (2009). https://doi.org/10.1007/978-3-540-68899-0
9. VDI/VDE. Status Report: Reference Architecture Model Industrie 4.0 (RAMI4.0). VDI/VDE Society Measurement and Automatic Control (GMA), 2015 July, Düsseldorf (2015)
10. VDMA. Industrie 4.0 Communication Guideline Based on OPC UA. VDMA, Frankfurt (2017)
11. Henßen, R., Schleipen, M.: Interoperability between OPC UA and AutomationML. Procedia CIRP **25**, 297–304 (2014)
12. Lee, B., Kim, D.-K., Yang, H., Oh, S.: Model transformation between OPC UA and UML. Comput. Stand. Interfaces **50**, 236–250 (2017)
13. IEC. OPC Unified Architecture Part 3: Address Space Model (IEC/TR 62541-3:2010). International Electrotechnical Commission, Geneva (2010)

14. González, I., Calderón, A.J., Figueiredo, J., Sousa, J.M.C.: A literature survey on Open Platform Communications (OPC) applied to advanced industrial environments. Electronics **8**, 510 (2019)
15. Kannengiesser, U., Neubauer, M., Heininger, R.: Subject-oriented BPM as the glue for integrating enterprise processes in smart factories. In: Ciuciu, I., et al. (eds.) OTM 2015. LNCS, vol. 9416, pp. 77–86. Springer, Cham (2015). https://doi.org/10.1007/978-3-319-26138-6_11
16. Christmann, D., et al.: Vertical integration and adaptive services in networked production environments. In: Felderer, M., et al. (eds.) ERP Future 2015 – Research, pp. 147–162. Springer, Switzerland (2016)
17. García, M.V., Irisarri, E., Pérez, F., Estévez, E., Marcos, M.: OPC-UA communications integration using a CPPS architecture. In: IEEE Ecuador Technical Chapters Meeting (ETCM). Guayaquil, Ecuador (2016)
18. Wrede, S., Beyer, O., Dreyer, C., Wojtynek, M., Steil, J.: Vertical integration and service orchestration for modular production systems using business process models. Procedia Technol. **26**, 259–266 (2016)
19. Reiswich, E., Fay, A.: Strategy for the amendment of plant information models by means of OPC UA. In: 2012 10th IEEE International Conference on Industrial Informatics (INDIN), Beijing (2012)
20. Kagermann, H.: Change through digitization – value creation in the age of Industry 4.0. In: Albach, H., et al. (eds.) Management of Permanent Change, pp. 23–45. Springer, New York (2015)
21. Lederer, M., Elstermann, M., Betz, S., Schmidt, W.: Technology-, human-, and data-driven developments in business process management: a literature analysis. In: S-BPM ONE 2020. CCIS 1278, pp. 217–231. Springer, Cham (2020)

Code Generation for Cloud-Based Implementation of Public Sector Processes Using a Pattern-Based Approach

Jan Gottschick[1]([✉]) [iD], Anna Opaska[1] [iD], Petra Steffens[2] [iD],
and Jaouhara Zouagui[1] [iD]

[1] Fraunhofer FOKUS, Berlin, Germany
{jan.gottschick,anna.opaska,jaouhara.zouagui}@fokus.fraunhofer.de
[2] Ingrano Solutions, Berlin, Germany
petra.steffens@ingrano-solutions.com
https://www.fokus.fraunhofer.de/dps

Abstract. For public sector digitisation, the working processes of public administration are recorded, documented and optimised. This paper is concerned with the question of how the resulting business process models can be used for the development of cloud-based systems in a model-driven software development approach. In doing so, it focuses on the formulation of a methodical and technological approach called Towerpark. Towerpark comprises two elements: a process modelling notation and a set of technical tools for the building of specific applications using code generation in the context of public administration. The Towerpark modelling notation (TMN) uses elements from the Business Process Model and Notation (BPMN) 2.0, whereas the Towerpark processing components rely on Kubernetes: from BPMN diagrams, Kubernetes manifests are generated, which can be deployed as specific applications inside a cloud infrastructure. We illustrate and evaluate our approach with a case study and give an outlook on further research activities.

Keywords: BPMN · DMN · Low-Code · eGovernment · Cloud Computing · Towerpark

1 Motivation and Objectives

In Germany, efforts to digitize the public sector can be assigned to largely three dimensions. On the **regulatory** dimension, federal and state laws have been passed, which are intended to facilitate electronic communication and transactions with public administration. The legal situation of electronic administration is shaped, in particular, by the federal "E-Government Act" [12], by state-specific eGovernment laws [11], and by the Online Access Act [5]. On the

strategic level, programs such as the National eGovernment Strategy [14], the Digital Agenda [10] and the Digital Strategy [7] have been created to advance digital government. In addition, overarching initiatives such as the "Föderales Informationsmanagement" (FIM) [4] were set off to harmonize administrative procedures across the federal, state, and local level and to standardize government processes. On the **implementation** level, numerous projects on communal, state, and federal level have been conducted over the last years to automate individual public sector services [6].

In the initiatives and projects on all three levels, the business processes underlying government services – be they government-to-government, citizen-to-government, or business-to-government - play a crucial role as the starting and end point of specific digitization efforts and as the target of regulation and strategy design. The objective of all such efforts is to replace current public sector as-is processes by future processes relying on IT applications, which offer automatic or semi-automatic solutions. The starting points for building solutions are manyfold: models of as-is processes, models of the target IT-based processes, high- and low-level specifications of the planned IT application.

Currently, the specification of as-is processes largely relies on the input of subject matter experts and the design and specification of the future IT applications on the input of IT experts and other stakeholders, including domain and legal experts.

For process modelling, Business Process Model and Notation (BPMN), in Version 2.0 an OMG standard since 2011 [3] is one of the most widely used modelling notations. For creating BPMN models for the digitization of public sector service processes, three roles are essential: the subject matter and methodical expert modelling the process and the IT developer transforming the model into executable code. There are two severe drawbacks to this approach:

- Modelling and mapping processes onto IT applications are two separate work steps. Given the scarcity of human and financial resources characteristic of the public sector, the necessity of such a two-step approach needs to be questioned.
- The development of digital public services including the design and implementation of underlying processes is usually carried out as an individual development project. Reuse potential of models and of their corresponding code is rarely realised.

In recent years, a new paradigm of software development has emerged, which aims at curing these problems: the low-code approach. This approach addresses a broad range of topics such as "process and data-oriented web and app development, but also artificial intelligence, interface and output generation, process control and automation, decision automation, data analysis, geodata processing and much more." [16]. Characteristic of low-code embracing development efforts in these areas is the vision of a) collapsing process modelling and code generation into one step and b) making model artifacts and the corresponding software components (microservices) reusable.

In this paper, we will describe the low-code approach Towerpark, developed within a research activity at Fraunhofer FOKUS. The Towerpark approach has two strategic objectives. It uses a restricted, specific form of BPMN to model public sector services, so that they can be understood both by actors participating in the process and by technical experts (e.g., software architects). Its second objective is to use low-code and advanced generators for translating models into executable code deployable in cloud-native infrastructures while at the same time avoiding the orchestration performed by classical BPM engines. This leads to the following research questions:

1. What could be a generic approach for digitizing public services applying low-code principles?
2. How should public sector service processes be modelled to adequately reflect both the domain and the technical view?
3. What would be a technical approach for transforming such models of public sector service processes into cloud-native solutions?

The paper is organised as follows: Section 2 provides an overview on the related work, Sect. 3 presents our proposed procedure for developing applications in Towerpark, Sect. 4 outlines the Towerpark Modelling Notation and Sect. 5 evaluates the proposed notation using a case study, Sect. 6 describes the implemented components while Sect. 7 presents our conclusion and thoughts on further research.

2 Related Work

Our research is initially based on established methods for model-driven software development (MDSD) [22] where parts of the application logic can be implemented in modelling instead of programming languages. In more detail, we define model-to-code translations, which we implement as template-based code generators. In order to define useful BPMN patterns and transformation rules for infrastructure code generation, we have furthermore researched common requirements and functionalities in specific applications in public administrations as well as Microservice [17,21] and Kubernetes patterns [23,24].

We propose an alternative to model-based process automation used in common Business Process Management Systems (BPMS). In contrast to our code generation approach, these systems use workflow engines, for instance the Business Process Execution Language (BPEL) engine or the Camunda Workflow engine to interpret process models (often in BPMN notation) at runtime. With the Zeebe Engine (https://github.com/camunda/zeebe), Camunda also provides a cloud-native BPM engine for microservice orchestration.

Workflow engines are often an integral part of process-oriented low-code platforms, e.g. Mendix (https://www.mendix.com), Pega (https://www.pega.com), Intrexx (https://www.intrexx.com), or A12 (https://www.mgm-tp.com/a12). Due to the increasing interest in low-code as a driver for digitizing public administration services, this technology is gaining ground in public administration, which also inspires the study of alternative solutions.

Several code generating approaches have been published which are based on BPMN or extended versions of BPMN. An excerpt of these approaches is given below:

– Chun Ouyang et al. [25] define a model-to-code translation from BPMN to Business Process Execution Language (BPEL) for a subset of patterns, with the aim of generating executable models from BPMN.
– Diaz et al. [26] define a method to generate code for user interfaces from BPMN models based on rules that were derived from seven projects from the Bizagi repository. In order to avoid ambiguity, the authors extend the BPMN notation with stereotypes.
– Gonzalez-Huerta et al. [27] propose a method for refining BPMN models that were created by process analysts into more unified BPMN models with computationally relevant properties. These refined models are then used to derive Unified Modeling Language (UML) models for designing software artefacts. The authors use pattern recognition to detect and correct incomplete BPMN patterns in the input model and differentiate between BPMN patterns and domain-specific patterns. Their approach is similar to ours in that it introduces patterns for the creation of a to-be BPMN model that takes into account the software system to be implemented. However, following the refinement, the software still needs to be fully implemented by software developers.
– De Moura et al. [28] and Schneid et al. [29] describe approaches for generating code for test cases from BPMN models in order to support automated testing in BPMS. De Moura et al. derive from a BPMN model a table of all possible process flows that serves as the basis for test code generation. Schneid et al. [29] introduce a no-code wizard-based test specification based on process analysis. In addition, Yotyawilai und Suwannasart [30] and also Paiva et al. [31] published about creating test cases with BPMN models.
– Kopp et al. [32] propose BPMN4TOSCA, a BPMN extension for the integraton of the OASIS Topology and Orchestration Specification for Cloud Applications (TOSCA), a standard for the specification of cloud-based applications. Furthermore, there have been efforts towards a mapping between TOSCA and Kubernetes API components [33]. This approach, however, focuses on technical models only and does not address the generation of infrastructure code.

3 Approach and Methodology

Traditionally, process-based software development is a multi-step, cross-level and cross-organizational procedure, in which several process models with different degrees of abstraction are created by different participants: in the first step, a process modelling expert, in cooperation with domain experts, builds an understanding of the existing business processes and documents them as process models on a **conceptional** level, e.g., in BPMN. These models are then usually extensively optimized in order to clarify the work processes and to prepare the technical implementation. In the next step, the process models are **technically**

refined by a technical expert or process engineer with regard to the software system to be implemented.

On the **implementation** level, the resulting technical models usually serve either as a basis for further software development or as orchestration descriptions in a BPM engine. Deviating from this, we first propose the process-based generation of cloud infrastructure code, e.g., for Kubernetes, in order to map process models directly into the cloud. The infrastructure code can be seen as a skeleton of a generic distributed application. To enable the generation of infrastructure code, we defined the Towerpark Modelling Notation (TMN), which can be used for technical refinement in order to create technical process models that combine the domain as well as the technical view. The automated mapping of the process documentation to an application in the cloud is possible with the help of adaptable software components that are associated with the predefined patterns that form the TMN, and with additional code generators.

Furthermore, we define additional implementation steps to enable **low-code development**, in which the generated application skeleton can be further refined for concrete domain-specific use cases. For the refinement, we implemented a prototypical integrated development environment (IDE) that adapts flexibly to the modelled technical process and allows domain and technical experts to create templates for specific applications by defining data models, views and component-specific models, such as Decision Model and Notation (DMN) diagrams. After these configurations, the specific application can be deployed to run on the technical infrastructure.

4   Towerpark Modelling Notation

The Towerpark Modelling Notation (TMN) is a catalogue of Towerpark patterns, each of which consists of the following parts: a BPMN pattern that can be used in the process model, associated infrastructure code templates, such as Kubernetes manifest templates, that enable the model-to-code transformation, and either associated standardised, partly configurable software components, that are referenced in the associated templates, or associated code templates for an extension of the IDE that allows the low-code development of the respective software components. In the latter case, the pattern furthermore defines associated non-generated artefacts, such as scripts or low-code models, that need to be provided.

Each process model that consists of BPMN patterns defined in the TMN can be translated into valid and complete infrastructure code. In our current implementation, we generate code for Kubernetes. However, the approach can be likewise adapted to, e.g., infrastructure-as-code languages like Terraform [34] and Nomad [18] for the deployment to virtual machines (Infrastructure-as-a-Service).

In this section, we describe the respective modelling and the associated implementation for selected TMN patterns. The TMN pattern catalogue is divided into the following categories: sequences, conditionals, parallelization, events,

external interfaces, lanes, and low-code. The selected patterns from the catalogue shown below represent their respective categories. The patterns are partly
based on experience and analysis of the architecture from existing solutions.
Although the catalogue represents a working status, it already covers representative application domains.

Figure 1 shows two process flows with two sequential tasks each. Each task
has a name, which relates to the microservice and optionally includes a usage
purpose (separated by a hash mark). In TMN, the two tasks can be seen as
microservices that communicate internally, using either REST calls or events, as
defined by the OpenAPI and AsyncAPI specifications [1, 19]. Events are used, if
the receiving task is a parallel multi-instance task. In the final application, the
event is sent via an event message broker, using event queue groups to ensure that
each event will be processed exactly once. The event topic, which is the name of
the event channel belonging to an event queue group, is prefixed in the process
model by a percentage sign. The data type of the payload is given inside pointed
brackets as a label of the connector. The schema of the data type is defined in
detail in a separate artifact, usually an OpenAPI or AsyncAPI specification. If
the type is not given, it will be inherited from the communication preceding the
previous task. The various kinds of tasks are described in Sect. 4.

Fig. 1. Task sequences

Figure 2 shows how conditionals are modeled in TMN. There must be one default
path, so that it is always guaranteed that one path is taken. All other paths are
guarded by a JSON Matching Expression path (JMESPath) expression [15] as
condition, which must evaluate to a boolean value. The input for which the
expression is evaluated is the payload (message) to be sent to the tasks to follow. The expressions should be unambiguous to ensure a deterministic behavior.
Each path can contain any kind of process and can use a different kind of communication protocol (REST/event).

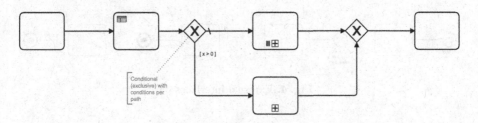

Fig. 2. Conditionals

Figure 3 shows the parallel execution of tasks or subprocesses. A copy of the message is sent to all parallel paths by the copier. The copier makes a note to whom it has sent the message. Each path can contain any kind of process. In addition, each path can contain a JMESPath expression as filter for specifying whether to forward a message only partially or not at all. If an optional merger is found, the merger collects the results of each of the preceding tasks of each path and merges the results to the final message. The final message is sent to the subsequent task as soon as all paths have finished their calculation. If one or more paths do not deliver a result, the execution will not finish. Therefore, processes should be encapsulated by a transaction, which will be described below. Each path can use a different kind of communication protocol (REST/event).

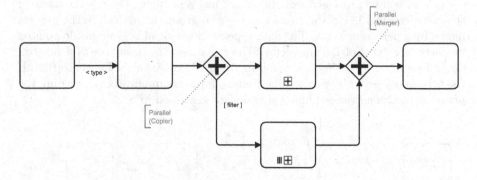

Fig. 3. Parallel execution of tasks

The patterns in Fig. 4 are used for communication from external services to the process using an API, or for communication from the process with external services. Requests from external services must use the given OpenAPI or AsyncAPI specification of the receiving task. If the default OpenAPI or AsyncAPI specification is used only, the scheme needs to be given. Resulting messages of the process can be forwarded to external services, using REST or event interfaces. The path to use of the given OpenAPI or the topic to use of the AsyncAPI define the target function of the service.

Fig. 4. External interfaces

The TMN is especially intended for low-code solutions. As stated previously, some patterns are not associated with existing software building blocks, but via the low-code extension of our development environment with code generators that create software from additional models. A low-code pattern (see Fig. 5) consists of a basic pattern, for example a business rule task, and a data object reference, which defines the related model and its model type marked by a hash mark. For example, a business rule can be implemented by providing a DMN [9] model ("# Rule"). The DMN model is used to generate the code for the microservice later to be deployed.

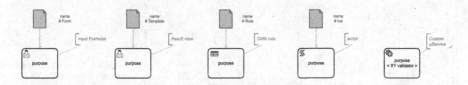

Fig. 5. Low-code patterns

The patterns shown above represent the core set of the Towerpark architectural patterns. The infrastructure code generated from the TMN models can configure all instantiated components and their interconnections so that the central orchestration by a business process engine is no longer required. The patterns simply describe the architecture of the modelled application.

5 Case Study: Parental Allowance

As required by the German Online Access Act (in German: Onlinezugangsgesetz [5], abbreviated as "OZG"), a central portal needs to be launched that offers citizen-to-government and business-to-government applications. In particular, it should allow citizens to submit an application for a statutory benefit, like parental allowance. The model in Fig. 6 shows this use case in a slightly simplified form. It does not include the user interface for the citizen nor for the government agent. The example shows the automated back office process, which is the focus of TMN. An application form received from a central portal as defined by the OZG will be automatically verified and checked. If the application is considered complete and correct, it is automatically approved and a notification is returned to the applicant. The application and the corresponding notification are stored for later use.

For better understanding, the process is logically divided into three phases: application, approval, and storage. It is important to understand that there are patterns (the tasks marked "# application receiver", "# parental allowance verify functions" and "# email sender"), which are implemented by reusable domain-specific microservices (components). Usually, these microservices only have to be configured for the use case at hand. The configuration has to be done by classical software programmers. For the other tasks, low-code components are used, which will be generated from their related models. The generators are typically programmed by software experts. Rules and templates should be maintainable by domain experts of the public administration. The more technical GraphQL model should be managed by a low-code expert together with the domain experts.

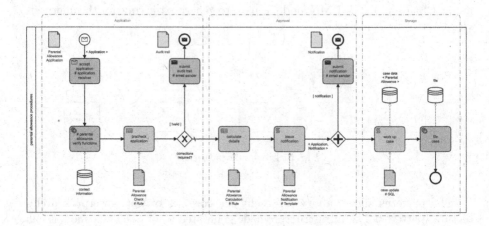

Fig. 6. Case study: parental allowance

The case study shows that the backoffice process can be described in a way, which on the one hand can be comprehended by the domain experts. On the other hand, the model can include the architectural patterns of TMN to provide the technical details for executing the BPMN model. In addition, the model reveals the new division of labour: who of the involved experts is responsible for which part of the implementation and its maintenance.

6 Implementation

We validated our approach by implementing an initial "Towerpark Toolset" as a proof-of-concept at Fraunhofer FOKUS. The toolset consists of a set of standardised, partly configurable software components that are associated with patterns of the TMN, several low-code generators for the respective low-code patterns and the major tool Navigator, which compiles TMN process models into infrastructure code. As the Towerpark system represents an open approach, it is provided that domain- and customer-specific building blocks can be added to the toolset.

Standard Microservices. We implemented a set of standardised reusable microservices that can be used to assemble generic applications and that are associated with some of the predefined TMN patterns. An example for a microservice that provides a frequently needed standard functionality is one for the conditional forwarding of messages, which is associated with the conditional TMN pattern.

Low-Code Generators. In addition to the pre-implemented standard microservices, our approach ensures that microservices can be generated from low-code models created by domain experts. For the proof-of-concept, we implemented the code generator Pharos that generates code for a microservice from a DMN diagram. The implementation of Pharos focuses on code generation based on rules which are part of DMN decision tables. The Pharos code generation translates each rule into an if-then-else-statement. The generated microservices can be packaged into a container image and inserted into the generated infrastructure code. In addition to DMN models, other models such as CMMN models are conceivable for code generation in Towerpark. The architectural patterns of TMN support various model languages for the low-code pattern. Thus, the approach is open for other specific models and their corresponding generators.

Navigator. The Navigator is a compiler written in the Rust programming language that on the one hand generates Kubernetes resources from BPMN XML, given that the modelled processes consist of the defined TMN patterns, and on the other hand generates also code to extend our IDE in accordance to the process model. The generated Kubernetes resources consist of manifest files for ReplicaSets, CronJobs and Services as well as of a customisation file (https:// kustomize.io/) that manages the creation of ConfigMaps and simplifies deployment. The resources serve as a blueprint for a cloud-native application, which can be complemented by Towerpark software components. The translation process is implemented as follows: initially, the Navigator deserialises a BPMN XML file into an internal data structure which is then transformed into a tree structure that represents the modelled processes. The Navigator then identifies the TMN patterns through pattern matching with a PEG grammar [13], using the PEST parser (https://crates.io/crates/pest). For each match, the parser creates an abstract syntax tree, which is used to extract relevant data for the specification of the associated Kubernetes templates. Finally, the resources are serialised into YAML files. In case of patterns for which non-generated artefacts need to be provided, these are assigned using the ID of the modelled BPMN task element. Because the TMN neither extend nor change the BPMN metamodel, common BPMN modelling tools can be used to create input models for the Navigator.

7   Conclusion and Outlook

Business process modelling in the public sector is an important, in certain cases even legally prescribed, endeavour. It also is a prerequisite for the automation of public sector processes and for efficient implementation and deployment processes. Ensuring that domain-specific models are mapped onto IT applications efficiently and adequately presents a major challenge. A model-based approach, in particular the low-code approach, would enable public sector domain experts to play a more active role in the technical creation and maintenance of IT applications and contribute to the transparency of IT solutions.

In this paper, we described the Towerpark approach for digitizing public services, applying low-code principles. It comprises the Towerpark modelling notation, the Towerpark toolset and a generic procedure for creating public sector applications from domain models. The Towerpark modelling notation aims at specifying both the domain processes and the software architecture of public sector applications. The focus of the Towerpark approach is the automation of backoffice processes. The Towerpark architecture, however, also supports the communication with user frontends through open interfaces. More generally speaking, it can be said that the Towerpark approach represents an open solution in two ways: it allows for the integration and exchange of tools and it is open for the integration of additional patterns if required.

There are a number of open research and practical issues, which need to be treated, in order to apply the Towerpark approach in real-life larger-scale projects and thus to promote its diffusion:

- optimization of the generated cloud code
- integration of additional architectural patterns and of their respective tools (e.g., generators or microservices)
- integration of additional low-code patterns and their respective tools (e.g., generators)
- extension of the approach to include patterns for specific technical and domain-specific aspects
- integration of domain-specific microservices
- generation of code for other technical infrastructures like IaaS (VMs)

In addition to these technical issues, the implications of low-code and model-based development of public sector applications should be empirically investigated.

In the light of our learnings and analyses from the application of the Towerpark approach, we are confident to claim that its potential for practical use and its benefits have been demonstrated successfully. Thus, we have been able to show that a typical government process, that of applying for parental allowance, can be implemented by using the proposed patterns and the code generation mechanisms. Even though the scope of this proof of concept is rather narrow, it shows that the Towerpark toolset can be used to generate a technical solution for public sector applications running in a cloud-native environment. To establish the general validity of the Towerpark approach though, the feasibility and practicality of mapping model fragments into RESTful methods and event-driven communication need to be demonstrated on a larger scale and in different industries.

References

1. AsyncAPI Initiative Homepage. https://www.asyncapi.com/. Accessed 27 Feb 2023
2. Business Process Model and Notation (BPMN) Homepage. https://www.omg.org/bpmn/. Accessed 27 Feb 2023
3. Object Management Group, ISO/IEC 19510:2013–07 (2013). https://www.iso.org/standard/62652.html

4. Bundesministerium des Innern: FIM E-Government mit Zukunft. https://www.bmi.bund.de/SharedDocs/downloads/DE/veroeffentlichungen/themen/moderne-verwaltung/foederales-informationsmanagement.html. Accessed 27 Feb 2023

5. Onlinezugangsgesetz, vom 14. August 2017 (BGBl. I S. 3122, 3138). https://www.gesetze-im-internet.de/ozg/OZG.pdf. Accessed 13 Apr 2023

6. Bundesministerium des Innern und für Heimat: Dashboard Digitale Verwaltung. https://dashboard.ozg-umsetzung.de/. Accessed 27 Feb 2023

7. Bundesministerium für Digitales und Verkehr, Digitalstrategie - Gemeinsam digitale Werte schöpfen. https://bmdv.bund.de/SharedDocs/DE/Anlage/K/presse/063-digitalstrategie.pdf. Accessed 27 Feb 2023

8. Case Management Model and Notation (CNMN) Homepage. https://www.omg.org/cmmn/. Accessed 27 Feb 2023

9. Decision Model and Notation (DMN) Homepage. https://www.omg.org/dmn/. Accessed 27 Feb 2023

10. Die Bundesregierung: Digitale Agenda 2014–2017. https://www.bmwk.de/Redaktion/DE/Publikationen/Digitale-Welt/digitale-agenda.pdf. Accessed 27 Feb 2023

11. Deutscher Bundestag: E-Government in Deutschland, vom 28.06.2019 (WD 3–3000 -134719), pp. 9–11. https://www.bundestag.de/resource/blob/655082/32a17c3834d5c5c5d6f5a7232f0491c0/WD-3-134-19-pdf-data.pdf. Accessed 27 Feb 2023

12. E-Government-Gesetz, vom 25. Juli 2013 (BGBl. I S. 2749). https://www.gesetze-im-internet.de/egovg/. Accessed 27 Feb 2023

13. Ford, B.: Parsing expression grammars: a recognition based syntactic foundation. In: Proceedings of the 31st ACM SIGPLAN-SIGACT Symposium on Principles of Programming Languages, pp. 111–122. ACM (2004). https://doi.org/10.1145/964001.964011

14. IT-Planungsrat: Nationale E-Government-Strategie Fortschreibung 2015. https://www.it-planungsrat.de/fileadmin/it-planungsrat/der-it-planungsrat/nationale-e-government-strategie/NEGS_Fortschreibung.pdf. Accessed 27 Feb 2023

15. JMESPath Homepage. https://jmespath.org/. Accessed 27 Feb 2023

16. Low-Code Association e.V.: The Low-Code Manifesto. https://www.lowcodeassociation.org/manifesto/. Accessed 27 Feb 2023

17. Microservice Architecture. https://microservices.io/index.html. Accessed 27 Feb 2023

18. Nomad Homepage. https://www.nomadproject.io/. Accessed 27 Feb 2023

19. OpenAPI Initiative Specification. https://spec.openapis.org/oas/latest.html. Accessed 27 Feb 2023

20. A thoughtful introduction to the pest parser, urlpest.rs/book/. Accessed 27 Feb 2023

21. Richardson, C.: Microservices Patterns, 1st edn. Manning, New York (2018)

22. Stahl, T., Völter, M.: Model-Driven Software Development. Technology, Engineering, Management, Wiley (2006)

23. Burns, B.: Designing Distributed Systems. O'Reilly (2018)

24. Ibryam, B., Huss, R.: Kubernetes Patterns: Reusable Elements for Designing Cloud Native Applications. O'Reilly (2023)

25. Ouyang, C., Dumas, M., ter Hofstede, A., van der Aalst, W.: From BPMN process models to BPEL web services. In: ICWS 06 - IEEE International Conference OB Web Services, Chicago (2006). https://ieeexplore.ieee.org/abstract/document/4032038

26. Diaz, E., Rueda, S.: Generation of user interfaces from business process model notation (BPMN). In: EICS 19 - Proceedings of the ACM SIGCHI Symposium on Engineering Interactive Computing Systems, pp. 1–5 June 2019. https://doi.org/10.1145/3319499.3328242

27. Gonzalez-Huerta, J., Boubaker, A., Mili, H.: A business process re-engineering approach to transform BPMN models to software artifacts. In: E-Technologies: Embracing the Internet of Things, pp. 170–184. https://link.springer.com/chapter/10.1007/978-3-319-59041-7_10

28. de Moura, J., Charão, A.S., Lima, J., de Oliveira Stein, B.: Test case generation from BPMN models for automated testing of web-based BPM applications. In: 2017 17th International Conference on Computational Science and Its Applications, 03–06 July 2017, Trieste, pp. 1–7 (2017). https://ieeexplore.ieee.org/abstract/document/7999652

29. Schneid, K., Stapper, L., Thöne, S., Kuchen, H.: Automated regression tests: a no-code approach for BPMN-based process-driven applications. In: 2021 IEEE 25th International Enterprise Distributed Object Computing Conference, 25–29 October 2021, Gold Coast, pp. 31–40 (2021). https://ieeexplore.ieee.org/abstract/document/9626192

30. Yotyawilai, P., Suwannasart, T.: Design of a tool for generating test cases from BPMN. In: 2014 International Conference on Data and Software Engineering, pp. 1–6 (2014). https://ieeexplore.ieee.org/stamp/stamp.jsp?tp=&arnumber=7062692&tag=1

31. Paiva, A., Flores, N., Faria, J., Marques, J.: End-to-end automatic business process validation. In: FAMS 2018 - The 8th International Symposium on Frontiers in Ambient and Mobile Systems, pp. 999–1004 (2018). https://www.sciencedirect.com/science/article/pii/S1877050918304666/pdf?md5=84182f8e0b708e00184b54c08478275a&pid=1-s2.0-S1877050918304666-main.pdf

32. Kopp, O., Binz, T., Breitenbücher, U., Leymann, F.: BPMN4TOSCA: a domain-specific language to model management plans for composite applications, business process model and notation, pp. 38–52 (2012). https://link.springer.com/chapter/10.1007/978-3-642-33155-8_4

33. Borisova, A., Shvetcova, V., Borisenko, O.: Adapting of the TOSCA standard model for the Kubernetes container environment, IVMEM - Ivanikov Memorial Workshop, pp. 9–14, September 2020. https://ieeexplore.ieee.org/stamp/stamp.jsp?tp=&arnumber=9356983

34. Terraform   IaC.   https://www.terraform.io/use-cases/infrastructure-as-code. Accessed 27 Feb 2023

Revisiting the ALPS - An Investigation of Abstract Layered PASS

Matthes Elstermann$^{(\boxtimes)}$ and Jivka Ovtcharova

Karlsruhe Institute of Technology, Karlsruhe, Germany
`matthes.elstermann@kit.edu`

Abstract. This work is a re-investigation of the concept and developed tools for the modeling approach called, Abstract Layered PASS (ALPS). The paper investigates the details of what is actually two separated extensions to the classical subject-oriented modeling approach with the Parallel Activity Specification Shema (PASS). One is the concept of Layered PASS, a way of modeling multi-behavior subjects and ad-hoc extensions, while Abstract PASS is essentially the theory behind declarative process modeling within the paradigm subject-orientation. Both ideas have been further refined since their first inception and are no longer pure conceptual ideas but rather are supported by functional tools and clear application scenarios. The overall goal of this work therefore is to integrate and unify previously fragmented concepts, the additions that have been made over the last years, often due to practical modeling concerns, and present their now existing formalization with an ontological definition that was developed alongside and is compatible with the formal OWL based exchange standard for PASS.

Keywords: ALPS · Subject-Orientation · PASS · abstraction · declarative process modeling

1 Introduction

At the S-BPM ONE 2014 conference two works were presented that discussed an editing concept for so-called multi-layered subject-oriented process models [14], as well as an extension to the Parallel Activity Specification Schema (PASS) [9] that would give *declarative* modeling means to the only explicit, subject-oriented process modeling language. Together with an earlier work that considered the use of an execution pattern from robotics to execute subjects from PASS process models with multiple behaviors [11], these three works laid down the foundation for a concept that summarizingly is called Abstract Layered PASS (ALPS).

This work now revisits and analyzes the ALPS concept itself, as well as the developments and advancements of the previous years, including now available modeling and handling tools. Furthermore it will be investigate in what relation to ALPS is currently in regards to standard PASS.

The overall goal here is to integrate and unify previously fragmented concepts, the additions that have been made over the last years, often due to practical modeling concerns, and present their now existing formalization with an

M. Elstermann et al. (Eds.): S-BPM ONE 2023, CCIS 1867, pp. 263–283, 2023.
https://doi.org/10.1007/978-3-031-40213-5_19

ontological definition that was developed alongside and is compatible with the formal OWL based exchange standard for PASS.

2 ALPS

As indicated in the introduction it is important to understand that Abstract Layered PASS is actually the combination of two separate but related concepts. First is the concept of (Multi) Layered PASS and secondly the concept of Abstract PASS.

2.1 Standard PASS

The content of this work heavily depends on and requires the reader to have a sufficiently detailed understanding of the modeling paradigm of Subject-Orientation and the Parallel Activity Specification Schema (PASS). Due to the size limitation of this article, only a very brief introduction can be given at this point for the purpose of defining what is considered to be 'Standard' or 'Simple' PASS.

Following [13], Subject-Orientation(SO) is *"a modeling or description paradigm for processes that is derived from the structure of natural languages. It requires the explicit and continuous consideration of active entities within the bounds of a process as the conceptual center of description. Active entities (subjects) and passive elements (objects) must always be distinguished and activities or task can only be described in the context of a subject. The interaction between subjects is of particular importance and must explicitly be described as exchange of information that cannot be omitted."*

This simple idea leads to a quite powerful change in perspective when it comes to modeling, if truly applied. While the notion of the active entity exist in all process modeling approaches, it is the focus and centering on them that makes SO unique. Also the explicit differentiation between active and passive entities is not to be underestimated since it is what makes subject-orientation not an alternative to something like object-orientation(OO), but rather into a paradigm that encompasses lesser methodologies like OO or the procedural paradigm.

Consequently, the Parallel Activity Specification Schema (PASS) is the only *formal and graphical, subject-oriented process modeling and description language consisting of two separate but interlinked diagram types called Subject Interaction Diagram (SID) and Subject Behavior Diagram (SBD).* Figure 1 shows a simple PASS process model where the SID contains two Subjects and the messages (Objects) they exchange, while their individual SBDs show what they either do for themselves in (yellow) Do States or how they interact with the other subject in this process via either sending information in (green) Send States or waiting for information in (red) Receive States.

Not shown in this simple example, but a part of the formal model exchange standard is the conceptual idea that a subject may have multiple behaviors beyond the so-called base behavior. These additional behaviors describe either Macros, a kind of sub-process that can be called within other states, or additional

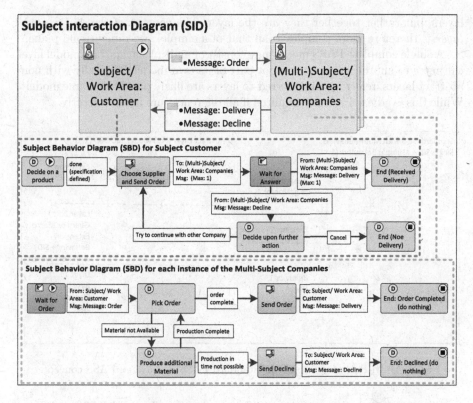

Fig. 1. Introduction to Standard PASS (example process) (Color figure online)

behaviors could describe so called Guards or Guard Behaviors, that are model mechanism to describe interrupts.

Subject-Orientation, PASS and the correlated discipline of Subject-Oriented Business Process Management (S-BPM) were created by and are founded on the works of Albert Fleischmann [16,17].

There are multiple tools supporting PASS editing [15] and as indicated, for the language itself there are formal definitions for its structure and execution [1,12].

2.2 Multi Layered PASS

In contrast to the later discussed Abstract PASS, Layered PASS is more an approach for *how* to model and structure PASS, rather than an extension to the modeling language itself.

The Concept of a PASS Model Layer: The core concept of Layered PASS is that of the titular *PASS process model layer*. In Layered PASS one *model layer* is always the combination of one SID with all SBDs connected to the contained subjects! Therefore one SID and its SBDs are not considered to be on separate layers, but rather together they *are* the layer. The concept of the ALPS *model layer* is therefore more complex than that of a simple, two-dimensional plane.

A single complete PASS model may consist of multiple layers, or a model layer can *refer* to another layer that is not part of its own model. Typically with non-abstract layers, referring and referred-to layers are likely part of the same model[1]. While this is advised it is not required if all references are made correctly.

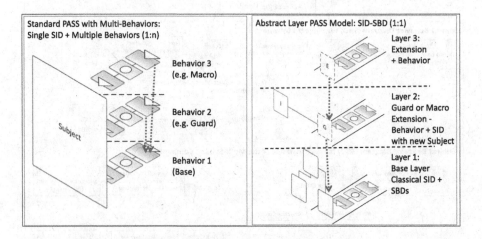

Fig. 2. Multi-Behavior Subject in Standard PASS vs Layered PASS concept

Figure 2 depicts the conceptual difference between Layered PASS and Standard PASS. In Standard PASS there are multiple behaviors per subject possible, but only one SID. In contrast to that, layered PASS keeps a 1:1 relationship between a subject and its behavior which, in turn, necessitates having an SID as the core of each additional layer containing so called *subject extensions* that refer to the additional behaviors. The types of behaviors basically correspond to the types of layers. For execution purposes layers in layered PASS have the same priority number system behind them as individual behaviors in multi-behavior, standard PASS have. However, not the single behavior has an execution priority but the whole layer, which, on the other hand, does not make any difference for the execution of individual subjects.

The big advantages of this concept are that, first it allows to keep the simple and intuitive relation of *one subject has one behavior*—a simple 1:1 relationship. Furthermore, it allows to model extended communication that may only be relevant on that layer. E.g. if an extension to an existing behavior introduces a new communication partner, this new communication partner subject can be added only there, without the need to modify the original SID. Similar aspects

---

[1] This is meant in a technical sense. Conceptually if one model layer refers to or links another layer, they together form a larger model context. Technically they are onle the same model if they have the same model-URI—assuming the use of the PASS OWL exchange standard technology.

are true for macros and guards, where this mechanism would allow to model the according concerns completely on the according layer, keeping especially the base layer SID free of possibly unnecessary technical details. Of course, if, e.g., it is important for a modeler to show the according guard messages on the base layer this can still be done in that SID. Layered PASS thereby gives a great degree of freedom for this kind of modeling.

Layered PASS Model Elements: As a consequence for considering layers not only as SBDs but as the combination of SBDs and SIDs, Layered PASS requires to extend the subject concept to work on SID extension layer. The graphical design for these are shown in Fig. 3.

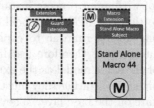

Fig. 3. Layered PASS SID Elements: Subject-Extensions (Standard, Guard, Macro) and the Stand Alone Macro

There are three types of so-called Subject-Extensions and the Stand Alone Macro Subject. In principle all of these are variants of the standard PASS Subject, that simply contains a "guard" or "extends" relationship.

The Subject Extensions are the main elements introduced by Layered PASS and layers that contain them in their SID are subsequently dubbed extension layers. Essentially, they are simple subjects with one behavior. But rather than being stand-alone, their behavior is an extension or addition to the behavior of a subject they are extending. Subsequently, they also *inherit*[2] send and receive capabilities of the subject they are extending.

All three extensions variants differ only in regards to which kind of behavior they are linked with:

Macro-Extensions are used to defined Macro-Behaviors that are already part of Standard PASS. In contrast to the Stand Alone Macros, Macro-Extension Behaviors are subject-specific. They can only be called in the states of the subject that is being extended, but therefore within the macro behavior all send and receive capabilities of the extended subject can be used legally.

Guard Extensions are used to model Guard Behaviors[3] which are the interrupt mechanism of PASS. Guard Behaviors start with special Receive States (Guard

---

[2] The extension concept is very similar to the inheritance concept in OO but adapted to the idea of Subjects. The only true addition made by the extension concept is that Subjects now have the data field to *"extend"* other Subjects and their behaviors.

[3] Like Macro behaviors Guard Behaviors also are part of Standard PASS.

Receive) describing that upon the reception of any message to be received in that receive state, the execution of the base behavior is interrupted. Guard Behaviors may end either like macros in generic *Return-to-origin* references that define to continue execution where it left off before the guard behavior was triggered. Alternatively the guard behavior may simply end its own end state or use a *State Reference* to a specific state off a base behavior.[4].

The last extension type is the general **Subject Extension**. Subject Extensions and their extension behaviors should be used only in cases where the original base model layer is not supposed to or cannot be modified. This could be the case when it is necessary to specific process variants that are only relevant for a specific sub-domain of the organization in which the modeled process is embedded. Another usage scenario is a situation where the base process model is already the foundation of a running process instance in a workflow engine. Instead of having to change the base model, a model extension could be added to a subject instance ad-hoc during runtime to cope with circumstances not envisioned in the base behavior. It is therefore less likely that Subject Extensions are modeled as part of the same model as the extended subject. Extension Behaviors do not have a start states. Rather they must start in at least one *State Reference* that extends a state on the base layer. They can end in their own end state or simply in another state reference guiding the process flow back to the base behavior. If the initial state reference of an Extension Behavior has one or more outgoing transitions with the same exit conditions as transitions of the extended state on the base layer, they basically overwrite the original process flow and reroute it, as is shown in the example extension process descriptions shown in Figs. 4 and 5. If they contain new transitions[5] they add new options to the according states.

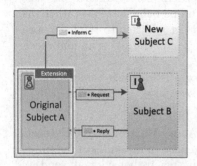

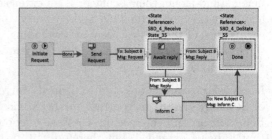

Fig. 4. Extension Layer SID with underlying base SID

Fig. 5. Extension Layer SBD of Subject Extension of Subject A with underlying base behavior

---

[4] An official specification for how especially the guard mechanism for layered models should be executed, was developed in parallel with this publication and should be published alongside this work at [4].

[5] This is only allowed for Do- and Receive States. Send State must still only have one outgoing transition which stays true even for extensions.

The final element shown in Fig. 3 that is not (yet) part of standard PASS is actually the most simple. It is called the **Stand Alone Macro Subject**. It is a subject that does not contain a standard base behavior, but rather a Macro Behavior that does not end with an End State but rather, as any Macro Behavior, with a *Return to Origin* state reference. Stand Alone Macros are being used to specify Macro Behaviors that are callable in the states of any subject. Logically therefore, the Macro Behavior of a Stand Alone Macro Subject can only send and receive messages defined for itself, but not those of other subjects, even if it is called within their behavior. Since they do not depend on any subject, they can be placed in the SID of the base layer of any model, if wished so.

2.3   Abstract PASS - Declarative Subject-Oriented Modeling

Even though not known and therefore stated at the time of conception, Abstract PASS essentially is the concept of having *Modeling by Restriction* or *declarative* modeling means with PASS. While there are classical approaches for declarative process modeling like ConDec [20,21] or DecSerFlow [21], ALPS is the only approach to do so within the modeling paradigm of subject-orientation.

For readers unfamiliar with the concept of declarative (process) modeling, in a nutshell, it is a modeling philosophy, where instead of a strict control flow, activities and especially the order of activities are not imperatively defined but rather restricted with various relative conditions.

From a (so-called) imperative[6] process modeling point of view, declarative description could be considered to be *"incomplete"*. A better view is to understand them as specifications that leave a greater degree of freedom for recipients of those specifications upon execution or implementation of such specs.[7]

In principle, this ideas is similar to the concept of *modeling by restriction* as mentioned by Fleischmann [18], however Fleischmann left it open whether the modeling language used would have explicit modeling capabilities to specify restriction or if that was a modeling method to be used with standard, imperative PASS that was about removing imperative elements.

In anyway, as envisioned in [9], in order to specify restrictions or declare preconditions, Abstract PASS requires additions to the PASS language. However, these mostly are variants of the standard PASS elements.

Abstract Model Elements SID: Figure 6 shows additional elements that can be used in abstract models.

---

[6] Usually, declarative (modeling) approaches are seen as counterpart to more classical description concepts that straightforward define how something is composed, made-up-of or, in the cases of processes, in what order activities must be done—this is referred to as imperative modeling [22,23].

[7] From this notion of having less defined or incomplete descriptions stems the name of *Abstract PASS* as this is similar as the concept of *Abstract Classes* or *Abstract Data Types* in object oriented programming. *Declarative PASS* would have been an equally good denomination. See also Sects. 2.3 and 2.5.

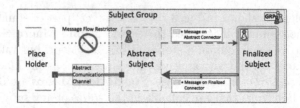

Fig. 6. Overview over declarative SID elements in ALPS

The only truly new element is the *Message Flow Restrictor* which does forbid any direct communication between the two subject connected by it[8].

The *Place Holder* simply is a kind dummy subject, that would allow to express something like *"any other subject"*.

The *Abstract Communication Channel* is a specification element that simply indicates that there is communication between two subject that is to be specified at a later point in time in an extending or implementing model. Theoretically the channel could be directed if only a one-way communication needs to be specified.

The *Abstract Subject* is nothing but a normal, Fully Specified Subject, but with an abstract (or incomplete) behavior (see next subsection). Abstract subjects, similar to abstract classes in programming, are the middle ground between Fully Specified Subjects and completely abstract Interface Subjects that do not have any behavior definition. In an implementing model, multiple-abstract subjects can be implemented by a single subject as long as no behavior rule is broken. Complementing this is the concept of the *Abstract Message Connector*. For most parts it functions as a Standard Message Connector. However, an Abstract Message Connector between two Abstract or Interface Subjects A and B allows to combine the two into one subject in an implementing model, where a Standard Message connector forbids this. If they are combined into one subject the according send and receive activities between A and B and the according messages do not need to be implemented.

Then there are elements that allow to group subjects. Firstly is the pure *Subject Group*, that next simply allowing to group subjects visually, can also be the target and origin of communication connections allowing to specify that a subject could send to or receive a message from all subject within that group. For modeling purposes this is only a simplification instead of having, e.g., the same message specified in the SID multiple times. Execution wise no precise concept has been derived beyond concept that would allow all subject within a group to have a shared input-pool. Secondly, is the *System Interface* as shown later in Fig. 17. It allows to group explicitly Interface subjects together in order to specify that an interface subject refers actually to complete subsystem of active entities and the contained interfaces subjects have to be at least some of them, thereby exposing some of the details.

Lastly on the SID side, ALPS contains the option to declare a subject or a message connector to be *finalized*. The implication of that is that, in contrast to

---

[8] Note, that in the example of Fig. 6, the Message Flow Restrictor and the Abstract Communication Channel would contradict each other and not form a valid model.

their standard variants, it would not be allowed to add further messages on them in implementing models. And it would not be allowed to add any communication means to a finalized subject (be it Interface, Abstract, or Fully Specified)[9].

Abstract Model Elements on SBDs: On the SBD side, ALPS also requires a few conceptual additions that are shown in Fig. 7.

Abstract Elements	Visual Representation	3. Abstract Process Specification/Verification /Complience Verification
Trigger Transitions (Do, Send Receive)	From: Sending Subject / Msg: Data Object → ; description ▶ ; To: Receiving Actor / Msg: Data Object	(afterwards-must-come) A *trigger transition* implies that after it is executed, the follow-up state must be visited. If states A and B are directly connected by a trigger transition T on specification layer X, it means that if A was left via T (with the according exit condition), B must follow. On implementing layer Y this must remain true, but other states between A and B are valid. It is not allowed to have the option to skip B after A was done --> **A triggers B.** *Standard transitions are both: trigger and precedence transitions.*
Precedence Transitions (Do, Send Receive)	From: Sending Subject / Msg: Data Object ▶ ; description ▶ ; To: Receiving Actor / Msg: Data Object	(must-come-before) A *"precedence"* transition implies that the follow-up state must not come before (cannot be reached before) the origin state is executed. So if state A and B are connected by succession/precedence transition T on specification layer X, it should not be possible to find a way via reverse/backtracking from B to a start state without going over A --> **executing A is the precondition for B** (but B can be skipped). *Standard transitions are both: trigger and precedence/precondition-transitions*
Final Transitions (Do, Send Receive)	description ▶ ; From: Sending Actor / Msg: Data Object ▶ ; To: Receiving Actor / Msg: Data Object ▶	A *final transition* defined on a specification layer X must exist exactly alike on an implementing layer Y with the same origin and target states (correctly implemented if abstract). No deviation from this schema is allowed on implementing layers. A *final send or final receive* transition may not specify a receiver or a message ("undef"). In that case a variance from the model spec is still viable. Otherwise they are fixed and stay valid only if the actual receiver on implementation layer (Y) is an heir/implementer of the original receiver or if the message is an heir/implemented of the original message/spec. Final Transitions may not target or originate in state groups.
Advise Transitions (Do, Send Receive)	advise --> ; To: Receiving actor / Msg: Data Object --> ; From: Sending Actor / Msg: Data Object -->	(afterwards/before should come) An advice transition has no meaning beyond defining one possible/the most likely outcome of a state and advising, that it is a good idea to execute the follow-up state next. All other possible states are also viable. It simply describes the most common path of progression of states inside a behavior advised by the modeler.
Flow Restrictor	⊘ ▷ ◁ ⊘ ▷	(Must-NOT-come-after) Specifies that after a certain state other state or group the target not allowed to be executed anymore. Flow-Restriction may be done bi-directional in order to exclude certain aspects.

Fig. 7. Overview of (declarative) elements and variant of SBD transitions in ALPS

Again, the only truly new element being introduced is the Flow Restrictor that forbids that two states connected by it are allowed in the same process flow upon implementation or execution.

All other elements shown and described in Fig. 7 are, again, simply variants of Standard PASS elements. They are required to express certain constructions with a little bit more detail. The explanations of their usage are given in the Figure. The base idea is that **Trigger Transitions** imply that a target state must come at some point in execution sequence, if the origin state was visited. *Precedence Transitions* require the origin state to be executed before the target state. In the context of ALPS, standard PASS transitions would allow that in-between two states additional states could be inserted for execution or implementing models. In contrast to that, *Final Transitions* forbid these additions. Lastly, *Advice Transitions* are but that; only an advice of what the intended execution order of some state could be but, without any rules behind that advice. Where Final Transitions are the most restrictive, Advice Transitions are the least or basically non-restrictive. Later shown Figs. 10 and 11 further outline the ideas behind it.

---

[9] As with the finalized-keyword in programming, this means that other, implementing or extending models (see sub-section on usage of Abstract PASS) would not be allowed to introduce changes. A modeler with access to this model, naturally, can still make changes.

While these transitions variants are the core of the declarative modeling approach, they do not allow to specify every conceivable aspect that could be restricted. Figure 8 shows visualization of the ability to declare states to be *abstract*, to be *final*, to limit their occurrence in loops or how often they could occur, as well as the option to specify rules and restrictions on groups of states.

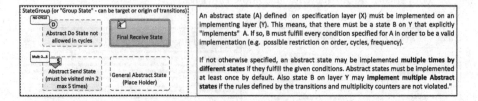

Fig. 8. Further specification means for states in Abstract PASS SBDs

Again, almost no new elements are introduced. The General Abstract State is basically only a generic place holder. All others are simply additional attributes that could be added to existing PASS states. As stated in Fig. 8, the specialty of specifying states to be *abstract* would allow implementing subjects to combine multiple of them into a singly state, as long as their type matches. Standard PASS states, in contrast, would require a modeler to implemented them as-is and not combine them. The only restriction that could be added to this, would be to declare a state to be *final*. This does forbid extending it and adding outgoing transition on an extension layers as it was described in Sect. 2.2.

What is being introduced by ALPS is the State Group or Group State as a model element with semantic meaning. In Standard PASS a State Group simply is a visual aid, to format an SBD and organize or structure it more pleasing. In contrast, within ALPS, groups are explicit elements of a specification and can be target or origin of transitions thus applying all pre- or post conditions to all states inside the group. This is useful, e.g., to specify that all activities in a group must be finished before a final report can be send.

Usage of Abstract Layered PASS: Now what is Abstract Layered PASS useful for? In principle, there are two possible usage concepts intended for ALPS that were implied in the previous two sections: direct or ad-hoc execution and specification adherence checking.

As far as surveyed, ad-hoc or direct execution is the more typical usage concept for any kind of declarative modeling. This is the case, e.g., for ConDec or DecSerFlow [20, 21]. Direct execution requires special workflow engines that can parse and generate execution options from an abstract or incomplete specification. Such an approach basically means *"filling out the blanks"* that are left by the incomplete specification. While this is a possible scenario for the usage of ALPS as well, no according workflow engine or even a specification for this kind of execution exist yet and also it is not what ALPS was originally intended for.

Following [9], the main intent of Abstract Layered PASS was an idea that, as far as known, does not exist as the usage scenario for any other declarative process modeling approach. The original idea was to use abstract models as specification modules to be *implemented* or *adhered-to* by other PASS models. The concept was derived from the difference between abstract definitions and concrete implementations in programming, where *interfaces* + *software contracts*[10] are a way to define an *Abstract Data Type* (ADT) and real classes later can implement such abstract specification. A compiler can then check whether the specification is adhered to, or not. In programming, an implementing class can actually *implement* multiple interfaces.

Figure 9 sketches this usage scenario. As depicted, this meant for situations where a general, but less restrictive process description is created first by a different modeler at a different time and even a different location than implementing models. Given a formal method/tool to validate the adherence, this is a great support for distributed modeling, even more so than the extension mechanism of layered PASS is. Also as mentioned, the idea is, that Subjects in implementing models could implement multiple abstract specifications and thus combine them into an actual executable process model that is compatible with multiple other models if all adhere to the same specification modules.

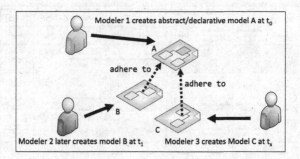

Fig. 9. Sketch for model creation with Abstract PASS as a specification other models

With these concepts, ALPS is a formal way within the domain of subject-oriented modeling for truly defining something that is sometimes dubbed a *behavioral interface*, especially in contrast to a normal/standard/fully specified behavior.

The tables of Figs. 10 and 11 show valid and invalid implementations of various abstractly defined behavioral interface specifications using Abstract PASS elements.

Examples: In the limited scope of this article, it is not possible to show an extensive example. Figures 12 and 13 demonstrate on a very small scale how an abstract general specification could be implemented by another model. It is a

---

[10] A concept of extended OO programming, where not only data types but also pre- and post conditions for method calls to and from classes can be specified. A feature rarely supported by default in most OO programming languages. Annotations like @Nonnullable would a primitive example.

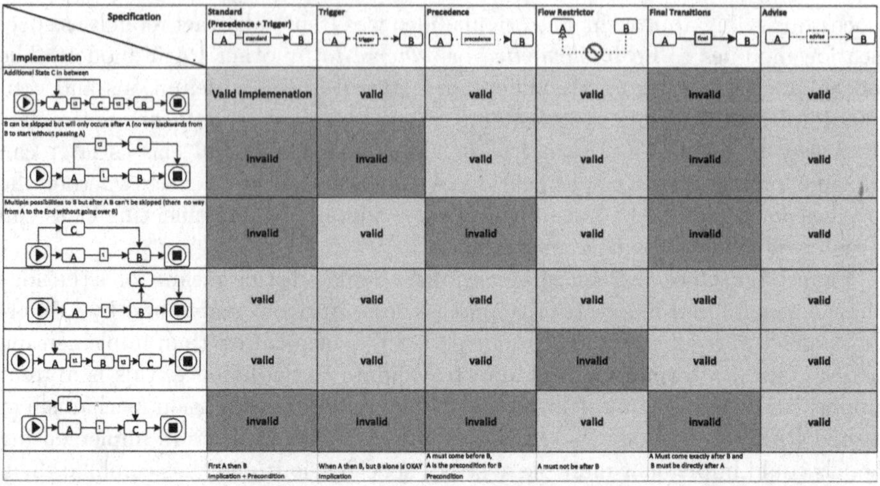

Fig. 10. Comparison ALPS specification to standard PASS implementation - Part A

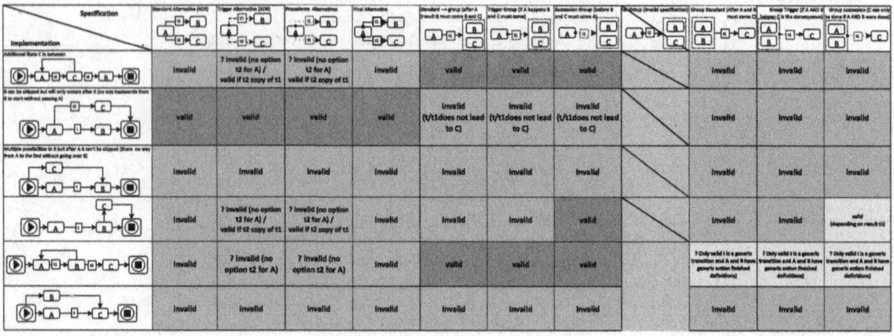

Fig. 11. Comparison ALPS Specification to standard PASS implementation - Part B - with groups an other extensions

formal representation or play on the idiom stating that *"the customer is king"*. Therefore, the king is a kind of customer and the King subject in Model B does implement the abstract Customer specification of Model A (Fig. 12. The subjects themselves and also the messages are allowed to be renamed[11] and fit to their new scenario.

Consequently, the behavior of subject King does adhere to the specifications of the abstract behavior of subject Customer. All states are implemented, even if their denominating has changed, and the specified order is not contradicted. It does not matter that additional Do-states have been added in-between and it can be seen that abstract behaviors do not need to have start or end states.

---

[11] Or rather the messages in Model B are extensions of their super classes. E.g., Command is considered a sub-class of the Request Message.

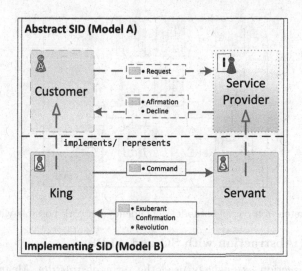

Fig. 12. Example: specification (Model A) and valid implementation (Model B)

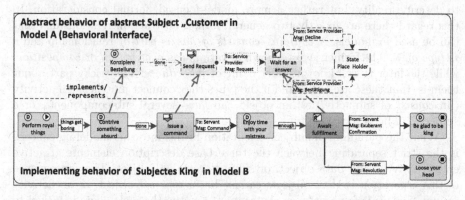

Fig. 13. Example Process Abstract SBD specification and valid implementing model (for subjects Customer and King in SID of Fig. 12)

2.4 Abstract and Non Abstract Layers

While being explained separately, Layered and Abstract PASS are a conceptual unit extends the modeling capabilities of standard PASS. Together they are used to form complex abstraction hierarchies. Figure 17 (at the end) gives a more concrete example of how multiple layers can interact.

However, the there shown examples still are hierarchical tree dependencies and ALPS is not limited to tree. The only intended rule for dependencies is to have "*a single direction of abstraction*", which is true for a tree structure. But with multiple specifications that could be adhered to, the model dependency graph can be a complex network or mesh. Figure 14 is a sketch of how such a dependency network of multiple different specifications and models could be structured at one point in time.

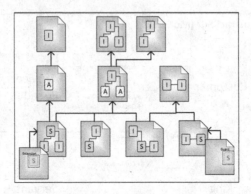

Fig. 14. Sketch of a complex model dependency network possible with ALPS

2.5   Formal Abstraction with SO and ALPS

The previous section extensively used the term *abstraction*. Meant is not the general interpretation of the term as it occurs in science whenever models are to describe reality, but rather a more model-focused, formal consideration. In this regard there are exactly two general, formal abstraction relationships that can be used in models. A *contains/consists of/has/is-part-of* relationship and a *is-type-of/is*. The former is also known in variants as *aggregation* or *composition*, while the later is well known under name of *inheritance*. The tricky part about them is, that these are only valid if the types they connect matches. An activity can *consist* of sub-activities, an object can *have* several sub-components, or a subject can be of a certain type.

What the paradigm of subject-orientation brings into this modeling concern is the strict separating between the three base description elements of active entity, activity, and data object, or subject, verb and object. The consequence of this separation is that subjects cannot be *"a type of"* object, or an activity cannot *"consist"* of subjects, as abstraction over the three elements is locked to its category. However, within these categories Abstraction can be used.

The Macro-mechanism is the *"consist-of"* abstraction mechanism for activities. The *implementation* concept of abstract states as sketched in Fig. 13 is the *"is-a-type-of"* mechanism for them.

For objects this is not explicitly shown here. However it was implicated that SO in general encompasses the concepts of Object-Orientation (OO) and the established mechanism of that paradigm can freely be used for data objects. The later discussed MS Visio based editor actually provides the classical OO means of *inheritance* and *composition*.

Finally, for subjects, the described mechanisms, be it the *implementation* of Abstract and Interface Subject, or be it the *extension* concepts for Macro, Guard or Extension Layers are essentially similar and fall under the *is-a-type-of* category. A *consist-of* mechanism is possible via a *Subject Group* and *System Interface Subject* elements of which the later is shown in Fig. 17. Both allow to define that a more general active entities (system) consist of sub-active-entities.

3 Tools for ALPS

In [14] and [9] ALPS was simply a concept, nothing more. This has change over the last decade and ALPS modeling is now fully usable.

3.1 Modeling

All examples are not simply pictures created in photo-shop, but where created with a dedicated editor that is build upon the Microsoft Office Visio. The main part was created as an VBA application directly build into the Visio stencils. This tool was detailed and explained in [15] and is available in its further developed version at [2].

The VBA solution is complemented by a separate Visio-Add-in developed in C# and available at [5]. This add-In feature only two, but very important functions. First is the import function allowing the import of ALPS model in the PASS OWL based exchange standard. And secondly, an actual functioning version of the *Layer Explorer* as original envisioned in [14]. This explorer allows to handle multi-layer model easily. It further comes with a support to easily "snap" especially subject-extensions and state reference to their counterparts on underlying layers, greatly reducing the modeling effort. Modeling layers is possible with just the stencils as they already allow to create Macro and Guard Extensions, but it is tedious as most mapping and matches need to be made manually. So usage of the add-in with the explorer is greatly advised.

Figure 15 shows both tools loaded and running in a Visio workspace. As far as currently known, this tool explicitly created for ALPS, is the only editor that allows to describe multi-behavior Standard PASS in general.

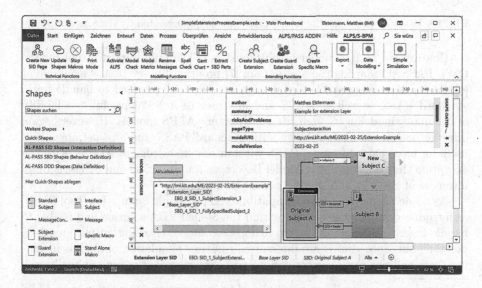

Fig. 15. Screenshot from ALPS Toolsuit embedded into MS Visio with Layer Model Explorer

3.2   Model Handling and Compatibility

The Visio stencils do not only allow to created ALPS models but also export them into the officially PASS OWL export standard as envisioned in [8]. However, the export is not only standard PASS but rather a version that is extended by the ALPS idea.

The core concept and structure of ALPS models as explained in this work is formally described in the ALPS ontology - an OWL file available at [3]. With this construction the ALPS_ont is actually the proof of concept for the claimed extensibility and backwards compatibility of the semantic PASS exchange standard. Figure 16 depicts the created setup and usage scenarios for the exported models. The chosen construction works in a way that indeed, all Layered PASS models are backwards compatible and should be understandable for tools that only now the Standard PASS Ont.

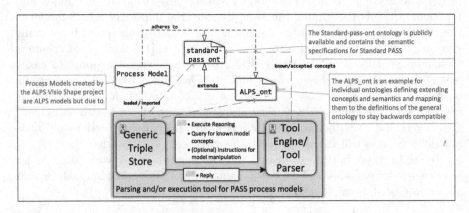

Fig. 16. Usage Concept for the ALPS Ontology as implemented by the alps.net.api [6]

However, to be fair, no such tools exist yet. The only importer tool for the OWL PASS standard is the alps.net.api [7] program library that is available at [6]. As its name suggest the alps.net.api was explicitly created to handle both, standard PASS as well as ALPS and any user of it will have full availability of handling, modeling[12], and im- or exporting ALPS models. However, again due the backwards compatibility with standard PASS, the alps.net.api allows users for most parts to model PASS without any knowledge of ALPS—with the exception that the concept of Model Layers, as a unit of SID and SBDs, is build into core of the API and therefore must be used.

As a side not in regards to compatibility: The Simple Simulation Tool (SiSi), as introduced in [10] was created within the Stencil VBA solution and is able to handle macro-behaviors on macro extensions. Model checking within guards is possible, but since guards are interrupts, run-time simulation of models including them will not work correctly. Similarly extensions layers are not really well

---

[12] Meant is, non-graphically manipulation of an in-memory representation of an ALPS model where program code is used to add and deduct elements.

supported by SiSi. However, both, guard and extension layers, both are tools for a different purpose than runtime-analysis via simulation and as such should not play a role for models that are intended as simulation basis.

3.3 Spec Validation

As indicate, the main purpose óf Abstract PASS is to use it as a specification means for other process models. To be of real usefulness, it was necessary to create a tool that can automatically verify that one model is adhering to the specification of another model and if not analyze what parts of the specification are violated. The according tool was created with Andreas Krämer and first released stand alone at [19]. However it now has been rolled up into and is standard part of the alps.net.api [6].

4 Summary and Outlook

This work was a presentation of developments over that last decade on the extensions of the subject-oriented modeling paradigm in form of the Abstract Layered PASS concept; from early project sketches to full usability. Even though ALPS may seem different from standard PASS on a first glance, it introduces only very few new elements while at the same time forming a *continuous* modeling canon of modeling means ranging from classical imperative process modeling to declarative specifications.

The only truly new elements introduced are Message and Flow Restrictors and Subject/State Groups as defining model elements. Other abstract model elements simply are variants of standard PASS elements. E.g. the different extension subjects are simply subjects that well *"extend"* another subject, with the only true addition being the *"extends"* property. The abstract subject simply is a subject with an abstract/declarative/incomplete behavior. And all *Trigger* or *Precedence* Transitions, at their core, still are Do or Receive transitions. Therefore all introduced and discussed tools are backwards compatible and many users may not even be aware that ALPS is always there if they need it.

Naturally, ALPS itself is an advanced modeling approach. It is neither intended nor useful for trivial situations and definitively not intended for beginning modelers that first should get an understanding of the subject-oriented paradigm itself before going abstract. ALPS with its formal modularization approach is useful when it comes to modeling processes in complex, ever-changing, socio-technical systems and when modeling happens distributed over time and space when different modules of process descriptions are created or changed at different times, by the different people, with different goals in mind. This situation is likely in large, international organizations with general directions and rules that have to be combined with local customs and regulations into actual purpose build processes. Another is possible the polar opposite in situations where processes have to be organized and fit cross-company in an network of

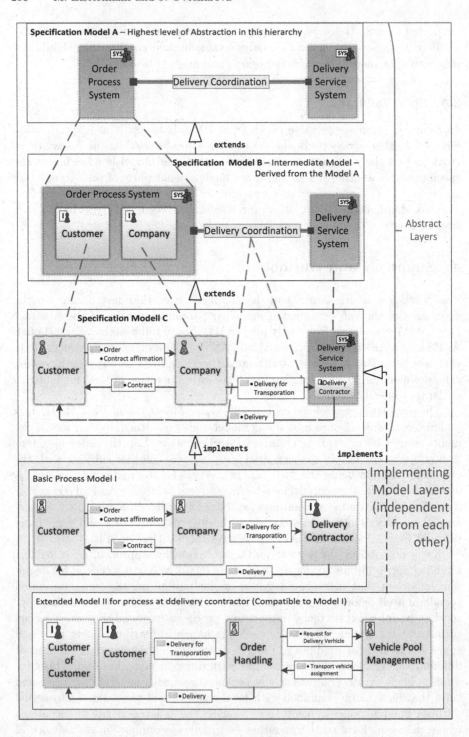

Fig. 17. The Concept of multi-layered, complex process systems (without SBDs)

multiple smaller organization. In both cases, having individual process specification and tools that can evaluated whether a given process description does violate other process specifications is almost mandatory. ALPS in conjunction with standard PASS can give process system modelers a greatest degree of freedom and especially flexibility when expressing such rules and the ALPS tools allow for exactly this kind of evaluation.

However, even while many developments have been made and ALPS has come far from its first conceptual ideas, there is research left to be done: first would be extensive modeling guidelines and example scenarios for abstract pass models to better guide modelers into this abstract domain. Also necessary are better tools that would allow to store and handle ALPS models remotely and make sure that rule adherence is always given. Other research directions that could be engaged would be tools that allow the quite popular topic of process mining to be done with subject-orientation/ALPS[13].

Secondly on the modeling side, ALPS is but a step into a formal extension to a concept for a holistic approach to subject-oriented process modeling. What is missing for that would be the ability to not only model active processes with subject, but also to have kind of passive processes that would specify what *can or cannot be done to or with* a data-object. Such passive specifications could then be used to verify if a given process model correctly handles an object. However, as of yet, this is merely a vague idea to complete the Grammar[14] of Subject-Oriented Process Modeling.

Last but not least, as mentioned, this work so far is focused on the modeling aspect of this abstract extension of subject-orientation. However, most declarative process modeling concepts intend the modeling to be used as a specification for direct executable process descriptions. The possible implications of this style of modeling on run-time behavior of a workflow engine has not yet been investigated for ALPS and the investigation and creation of an according engine for ad-hoc execution of abstract models is a challenging goal of for future works.

References

1. Börger, E.: A subject-oriented interpreter model for S-BPM (2012). https://www.di.unipi.it/~boerger/Papers/Bpmn/SbpmBookAppendix.pdf
2. Elstermann, M.: Alps-visio. https://subjective-me.jimdofree.com/visio-modelling/. Accessed 24 Feb 2023
3. Elstermann, M.: Reference-execution-model-for-PASS. https://github.com/MatthesElstermann/ALPS_ONT/tree/main. Accessed 24 Feb 2023
4. Elstermann, M.: Proposal for a recursive interpreter specification for pass in pass. In: Elstermann, M., et al. (eds.) S-BPM ONE 2023. CCIS, vol. 1867, pp. 187–201. Springer, Heidelberg (2023)

---

[13] Which naturally would be called *Mining in the ALPS*.

[14] In this regards to Grammar, standard PASS represents the standard *active sentence*, ALPS extends the grammar by *subjunctive* modeling expressions. This Ultimate PASS (working title) would now comprise the *passive tense*.

5. Elstermann, M., Gnad, L.: Alps-visio-add-in. https://github.com/ MatthesElstermann/ALPS-Visio-Add-In. Accessed 24 Feb 2023
6. Elstermann, M., Gnad, L.: Alps.net.api. https://github.com/I2PM/alps.net.api. Accessed 24 Feb 2023
7. Elstermann, M., Gnad, L.: An im- and export library for the subject-oriented exchange standard. In: Elstermann, M., Betz, S., Lederer, M. (eds.) Subject-Oriented Business Process Management. Dynamic Digital Design of Everything – Designing or Being Designed?, S-BPM ONE 2022. CCIS, vol. 1632, pp. 23–40. Springer, Cham (2022). https://doi.org/10.1007/978-3-031-19704-8_2
8. Elstermann, M., Krenn, F.: The semantic exchange standard for subject-oriented process models. In: Proceedings of the 10th International Conference on Subject-Oriented Business Process Management, pp. 1–8 (2018)
9. Elstermann, M., Ovtcharova, J.: Abstract layers in PASS – a concept draft. In: Zehbold, C. (ed.) S-BPM ONE 2014. CCIS, vol. 422, pp. 125–136. Springer, Cham (2014). https://doi.org/10.1007/978-3-319-06191-7_8
10. Elstermann, M., Ovtcharova, J.: SiSi in the ALPS: a simple simulation and verification approach for PASS. In: Proceedings of the 10th International Conference on Subject-Oriented Business Process Management, pp. 1–9 (2018)
11. Elstermann, M., Seese, D., Fleischmann, A.: Using the arbitrator pattern for dynamic process-instance extension in a work-flow management system. In: Derrick, J., et al. (eds.) ABZ 2012. LNCS, vol. 7316, pp. 323–326. Springer, Heidelberg (2012). https://doi.org/10.1007/978-3-642-30885-7_23
12. Elstermann, M., Wolski, A., Fleischmann, A., Stary, C., Borgert, S.: The combined use of the web ontology language (OWL) and abstract state machines (ASM) for the definition of a specification language for business processes. In: Raschke, A., Riccobene, E., Schewe, K.-D. (eds.) Logic, Computation and Rigorous Methods. LNCS, vol. 12750, pp. 283–300. Springer, Cham (2021). https://doi.org/10.1007/ 978-3-030-76020-5_16
13. Elstermann, M.: Executing Strategic Product Planning - A Subject-Oriented Analysis and New Referential Process Model for IT-Tool Support and Agile Execution of Strategic Product Planning (2019)
14. Elstermann, M., Ovtcharova, J.: An editing concept for PASS layers. In: Zehbold, C. (ed.) S-BPM ONE 2014. CCIS, vol. 422, pp. 137–146. Springer, Cham (2014). https://doi.org/10.1007/978-3-319-06191-7_9
15. Fleischmann, A., Borgert, S., Elstermann, M., Krenn, F., Singer, R.: An overview to S-BPM oriented tool suites. ACM, Darmstadt (2017)
16. Fleischmann, A., Schmidt, W., Stary, C., Obermeier, S., Börger, E.: Organization-specific implementation of subject-oriented processes. In: Subject-Oriented Business Process Management, pp. 173–188. Springer, Heidelberg (2012). https://doi. org/10.1007/978-3-642-32392-8_9
17. Fleischmann, A.: Distributed Systems: Software Design and Implementation. Springer, Heidelberg (1994). https://doi.org/10.1007/978-3-642-78612-9
18. Fleischmann, A., Schmidt, W., Stary, C.: Subject-oriented business process management. In: vom Brocke, J., Rosemann, M. (eds.) Handbook on Business Process Management 2. IHIS, pp. 601–621. Springer, Heidelberg (2015). https://doi.org/ 10.1007/978-3-642-45103-4_25
19. Krämer, A.: ALPS verification. https://github.com/andikra/ALPS-Verification-Thesis. Accessed 24 Feb 2023
20. Pesic, M.: Constraint-based workflow management systems: shifting control to users (2008)

21. Pesic, M., van der Aalst, W.M.P.: A declarative approach for flexible business processes management. In: Eder, J., Dustdar, S. (eds.) BPM 2006. LNCS, vol. 4103, pp. 169–180. Springer, Heidelberg (2006). https://doi.org/10.1007/11837862_18
22. Pichler, P., Weber, B., Zugal, S., Pinggera, J., Mendling, J., Reijers, H.A.: Imperative versus declarative process modeling languages: an empirical investigation. In: Daniel, F., Barkaoui, K., Dustdar, S. (eds.) BPM 2011. LNBIP, vol. 99, pp. 383–394. Springer, Heidelberg (2012). https://doi.org/10.1007/978-3-642-28108-2_37
23. Prescher, J., Di Ciccio, C., Mendling, J.: From declarative processes to imperative models (2014). https://citeseerx.ist.psu.edu/viewdoc/download?doi=10.1.1.662.5516&rep=rep1&type=pdf#page=170

Author Index

A
Auer, Thomas 45, 121

B
Betz, Stefanie 180
Bönsch, Jakob 63

D
Dittmar, Anke 83

E
Elstermann, Matthes 63, 180, 187, 263

F
Fleischmann, Albert 3
Flügge, Wilko 111
Forbrig, Peter 83

G
Gaawar, Paramvir Singh 151
Gniza, Reinhard 3
Gottschick, Jan 250

H
Hauck, Svenja 63
Hein, Michael 55
Heininger, Richard 202, 223

J
Jagusch, Konrad 111
Jericho, David 111
Jost, Thomas Ernst 202, 223

K
Kannengiesser, Udo 240
Krenn, Florian 240
Kühn, Mathias 83

L
Lamprecht, Axel 131
Lederer, Matthias 3, 17, 180
Liepert, Constantin 131

M
Moya, Ana 55
Müller, Harald 240

O
Opaska, Anna 250
Ovtcharova, Jivka 63, 263

P
Piller, Christoph 163

R
Reimann, Janina 55
Rösl, Stefan 45, 121

S
Schieder, Christian 45, 121
Schmidt, Werner 180
Sender, Jan 111
Stary, Christian 91, 131, 202, 223
Steffens, Petra 250

T
Thummerer, Julia 17

U
Umlauft, Alexandru 83

W
Widenhorn, Andreas 151

Z
Zouagui, Jaouhara 250
Zügn, Dennis 131

M. Elstermann et al. (Eds.): S-BPM ONE 2023, CCIS 1867, p. 285, 2023.
https://doi.org/10.1007/978-3-031-40213-5

Printed in the United States
by Baker & Taylor Publisher Services